CONSTRUCTIVE
Theology

CONSTRUCTIVE Theology

A Contemporary Approach to Classical Themes, with CD-ROM

A Project of the Workgroup on Constructive Christian Theology

Serene Jones and Paul Lakeland
editors

Fortress Press
Minneapolis

CONSTRUCTIVE THEOLOGY
A Contemporary Approach to Classical Themes, with CD-ROM

Copyediting and CD-ROM editing: Beth Wright
Cover design: Brad Norr Design
Interior design: James Korsmo
Typesetting and CD-ROM development: Scribe, Inc. (www.scribenet.com)

Library of Congress Cataloging-in-Publication Data

Constructive theology : a contemporary approach to classical themes with CD-ROM / edited by Serene Jones and Paul Lakeland.

p. cm.
"A project of the Workgroup on Constructive Christian Theology."
Includes bibliographical references and index.
ISBN 0-8006-3683-X (alk. paper)
1. Theology, Doctrinal. I. Jones, Serene, 1959– II. Lakeland, Paul, 1946–

BT75.3.C66 2004
230—dc22

2004018099

The paper used in this publication meets the minimum requirements of American National Standard for Information Sciences Permanence of Paper for Printed Library Materials, ANSI Z329.48-1984.

Manufactured in the U.S.A.

09 08 07 06 05 1 2 3 4 5 6 7 8 9 10

Contents

Preface

The enterprise of Christian theology today is both varied and exciting. In this book, we want to invite you to enter into this world, to participate in the activity of religious reflection along with the group of people whose thought you will encounter in the pages that follow. "We" are a group of some fifty theologians and scholars of religion. We belong to many Christian traditions, and we do not all share the same convictions about how theology needs to be done, or what its precise role may be in today's world. But we are all—Protestant and Catholic, women and men, people of color and Caucasions, gay and straight—committed to working in collaboration to uncover the continuing importance of the ancient traditions of Christianity for the very different world of today. This book is testimony to these commitments.

There are so many things in the Christian theological tradition today that we can no longer take for granted. While many people remain proudly members of this or that historic Christian church or denomination, many others move much more freely between traditions or construct a personal religious outlook that draws elements from various places both inside and outside the Christian tradition. Still others live more or less comfortably on the edge of religious conviction but retain a sense of what Christianity was and is and how it may be of continuing importance to the world. Representatives of all these approaches are included within the authorship of this book, just as you, our reader, will in all probability find yourself somewhere in this spectrum.

At the same time as we recognize, celebrate, and illustrate pluralism, we also offer here a vision of the common historical foundations that lie behind today's very different situation. Ancient traditions and teachings remain alive in us even as, and perhaps especially when, we try to speak to the world of today. To adapt a wise and witty saying that has been attributed to many different authors, while we reject a traditionalism that is "the dead faith of the living," we believe in the continuing importance of that tradition that is "the living faith of the dead."

One of the striking things about the world of Christian scholarship at the present time is the degree of collaborative work. No current approach to Christian theology, we are confident, exhibits more evidence of this working together than the one that lies before you. We warmly invite our readers to join us in the extended argument that is Christian theology today. You will find here the fruits of five years of discussion and collaboration, and it can only be improved by the contribution that you will make as you engage with us in constructing theology anew.

Finally, we must recognize those individuals and groups who have made this work possible. We have received substantial funding from the Louisville Institute and the Wabash Center for Teaching and Learning in Religion and Theology. We are grateful for the confidence they have shown in us, without which we could not easily have reached this point. We are also enormously grateful to the staff of Fortress Press, particularly Michael West, who has undertaken here an editorial task of monumental proportions, and has never—to our knowledge—despaired in the least of its coming to fruition. Finally, to all those past members of the Workgroup, whose labors built up both the traditions we inherited and the healthy financial situation that helps to support our meetings, we express our gratitude and our hopes that they too will find this text a worthy Workgroup venture.

Serene Jones
Paul Lakeland

Contributors

Victor Anderson is Associate Professor of Christian Ethics at Vanderbilt Divinity School, Nashville. His research interests include ethics, American philosophy, and African American religion. He is author of *Beyond Ontological Blackness: An Essay on African American Religious and Cultural Criticism* (Continuum, 1995) and *Pragmatic Theology* (SUNY Press, 1998).

Ellen T. Armour is R. A. Webb Professor of Religious Studies at Rhodes College. She is the author of *Deconstruction, Feminist Theology and the Problem of Difference: Subverting the Race/Gender Divide* (University of Chicago Press, 1999).

Karen Baker-Fletcher is Associate Professor of Systematic Theology, Perkins School of Theology, Southern Methodist University, Dallas. She is author of *Sisters of Dust, Sisters of Spirit* (Fortress Press, 1998) and *A Singing Something: Womanist Reflections on Anna Julia Cooper* (Continuum, 1994).

Paul E. Capetz, Associate Professor of Historical Theology at United Theological Seminary of the Twin Cities, has authored two books, *Christian Faith as Religion: A Study in the Theologies of Calvin and Schleiermacher* (University Press of America, 1998) and *God: A Brief History* (Fortress Press, 2003). Formerly an ordained minister in the Presbyterian Church (U.S.A.), he voluntarily set aside his ordination to protest the church's anti-gay stance.

Don H. Compier is Dean of Community of Christ Seminary at Graceland University in Missouri. Among his works is *John Calvin's Rhetorical Doctrine of Sin* (Mellen, 2001).

M. Shawn Copeland is Associate Professor of Systematic Theology at Boston College and adjunct Associate Professor at the Institute for Black Catholic Studies, Xavier University of New Orleans. President of the Catholic Theological Society of America, her research and writing focus on political theology. She is co-editor of *Feminist Theology in Different Contexts* (Orbis, 1996) and *Violence against Women* (Orbis, 1994).

Paul DeHart is Assistant Professor of Theology, Vanderbilt Divinity School, Nashville. His work is concentrated in the area of modern Christian thought, especially the doctrine of God, and he is author of *Beyond the Necessary God: Trinitarian Faith and Philosophy in the Thought of Eberhard Jüngel* (Oxford, 1999).

James H. Evans Jr. is Robert K. Davies Professor of Systematic Theology, Colgate Rochester Crozer Divinity School. Among his many works is *We Shall All Be Changed: Social Problems and Theological Renewal* (Fortress Press, 1997). He is currently completing a research project on Back to Africa movements in the United States, as well as a volume on devotional theology.

Francis Schüssler Fiorenza is Stillman Professor of Roman Catholic Theological Studies at Harvard Divinity School. His longstanding interests in foundational theology, political theology, and hermeneutics figure in his 100 essays and his books *Foundational Theology: Jesus and the Church* (Crossroad, 1984); *Systematic Theology: Roman Catholic Perspectives*, edited with John Galvin (2 vols., 1991, Fortress Press) and *Modern Christian Thought*, volume 2, *The Twentieth Century*, written with James Livingston (Prentice-Hall, 2000).

Mary McClintock Fulkerson is Associate Professor of Theology at Duke Divinity School. She is author of *Changing the Subject: Women's Discourses and Feminist Theology* (Fortress Press, 1994). Her current project is a theology of redemptive place based on an ethnographic study of an interracial church.

Michelle A. Gonzalez is Assistant Professor of Theological Studies at Loyola Marymount University. She is the author of *Sor Juana: Beauty and Justice in the Americas* (Orbis, 2003).

Roger Haight, S.J., is currently engaged in teaching and research in the area of the church. Among his works are *Christian Community in History* (Continuum, 2004) and *Jesus, Symbol of God* (Orbis, 1999).

Bradford E. Hinze is Associate Professor of Theology at Marquette University. Among his works is *Spirit in the Church and the World* (co-editor; Orbis, 2004). He writes on the dialogical and trinitarian character of the church's identity and mission.

Peter C. Hodgson is Charles G. Finney Professor of Theology, Emeritus, Divinity School, Vanderbilt University. Among his books is *Mystery beneath the Real: Theology in the Fiction of George Eliot* (Fortress Press, 2000). His current project is a work on Hegel and Christian theology to be published by Oxford University Press.

Barbara A. Holmes is Associate Professor of Ethics and African American Religious Studies at Memphis Theological Seminary. Her latest book is *Joy Unspeakable: Contemplative Practices of the Black Church* (Fortress Press, 2004).

Dwight N. Hopkins is Professor of Theology at the University of Chicago Divinity School. Among his books is *Down, Up, and Over: Slave Religion and Black Theology* (Fortress Press, 2000). His current project is *On Being Human: Black Theology Looks at Culture, Self, and Race.*

Leonard M. Hummel is Assistant Professor of Pastoral Theology and Counseling at Vanderbilt Divinity School in Nashville. He is author of *Clothed in Nothingness: Consolation for Suffering* (Fortress Press, 2003). His forthcoming work is *Chance, Necessity, Love: A Practical Theology of Cancer.*

Ada María Isasi-Díaz is Professor of Ethics and Theology at Drew University, Madison, New Jersey. Among her many important writings are *Mujerista Theology* (1996) and *En la Lucha/In the Struggle* (Fortress Press, 2d ed., 2004).

David H. Jensen is Associate Professor of Constructive Theology at Austin Presbyterian Theological Seminary in Texas and has written in the areas of Christology, interfaith dialogue, marriage, and the family. He is the author of *In the Company of Others: A Dialogical Christology* (Pilgrim, 2001). His most recent book develops a theology of childhood. He is a member of the Presbyterian Church (U.S.A.).

William Stacy Johnson is Arthur M. Adams Associate Professor of Systematic Theology at Princeton Theological Seminary. Among his books is *The Mystery of God: Karl Barth and the Postmodern Foundations of Theology* (Westminster John Knox, 1997). He is currently working on a constructive approach to the meaning of revelation in a postmodern, post-Holocaust, post-Christendom age.

Serene Jones is Titus Street Professor of Theology at Yale University Divinity School, where she also holds appointments in Women and Gender Studies and African American Studies. Her research areas are contemporary theology, women and religion, globalization, and the Calvinist theological traditions. Among her books is *Feminist Theory and Christian Theology: Cartographies of Grace* (Fortress Press, 2000).

Margaret D. Kamitsuka teaches Gender and Religion at Oberlin College and has written articles appearing in *Journal of Feminist Studies in Religion* and *Journal of Religion.*

Catherine Keller is Professor of Constructive Theology at the Theological and Graduate Schools of Drew University in New Jersey. Among her works are *Face of the Deep: A Theology of Becoming* (Routledge, 2003) and *God and Power: Counter-Apocalyptic Journeys* (Fortress Press, 2005).

Kris Kvam is Associate Professor of Theology at St. Paul School of Theology in Missouri. Among her interests is gender in religious traditions, and she is co-editor of *Eve and Adam: Jewish, Christian, and Muslim Readings on Genesis and Gender* (Indiana University Press, 1999).

Paul Lakeland is Aloysius P. Kelley, S.J., Professor of Catholic Studies at Fairfield University in Connecticut. Among his works are *The Liberation of the Laity: In Search of an Accountable Church* (Continuum, 2003) and *Postmodernity: Christian Identity in a Fragmented Age* (Fortress Press, 1997).

Walter J. Lowe is Professor of Systematic Theology at Candler School of Theology, Emory University. His work ranges across hermeneutics, Continental philosophy, and theology. He is author of *Evil and the Unconscious* (Scholars, 1983) and *Theology and Difference: The Wound of Reason* (Indiana, 1993).

Charles T. Matthewes is Assistant Professor of Religious Studies at the University of Virginia. He is author of *Evil and the Augustinian Tradition* (Cambridge, 2001).

Joy Ann McDougall is Assistant Professor of Systematic Theology at Candler School of Theology, Emory University. Her research interests include twentieth-century German theology, political and liberation theologies, and feminist-womanist debates in the doctrines of God and Christology.

Sallie McFague is Distinguished Professor of Theology at the Vancouver School of Theology in Canada and author of several books on theology and ecology, including *Life Abundant: Rethinking Theology and Economy for a Planet in Peril* (Fortress Press, 2000).

Ian A. McFarland is Senior Lecturer in Systematic Theology at the School of Divinity, King's College, University of Aberdeen, Scotland. He is author of *Difference and Identity: A Theological Anthropology* (Pilgrim, 2001) and *Listening to the Least: Doing Theology from the Outside In* (Pilgrim, 1998).

M. Douglas Meeks is Cal Turner Chancellor Professor of Theology and Wesleyan Studies at the Divinity School of Vanderbilt University. Author of *God the Economist: The Doctrine of God and Political Economy* (Fortress Press, 1989), his chief area of teaching and research is Christian doctrine and social theory. He is working on a book tentatively titled *Spreading the Lord's Table: The Church in the Global Economy*.

Linda Mercadante is B. Robert Straker Professor of Theology at the Methodist Theological School in Ohio. Author of *Victims and Sinners: Spiritual Roots of Addiction and Recovery* (Westminster John Knox, 1996), she specializes in issues of theology and culture and is ordained in the Presbyterian Church (U.S.A.).

Amy Plantinga Pauw is the Henry P. Mobley Jr. Professor of Doctrinal Theology at Louisville Presbyterian Theological Seminary in Kentucky. Among her works is *"The Supreme Harmony of All": The Trinitarian Theology of Jonathan Edwards* (Eerdmans, 2002).

Jim Perkinson directs the Doctorate in Ministry program at Ecumenical Theological Seminary, Detroit, and is Associate Professor of Religious Studies and Philosophy at Marygrove College there. He is also a hip-hop poet of increasing renown.

Jamie T. Phelps, O.P., is since 2003 Director of the Institute for Black Catholic Studies and Professor of Systematic Theology at Xavier University, New Orleans, where she began after a dozen years as Professor of Doctrinal and Mission Theology at Catholic Theological Union, Chicago. Along with many scholarly publications, she is editor of *Black and Catholic: The Challenge and Gift of Black Folk* (Marquette, 1997).

Darby Kathleen Ray is Associate Professor of Religious Studies at Millsaps College in Mississippi. She is the author of *Deceiving the Devil: Atonement, Abuse, and Ransom* (Pilgrim, 1998).

Stephen G. Ray Jr. is Assistant Professor of Theology and Philosophy at Louisville Presbyterian Theological Seminary in Kentucky, and author of *Do No Harm: Social Sin and Christian Responsibility* (Fortress Press, 2003).

Joerg Rieger is Professor of Systematic Theology at Perkins School of Theology, Southern Methodist University. Among his most recent books are *God and the Excluded: Visions and Blindspots in Contemporary Theology* (Fortress Press, 2001) and *Opting for the Margins: Postmodernity and Liberation in Christian Theology* (Oxford University Press, 2003).

Cynthia L. Rigby is W. C. Brown Associate Professor of Theology at Austin Presbyterian Theological Seminary in Texas and the co-editor of *Blessed One: Protestant Perspectives on Mary* (Westminster John Knox, 2002).

Kathleen M. Sands is Associate Professor of Religion at the University of Massachusetts, Boston. Among her works is *Escape from Paradise: Evil and Tragedy in Feminist Theology* (Fortress Press, 1994). Her recent research focus is religion in public life.

Michele Saracino is Assistant Professor of Religious Studies at Manhattan College. She is interested in the connections among Catholicism, critical theory, and culture. She is author of *On Being Human: A Conversation with Lonergan and Levinas* (Marquette University Press, 2003).

Laurel C. Schneider is Associate Professor of Theology, Ethics, and Culture at Chicago Theological Seminary. She is author of *Re-Imagining the Divine: Confronting the Backlash against Feminist Theology* (Pilgrim, 1998).

Craig Stein holds a doctorate in theology from Candler School of Theology, Emory University, and has taught at Union Theological Seminary, Richmond, Virginia, as Assistant Professor of Theology.

Kathryn Tanner is Professor of Theology at the University of Chicago Divinity School. She is author of several volumes, most recently *Theories of Culture: A New Agenda for Theology* (1997) and *Jesus, Humanity, and the Trinity: A Brief Systematic Theology* (2001), both from Fortress Press.

John E. Thiel is Professor of Religious Studies at Fairfield University. His most recent books are *God, Evil, and Innocent Suffering: A Theological Reflection* (Crossroad, 2002) and *Senses of Tradition: Continuity and Development in Catholic Faith* (Oxford University Press, 2000).

Deanna A. Thompson is Associate Professor of Religion at Hamline University, St. Paul, Minnesota. She is the author of *Crossing the Divide: Luther, Feminism, and the Cross* (Fortress Press, 2004).

Mark I. Wallace is Associate Professor of Religion at Swarthmore College. He is the author of *Fragments of the Spirit: Nature, Violence, and the Renewal of Creation* (Trinity Press International, 2002) and *Finding God in the Singing River: Christianity in an Environmental Age* (Fortress Press, 2005).

Sharon D. Welch is Professor of Religious Studies at the University of Missouri, Columbia, and the author of *A Feminist Ethic of Risk* (rev. ed.; Fortress Press, 2000) and *After Empire: The Art and Ethos of Enduring Peace* (Fortress Press, 2004).

Tatha Wiley teaches at United Theological Seminary of the Twin Cities, St. Paul. She is author of *Original Sin: Origins, Developments, Contemporary Meanings* (Paulist, 2002), editor of *Thinking of Christ: Proclamation, Explanation, Meaning* (Continuum, 2003), and author of *Paul and the Gentile Women* (Continuum, 2005).

Introduction

Theology as Faith in Search of Understanding

It is a continual theme of Christian theology that every new generation must take up the task of "faith in search of understanding" with fresh vigor and creativity. Over the centuries, this task has been undertaken by many, sometimes in the midst of enormous social crisis, sometimes in the stayed quiet of history's rare moments of peace. It is a task that has been embarked on when Christian theology has voiced the thoughts of the powerful and also in cases when only stifled whispers of a repressed and silenced faith could be heard. It is a task as hard as it is rewarding, as fraught with tensions as it is guided by grounding wisdoms, a task both invigorating and daunting, an enterprise filled with as many surprises as familiar truths.

In the pages of this book we offer you a glimpse of what this task looks like when undertaken by a committed, diverse group of theologians who stand at the beginning of a new millennium and in the center of the world's most powerful empire and ask again: How should the Christian faith be understood today, here and now, in this place and time? No one doubts that religious beliefs have the power to tear down cities as well as build up nations, that theology has the capacity to save lives as well as to take them. Each of us thus recognizes that faith matters profoundly and therefore theology really is a life-and-death endeavor. We also acknowledge that simple answers are not easy to find and that the faith we seek to comprehend is alive in the world and yet elusive and pluralistic in its forms. Such a challenge has made the writing of this book an exercise in collaborative humility. As theologians, we are committed to speaking boldly about a faith we passionately hold; as scholars and activists, we remain aware of the complexity, multiplicity, and indeterminacy of our project and its claims. Fortunately, we find this challenge an exciting one, a fact that puts us in the good company of generations of theologians who have struggled with precisely this tension.

The writers of this book have chosen to refer to ourselves by the rather mundane name "The Workgroup on Constructive Christian Theology." This title tries to say simply what we do: each year, we gather as teachers of

Christian theology to *work* to put our creative energies together and make theology. We do so as a *group*; it is a collective endeavor from its beginning to its end. And our goal is to be *constructive*. We are not interested in merely describing what theology has been; we are trying to understand and construct it in the present, to imagine what life-giving faith can be in today's world. In doing so, as with any construction job, we are attempting to build a viable structure. In our case, that structure is an inhabitable, beautiful, and truthful *theology*. Our biggest hope in writing this book is that those who read it might be inspired to do the same: to collaborate in writing new scripts for the deep wisdoms that live in your faith and, in doing so, to engage with vigor and passion in the enterprise of *fides quaerens intellectum* (faith in search of understanding).

A Short History of the Workgroup

Like all theological endeavors that seek to understand the Christian faith, our project has a particular story behind it, one that stretches back several decades and includes within it a unique history of personalities, topics, and social challenges. The present book is the fourth in a series of textbooks produced over the past thirty-five years by consecutive generations of the Workgroup, each of which has been committed in its own distinctive way to the task of doing constructive theology in an open and engaged manner.

Critically Liberal Theology

The first two volumes, *Christian Theology* (1982) and *Readings in Christian Theology* (1985), represented the best theological thinking of a generation of scholars responding to the need for a popular theology textbook that could articulate for students a vision of faith that was theologically traditional and at the same time socially liberal and intellectually critical. For them, writing in the early eighties, this required sympathetic engagement with what many less sympathetic, conservative Christians regarded as threatening forces, such as the growing appeal of scientific and historical knowledge and the liberal social change that antiwar activism, the civil rights movement, and the women's movement had prompted in churches across North America. Like the writers of the present volume, this first generation was convinced that a strongly progressive political vision and classical theology were well-suited companions, a sense first nurtured in them by their own teachers, figures like Paul Tillich, H. Richard Niebuhr, Karl Rahner, and Karl Barth. Their texts were far-reaching in the scope of topics they treated and in the range of their audiences, a fact attested by their continued use in many of our theology classrooms today.

Postmodern Liberation Theology

Twelve years later, the second generation of Workgroup theologians published a sequel to the first two, entitled *Reconstructing Christian Theology* (1994). While they retained a commitment to writing vital, emancipatory theology, they recognized that their audiences had changed and that they faced a new set of challenges. Their predecessors' confidence in liberalism and critical modernism had begun to crumble under the weight of a variety of political and intellectual forces that pushed this second group to take even more seriously than before the contextual character of theological reflection. On the political front, the book listened closely to the voices and concerns of womanist, *mujerista*, feminist, lesbian and gay, disabled, and environmentalist activists and theologians in North America and tried to show that rethinking our assumptions about such things as race and gender also requires rethinking our basic theological assumptions about who God is (Is God masculine, feminine, Hispanic, African American, etc.?) and who we are (Are we women, men, gay, straight, subjects, persons, creatures, human beings, etc.?).

Similarly, this second generation attended to the revolutionary claims of liberation theologians speaking from the so-called third world about the legacies of colonialism and correlative issues of economic and cultural justice, pointing out that when it comes to community formation, theology can just as easily be used to oppress people as to liberate them. On the philosophical front, the destabilizing claims of postmodernist theory in all its varieties pressed this group of theologians to think even more critically than their teachers about the fragility of truth claims and the illusory character of "principles" and "natures," such as the seeming givens of race and gender, to name just two. In response to all these challenges and possibilities, the book offered a theological vision based on a thoroughgoing marriage of faith claims and political contexts. In doing so, it both followed through and courageously challenged the claims of the text before it.

A New Constructive Theology

A decade later, the Workgroup underwent yet another reconstruction and, with many new theologians on board, began the third phase of this ongoing conversation. This book is the product of that phase. Like our predecessors, we are determined to keep faith vitally connected to the present-day world and its pressing concerns, and, as in the previous volumes, we seek to do this in a collaborative, critical, and constructive mode. But we also face a new set of challenges. We continue to be inspired by the liberal theological agenda expressed in the first set of volumes, and we share the political and social concerns of the second volume as well, but we find ourselves living in different times and speaking to a very different generation of students.

While some of our students could benefit from liberal and liberationist critiques of an overconfident, complacent, but well-formed faith (the task that rightly marked the endeavor of the previous volumes), many who enter our classrooms today know little to nothing about Christian theology and have only a rudimentary familiarity with Christian scriptures. They have no living memory of the Vietnam War; most of their mothers work; they accept racial, ethnic, and religious pluralism as an established fact of North American life; and they have only sporadically attended church and have usually done so in at least three different denominations. They come to our classrooms because they are interested in spirituality and in exploring the deep questions of life, but they are not traditionally "churched." They also come seeking a sense of communal belonging, a connection to traditions. They have an earnest desire to be more socially involved and politically active, but they are not engaged, for the most part, in longstanding religious communities or active political organizations. Our students are thus restless and, to a large degree, theologically rootless. They are looking for bold visions of hope in an age when liberal mainline churches are struggling to survive and when possibilities for emancipatory social change shrink daily. In this context, they are asking us, their classroom professors, for help in figuring out how to build a liberating "spiritual" path to the future.

Oddly, this means that we are required to teach our students the basics of Christian theology while at the same time trying to teach them to be creative and critical with respect to its rich and conflicted heritage. This has put us in the exciting but unusual position of being both Christianity's wise conservators and its harsh critics—all the while trying to construct bold visions of hope and justice for a world in desperate need of them.

How does a group of theologians go about doing this? We had no clear answer to this question when we first began discussing the writing of this book. We were not even sure how to get started. This was in part due to the large size of the group. In previous generations of the Workgroup, the number of theologians working together had been limited to fifteen. For this book, the group had been intentionally expanded to include over fifty teachers of theology; with this increase in size came an unprecedented level of diversity, a fact that we all realized could either energize or paralyze us. Not only are we diverse with respect to race, gender, class, sexual orientation, ethnicity, and region (to name only a few of the most obvious differences), but we hail from ecclesial backgrounds ranging from Southern Baptist to Roman Catholic and teach in a variety of institutions, from small church-related colleges and seminaries to big state universities and divinity schools. Moreover, our age range is wide, running from seventy-something all the way back to the mid-twenties.

How does a group this large and diverse find enough cohesion to write a collaborative textbook filled with boldly articulated theological visions? One obvious answer might have been for us to have decided from the outset on a shared *methodology* for doing theology. For most of the twentieth century, shared method—a common perspective on the proper task and form of theology—had been, in fact, the key point of agreement around which major "schools of theology" formed and out of which grew the rationale for numerous collaborative endeavors such as ours. If we had chosen this formal, conceptual route, the options before us would have been dazzling: we could have been liberals, postliberals, or liberationists; feminists, Neoorthodox dogmaticians, or process thinkers; historicists, pragmatists, cultural theorists, or postmodernists of either the Derridian or Marxist variety; and so on. Clearly, differences concerning method constituted one of the group's most unwieldy forms of diversity. It quickly became apparent that if we wanted to reach a methodological consensus about this book before we started writing it, the project might well remain just an editor's wild fantasy.

So we decided to talk about something we all held in common: teaching, that activity to which we are all deeply committed. We asked: Who are our students? What sort of issues and challenges enter our classrooms daily? What kind of pedagogical practices do we find most useful? What are the core theological insights we find ourselves actually teaching? Perhaps most important, what do our practices suggest about what we believe theology is? At the end of a hard day of work, what kind of theology have we passed on to our students—sometimes to our own surprise? What theological visions are embedded in our activities as professors, day in and day out? And how might we write a text that reflects this reality?

We soon discovered that we shared much more than we had imagined, and it was out of the soil of these conversations that this book grew. Amazingly enough, a strong shared understanding of theology also emerged, and along with it—surprise, surprise—we even discovered a few of those collectively held methodological insights that at first seemed so elusive.

What does this understanding of theology look like? Below, we offer a rough summary of its main features, a sketch of its principal contours, and its central concerns. But before turning to that account, it is important to note that we believe the best answer to the question of "What kind of theology are we doing here?" is not to be found in these summary comments. Rather, the best answer is one that readers themselves should discover after having grappled with the text for a while. To this end, we ask that you let yourself be pulled into the worlds of reflection that lie in the pages ahead; follow along with the book's thinking process, engage its play of mind, its multiple images and arguments, its literary form, and its unfolding and unfinished but carefully considered dramas of thought. After living with the book for a time, step back and reflect on the kind of imaginative thinking it has encouraged in you. What flights of theological fancy has it provoked? What shifts in perspective has it encouraged? Which parts have irritated and disturbed you, and which sections have delighted you? What, if any, new ways of understanding the Christian faith were opened up to you? The insights that come to you in this reflection may well be your best answers to the question, What is theology? All this is to say that, finally, the best way to understand what we are doing here is for you to engage actively in our process of doing it.

What Is Constructive Theology?

A Focus on Classical Themes

There are many ways to organize a text in constructive theology that seeks to speak meaningfully to today's world. One could identify, let's say, a set of pressing social themes—U.S. imperialism, gender, the deepening of racial divisions in North America, the environmental crisis, the state of the family—and explore what difference faith makes to how we think about them. One could similarly take a number of more abstract topics, such as love, justice, forgiveness, hospitality, and peace, and flesh out what each might mean to us today when considered in the context of a comprehensive reach of faith. Likewise, one could divide up chapters according to present-day theological schools of thought—liberal, liberationist, postliberal, evangelical, and so forth—and demonstrate the difference each makes to how we understand faith claims. Along similar lines, the focus could fall on a list of contemporary theologians whose works stand as markers of the age—a list that would no doubt include many of our authors and would highlight the fact that scholars with different backgrounds and church commitments craft theological visions that are strikingly different in tone and texture.

In addition to these possibilities, there is another, more traditional option for organizing a book in constructive theology, and that is to divide the text according to the classical doctrinal pattern, addressing subjects like God, Christ, Atonement, and Life Eternal. A brief glance at our table of contents should make it clear that this last, rather old-fashioned option is the one that won out in our deliberations on organization. In the following chapters of this book, we explore six of these classical themes: God, Human Being, Sin and Evil, Jesus Christ, Church, and Spirit. We also explore, as themes running throughout each of these chapters but not independently treated, the classical themes of creation, redemption, and the future.

Why did we choose this approach? The answer is pragmatic. Since our students know so little about the history of Christian theology and have limited training in the tradition, this pattern seemed best suited to teaching "the basics." In a primer on Christian theology, we should teach primary things, and for theologians like ourselves, that is what this list of classical themes represents. They are those primary themes that have emerged, again and again over the centuries, when Christians have attempted to organize comprehensively their thoughts about the faith they hold.

Admittedly, this list of themes has undergone significant changes over time; the content of each specific topic has been contested and renegotiated by constantly shifting communities and cultures (a subject we return to often in the book). And yet people of faith have continued to ask some basic questions: What does the word *God* mean? Who is Jesus? What makes a group of people a church? Why are there evil, sin, and suffering in the world? How do we think about the power of the Spirit in our lives? And perhaps most perplexing of all, how did we get here, and what on earth are we supposed to do with ourselves? Who are we? What awaits us in the future? Wherein lies our hope in the present? The fact that generation after generation of Christians seems to ask these or similar questions and thus engages these basic themes is what makes this list *classical.* As topics, they seem to be as enduring as they are comprehensive and as sturdy as they are malleable.

Theology and Doctrines

In the field of theology, these themes are often referred to by the more formal word *doctrines* (the doctrine of God, the doctrine of sin, and so forth), a practice we follow in this book. It is important to acknowledge from the outset, however, that we were initially reluctant to use the term. Why? Because to the postmodern ears of many of our students, it has negative associations. For some, it conjures up images of ironclad statements ("Christ's death atones for our sins") to which they must assent under the threat of heresy. Such heavy-handed statements, they further imagine, are carefully calculated, highly abstracted, and tightly regulated truth claims or propositions ("the Father, Son, and Holy Spirit are three consubstantial persons") that represent the timeless data of faith. Given that in our churches and popular culture many of these classical doctrines are invoked in a language that sounds old and incomprehensible to today's ears ("the church is one, holy, apostolic, and catholic"), it is not surprising that many of our students view these kinds of doctrinal claims as things to be avoided, not embraced, particularly if one wants to construct a liberating, pertinent theology for our world.

Such a view of doctrine could not be further from the understanding of the term operative in this book. For us, doctrines are something quite different. At one level, the term *doctrine* is simply another name for those compelling themes or living topics that repeatedly emerge when Christians reflect on the beliefs and the complex ways of life they embrace and try to give some ordered, comprehensive account of the theology embedded in their practices. In other words, the list of classical themes we work with in the chapters ahead is, in fact, nothing more than a list of the classical doctrines of the church.

If they are the same thing, one might ask, why invoke the language of doctrine, given its complicated associations? Why not just stick with *themes*? One reason is that the term *doctrine* has a richer history of usage by theologians, both in the past and present, and that history carries with it a fuller, more nuanced understanding of the nature of theological claims. To us, the term *theme* seems flat and monotone. *Doctrine,* on the other hand, sounds not only compellingly authoritative but also round, full, and ripe with significance. Whereas *theme* evokes images of a single idea that can be identified and traced through a body of literature, *doctrine* opens onto vaster worlds of meaning and possibilities; its referents thus seem more far-reaching.

Doctrines as Theological Geographies

A helpful metaphor we have used for this particular understanding of doctrines is that of *theological geographies*. According to this image, doctrines are like maps—they are theological geographies drawn to guide Christians as they struggle to understand their faith. To grasp this metaphor, it may help to think, first, about the complex mental world of our deeply held beliefs about God—a rather large territory, to say the least. Next, try imagining this world of beliefs as a landscape—a vast and complex terrain holding within its borders all those images, stories, concepts, practices, and feelings that make up the sum total of "what we believe in." Now, with this image in mind, try to imagine drawing maps of this landscape. Ask yourself, What would well-crafted pictures of it look like? These maps are what we call *doctrines*; they are collectively rendered maps that Christians have drawn over the years in order to help them find their way around this complex terrain of faith. When they are accurate, these sketched-out and patterned maps can be laid over our faith lives, helping us to see Christianity's content and order with a clarity we might not otherwise have.

When viewed from this cartographical perspective, the theologian-authors of this book are perhaps best understood as artful geographers or skillful mapmakers. Picking up a variety of tools—history, scripture, traditions of creeds and dogmas, cultural analysis, prayerful reflection, commonsense experience, social and linguistic theory, poetic images, and so on—we put them to work in order to draw for our students a helpful sketch of the basic lay of the land with respect to Christian convictions about God and the world. Like any good mapmaker, we do not do this just for the descriptive pleasure of charting; we do it in the hope that our maps might help individuals and communities make informed, reflective judgments about the shape of faithful Christian living. In this regard, we are mapmakers with a normative and pragmatic commitment, namely, the goal of enabling responsible faith.

This task is both constrained and open-ended. On the one hand, we are bound by the given contours of the terrain we are trying to draw. For example, just as a geographer cannot simply conjure up mountains where there are none, theologians who are mapping the terrain of Christology cannot conjure up any kind of Jesus they want. There are definite constraints on the enterprise. In this case, these constraints comprise the fact that Jesus was a first-century Jew from Palestine whose life, death, and resurrection are narrated in the New Testament, a collection of books that Christians hold as the authoritative word about Jesus. On the other hand, as theological geographers, we also have permission to be quite creative with respect to what we choose to highlight and how we decide to render it. Even though geographers cannot make a mountain, they can decide to rename it or use different colors to mark it. Similarly, even though theologians cannot simply invent any kind of Jesus they want, they can still decide to ask new and different questions about who he is and what his message means and, in doing so, highlight different dimensions of the scriptural story and the history of its interpretation. One could depict him as a revolutionary or just a nice guy or a holy prophet or a model of transgendered masculinity, or, perhaps most strangely, the Son of God. Chances are that if these depictions are well-crafted, they all respect the constraints listed above, but each offers us a very different picture of this figure who sits at the heart of the Christian imagination.

It is also interesting to think about the pragmatic aims of mapmaking, particularly as it applies to theologian-cartographers. In the field of geography, there is usually a very practical reason for taking the time to draw a map of a given terrain, like a mountain. People might want to explore it for pleasure or for putting a pipeline through it or for determining how to build a new highway around it. Similarly, theologians engage in doctrinal mapping for pragmatic reasons, the most central one being that of helping Christians understand their faith and live it more responsibly; in short, the goal is to make us personally and collectively better Christians. In the pages ahead you will no doubt find that what being a better Christian entails is a widely debated topic, one that theologians have argued about for centuries.

Just as a geographer's drawing of a mountain has the power to influence a hiker's decision about whether to climb it or a community's decision about whether to put a highway around it, so too with theological mapmaking. The way we choose to color in the lines of a doctrine and to shape the language through which it is presented affects people's decisions not only about its truth but about the way they choose to live in light of it. In this book you will discover myriad instances of this normative dimension of mapmaking. As theologians, we are not writing from a disinterested perspective. We believe that the theology presented here really matters, and we hope that our readers will find it compelling and perhaps even life-altering.

The Relation among Doctrines, Beliefs, and Everyday Life

To draw a map, first one has to identify the terrain to be represented. In the case of theology, identifying the particular territories of beliefs and practices that doctrines are going to map is not an easy or even straightforward endeavor. Faith is a complex matter; like any form of life, it consists of beliefs, actions, attitudes, and patterns of behavior that are often hard to identify, much less distinguish from one another and then define. Thus, at times we may not know what it is we believe theologically or why we undertake the specific faith-practices that we do, but we nonetheless do them over and over again just as we are constantly reenacting particular theological habits of thought in the course of our daily lives. Furthermore, our religious beliefs can almost never be separated from other beliefs, actions, and attitudes that we hold and that also shape us, such as our culturally constructed beliefs about what it means to be a woman or a citizen or a student of theology.

It is also the case that people are often not aware that they have deeply held beliefs about such matters until their normally accepted ways of acting and thinking are challenged, perhaps by an event that exceeds their interpretive capacity or by a disagreement among friends on an issue about which they had assumed there was consensus. When such events happen, these previously commonsensical or unconscious thought patterns come to the surface of our reflective minds; we are forced to articulate these patterns and may also be prompted to change or adapt them to fit the new situation. When this occurs in the context of our religious beliefs, faith begins to "seek understanding," and the activity of self-conscious doctrinal mapping commences as a way of solving a problem or responding to a new situation.

This does not mean, however, that our beliefs only matter when we are faced with crisis or novel circumstances. Our religious beliefs, like other beliefs, are constantly exerting pressure on all that we know and do, from deciding on what to eat for dinner to thinking about U.S. foreign policy to grieving the loss of a friend. Beliefs are, in each of these instances, profoundly shaping not only how we perceive our world but also how we engage and respond to it. For this reason, the influential scope of doctrines on our daily lives is similarly comprehensive in its reach. Doctrines stretch into every corner of our lived experience. Likewise, because beliefs live deep in our imaginations, the material that doctrines map is often more the stuff of dreams, images, memories, emotions, and all the other things that compose our daily thoughts than it is the stuff of rational concepts and philosophical arguments.

Note that according to this definition, beliefs and doctrines are not identical. They describe two different but interrelated realities. Consider the fact that because beliefs are so fluid, incoherent, and often inarticulate, they are almost impossible to pin down and then precisely map out. Coursing through the terrain of lived experience, they resist calculated, analytic form. Constructive theologies like ours, however, are quite different; our work in this text consists precisely in making a series of carefully formed maps. Their purpose is to impose calculable form upon a messy, indeterminate terrain and thereby impose enough order that we can reflect on it. Again, doctrines do this by depicting the lay of the land with respect to our faith, so that as communities of reflection we might have some sense of where we have been, where we are, and where we might be going. In the following chapters this is what we hope you will find—a series of theological geographies that suggest a way of traveling through the terrain of faith in a manner that facilitates communal conversation and proves both illuminating and liberating.

The Structure of Our Doctrinal Maps

There is, indeed, much more to be said about this activity of mapmaking and the exciting questions and possibilities it opens up for imagining what contemporary theology might be and do. We hope that as you travel through this book, some of your questions will be addressed in the substance of the chapters just as other, not previously considered queries and insights will emerge and be pressed. To usher you into the body of the book with some sense of confidence, we will first explain something about its structure. In addition to helping you understand the flow of the book, explaining our structure also gives us a chance to identify several assumptions about theology that are present in the book but not always in explicit form.

Vignettes

At the beginning of each chapter, we offer a series of short vignettes. These are pithy stories or images that we think paint interesting pictures of how the particular doctrine we are treating actually plays itself out in our everyday worlds. We have collected many of these vignettes from our students and from news headlines; we thus hope they stir in our readers a sense of recognition or identification. However, we also throw in a few that might sound strange, surprising, or even disturbing, vignettes that capture something of the oddity, intensity, and plurality of Christian beliefs and experiences. We hope that in reading the vignettes you are provoked to respond to the chapters' beginnings with some of your own and others' stories.

One reason we choose to begin this way is that, as mentioned above, we think of doctrines not as abstracted, other-worldly statements with no pertinence to today's world but rather as connected to all dimensions of our lives. We believe that they affect and move us in ways both familiar and unexpected and often become apparent to us not through consciously articulated convictions but through reflection on some of the ordinary things we do, because of our faith, on a day-to-day basis. By starting with these stories, we start with a genre of expression that is, in many ways, better suited to grasping the detail and shape of those ordinary actions than more theoretical language.

A second, related, reason for beginning with narrative and images that evoke specific contexts is to help readers see that the meanings that doctrines take on are profoundly shaped by the local environment in which they are engaged and hence by the particular people and communities they are addressing and by whom they are addressed. Note that this claim about the highly particular character of theological meaning-making is not designed to relativize and thereby curb the authoritative reach of the faith claims Christians make. Quite to the contrary, it insists that we acknowledge the theological character of even the most idiosyncratic and endlessly particularized dimensions of our varied human lives.

The State of the Question

Having put forth these short scenes and stories, we then turn to the second section of each chapter, "The State of the Question." This section is designed to give readers a condensed version of the main issues treated in the chapter. Here we lay out what we consider to be the central questions that contemporary people are asking about doctrines such as God, Evil, and the Spirit. We then outline briefly a few answers offered by theologians both in the present and in the past, pointing out as we go that while some of our present-day concerns are unique to our age, others are rooted in debates that started centuries ago.

In contrast to the lively feel of the vignettes, this section is presented in much more analytically precise language. It introduces some of the technical terms we are using and also identifies, at a conceptual level, the most important cartographical lines for our map of the doctrine. In other words, it provides the basic geographical grid work upon which the rest of the chapter builds.

Scriptural Geographies

With this grid work in place, the chapter now begins the process of giving form and color to the theme at hand. The first layer of mapping traces out the scriptural context of each doctrine. Why begin here? As Christian theologians, we accept the basic claim that the Bible serves a normative function in the life of faith. What we hope readers discover in this section is the complex process by which this norming is accomplished. To explain this, we do not lay out a carefully formulated theory of interpretation, however, nor do we delve into debates about such topics as inspiration, historical truth, canonical borders, and so on. If this were a book mainly on scripture and theology, these would be questions we would gladly engage. For our purposes here, it is sufficient to highlight only the most important scriptural scenes with which particular doctrines have been in conversation. For example, it is hard to talk about the topic of evil without exploring the story of Adam and Eve and the fall; so in the chapter on Sin and Evil, the Adamic myth is directly explored. As another example, we could not treat the Spirit without mentioning Acts' account of Pentecost, an account that grounds a good portion of that chapter's reflections.

As you read through these scriptural portions, we encourage you to dig more deeply than we do into passages about which you are curious, those you like as well as those you do not. As you do so, pay attention not only to how that biblical text might inform a particular doctrine but also to the interesting ways in which a doctrinal view may in turn inform the way you read a biblical story or poem. Examine, for instance, how your present-day understanding of what a church is—a view most likely shaped by the church communities you have been a part of—affects the way you read the tale of Pentecost or the story in which Jesus calls Peter a rock. Do you imagine church as a community of folks sitting around a campfire singing into the night or as lines of bowed bodies taking communion in a high-ceilinged cathedral? Chances are that your answer to this question will substantively affect how you imagine the interaction between Jesus and Peter or the babbling voices of Spirit in Acts. As another example, consider when you read of the Devil's temptation of Jesus: What images of evil come to mind? What kind of people do you see? What historical events come to mind? And what do these images tell you about the doctrine of sin that is informing your reading of this mysterious story? By asking questions such as these, we hope you can begin to have a sense of the complicated ways in which the strange world of scripture intermingles with the world of doctrine, both of which in turn infuse our everyday imaginations with grace-filled possibilities and promise.

Historical Theological Geographies

In addition to scripture, each of our chapters offers extended discussions of how particular doctrines have been shaped throughout history. Moving from the biblical world and the early church through the Middle Ages and Reformation and into the present, we explore the varied ways communities of faith have mapped out topics such as God, Christ, and church. What is so striking about this history is not just that the enduring questions are asked but also that the answers offered can take radically different shapes in different times and places. For example, in the early church, nothing was more important to theologians than hammering out the distinctions that mark the relations between the persons of the Trinity. By the time the Reformation rolled around, however, these distinctions were commonly accepted; the hot topic was not, therefore, the Trinity but the nature of God's sovereignty and the scope of God's power. Similarly, consider that for many Christians today both the Trinity and sovereignty are a crucial part of their view of God, while the challenge of religious pluralism seems to loom even larger, raising for us questions about the relation between Christian notions of the Divine and other views of the Deity, something our Reformation forebears could have hardly imagined. These sections on the history of doctrines are also designed to illustrate not just changes that emerge across time but also the diversity of opinions that each age holds within itself and to describe why at times one view comes to dominance while others are downplayed or, in the extreme, ruled heretical.

Our hope in these sections is that you will be able to appreciate the place of history in many of your presently held beliefs. In a world in which things change rapidly and we rarely have enough time to eat breakfast, much less study documents from the fourteenth century, it is easy to feel like our experience of God is radically new. While it is true that faith must be renewed and rejuvenated every minute of our lives if it is to be relevant and alive, it is also the case that our capacity to imagine God and to engage in age-old faith practices such as praying is shaped by the beliefs and practices of the generations of Christians who have gone before us. We hope you will find that this legacy is filled with as many eccentric ideas and strangely exciting possibilities as it is with outdated insights and problematic propositions. It is a history, we believe, full of truly unconventional conventions, a reality that makes doing constructive theology an archival adventure.

Contemporary Doctrinal Geographies

In the final and longest section of each chapter, we bring you directly into the world of contemporary theology by offering a series of present-day perspectives on a single doctrine. These are the most creative pieces in our text. In each "constructive proposal," you meet one of our authors as they present in their own distinctive voices their theological assessments of the classical themes at hand. Note that these are the only sections in the book where individual writers are identified. We inserted authorial names here to make the point that collaborative theology does not require that all of our particular voices be blended into a single one. While we do believe that collective visions are possible and collaborative scholarship is quite doable, we also want to honor the fact that there is room for an acknowledged and celebrated plurality of individual voices.

In these sections you will also find many of our political and social assumptions about theology explicitly named and addressed. As a group, we are committed to constructing theologies that are both anti-racist and anti-imperialist, both peace-seeking and gender-troubling, both globally aware and locally grounded, both economically progressive and critically engaged with the reality of global capital, and both nonhomophobic and nonheterosexist. We hold to a theology that is harshly critical of the status quo and its abuses of power and knowledge, but we also remain humbled by the dazzling complexities of the social worlds we all inhabit. In this lies our awareness that we are often implicated in the very social harms that we contest. Finally, we are compelled by a theological vision whose goal is the flourishing of all parts of this richly complex world we call "creation"—a world brought into being, sustained by, redeemed by, and ultimately consummated by the one we call "God Most Holy."

Embedded in most of these theological commitments is a series of theoretical perspectives shared by the group. We share the view that the structures of oppression and harm that shape our world not only are present in external institutional structures and economic programs but also live in the depths of our language and in the varied play of our shared cultural imaginations, both of which are intertwined with our theology. In this regard, we maintain that words matter profoundly and that ideas are never simply innocent or passive signs but always politically interested and socially active performances. Additionally, we hold that language and the cultural imagination are places where power relations between people are negotiated and enacted. As such, in the turn of phrase or the tweaking of an image, language enacts social scenes in which some lives are thwarted while others are encouraged.

These themes at the end of each section influence how the vignettes as well as scripture and doctrinal history are brought together. Additionally, they appear again and again in the chapters in the form of dialogue boxes, one of the most innovative features of this book.

Special Questions

You will notice that popping up here and there are two-column boxes filled with a rather odd collection of writings. At times, they express a view that does not quite resonate with the one discussed on the main part of the page. They may state a contrary opinion or ask questions, or they may represent the view of a well-known personality who has a strong position on the topic at hand. We have entitled these *special questions*.

Throughout our own process of writing this book, such exchanges of a sort were always present in our conversations with one another. We were always talking back and forth with each other about God, church, Christ, and so on—to say nothing about all the other political, social, theoretical, and philosophical debates and arguments peppered throughout our writings. Rather than seeing these disagreements or simple differences as a problem, we see them as an important part of what keeps constructive theology alive and vital in today's world. We hope that as you read, you have your own pen poised to fill in the margins with dialogues of your own.

Missing Maps

As with any geographical enterprise, the map of Christian theology presented here is far from complete. Although we have tried to cover what we believe to be the most important themes, there are several topics that we missed. The most obvious of these are the classical doctrines of Creation, Redemption, and Eschatology (Last Things). There is no distinct chapter in which we discuss what it means to say that God creates and sustains the world. Similarly, there is no extended discussion of what it means to say that God redeems the world—the claim that we are saved. And the insistent

Christian question about what awaits us at the end of time, be it at the end of our days or of history itself, is never addressed here as a topic specific unto itself. Looking at these absences, one might suppose that we considered these doctrines less important than the ones treated. This is decidedly not the case. They are absolutely crucial themes in our classroom teaching and in our broader theological contexts, and because of this, they are treated in the book, but in a rather different manner from the others. We recommend that you look for them as themes running across all the chapters; in other words, you will find them systematically integrated into the other doctrinal conversations. In particular, the chapter on Human Being includes explicit discussions of Creation and Eschatology, as does the chapter on the Spirit. The chapters on Jesus Christ, God, and Spirit have extensive sections discussing Redemption, and in the chapters on Sin and Evil and on Church the theme of hope echoes loudly. As you begin to notice how these themes crosscut the divisions of our chapter headings, you may also trace the ways *all* the doctrines cross-fertilize. God and Spirit speak to each other, as do Church and Evil and Jesus Christ and Human Being—and the list of intersections could go on.

There are other missing maps in the geography we lay out here. Although our authors admittedly represent a wide range of perspectives, we realize that our theology primarily represents Christianity as it has developed out of the Western Augustinian heritage. It is a tradition of theological reflection that our writers are deeply familiar with, one so comfortable to us, in fact, that we are often unaware of its presence and hence rarely pause to note it. We acknowledge, however, that North American theology today includes many other Christian voices. In particular, we note the absence in our text of the Eastern churches and the under-representation of historic Anabaptist fellowships and Pentecostal communities of faith. Let us hope that the next incarnation of the Workgroup will be expanded to include these and as yet unimagined voices speaking from our U.S. context.

1

God

Ellen T. Armour, Paul E. Capetz, Don H. Compier,
Laurel C. Schneider (chapter editor)

A church in a big city decides to respond to the increasing number of immigrants from Muslim countries living in its neighborhood: adult education program participants begin to study Islam. Some members of the church wonder whether Christians and Muslims worship the same God or different gods.

◆

A seminary student, called to ministry out of her large Afrocentric church congregation, questions why her systematic theology class privileges the concepts of God that come predominantly from white Eurocentric theologians.

◆

A young woman who has had great difficulty establishing and maintaining good relationships begins to see the source of her problems in a childhood dominated by an abusive and violent father. Her response is to reject all language, images, and concepts for God that are male, especially those that emphasize the fatherhood of God. She finds she can no longer enter a Christian church without feeling sick to her stomach.

◆

A high school student taking a biology class asks his pastor, "How can we believe in a God who created the world out of nothing, when science is telling us that the cosmos evolved naturally?"

State of the Question

All theological construction comes out of and is largely shaped by particular social, political, economic, cultural, and historical dynamics. Even the kinds of questions we choose to pursue in theology are profoundly shaped by those same forces, but not in some linear cause-and-effect way. Our probing represents a much more complex and interesting interweaving of mutually dependent influences. As authors of this book, we begin to envision and discuss how we understand divinity and the sacred today. Yet in the same breath our shared commitments to theological reflection that recognizes the social location and specificity of every claim mean that we must explore what our particular investments in ideas of the divine might be. Why indeed do we seek to construct new concepts? Why now? And while we seek to keep in mind these questions of context, we can never forget that tradition has played a very strong role in shaping our present situations. So our constructive task as it relates to concepts of God for our contemporary scene also involves identifying and working with the effects of inherited concepts on the present. We remain accountable *to* as well as *for* our inherited traditions even as we may criticize or celebrate them.

Perhaps one of the most distinguishing features of our contemporary horizon resides in our understanding of language. We no longer believe that we can simply seek the best translation of traditions and doctrines into today's parlance. For neither tradition nor our mode of expressing it is a given, inert entity. We are more aware of the structural dimensions of language and the productive dimensions of culture. These realities must be carefully scrutinized as we endeavor to articulate ideas, traditions, and doctrines in more effective, accountable, and truthful terms. Neither tradition nor present modes of interpretation and experience are objective matters; both entail particular investments and influences. The very question of where to begin our reflection, in other words, has become extraordinarily complex.

Nonetheless, we can still identify key features of this particular, millennial point in theological history. We can distinguish relevant forces that shape and give a particular meaning to the way we ask our questions here and now. We are engaged in this thinking and writing in the aftermath of the attack on New York's World Trade Center and in the midst of the United States' declared "war on terror," which resulted in the invasion of Iraq. We recognize anew that ideologies of faith, coupled with global economic and military tensions and legacies of domination, demand our best and most critical work as contemporary theologians. We cannot afford to ignore the particularities of the global context that increasingly shape both our questions and the resources we have for answering those questions.

Aware of the ever-present risk of oversimplification, we might try to describe our current position in history as one characterized by pluralism, critique and retrieval of traditions, and syncretism. Theological approaches to concepts of God now develop in a context of greater religious multiplicity than perhaps ever before. Theism, for example, is not a concept that Christian theologians can take for granted any longer. This is particularly the case as the practical authority of mainstream liberal religious institutions continues to diminish in public and private life. Contemporary persons in the postindustrial West increasingly see their own spiritual lives in highly individualized, syncretistic, or postdenominational terms. The mainline denominations, so closely associated with the cultural privilege of Protestantism in Europe and North America over the past several centuries, can no longer take for granted a strong membership in those regions. Church theologies that encourage denials of pluralism and cultural change attract huge numbers of people worldwide but at the same time lose them in huge numbers, at least in North America.

Within this milieu of cultural flux and diminished ecclesial authority, we share with our predecessors enduring questions about the meaning and possibilities of speaking about divinity, world, and humanity. We are shaped by Christian cultures and histories. We also live in a time of immense religious experimentation, disaffection, and adaptation. As always, we are constrained by a variety of new and old sources. The newer influences include growing social, cultural, and religious plurality; syncretism in both mundane and esoteric affairs; advancing globalization that both uncovers and threatens real difference and plurality; postmodern concerns about the nature and accessibility of truth-claims; scientific disruptions of Cartesian and Newtonian certainties; and heightened concerns about global social justice.

Finally, other religious traditions, particularly nontheistic ones, have begun to influence significantly Christian religious practices and the intellectual milieu in which contemporary persons consider religious ideas. Science adds daily to the intellectual content of our considerations. Modern scientists and other scholars are deconstructing traditional presuppositions about the separation of body and spirit, raising new questions about the ancient theological conflict between apophatic and kataphatic claims about God (see page 34). For example, questioning the traditional argument that God's absolutely spiritual nature is radically distinct from the world leads to negative *and* positive implications about divinity. The globalization of economics and media, along with the commodification of cultures, challenges the content and political investments of our theological constructs. Meanwhile, postmodern theories introduce interesting complications by reminding us of the partiality of every resolution. In sum, we are challenged to rethink more than just the *content* of our claims about God or divinity. We must think ever more rigorously about the complex investments and influences that shape us before we even begin, for these will be wielded productively, for good or ill, in our theological constructions.

The task of constructive theology, as we have said, requires attention both to the particular shaping influences of the time and place in which one seeks God, and to the shaping influences of the long and rich history of ideas about God that come to us from tradition. We cannot think about divinity apart from these influences. In this chapter, therefore, we will begin with the history that shapes us before moving on to our own preliminary sketches for constructing concepts of God.

A Brief History of God

The history of Christianity's doctrine of God may really be a history of *doctrines* of God since Christian theology is the result of an ever-expanding circle of peoples who brought to the question of God their own social, cultural, and historical concerns and demands. Indeed, from the earliest attempts of Christians to articulate and determine their doctrinal positions on God, many divergent strands came together out of Hellenistic, Jewish, and other Near Eastern traditions to form a new synthesis. To put it bluntly, the emergence of classical Christianity in its so-called orthodox forms as well as its "heretical" forms is a thoroughly syncretistic phenomenon and, as such, represents a lengthy attempt to blend traditions that may not cohere with one another as neatly as we ordinarily like to believe. Reconstructing a doctrine of God for our time in such a way that it retains grounding in Christian tradition may mean not only having to recognize this syncretistic heritage but also having to choose from among these various strands in order to develop a coherent theology.

Ancient Israel

One key historical origin of Christianity's doctrine of God lies in the obscure prehistory of Israelite religion. Early Israelite religion and mythology originated in a matrix of cultures of the Mediterranean and North African region often called the Fertile Crescent. Like all other ancient Near Eastern people, the earliest Israelites assumed the reality of what we call "deities" or "gods," that is, personifications of the powerful forces with which all humans had to come to terms for survival. And like most ancient peoples in that region, the Israelites believed that these "personal" gods could be related to and appeased by appropriate rituals (religion).

Polytheism was characteristic of the ancient Near East. The religion that traces its origins to the story of the exodus of Hebrew slaves from Egypt and their wanderings in the desert near Mt. Sinai was not "monotheistic" (believing that only one god exists) but rather "henotheistic" (serving only one god despite the existence of other gods). From what can be ascertained about the historical development of Israelite religion from the Mosaic period (c. thirteenth century B.C.E.) to the Babylonian Exile (sixth century B.C.E.), it seems clear that monotheism was not characteristic of any religion in this early period.[1] The twelve Israelite tribes, which eventually coalesced into a single nation in the tenth century B.C.E., were unified officially by their worship of the god named "Yahweh." The relationship between Israel and Yahweh was codified in a suzerainty covenant recorded in the Book of Exodus that governed matters from the sacred to the mundane. The biblical record suggests that syncretism played a large role in the religious life of Israelites: worshipping the gods of the indigenous Canaanites alongside Yahweh (see the contest between Yahweh and the Canaanite god Baal in 1 Kings 18). Archeological finds include statuettes representing Yahweh (a male god) with his female consort, often called Astarte or Asherah, indicating the blending of Israelite and Canaanite traditions.

In later centuries, when the nation was divided into two kingdoms, prophets inveighed against this syncretism and the popular religiosity to which it gave expression. When the northern kingdom of Israel was swallowed up by Assyria and the southern kingdom of Judah exiled to Babylon while Solomon's temple at Jerusalem was destroyed (722–587 B.C.E.), the people assumed that their god Yahweh had been defeated by the stronger gods of the Babylonians (see Ps. 137:4). But the prophets and ancient Israelite historians, in a theological move that would echo down the millennia, interpreted these national crises as Yahweh's punishment of his people for their infidelity to the Sinai covenant. The exile was not a defeat but a victory for Yahweh over his people. And the fact that Yahweh could use a foreign people with foreign gods as instruments of his righteous purpose suggested a wider divine power and scope than had hitherto been the case. This retrospective retelling of the nation's story by ancient Israelite historians also accounts for the remarkable historical fact that what we now know as the religion of Judaism with its monotheistic theology was born out of the ashes of the older religion of Yahwism with its henotheistic theology.

Whereas previously Yahweh had been imagined to be the national god of Israel exerting his power locally within a larger context of national deities, Israel's god came to be viewed as the only deity in existence (see the Book of Isaiah, beginning with chapter 44). Increasingly, the theologians of this emergent religious view drew sharp distinctions between idolatry, or the worship of so-called gods who are in fact not gods at all, and worship of the one true God who created the world (see, for example, Isa. 44:9–19 and Jer. 10:11). In monotheism, there are only two categories: the creator and the creation. Monotheism, in this sense, is the indispensable presupposition of Judaism as well as the other two religions that derive from it, namely Islam and Christianity (though, as we shall see, the church's trinitarian Christology will pose a serious question about the extent to which monotheism remains intact here).

Emergent Christianity

Christianity emerged at the intersection of Judaism and Hellenism. When the Jews came into contact with the culture of the Greeks through the dissemination of Hellenism on the heels of the military conquests of Alexander the Great (fourth century B.C.E.), their ability to maintain a distinctive way of life as a people was seriously threatened. They faced the challenges that many traditional, indigenous cultures struggle with today, for example, in the face of expanding Western capitalism. As Hellenism spread across the ancient Near East, some Jews found it so attractive that they aspired to complete assimilation through an erasure of the marks of Jewish identity. Others shunned and denounced Hellenism as nothing more than Gentile idolatry. But some took a moderate position between the two extremes. Philo of Alexandria (c. 13 B.C.E.–45 C.E.), a contemporary of Jesus and Paul, advocated observance of the letter of the Jewish law and appreciation of the brilliant intellectual accomplishments of the Greeks. Philo's allegorical readings of biblical texts demonstrated his view that Greek philosophy and Judaic tradition led down the same path. Philo's was a balancing act that set the pattern for the classical Christian tradition: Greek polytheism was emphatically rejected as idolatry, but Greek philosophy was retained and integrated as much as possible with the biblical tradition. The importance of this posture toward Greek philosophy on the part of Hellenized Jews for the subsequent development of Christianity cannot be overemphasized.

Greek philosophy had achieved its greatest accomplishments in the fifth and fourth centuries B.C.E. under Socrates, Plato, and Aristotle, all of whom set the stage for a merging of Jewish monotheism with Greek philosophy through the rigorous scrutiny of reason that they applied to all assumptions of Hellenistic culture, including its pantheon of unscrupulous, unpredictable, and generally unreasonable gods. While criticism of the gods was not the primary concern of these Greek philosophers, the effect of their method of philosophizing did a great deal to undermine faith in inherited religious beliefs and, perhaps ironically, render Judaism increasingly attractive to many intellectual Gentiles who perceived in its monotheistic theology, its high ethical code, and its nonsacrificial form of worship in the synagogues a rational approach to religion (these Gentile admirers are mentioned in Acts 17:4, 17, and 18:7 and were prime targets of early Christian missionary activity). In Rom. 12:1–2 Paul even depicts the Christian religion according to the philosophical category of "rational" (translated "spiritual" in the NRSV, but the Greek word *logikē* means "logical" or "rational"). A critique of polytheism became a point of contact between Jerusalem and Athens, where the traditions of Judaism and Hellenism converged. From the Jewish side, of course, this critique was an expression of monotheistic theology, while from the Greek side it was philosophy's insistence that all beliefs be tested by the criterion of reason since it is only on this basis that human beings may live a life of virtue. The Christians were particularly eager to appropriate this philosophical heritage against the charges of Roman citizens who accused them of being atheists on account of their refusal to worship the gods of Rome.

Christians as Atheists

In Acts 17:16–34 Luke presents the apostle Paul engaged in dialogue with representatives of the leading philosophical schools of his day (Epicureanism and Stoicism).

> While Paul was waiting for them in Athens, he was deeply distressed to see that the city was full of idols. So he argued in the synagogue with the Jews and the devout persons, and also in the marketplace every day with those who happened to be there. Also some Epicurean and Stoic philosophers debated with him. Some said, "What does this babbler want to say?" Others said, "He seems to be a proclaimer of foreign divinities." (This was because he was telling the good news about Jesus and the resurrection.) So they took him and brought him to the Areopagus and asked him, "May we know what this new teaching is that you are presenting? It sounds rather strange to us, so we would like to know what it means." Now all the Athenians and the foreigners living there would spend their time in nothing but telling or hearing something new.

Then Paul stood in front of the Areopagus and said, "Athenians, I see how extremely religious you are in every way. For as I went through the city and looked carefully at the objects of your worship, I found among them an altar with the inscription, 'To an unknown god'. What therefore you worship as unknown, this I proclaim to you. The God who made the world and everything in it, he who is Lord of heaven and earth, does not live in shrines made by human hands, nor is he served by human hands, as though he needed anything, since he himself gives to all mortals life and breath and all things. From one ancestor he made all nations to inhabit the whole earth, and he allotted the times of their existence and the boundaries of the places where they would live, so that they would search for God and perhaps grope for him and find him though indeed he is not far from each one of us. For 'In him we live and move and have our being'; as even some of your own poets have said, 'For we too are his offspring'.

Since we are God's offspring, we ought not to think that the deity is like gold, or silver, or stone, an image formed by the art and imagination of mortals. While God has overlooked the times of human ignorance, now he commands all people everywhere to repent, because he has fixed a day on which he will have the world judged in righteousness by a man whom he has appointed, and of this he has given assurance to all by raising him from the dead."

When they heard of the resurrection of the dead, some scoffed; but others said, "We will hear you again about this." At that point Paul left them. But some of them joined him and became believers, including Dionysius the Areopagite and a woman named Damaris, and others with them.

The significance of this depiction of Paul as a Greek philosopher would become especially important as Christians were accused of atheism. The most important Greek philosopher was Socrates (fifth century B.C.E.), who was condemned to death by his fellow Athenians ostensibly for atheism. Christians were quick to see the parallel between the Greek charges against Socrates and the Roman charges against them. In the centuries following Paul, this Christianization of Greek philosophy became an important feature of classical Christian theology.

Yet another influence on the early development of Christian ideas about God is apocalypticism, which stands in utter contrast to the convergence of Greek philosophy with Jewish monotheism. The expectation of a divine eruption into history to cleanse and redeem the world, apocalypticism is a movement that arose in Judaism, probably in response to Persian influences dating from the end of the Babylonian Exile. In the Hellenistic era apocalypticists took a very dim view of all Gentile influence, equating it with idolatry. Emblematic of apocalypticism was the response to the profaning of the temple in Jerusalem in 168–167 B.C.E. by the Seleucid (Syrian) ruler Antiochus IV Ephiphanes, who turned the temple into a syncretistic shrine of Yahweh,

Baal, and Zeus. Shortly after this event, one group of Jews withdrew from mainstream society altogether and founded a monastic community at Qumran, near the Dead Sea. There they awaited a figure called "the messiah" (Hebrew: "anointed"), who would overthrow the Gentile rule of Israel and restore the temple to its pristine, monotheistic purity.

The theology of this and other Jewish communities like it focuses on eschatology, that is, the events believed to characterize the end of time. Their eschatological beliefs are called apocalyptic, or, "disclosed," because they claimed that what is to transpire in the last days was revealed to them by God through ancient prophecies now coming to fulfillment in their own generation, which is the last generation before the end (see, for example, the Book of Daniel, which represents this sort of perspective). Apocalypticism provided a significant matrix of beliefs evident in the preaching of John the Baptist, Jesus, and the first Christians, and so it contributes to the early shaping of Christian ideas about God.

Essentially, apocalypticism represents a break with the ancient Israelites' view of history, that is, that the evils experienced by Israel were God's punishments of the people's sin. Apocalypticism finds this reading of history a bit facile, probably in part because Hellenistic influences led to a demand for rationality in the actions of a God who appeared to be punishing the just along with the unjust. Apocalypticism addresses this problem by positing history as the site of a cosmic battle between God and the forces of evil (often figured in later Christian tradition by Satan). God will ultimately triumph, but in the meantime, the just and the unjust suffer. What is more, the epochs of history are predetermined to become increasingly evil until the time when God sends his representative (the messiah) to defeat Satan and his army (the demons). Afterwards, the rule (or "kingdom") of God will be definitively established, the wicked will be punished, and the righteous dead will be raised again to life so that they may inherit the reward for their virtue (Dan. 12:2–3).

It is clear in the rise of apocalypticism that the older theological perspective that viewed history as the realm of God's redemptive acts was found wanting in its ability to explain the various evils to which Israel was subjected by its foreign rulers. Instead, apocalyptic Jews and the first Christians shifted to a preoccupation with creation ("What kind of world is this?") and to the ardent expectation of a new creation, since the old one is completely under the sway of demonic forces that prevent God's elect from living according to the original terms of the covenant. What is striking here is that a form of dualism has entered what was originally a monotheistic framework drastically modifying its theology. When apocalyptic ideas encounter philosophical dualisms (between mind and body or ideas and matter, for example), Christianity will struggle to account for the existence of evil and still maintain the goodness of God and of the material world.

Christianity's emergence as a religion distinct from Judaism cannot be explained by reference to what Jesus taught about God or the Torah or any other matters under debate among Jews at that time. The novelty of the Christian message emerged only after the Romans had crucified Jesus and his disciples proclaimed that God had raised him from the dead and his return in glory as Lord and Messiah was imminent (see Mark 15:26; Luke 24:21). The early church proclaimed Jesus' death and resurrection as God's decisive act inaugurating the new age.

The crucial transitional figure here is the apostle Paul, who understood his distinctive mission as taking the gospel message to Gentiles. If we look at the letters of Paul to his Gentile converts, we see the beginnings of the distinctively Christian problematic in speaking about God, which will later become explicit in the debates about Christology and the trinity. Paul speaks of Jesus as "God's son" and insists that Christians receive "the Spirit" upon baptism, enabling them to participate in the benefits of Jesus' own relationship to God as Father (see, for example, Gal. 4:6). The relations between these three terms (God the Father, Jesus the Son, and the Holy Spirit) are not clarified by Paul, though it is clear that they were part and parcel of Christian theology from the earliest days. Paul believed the outpouring of God's spirit upon humanity marked the first step in the fulfillment of eschatological hope (Rom. 8:23). He did not conceive of Spirit as the third person of the trinity (this notion developed later) but rather as the power that breaks the bond of the demonic forces of sin and death. The Christian who dies and rises again with Jesus through baptism is enabled thereby to live in obedience to God in the triumphal "new creation."

It should not be surprising that, in the multicultural context of Paul's missionary activity, translation issues would lead to divergent interpretations of basic Christian ideas. For example, within a Jewish context, speaking of Jesus as God's son can be understood merely as an honorary title; after all, the kings of Israel were called sons of God (see Ps. 2:7). But given their polytheistic context, it is easy to imagine that the Gentile converts interpreted such language through the lens of their own cultural myths, which told of the gods and goddesses having children of their own. This procreative interpretation of God and Christ speaks to the resilience of culture and to the power of syncretism, despite later Christian apologists who fought against this (mis)interpretation. In any case, the innovation of Christianity lies in the claims it makes on behalf of Jesus and his relationship to God. The problem of Christian theology, which it attempts to resolve with assistance from Greek philosophical categories, is reconciling this high estimate of Jesus as God's son with Jewish monotheism.

Messiah was a Jewish term reflecting Jewish hopes for God's overthrow of Gentile rulers and restoration of Israel's purity as a nation. The early Christian evangelists had to find categories for interpreting Jesus' theological significance that would appeal to non-Jewish converts. The most enduring of these attempts was the development of the term *logos* (meaning "word" or "reason"), found in the prologue to the Gospel of John. The *logos* was an attractive concept for a variety of reasons. For one thing, it enabled Hellenistic Jews such as Philo and later Christian apologists to explain how the pagan philosophers could have access to sublime truths about the divine in the centuries before Jesus. The answer was that Socrates, Plato, and the others who taught doctrines compatible with Jewish and Christian theology were believed to be inspired by the *logos*, the divine reason permeating the world. For another thing, *logos* rendered the church's claims intelligible in terms other than those of apocalyptic theology, which had not succeeded in predicting the imminent return of Jesus and, with the growing ranks of Gentile converts, had ceased to make sense as a purely Jewish movement of purification.

"Heresy" versus "Orthodoxy": The Conflict over Gnosticism

In the second century C.E., as Christian communities continued to expand and incorporate new Gentile communities, problems with Christian language about God became more evident. Gnosticism and Marcionism were two schools of thought popular among early Christians that evoked passionate internal debates. Eventually refutation of these "heresies" demanded that the church make crucial decisions regarding what became the foundation of "orthodox" or "catholic" trinitarian theology. In different ways the Gnostics and Marcionites challenged Christianity's claim to be a monotheistic religion in basic continuity with Judaism.

Marcion (c. 70–150) was motivated primarily by soteriology, or concerns about the saving or redeeming work of God. He insisted that Christians repudiate Judaism, since the way of salvation taught in the Old Testament ("works of the law") was diametrically opposed, he claimed, to the way of salvation taught in the New Testament ("faith in the gospel"). This difference implied to Marcion dual gods: Jews worshiped a different god from the God who sent Jesus. He claimed that the God known by Christians as "the Father of our Lord Jesus Christ" is not the one known among the Jews as "Yahweh," since the Jews serve a god of justice and law whereas Christians are redeemed by a god of grace and mercy. The identification of these two gods as one and the same was, in Marcion's view, the original Christian heresy that falsified Jesus' thoroughly anti-Jewish message.

The Gnostics developed a more extreme form of dualism that was heavily indebted to cosmological considerations. For them, the fundamental metaphysical antithesis was ethical: matter, which is evil, and spirit, which is good. The God who sent Jesus is the spiritual principle, whereas the god who created the world is the material principle. Positing an evil deity (reminiscent of apocalypticism's Satan) now responsible for creation of the material world itself (rather than responsible only for the evil doings of humankind) was persuasive to many as an answer to the vexing problem of evil, ensuring influence on Christian doctrine despite being declared heresy by the emerging "orthodox" church.

The church's rejection of Marcion and the Gnostics was momentous for the subsequent development of Christianity. This is evident in the formation of the Christian canon, or Bible. First, what may appear to have been a mere editorial decision to include the Hebrew Bible within the Christian scripture is actually pivotal, since it identifies the God who created the world with the God who redeemed it. "Old" and "New" Testaments are not reflections of antithetical principles of salvation but are actually different forms of one salvific activity of God, consummated in Christ. Moreover, identifying the God who sent Jesus with the God of Israel entails that, contrary to Gnostic rejection of the body and everything associated with matter as evil, the Christian view emphatically affirms the basic goodness of creation and of matter.

The orthodox insistence upon the goodness of the world against all forms of dualism is captured in its affirmation that God created the world out of nothing (*creatio ex nihilo*). This doctrine eliminates any role for an ultimate principle other than God in the constitution of the world. Here, orthodox Christianity breaks not only with Gnosticism, but with its own Greek and Jewish roots. Platonic philosophy and the first creation story in Genesis depict creation as bringing order out of a preexisting material chaos. The orthodox doctrine insists that the one God created matter and did not merely impose order upon it.

Among classical theologians it is Augustine of Hippo (354–430) who most seriously grapples with the implications of this doctrine for understanding the origins of evil in a world wholly made by a good God. In his early adulthood Augustine was a follower of Manicheism, which like Gnosticism advocated a cosmic dualism. He ultimately became a Christian through the influence of Christian Neoplatonism. Using Platonic resources he espoused a metaphysical argument in which evil is not a substance in competition with goodness. Evil, rather, can only be thought of in completely negative terms as a privation, or lack of goodness. His thought is difficult to grasp, but its point is to allow for a ringing endorsement of the goodness of God and God's creation according to the principle that "being as being is good" (*esse qua esse bonum est*). In theological terms, whatever God creates is good (Gen. 1:31).

So, according to Augustine, there cannot be a being who is completely evil, since to have existence at all is good. Augustine uses this insight to develop a theodicy that avoids making God responsible for evil without resorting to a Gnostic or Manichean dualism. The roots of the problem of evil in his view are existential, not cosmological or metaphysical. Evil arises out of the misuse of good: the result of a free decision on the part of a suddenly prideful rational creature to turn away from God, who is the overflowing source of all being and hence of all goodness. Of course, why intelligent creatures would turn away from God in this manner is impossible to explain, but that is exactly Augustine's point: sin is irrational.

"Heresy" versus "Orthodoxy" II: Trinitarianism

From the end of the second century, the orthodox or catholic church established three apostolic (consciously linked to the disciples Jesus commissioned) structures of authority: the Rule of Faith (later to become the Apostles' Creed), the canon of early Christian scripture (the New Testament), and the episcopacy (authorized by apostolic succession). These three sources or criteria for Christian doctrine were mutually reinforcing: the scripture was interpreted in accordance with the creed, which was upheld by the bishops. While this provided a bulwark against the remnants of divergent (heretical) movements of the second century, it did not prevent the irruption of controversies in the early fourth century. Here again, Christology was the sticking point; this time trinitarian theology, which distinguished Christianity from other monotheistic religions, would be the result.

In essence, trinitarianism emerged out of the attempts of early church theologians to incorporate worship of Jesus into the monotheistic theology so clearly defended by the church in the second century. Orthodox Christianity's basic premise rests on its claim that Jesus is the *logos* incarnate. God's *logos* is the divine reason that permeates the created order and that renders the world intelligible as a revelation of God to the human mind (the finite *logos).* So the "image of God" (*imago Dei*) in human beings is assumed to be their endowment with a rational soul (Gen. 1:26). But what is the relation of the *logos* to God? In what sense is the *logos* distinct from God? In what sense is the *logos* God? This is the basic issue raised in the prologue to John's Gospel (John 1:1).

In the early fourth century a church elder from Alexandria named Arius claimed that "There was a time when he [the *logos*] was not," setting off a firestorm of controversy. Arius was concerned to preserve the monotheistic unity of God against emerging views of Jesus' divinity. By claiming that there was a time when the *logos* was not, he attempted to argue that the *logos* is not coeternal with God but is a creature of God. He appealed to scripture, in which the divine Wisdom speaks as a personified figure and says, "The Lord created me at the beginning of his work, the first of his acts of long ago." (Prov. 8:22). Arius naturally connected *sophia* (Wisdom) to the reason or mind of God spoken of in John 1. As the first creature of God through whom God subsequently created all other works, the *logos* is not identical to God and received "divinity" as an honorary title only. In Arius's view, the strength of this interpretation is that it preserves the church's monotheistic premise while retaining a high status for Christ.

The problem with this formulation is the implication that the church's worship of Jesus is idolatrous. Athanasius, Arius's principal opponent, argued moreover that nothing but true divinity can save creatures from death (which, by this time, had become the fundamental existential question for Christians). This dispute threatened to split the church. Bishops aligned themselves with one side or the other, prompting local schisms. The stakes in this controversy were much higher than in previous controversies. The Roman emperor Constantine had aligned his interests with Christianity, seeing it as a potential force for unifying his unwieldy and diverse empire. For this purpose, he needed a uniform theology expressed in clear, teachable doctrines and could ill afford a divided church. Thus, he called the bishops together at Nicaea and demanded that they resolve the controversy once and for all. The combination of imperial demand and internal pressure to resolve growing disputes about the nature of divinity culminated in the orthodox doctrine of

Jesus Christ's full divinity (the Nicene Creed of 325 and 381) and full humanity (the Chalcedonian definition of 451). Athanasius's Christology, which won in Nicaea, finds official formulation in the Nicene Creed. The *logos* incarnate is "very God of very God," "begotten, not made," "of one substance with the Father," and "there was never a time when he was not." All of these various phrases are intended as refutations of Arius and as affirmations of the full divinity of Jesus. The addition of Chalcedon establishes as orthodoxy the claim that the Word (*logos*) incarnate in Jesus is of the same substance (*homoousios*) with God and that Jesus is, nevertheless, fully a human being in body and soul (*homoousios*, the same in substance to us as well).

At the same time that christological questions were being debated in the fourth and early fifth centuries resulting in affirmations of Jesus' full divinity, the doctrine of the trinity was being worked out by the Cappadocians (Gregory of Nyssa, Gregory Nazianzus, and Basil of Caesarea). They came up with the formula that God is "one divine nature in three distinct persons." In this way it was believed that there is one God (monotheism), although there are real distinctions within God that necessitate our speaking of God as Father or Son; once this formulation is worked out, the question of the Spirit falls into place of its own accord. Whereas God is defined as "one divine nature [Greek: *ousia*, Latin: *essentia*] in three persons," Jesus Christ is defined as "one person in two natures" (divine and human). In this way the Son or Word (the second person of the trinity) is said to have been incarnate, thereby preserving the distinction between the Father and the Son at the same time that the full and unqualified divinity of Jesus Christ is affirmed. This christological-trinitarian formula is the foundation of all subsequent theological developments in Eastern Orthodoxy, Roman Catholicism, and classical Protestantism.

The trinitarian theology of the orthodox church (God is "one nature in three persons") emerged as a result of its christological claims to protect the church's affirmations of Christ's divinity from detracting from its earlier monotheistic commitments against Marcion and the Gnostics. This was no small task for the early church theologians: to continue to assert God's oneness as creator and redeemer (against the Gnostics and Marcionites) and yet to proclaim the full divinity of the man Jesus. These distinctions within God are more than linguistic or grammatical rules for speaking of God, though they are surely that as well. They are believed to correspond to the very being of God. They refer to what is called the "immanent" trinity (that is, contained within the divine being), not only to what is called the "economic" trinity (how God relates to creatures in the order of salvation). The trinitarian assertion of one nature in three persons allows theoretically for this apparent contradiction to resolve itself. How successfully trinitarianism reconciles monotheism with a high Christology remains an important question among theologians today. It is an especially critical issue given that Jews and Muslims reject the trinity as "tritheistic" and that within Christianity itself there have always been unitarian reactions to trinitarianism.

The Medieval Synthesis: How to Know and Speak about God

If concerns about salvation and Christology dominated developments in concepts of God in the first several centuries of Christianity's existence, the next major developments were prompted by concerns about the relationships between the finite and the infinite and among faith, reason, and language. What can reason demonstrate to us about God? Where does reason meet its limits? What can be said about God by finite creatures? Where does language meet its limits? Anselm (1033–1109), Archbishop of Canterbury, brought faith, reason, and language together in his ontological proof for God's existence. It is obvious from what God is that God must exist, he argued. Even those who deny God's existence mean by God "that than which nothing greater can be conceived." Since it is better to exist in reality than merely in the imagination, God must exist, else we could conceive of something greater: namely, a god who *actually existed.*

Creative solutions to questions about the limits of language and reason also emerged out of monastic communities, which grew and diversified during the medieval period. The tradition of Christian asceticism, which dates back to the first decades after Christ's death, took on new forms through institutionalized practices of spiritual discipline. Both men and women were drawn to the monastic life, which in some cases even enabled the theological contributions of some women to be heard (see, for example, works by Teresa of Avila [1515–1582], Hildegard of Bingen [1098–1179], Julian of Norwich [1343–1413], and Marguerite Porete [c. 1280–1310]).

Because union with God became one of the primary goals of spiritual discipline, the limits of language itself—the challenge of speaking adequately about direct experiences of union with God—helped contribute to a philosophy of language in relation to God. In particular, medieval theologians saw the value of making a distinction between apophatic and kataphatic approaches to speaking about God. *Kataphasis* says what God is, *apophasis* what God is not. Together, *apophasis* and *kataphasis* attempt to preserve the distinction between creator and creature, the infinite and the finite, that is crucial to monotheism. While *kataphasis* attributes to God all good things supereminently (God is goodness itself), *apophasis* reminds us that the gap between the finite and the infinite is such that the truest statements we can make about God indicate only those things that God is not. Negative theology, or the *via negativa*, also enabled Christian theologians to defer the question of just how trinitarian terms refer to God. God is both one and three, though the mystery of God completely exceeds our capacities to understand how this is so.

Thomas Aquinas (1225–1274), who is considered to be Roman Catholicism's greatest theologian, developed a sophisticated understanding of theological language as "analogical," combining both apophatic and kataphatic approaches. He argued that what we may say positively of God, such as "God is wise," does point to something real in God, but we have to recognize that these positive attributes do not mean the same thing as they do when we say them of creatures. Analogy, for Thomas, is the mean between the extremes of a univocal use of language for speaking about God and creatures and an equivocal use of terms, that is, for indicating a similarity within a difference. In this sense we must recognize that the kataphatic alternative does not really depart from the basic requirements of the apophatic tradition that there are definite limits to what human beings can say about the divine. When we say that God is infinite and eternal, for example, we are saying that God is not finite and not subject to time.

What Can We Know about God?

Apophasis and *kataphasis* provide a helpful way of thinking not just about what we can say about God, but also what we can know about God. Aquinas, for example, argued that God's existence could be known (though God's essence remained unknowable) through observation of God's effects in the world. The presence of motion and causation, for example, in the world requires that we posit the existence of a Prime Mover and a First Cause; that is, God. However, while reason could prove that God exists, it offered no access to God's essence; that is, how or what God is in Godself. Access to God at that level comes only through revelation and is limited by our finitude. We will only know God in Godself in the afterlife, where full union with God is achieved.

The Protestant Reformation

For the most part both Martin Luther (1483–1546) and John Calvin (1509–1564) worked within the broad outlines of the classical doctrine of God that had been established by the orthodox trinitarian-christological creeds during the first centuries of the church, or what is called the patristic period. They were more concerned with the correct doctrine of salvation ("justification by faith alone") than with new questions about God. Their reorientation of church authority, however, opened a gateway to modernity that would eventually have huge implications for how Christians think about God. Calvin argued strenuously for a view of God as a cosmic micromanager who determines all that happens in the world on a moment-by-moment basis. While not novel, this influential articulation of the doctrine of providence would become highly problematic at the dawn of the modern era.

In general it is best to say that the Protestant Reformers assumed their continuity with orthodoxy, although their emphasis upon the Bible as the sole criterion of what is valid in the post-biblical traditions of the church (*sola scriptura*) did open the way for others to question whether the doctrine of the trinity could actually be substantiated by appeal to the New Testament. Michael Servetus (1511–1553), a forerunner of modern Unitarianism, was burned at the stake in Calvin's Geneva for denying the doctrine of the trinity, which he insisted was not in accord with scriptural teachings. Servetus was ahead of his time. It was not until the emergence of the scientific revolution and the Enlightenment that both Lutherans and Calvinists would begin to take seriously the problems raised by orthodox views of God and begin serious revisions of the older tradition, revisions still going on today.

The Crisis of Modernity

By the end of the medieval period, revelation had superceded reason as the criterion of theology. Theology, to use the Augustinian phrase, became the enterprise of "faith seeking understanding" (*fides quaerens intellectum*), an attempt to show that what Christians believe on the basis of the authority of revelation is reasonable even though it cannot be rationally determined apart from faith.

The Enlightenment, launched by the scientific revolution, would harden the lines between faith and understanding, revelation and reason, though one could not predict this outcome from what led up to it. The

Enlightenment brought about significant challenges to the way Christians thought about and talked about God. Though it ostensibly began in the seventeenth century in Europe, the scientific revolution was in fact the result of a long and slow evolution of ideas that went back to Aristotle. Ideas about the physical universe in the Christian West were subject to doctrine and the authority of the church from Constantine forward. Aristotle's experimental method and emphasis on the accessibility of truth through direct observation fell out of favor in the Christian world, as imperial politics relied less and less on an educated populace, supporting the evolution of doctrines that increasingly required affirmation by faith rather than by reason. But, in large part thanks to Muslim philosophers who kept Aristotle's works alive and who laid the foundations for modern science, Thomas Aquinas saw in the empirical approach to truth a powerful avenue for a Christian theology that need not be opposed to reason. His cosmological proofs for God's existence (described page 35) reflect this view. Since God had created the earth and its inhabitants according to his will, Thomas asserted, the study of creation witnessed to God's existence and to the divine purpose.

Thus, whole new avenues of research and thought opened for scholarly priests who fully believed that "natural philosophy" would provide nothing but support for God's revelation in scripture and history. What happened, of course, is a different story. The priestly natural philosophers began to discern significant differences between the claims of scripture and church tradition and the workings of the earth and stars. Even more significant, they also began to discern differences between nature and the teachings of the church. Galileo Galilei is perhaps the most famous of these early philosophers. His confirmations of a sun-centered universe virtually eliminated the ancient three-tiered universe upon which popular religious assumptions of heaven and hell resided. With the realm of creation suddenly thrown off-kilter, many assumptions about God, God's place in heaven "above the stars," and the reliability of scripture and tradition came into question.

Despite the Roman church's resistance, empirical science as a means toward truth took root in a Christian world that was, thanks to the Protestant Reformation, ready to doubt the reliability of church authorities. As scientific legitimacy rose and ecclesial authority receded, the popular language and worship of a God imagined in royal, personalistic terms who occupies a real place (heaven) and who conducts miracles that contradict nature became increasingly difficult for theologians to support, despite the fact that premodern ideas about God's personhood and "place" in heaven remained strongly embedded in liturgies, hymns, and sermons. Apophatic appeals to claims about God beyond being and beyond nature were increasingly difficult to understand and, for Protestants in particular, increasingly difficult to preach.

As the Enlightenment period progressed, the authority of church officials to determine truth-claims about God eroded further as philosophers asserted that human beings (men in particular) are each endowed with the capacity to employ reason and so to discern individually the false from the true. Immanuel Kant (1724–1804) summed up the spirit of this age with the words "dare to think!" While the orthodox doctrine of God did not change substantively in the Enlightenment (indeed, the churches have not officially changed it since the Nicene Creed), theological debates about the coherence and persuasiveness of the doctrine of God have intensified in the West since the Enlightenment.

Christian theologians in modernity therefore found themselves in an era of hyper-rationalism in which arguments about God must attend to scientific claims about the world insofar as God is creator of that world and insofar as moderns understand reality to be, fundamentally, subject to reason. Deism emerged as one theological response to this new challenge. If God is real, good, and perfect (which Christians do assert), then according to the deists God must therefore be reasonable. Isaac Newton made this argument in the eighteenth century when justifying his claims for universal physical laws that the Designer (God) could not break to remain perfect. Popular among the educated writers of the American Constitution (Thomas Jefferson in particular), deism also evolved increasingly into a progressive view of the human soul as itself a part of divinity. Deist theologians like Matthew Tindal (1655–1733) were influenced by both the new science and Enlightenment humanism and argued that miracles, mystery, or anything not accessible to reason are impossible and untenable. The Protestant Reformation had dethroned the church as authority for truth but had asserted that the biblical scriptures were a sufficient and even superior alternative. With new science and the Enlightenment, however, even the Bible was now no longer for educated persons an unquestionable source of information about reality, mundane or divine.

It should not be surprising that deist challenges to orthodox understandings of God drew heavy criticism and strong reactions in favor of orthodox, trinitarian understandings of divinity and in favor of some level of mystery. Also, empiricism was quickly understood to have limits. Both David Hume (1711–1776) and Immanuel Kant demonstrated the role of human perception in observation and the limits it places on empiricism for proof. In addition, partly in response to the hyper-rationalism of the new science, and in response to the growing diversity of Christian (and non-Christian) expression throughout the world, some late Enlightenment theologians began to turn away from attempts to reconcile ideas of God with the rapidly shifting outer or "objective" realm of science toward more individual, inner, and "subjective" feeling, intuition, and piety as the means to understanding and conceiving of God. While some theologians (like Friedrich Schleiermacher, 1768–1834) worked to make the existence of God rationally coherent through examination of human experience and theories of religious self-consciousness, others rejected the search for coherence entirely on the grounds that the doctrine of God need not be coherent to be true, since God is beyond human understanding. This allowed orthodoxy to reassert itself in some communities unwilling to continue the struggle to square modern ideas of reality with traditional doctrine.

One way of thinking about the impact of modernity on theology and the doctrine of God in particular is through the concept of history. Prior to the Enlightenment, theology was more credibly received as unchangeable truth elucidated by great minds or "revealed" supernaturally. History, in this view, is merely the neutral timeline in which these unchangeable truths unfold. After the Enlightenment, history itself, or the ideas and perceptions rooted in particular times and places, came to be understood as a formative influence on truth, including religious truth. The expansions and contractions of imperial colonialism exposed Christians to the existence of other religions. This presented a new problem to Christian theology: how to reconcile Christian claims to exclusive truth with the presence of diverse traditions. Arguably the most important philosopher of religion in the nineteenth century, G. W. F. Hegel (1770–1831), looked at history as a road map of human progress with Christian trinitarianism the highest achievement. His argument suggested that religion, like all other spheres of worldly existence, is profoundly historical, processive, and dynamic in character, revealing an infinite Spirit realizing itself in the finite and carrying the finite ever further toward its fullest self-realization. So for Hegel the Christian claim that God has become incarnate in a human being (carried forward in the realization of the Christian community and Christianized history) represents the culmination of an incarnation that has been occurring since the advent of religion. Hegel thus introduces into the Godhead itself the very process of historicization and concretization even as he infinitizes and spiritualizes the stuff of everyday reality (insofar as it is caught up in the sweep of Spirit's, or *Geist's*, self-realization).

While Hegel's work itself remains difficult and abstract, the impact of his thinking on theologians' attempts to rationalize the doctrine of God for modernity is great. Using Hegel's ideas of historical consciousness, Ludwig Feuerbach (1804–1872), for example, went so far as to argue that a God independent of human imagination is not available to human thought and that "theology is anthropology." What he meant is that ideas about God are really ideas about the human being purified of its limitations and projected onto the infinite. Feuerbach saw this as a positive claim for religion: rather than displacing idealized humanity onto a screen (God) that does not exist (and thus evading our responsibility for making the world a better place), humanity should seize upon the idea of God as the ideal toward which it, as a species, should strive. Making the human race better will necessarily result in making the world a better place for human beings.

Modernity, in the form of science and its view of truth as ultimately available and rational, yielded several significant trajectories in Christian thinking about the God who, remaining distinctly unavailable for observation and testing, poses problems for the modern mind. One trajectory allowed that, without rational proof, no God could be said to exist. Any talk of God is therefore completely in error or should fall within the category of psychology and be treated in that realm (Feuerbach's argument for God as a culturally shared projection of human imagining would fall into this category). Other trajectories allowed for God's independent existence and insisted that this God is consistent with modern ideals of human liberty and flourishing. Still others asserted God's complete otherness as a challenge not only to all human *theological* understanding but to *all* human understanding (in science, philosophy, ethics, and so forth).

We can see, therefore, why Catholicism and Protestantism have each produced movements that simply refuse to grant modernism any authority and assert instead ongoing belief in the literality of many doctrines and other aspects of tradition, for example, specific scriptural texts, the Virgin Birth, substitutionary atonement, miracles, and divine providence. For those on this path, the doctrine of God has little to do with congruity with science or reason and much more to do with affirmations of divine creative, providential, and salvific power in spite of or even against modern difficulties with how such a God can make sense. On the other hand, Kant's equation of religion with morality gave impetus to those concerned about social justice, allowing some to begin to focus on God as the lover of justice. This activist God, already in the nineteenth century central to African American Christian theology, became a central idea within such diverse venues as the labor movement, abolition movement, the African American women's club movements, the temperance movement, and women's movements.

The crises of two world wars and failed post–Civil War Reconstruction in the United States threw cold water on the alignment of Christianity with confidence in human progress. In these events, human beings had shown themselves capable of immense evil. With the advent of the nuclear age, humanity now possesses the capacity to destroy not just individual lives, but life itself. Theology needed to give an account of God in this context, an account that would neither belittle the massive and systematic suffering nor discount modern knowledge of the world in all of its complexity. Two German Protestant theologians, Paul Tillich (1886–1965) and Karl Barth (1886–1968), emerged in this period with substantive responses. Though both were motivated by strong iconoclastic impulses, their theological positions took very different forms. In line with the mystical tradition of *apophasis* but with new conversation partners (such as the philosopher Martin Heidegger and the modern depth psychology of Sigmund Freud and Carl Jung), Tillich spoke of the God beyond the kingly God of myth, the "ground of being." Tillich claimed that humanity is inherently connected to this transcendent ground. Access to this ground comes not only through the revealed traditions of various religions but also through other aspects of human culture (great art, philosophy, and so forth). Karl Barth, on the other hand, railed against liberal conceptions of a God accessible to human construction of any kind. He agreed with Feuerbach that humans create most of what we think of God, but he used this argument to reassert the radical otherness of God and God's distance from human affairs in all of their complexity. "Let God be God!" was his refrain, and by it he meant to restore to Christian understanding a genuine transcendence of divine power and existence. The resulting humility in human understanding of God and of the world is necessary, he believed, to avoid the kind of idolatry that mistakes patriotism for divine right.

Another approach to the doctrine of God that emerged in the early twentieth century is process theology. Based in a metaphysical system developed by mathematician and philosopher Alfred North Whitehead (1861–1947), process thought sought to close the gap between theology and physics, a gap many had begun to take fully for granted. Process thought aligns theism with modern science while acknowledging the reality of radical evil. Whitehead and his followers departed from orthodox claims of divine eternity and infinity by locating God within (and materially bound to) the process of history as the evolutionary "lure" toward increasingly complex and realized existence.

Together these theologians began to open the doctrine of God for more radical reconstruction by recognizing more explicitly its historic dependence on human construction and by claiming an imperative toward "new" language, images, and concepts that would theoretically allow Christian theology to be both more persuasive and more consistent with historic ideas about divine love and creativity.

Social Movements of the Twentieth Century

By the late-twentieth century Christian theology was dominated by two major, related concerns: the rise of various movements for social change around the world and the challenge of religious pluralism. Political movements for liberation based on essential claims of human rights found parallels in theologies of liberation, which were founded on essential claims of the gospel as good news to the poor and oppressed. In addition, the extension of the reach of capitalism and its technologies across the globe brought a reconsideration of the traditional view that Christianity is the best and truest religion. Because the monotheistic and trinitarian theism of Christianity is basically incompatible with nontheistic traditions like Zen Buddhism or with monistic religions like Hinduism, some theologians have sought to relativize "God" as one name among many for ultimate reality.

Many North Americans may think immediately of the civil rights and women's movements as paradigmatic of late-twentieth-century popular concerns for social justice and equality that have had profound repercussions in theology. However, these movements also had some connection to issues of religious pluralism. Dr. Martin Luther King, Jr.'s (1929–1968) philosophy and practice of nonviolent resistance owed much to the work and thought of Mohandas K. Gandhi (1869–1948). Howard Thurman (1900–1981), an important source of spiritual leadership and theological support for the civil rights movement's leaders, envisioned and even founded a church built on the practice of pluralism. The North American women's movement of the 1960s and 1970s influenced the emergence of feminist theology, which posed central challenges to the most ancient concepts of God. In 1973 Mary Daly (b. 1928) coined what would become a foundational challenge for constructive theology in its relationship both to traditional sources and to worship practices. She wrote, "If God is male, then the male is God."[2]

Liberation theologians in Latin America, Europe, and North America began arguing for revisions of images and of basic conceptions of divinity because of the deep intertwining of problematic European or white cultural values and masculinity in the doctrine of God dating back to its origins. Central to these theologies around the world is the insight that ideas are shaped by one's social location. Reading through the eyes of the poor in Latin America, for example, highlights with new intensity a "preferential option for the poor" exercised by the God of the biblical tradition. Reading through the eyes of the heirs of slaves in the United States draws from the Exodus tradition as picked up by the prophets and by Jesus a concern for political as well as spiritual liberation. From the intersections of these locations and movements for liberation come critiques of oppressive presuppositions in the doctrine of God as well as creative reconstructions of alternatives to it.

Some Peculiar Challenges of Our Time

Pluralism and Syncretism

Before we can at last turn to the question of our own propositions for reconstructing the doctrine of God, we realize that in addition to the weight and shaping influence of tradition and history on our work there are the facts of our contemporary scene that distinguish this time from those of our predecessors. Most notably, our awareness of Christianity's ambiguous impact on culture expands the boundaries of constructive theology's audience beyond those who identify themselves as Christians. Concepts of God have political and ethical consequences that reach far beyond the religious and communal bounds of those who espouse them. Western countries and individuals have often invoked God's name to justify their actions. We must consider the ethical and political implications inherent in any constructed concepts of God. Since such claims affect Christians and non-Christians, Christian theologians must consider the practical consequences of their claims for adherents of other religious and secular traditions.

Encounters with other religious traditions are not new to Christianity, but two factors are unique to our context. First, we have become more familiar with other faiths and more aware of the relationship between Christian claims of superiority and Western imperialism. Most contemporary theologians can therefore no longer defend Christian triumphalism either intellectually or ethically. Globalization means that even persons without theological education have had contact with practitioners of various religious traditions. We observe many new forms of religious syncretism. Christians may practice Buddhist meditation. In many urban settings Christians regularly cooperate with Jews, Muslims, and Hindus in social justice ministries. A constructive theology of God must be attentive to these new realities. How do other religious traditions challenge traditional Christian views of God? And what resources for reconstruing the divine do they offer? Given our troubled imperialistic past and the current trend to commodify religion, how can Christian theology responsibly engage with other traditions without doing further violence to them?

Critique and Retrieval of Traditions

Throughout its history Christian theology has often turned to philosophy as a resource for aiding its critical and constructive thinking about the divine. Today's philosophical scene is also characterized by considerable pluralism. In a variety of ways different thinkers continue to offer new angles of vision on enduring problems facing Christian inquiries into the divine. Process philosophy, for instance, presents the possibility of theological alternatives for dealing with familiar dilemmas (theodicy, for instance) in ways that promise congruence with contemporary scientific cosmologies and ecological concerns.

The philosophers of the phenomenological and post-structuralist traditions of Continental thought have raised particularly cogent questions with implications for theology. In a number of ways these trends return to issues raised in earlier centuries. Through the divergent accounts of interpretation provided via Hans-Georg Gadamer (1900–2002), Paul Ricoeur (b. 1913), Jacques Lacan (1901–1981), and Jacques Derrida (1930–2004), the relationship between language and reality is back on the agenda. Though they differ profoundly in many respects, these philosophers present Christianity with a new insight: human beings and human culture are deeply embedded in language. This insight has provoked a variety of responses. The "death of God" theologians of the 1970s and 1980s saw in this insight confirmation that finitude is all we have and whether God actually does or does not exist is less the point than that the problematic "objective" God of metaphysical or onto-theology be recognized as dead, particularly in a religiously plural world. Most theologians reject more extreme versions of this perspective but embrace the attention to language and its effects that these insights encourage. For those theologians interested still in speaking of divinity that exists beyond the bounds of human language and knowing, questions about the capacity of language to refer in some meaningful way to God have reappeared and, along with them, resurrection of interest in apophatic theology.

Contemporary philosophical reflection, then, calls us back to consider the ongoing relevance of old and venerable strands of Christian tradition. And our recognition of religious pluralism leads us to acknowledge that these questions have characterized other religious traditions as well, including the nontheistic ones.

Without denying the ongoing importance of conversation with philosophy, theologians are also turning to other disciplines to understand and grapple with our contemporary context in thinking about God: sociology, anthropology, and phenomenology of religion. If theology is to speak effectively to Christians in their diversity, it needs to draw on the best analyses of Christian communities and practices, as well as beliefs. Of course our setting also demands better understanding of other religious traditions. Feminist, post-colonial, and queer theorists are other important conversation partners for many constructive theologians as we explore more deeply the relationship between theological concepts and identity formation and its limits.

The following four constructive proposals are attempts to respond to these contemporary challenges. Each proposal represents a different theological perspective on the question of conceptualizing God and is authored singly, but each also bears the marks of ongoing dialogue and exchange between the writer and other participants in our workgroup. None claims to be a definitive statement, but rather all aim to serve as examples of the important differences that can ensue in theology even among theologians working closely together. We hope that they will challenge and encourage your own constructive work. Clearly, many more positions can be articulated that come close or diverge widely from these, while still taking seriously the challenges of Christian history and of the contemporary scene.

Constructive Proposals

Beyond Atheism and Theism

Ellen Armour

Our description of the history of concepts of God in Christian theology posits our time as *postmodern*, in the sense that many of the founding assumptions of modernity have come into question in recent decades. It is not our contention that Western culture has successfully dispensed with those founding assumptions and replaced them with others; rather, in many ways, Christian theology continues to work its way through them.

One of those founding assumptions is, to my mind, a particularly strong hallmark of modernity that will not be easily superceded. That is the place it has assigned to religion. As noted in our historical section, modernity responded to the challenges that science and history posed to traditional religious authorities by separating the secular from the sacred, faith from reason. God-talk was profoundly affected in method and content by attempts to respond to the modern worldview. Because God was no longer available to us through nature (as was the case in medieval theology), gaining access to God required going through the being who sought that access: the human subject.

I see the impact of this legacy in my students. Mostly from the Bible Belt, students in my classes at Rhodes College (a church-affiliated college in Tennessee) are largely Christians of various stripes and levels of devotion. However, to a person they conceive of religion as primarily a matter of faith, which they define as belief in something even though it cannot be proven. God's existence is the quintessential case in point. The project of proving God's existence is to their minds fruitless. One either chooses to believe or one does not, but reason has little if anything to do with it. Being religious (in its Christian form) is to their minds fundamentally a matter of believing that God exists and that Jesus died for their sins. That is, what is fundamental and salvific is holding certain *ideas* to be true, whether they accord with reason or not. When pushed, they admit that certain practical actions follow from faith commitments, but those practical actions are matters of personal morality, not social policy or communal commitments.

Historical study gives us a new perspective on our present; that is, knowing something about how our foremothers and forefathers understood and practiced Christianity allows us to see our own ideas and practices with new eyes. The bifurcation between faith and reason that is symptomatic of our time would be quite foreign to figures like Anselm and Thomas Aquinas, central figures in the history of God-talk. Famous for their proofs for God's existence, they were confident in faith and reason's compatibility and saw faith and practice as inseparable. Anselm, the originator of the ontological argument for God's existence, grounds this proof in the practice of prayer. The *Proslogion* opens with an address to God, in which Anselm says, "I do not seek to understand so that I may believe, but I believe so that I may understand." Thomas, a strong critic of the ontological argument, grounds his cosmological proofs for God's existence in the claim that knowing that

God exists is a very limited form of knowledge, in two senses: (1) it is not knowing God as God is in Godself (*in esse*), and (2) it is not knowing God in the sense of union with God, which Aquinas understood to be the *telos* (end or goal) for which human beings were created. Thus, whatever it might mean to "have faith," clearly, for Thomas, it means much more than simply taking as fact the existence of God.

Certain Christian predecessors would also trouble the line of demarcation separating theism and atheism. Pseudo-Dionysius (fifth century), anonymous author of *The Divine Names* and important predecessor to Thomas, distinguished between two ways of talking about God: the *via affirmativa* and the *via negativa*. The affirmative way uses what the contemporary theologian Edward Farley calls "omni-language" to assert the difference between God and humanity. In this mode, Christians say that God is omnipotent (all-powerful), omniscient (all-knowing), eternal (not subject to time). However, these words have little positive content, since as finite beings we cannot know what it is to be "omni" anything. Moreover, the point of God-talk is not simply to name God correctly in order to ensure that we hold proper ideas about divinity in our heads; it is, rather, to know and experience God. This requires the *via negativa*, the mode of talking about God that denies *all* attributes to God including the positive ones. *The Divine Names* is no mere intellectual exercise but quite literally a *via* (path) toward mystical union with the divine. It is a way of ascent that takes the supplicant to the experience of ineffability, to the point where words are exhausted. This is what it is to know God, according to the mystical tradition. "I pray God to free me from God," was Meister Eckhart's (1260–c. 1327) famous prayer. Mystics and visionaries male and female saw this path as bodily as well as intellectual. Specific bodily practices and disciplines prepared one for divine union; the experience of divine union brought with it, on occasion, certain bodily manifestations and obligations (for example, in the life of Julian of Norwich).

I am not advocating that we somehow turn the theological clock backwards and reenter the medieval mind-set. I mention this strand of the tradition for two reasons: first, as noted above, contextualizing the present via a glance at the past counters our cultural and historical myopia; we tend to think that it has always been this way. It is important to see that it has not. Second, as we said at the outset, although addressed to contemporary concerns, constructive theology is always in conversation with the tradition. Contemporary theologians seek out in the tradition those elements that seem particularly relevant to contemporary concerns.

Another feature of the contemporary Christian scene is an interest in spirituality. To return to my students again, I find that they distinguish frequently between "spirituality" and "religion." The legacy of modernity is evident in what they seem to mean by this distinction, but their terminology also begins to exceed the modern paradigm in some ways. *Spirituality* is their term for one's private religious life. It includes beliefs, but also one's devotional life. *Religion* is their term for the corporate and institutional religious life. It includes doctrines and scripture, church services, congregational and denominational structures. One can be spiritual without being religious; one can also be religious without being spiritual. However, genuine religion is spiritual.

In using this terminology, my students are reflecting a current trend in contemporary religious life, the renewed interest in spirituality evident both within and outside even the Protestant church, within and outside Christianity. Outside Christianity the neo-pagan movement, for example, defines itself as spirituality rather than religion. Among the mainline Protestant churches in my own city, at least one has constructed a labyrinth for walking meditation, at least one has hired a minister of spiritual formation, and at least two sponsor weekly Taizé services (musically based meditation services). Christians are turning to yoga and to Buddhist meditational practices as resources and strategies for cultivating their religious lives. Not coincidentally, we have witnessed a resurgence of interest in medieval Christian mysticism. Note, for example, the recent popularity of medieval Christian religious music (for example, the recording *Chant* by the Benedictine monks of Santo Domingo de Silos Priory and contemporary performances of music by the medieval female visionary Hildegard of Bingen). Witness as well the interest in secular academic circles in medieval mysticism.[3] Insofar as this terminology follows the split between public and private, it reflects the contours of modernism. However, since both *religion* and *spirituality* as categories include practices as well as beliefs, we see perhaps the beginnings of a break with modernity. In this event I see opportunities for taking constructive theological reflection beyond the division between faith and reason and the stark alternative it offers between atheism and theism.

Suppose that, rather than asking what Christians believe about God, we were to ask about the work certain concepts of God do? That is, what practices do particular concepts enact and maintain? What practices do they render obscure? Conversely, what concepts of God might support practices that we want to invite and sustain? Among the most important contributions to theology of the contemporary era is the work of feminist theologian Sallie

McFague on critiquing dominant models of God and developing new ones. McFague's work springs from what she (and a number of others) perceives to be the central issues of concern for our day and age: specifically, the contribution that theology makes (wittingly or unwittingly) to issues of ecological and social justice. In her book *Metaphorical Theology* McFague argues that the model of God as Father, Lord, and King that dominates Christian theology is not only anachronistic (given contemporary political systems) but dangerous. It justifies a system of domination that grounds and sustains social hierarchies (patriarchy, for one) and a hierarchical relationship between humanity and nature. Nature (imaged as female) is understood as raw material to be exploited by its human master (imaged as male), made in the image of God. McFague suggests that the patriarchal monarchical model of God has helped to bring us to the nuclear and ecological crises that our age confronts. Christianity's ability to respond to these crises will surely be hampered, McFague's analysis suggests, if it persists in thinking of God in these terms. McFague turns to the theological tradition and to other cultural resources that intersect with it in order to develop alternative models for God (as lover, mother, and friend; the world as God's body) that are more suitable for our time.

It is not difficult to imagine the kind of life practices (private, public, religious, moral) that individual or communal religious lives would call into being and sustain by incorporating these models into their worship practices. Indeed, it is encouraging to see the degree to which the challenge of thinking in new models has been taken up by liturgists and hymnodists in the years since McFague's work became public.

A couple of years ago I presented McFague's work to an adult lay audience at a local Presbyterian church. My audience had no trouble naming the dominant image of God, and several were able, without any prompting, to identify its gender as a problem for some women. When I asked them to suggest alternative images for God that were significant to them, I was surprised when the first image they listed was "rock"—hardly personal or anthropomorphic! In retrospect, perhaps I should not have been so surprised. After all, this is a common image for God in biblical and liturgical traditions. And the connotation that this image carried for my audience was quite traditional. The distinction between the "is" (aptness) and "is not" (inaptness) of this metaphor for God was clear to them. God did not resemble a rock in any material way, in their minds; rather, "rock" signified divine strength and reliability. When I explored this image further with my audience, it was clear that they had not connected it immediately to issues of ecological injustice, although as we explored other natural images for God, those possibilities in nature imagery became clearer to them.

Up to this point in my description of this experience in lay education, I have used the term *image* or *metaphor* rather than *model* to describe how "rock" functions. This terminology is quite deliberate on my part. McFague defines models as extended metaphors; like all metaphors, they work via their similarities to and differences from that to which they are applied. Becoming a model, though, requires a metaphor that offers arguably more similarities than differences, more hooks from which to hang attributes associated with the imaged thing. It is not at all clear that "rock" or "river" offers enough hooks to work well as a model for God. But recall that my project set out to articulate a constructive position that is neither atheistic or theistic. What might images drawn from nature offer that project?

Here I must turn to the work of French philosopher, linguistic theorist, and psychoanalyst Luce Irigaray (b. 1930). The complexities of her thought mean that I cannot do it justice in the limited space available to me, but I will do what I can to sketch out the insights that are most pertinent here. Irigaray uses her three areas of expertise and training to develop theories (and, to some extent, practices) that can promote "sexual difference," that is, an economy (monetary, linguistic, sexual, and so forth) that makes space for genuine difference between the sexes. Our current economy, she argues, is one of sexual *indifference*. It construes woman as nothing more than man's other, defining her in terms of what she lacks that he has. This effectively renders her not different, but the same with less.

Religion is integral both to Irigaray's critique of the current economy and to her imagining what will replace it. Like a number of feminist theologians in this country, Irigaray sees a connection between imaging God in masculine terms and the current economy of sexual indifference. In a twist on Feuerbach she argues that the male God is simply the male subject purified of limitations and flaws and projected onto a divine other. By reflecting man back to himself in idealized form, God reassures man that he really does have what the economy tells him he has, even if only in derivative measure (compared to God). In this respect, religion specifically, Christianity plays a central role in sustaining the economy of sexual indifference.

Irigaray suggests a couple of routes out of this dilemma, including one that I find particularly intriguing for any attempt to move beyond the modernist dilemmas of faith versus reason and atheism versus theism. She notes that the raw material that sustains the economy of sexual indifference (nature, for example) is frequently marked as feminine. In the work of the philosophers, she finds evidence of what she calls "sensible transcendentals." These are raw materials (earth, water, air, fire the pre-Socratic elements), or sensibles, out of which these thinkers unwittingly construct their work. These sensibles are transcendent in at least two senses. The work of these philosophers would collapse without the material infrastructure that sustains them. That these elements perform this essential labor goes unnoticed by the philosophers and thus, in a certain sense, transcends their control.

Although she does little or nothing to develop this insight, Irigaray makes the intriguing suggestion that these sensible transcendentals hold potential for a new connection to the sacred—one that would support and sustain attention to sexual differences. The constructive possibilities for taking God-talk beyond the current impasse of faith versus reason and theism versus atheism intrigue me. First, a theological appropriation of sensible transcendentals renders moot certain aspects of the conflict between faith and reason and its limited choices between theism and atheism. One does not have to decide whether or not to believe in the existence of earth, fire, air, or water. Because they are sensible, a theological appropriation of the elements refocuses attention from an invisible, disembodied-but-agential transcendence (the God of traditional theism) to a (more or less) visible, embodied, impersonal transcendence. That said, of course, we are a considerable distance from the notion of a personal deity (though we may be closer to divinity). We are not at all distant from vital aspects of the Christian tradition, however. Clearly, earth and water would connect quickly and easily to the images of rock and river that emerged in my discussions with local laypeople. Water is, of course, of rich symbolic importance in the Christian tradition. The waters of baptism signify and accomplish the move from sin to redemption, death to rebirth. Fire is the traditional symbol for Holy Spirit, the third "person" of the trinity (intriguingly, the one who is arguably the least person-able and least person-ified). Air, too, is rich in imagery as the medium through which Christ ascends, thus linking the heavens and the Earth, the human and the divine.

Thinking theologically through the elemental is also congruent with my desire to move away from a concern with beliefs about God to the work that certain concepts of God (or of the divine) do. Thinking through the elements refocuses our attention on ritual rather than belief. The central rituals of Christianity, baptism and Eucharist, connect immediately with water and earth (out of which grow the raw materials that become bread and wine). Air and fire also call our attention to ritual, though in different ways. I have noted above the renewed interest in spirituality, particularly in various forms of meditation. Centered breathing is a crucial element of most forms of meditation of which I am aware. Fire, as I noted above, is a central symbol for the Holy Spirit, depicted in Acts 2:3 as descending like "tongues, as of fire" on the day of Pentecost. The reader who is familiar with the biblical account of Pentecost will recall the effect of the descent of the Holy Spirit: the invocation of a diverse Christian community as each heard the gospel message in his or her own native tongue.

Thinking constructively through the elements also refigures the relationship between the divine and the human, transcendence and immanence. In traditional theism, God is a bigger, better version of us. God transcends us both as source of our existence and as what lies beyond our grasp and beyond our limitations. Divinity conceived as elemental, while not a deity per se, remains that in which we "live and move and have our being" (Acts 17:28). Air transcends us in both ways: without it, we literally could not exist, yet it does its work almost invisibly. It is immanent as well as transcendent, as much "in here" as "out there."

What work would such theological thinking do? What implications for living the Christian life arise from such a theology? Considering the elements as windows to the sacred implies a critique of the instrumental approach to the world that has brought about the ecological crisis. After all, we are quite literally sustained by the elements physically and spiritually. We have, then, religious and moral obligations to the natural world. Awareness of its fragility (and of the fragility of divine transcendence) also brings about a different configuration of the relationship between religiosity and mortality. Again, if my students are reliable examples, many Christians think of their religion as a matter of a vertical relationship between them and God that promises them ultimate escape from mortality. Clearly, thinking theologically through the elemental offers a different relationship to mortality. Rather than promising an escape from it, it confronts us with it. Rather than transcending the body (as traditional omni-language does), the elementals figure an embodied transcendence.

Finally, thinking divinity through the elements also refigures the relationship between unity and diversity. Sensible transcendentals do not map neatly onto a unitary deity. Indeed, I would argue that this is part of their value to us. The event of Pentecost (the descent of the Spirit as fire) plays quite intriguingly with the issue of difference and community. Community is produced not in spite of (linguistic) difference but through it. Thus theological reflection on divinity through sensible transcendentals has immense and fruitful implications for a multicultural, pluralistic world.

God Is Love: Theological Reflections on the Spirituality of Young Adults

Don Compier

As a human discourse theology cannot pretend to utter timeless truths. Theology is rhetorical, seeking to persuade through successful communicative performances. Individual theologians always write for specific audiences with specific purposes at specific historical moments.[4] This essay has its own ax to grind!

As I survey the current state of mainstream religion in the United States (to be sure, without much sociological sophistication), I am struck by the almost complete absence of young adult voices. Even when persons representing the cohort of eighteen- to thirty-five-year-olds show up, they do not seem to find space to speak in their own dialect. As I look at ecclesial and academic (and indeed political) leadership around the nation, I sense that we are doing a rather poor job of passing the baton to the next generation. One finds a great deal of literature in various genres decrying the supposed deficiencies of up-and-coming leadership prospects and precious few concrete proposals for training or mentoring, let alone providing genuine opportunities for the acquisition of indispensable on-the-job training. I am deeply concerned about the graying of the church and the academy. Of course we must value the wisdom of senior colleagues and the important traditions they represent. But their precious heritage will not survive if we do not actively encourage the emergence of their successors.

I contend, then, that contemporary doctrines of God (and all theological subjects, for that matter) must attempt to respond to the voices, the questions, and the yearnings of young adults. In this enterprise we can overcome the supposed incompatibility among theological schools such as Barthianism, correlational methods, and theologies of liberation.[5] Like theologies of the Word of God, theologies sensitive to the presence of young adults will seek to serve effective preaching. The often misunderstood and unjustly neglected "classical" Christian traditions should indeed be proclaimed anew. Yet our communication of the gospel will fall on deaf ears if we do not achieve a deeper understanding of youth cultures. At their best, correlational theologies that, in Tillich's terms, attempt to link theological "answers" to existential "questions" foster a robust dialogue with contemporary culture. And if, as I contend, young adults today are characterized by a profound search for personal, social, and ecological liberation, our conversations must move beyond indispensable philosophical mediation to engage in what Rebecca Chopp has called "critical praxis correlation."[6] This emphasis is typical of theologies of liberation, which test doctrinal thinking by probing its fruitfulness for the promotion of transforming social engagements. If we are serious about such an examination, we must acknowledge the gravity of a number of critiques leveled at the Christian tradition itself.

In short, I contend that theology in the United States at the beginning of the twenty-first century must pursue the genre of apologetics. I used to say that apologists offer a defense of Christian faith in light of current critiques. After becoming more familiar with the work of Friedrich Schleiermacher, I have had to revise my views. He models a way of approaching apologetics as genuine dialogue, not defensive arguments. On the one hand his address to "cultured despisers" translates the good news into terms intelligible to contemporary persons. Yet on the other hand he readily acknowledges the validity of some of the Enlightenment and Romantic critiques of established Christian thought and practice.[7] Apologetics, then, is a communicative act involving repentance and prospects for reconciliation and renewal.

All good theology begins with careful listening. Marcus Borg has argued that Jesus became attuned to both the Spirit and his society.[8] We are fortunate that in our day mystical writings draw the attention of an increasing number of scholars. I am convinced that the experiences of the great spiritual authors offer fresh and vitally important vantage points that should inform our formulation of doctrines of God.[9] As it turns out, spirituality has become a very popular topic among young adults as well.

As something of a novice in this field, at present I can only draw tentative conclusions about the lessons theology might derive from the renewed appreciation for living spiritual traditions. I am beginning to sense, in addition, that the enlargement of our literary horizons to include mystical texts may recast the long-established lines of argumentation about theodicy, the "defense of God." With the advent of the modern era, the problem of evil has presented one of the principal apologetic challenges. The genocidal horrors of the bloody twentieth century have deepened this grave concern. My unscientific survey of popular culture (film, music, comic books, and so forth) suggests that the problem of evil continues to vex contemporary persons. This dimension of the debates of modernity constantly attracts new interlocutors. While not lacking in philosophical sophistication, young adults tend to personalize the issue, to voice its emotional resonance. In ways reminiscent of literary giants like Voltaire (1694–1778) and Fyodor Dostoevsky (1821–1881) rather than philosophers like Gottfried Wilhelm Leibniz

(1646–1716) or David Hume (1711–1776), they express anger, fear, and bewilderment (for example, the graphic novel series *Preacher* and the musical work of Smashing Pumpkins, in particular their song "Bullets with Butterfly Wings"). Like the practitioners of protest theodicy before them, the upcoming generations understand that evil is a spiritual issue. Our conceptualization of the dilemmas that suffering poses becomes a vital part of the emergence of our fundamental dispositions toward the world, including its possible transcendent dimensions.

The experience of suffering, of course, has been addressed in spiritual writings for a very long time. At the risk of enormous oversimplification, I make bold to draw two conclusions from this large body of work. First, I find it remarkable that the God the mystics claim to experience is not primarily categorized in terms of power or certainly not in tropes depicting control and force. I am struck by the repeated discussion of God's silence, the withdrawal of the divine, and the patient unobtrusive presence of the holy.[10] Second, one cannot miss the frequent lyrical descriptions of divine love.[11] Moreover, these themes tend to merge. God's strength is depicted as the undiminished vitality of the persistent lover. From the perspective of spirituality, then, we might say that God's power *is* love and that God's love *is* power.

The long traditions of Christian reflection on the trinity also undergird these equations. Trinitarian doctrine makes the radical claim that the God of monotheism *is* a true beloved community. In Augustine's influential formulation, three irreducibly distinct persons are indissolubly united by bonds of deep mutual love. God's own being, then, is seen as one characterized by relationships of self-giving, reciprocal compassion, respect, and sharing.

Lest we are left with the impression of a somewhat narcissistic deity, Christian theology has provided balance by stressing the "overflowing" nature of the divine love that ever seeks that which is wholly other or outside of God's self. The Jewish philosopher Emmanuel Levinas (1906–1995) helps us to understand that this theme is central to the understanding of creation in the biblical traditions. The love that constitutes the very being of God can only become effective if God permits the existence of a truly independent universe. It is true that Christian theologians often refer to the dependence of creation on God for its very existence. Some influential thinkers, notably Calvin, even depict God as the second-to-second micromanager of all that is! Yet the theme of creation as "not God" recurs again and again across the centuries. God must constantly work out a relationship with a reality that God may have willed into being but that nevertheless now has a reality of its own.

Such a realization might lead to a discursive shift in theodicy. We are still in the grips of Hume's powerfully articulated fork or triangle. In his classic argument the Scottish philosopher of the eighteenth century demonstrated that one cannot rationally maintain three affirmations, namely that God is all-powerful, God is wholly good, and that evil is real. For if genuine evil exists, either God willed it (thus forfeiting omnibenevolence) or could not prevent it (in which case God is not omnipotent). According to this formulation, we must choose between God's power and God's goodness (love), or we risk denying the reality of evil.[12] But what if God's "moral" attributes (steadfastness, compassion, and so forth) and "metaphysical" attributes (eternity, independence from the world, and so on), are one and the same? We might then engage in fresh inquiries into the nature of both love and power.

Still in the thrall of (post)romanticism, I believe that we have spoken rather sloppily in our theological conversations about love. The word *love* has become one of those concepts that everyone presumes to understand, so taken for granted that almost no one really grasps what in fact we are talking about. Attention to spiritual experiences can put flesh on conceptual bones. Through the lenses offered by thinkers such as Jacques Derrida and Levinas (themselves informed by currents of mystical thought), I contend that love (*agape/caritas*) is respect and solicitous care for the other as other. Resisting all attempts at assimilation, it wishes to maintain the separate, concrete dignity and relative autonomy of each agent as the basis for true relationships and true community. In the language of Mark McIntosh, God is "drawing intimacy and joy out of difference without washing out otherness."[13] If we affirm that God *is* love, and if we accept my proposed definition of *agape/caritas*, the divine simply cannot do anything else, not because of limitations in power but because the Holy One has a certain type of character and not another.

The Theories of Levinas and Derrida

It is important to understand some vital differences between these philosophers' positions and the ethics and politics that they might engender from that of modern liberalism. Within modern liberalism, respect for the other is grounded in respect for the self. I respect the other because I consider the other as another like me. In theory, this plays out politically as tolerance. However, in practice, tolerance sustains itself only as long as real difference stays submerged. Once difference rises to the surface (as, for example, when the population of Latinos in the United States becomes large enough that whole neighborhoods become Spanish speaking and the need for English language instruction grows), tolerance fails when the illusion of sameness can no longer be maintained.

Levinas's position on the relationship between self and other is diametrically opposed to that suggested by liberalism. The demand of the other simultaneously calls me into being as an ethical subject as subject-in-relation. I bear the other within me, in a sense; thus, any claim to self-sameness or self-mastery is forever postponed. Yet the other is not my master either. Its demand, "Thou shall not kill (me)" can be met with either an ethical response or its refusal (murder).

Likewise, Derrida's work refigures the relationship between self and other, with consequences for ethics and politics. First, our ethical obligation to the other is absolute, yet structurally infinite and unfulfillable. By responding to any particular concrete other, I am necessarily ignoring the needs of another concrete other. Yet responding to one does not release me from my obligation to another. Thus, ethics is simultaneously utterly impossible and utterly necessary. Second, others refuse to stay neatly in their places. Though always subject to the demand that they be like us, those deemed "other" (for example, because of sexual or racial differences) also exceed the boundaries of this demand. It is out of this excess that the possibilities of political transformation arise.

I believe that thinking along these lines permits using the best insights of recent doctrines of God and theodicies while avoiding their pitfalls.[14] Some examples: The core insight of the free will defense (evil results from wrong human choices) is conserved, but without having to define human freedom in voluntaristic terms. Freedom then refers to realization of our communal destiny, not unfettered consumer-like choices. Soul-making theodicy's emphasis on the development of moral character (without evil, how would humans mature in the struggle against wrong?) may be preserved, but without assuming that God has chosen to make certain persons' suffering an object lesson for the rest of us. Recourse to divine mystery (our feeble human minds cannot comprehend why evil exists) can now be interpreted as an expression of the ineradicable value of otherness. If we are to respect differences, we must first acknowledge that God's ways are not our ways. Jürgen Moltmann's (b. 1926) ideas about a suffering God are freed of their potential for a sort of trinitarian solipsism.[15] A loving God cannot be unmoved by human (or animal) pain, yet God's actions in history and nature primarily represent compassion for distinct created others, not for diverse personae of the divine self.

Above all I believe that a doctrine of God deriving from and stressing mystical otherness offers a viable and sympathetic alternative to most process thought. When I have read works in the tradition of Alfred North Whitehead, I have always been troubled by (1) the tendency toward aestheticism (not the same as aesthetic sensibilities!) and (2) the absence of eschatology (judged by the criteria of hope and imagination). First, process thinkers sometimes tend to use language that seems to indicate that beauty is a higher good than love. Of course appreciation of what is pleasing and attractive is a vital element in amorous experiences (and not only erotic ones), yet as an end in itself it does not readily encourage regard for all others on their own terms. Attention to spiritual lives must involve appreciation for beauty. I believe that emphasis on the priority of otherness preserves the proper tension between art and ethics from its collapse in aestheticism.

From the perspective of suffering, the wan portrayals of the eschaton in process thought present a far more serious problem. As African American spirituals suggest, oppressed persons long for future liberation and justice. The ability to articulate "well-founded hope" (Hendrikus Berkhof) affects the capacity to resist and continue struggles when the odds are long. Process theology places such a premium on freedom that it risks pulling up the anchor steadying the ship in the midst of storms (see The Letter to the Hebrews). Yet eschatological alternatives offered by thinkers such as Moltmann and John Hick (b. 1922) beg the question of why God can make it all better later yet lacks the power to prevent serious harm in the first place.

A radical commitment to a theology of divine love offers a way to avoid either extreme. When we reflect on the human experience of love and on the frequency of erotic imagery in spiritual discourses, other possibilities present themselves. Love does not control. It cannot micromanage. To do so would amount to destroying the otherness of the beloved. But lovers can do more than lure and persuade: they can woo. Human love, of course, comes and goes, lacking perfect steadfastness. Yet we know that if we continue to love someone as best we can, in time persons tend to respond to our careful regard. In the beginning love lacks the strength of force, but over the long haul its power tends to increase and accomplish more than coercion. If these generalizations hold in the case of fallible human love, we can extrapolate to envision the long-term effects of God's unwavering, perfect, ever-present, and everlasting charity. Such a theology accepts the tragic inevitability of genuine evil in our present existence. Yet it can persuasively articulate genuine grounds for hope in the future triumph of the divine care.

These reflections already begin to suggest that emphasis on the priority of divine moral attributes reinforces themes found in theologies of liberation. As thinkers such as Gustavo Gutiérrez (b. 1928) and Jacquelyn Grant (b. 1948) emphasize, thinking proceeding from the "underside of history" must focus on critiques of the erasure of the agency and subjectivity of the oppressed.[16] My proposed stress on the relationship between love and otherness would then imply that the Holy Lover is offended by structures that objectify persons, excluding them from the capacity to participate in the web of genuinely loving relationships. Liberation theology's stress on God's preferential option for the poor (or, in James Cone's formulation, the Blackness of God)[17] then expresses the notion that a deity who values the autonomy and dignity of each creature must first work to overcome the forces that stand in the way of the capacity to exercise genuine personhood. Liberation (or at least the initial stages of consciousness raising, recovery of the voices of the silenced and marginalized, and so on) is the indispensable prerequisite for entry into the beloved community that maintains difference and otherness. Liberation offers a concrete exemplification of what love is and of what love requires.

At the same time theologies of divine love can help address certain gaps in the treatment of theodicy in liberation thought. In his early work Gutiérrez, for instance, tended to go too far in his exultation of the emancipatory power of God, leaving at least some readers wondering how this almighty deliverer could allow the poor to suffer so much in the first place. When he at last faces the problem of evil squarely in his book on Job, I was left unsatisfied by the inconclusiveness of his restatement of Barthian themes. Similarly, Cone shifts the ground toward anthropodicy (defense of humans in light of the problem of evil), seemingly leaving the question of divine responsibility in limbo.[18] I have the uneasy feeling that such reflections, in spite of the immense richness of their contextual awareness, in the end do little to move us beyond Immanuel Kant's moralism, which, as Friedrich Nietzsche (1844–1900) grasped, in the end really requires no conception of God at all.

A theology stressing God's character as love that values otherness can retain the rhetorical force of liberationist emphases on the solidarity of God with the oppressed, yet make sense of the delay of parousia or utopia and still offer a hope that steadfastly braces persons to continue the long struggle toward justice. I dare to hope that my synthetic constructive proposals may prove timely, for many writings suggest that chastened liberation theologians are reformulating their doctrines for service over the long haul. Serendipitously, they are reemphasizing spirituality in the process.

And thus I circle back to where I began. For I detect great interest in liberation among young adults. While disconcerting signs of reaction cannot be ignored, feminism, the civil rights movement, the emergence of post-colonialism, and the movement for gay and lesbian rights seem to have left an indelible imprint. In particular, signs of growing ecological awareness and international experiences offer reasons for hope. Apologetics emerging from genuine dialogue with younger voices must therefore take matters of justice with the utmost seriousness. Current theologians must demonstrate a willingness to be called to account for our complicity, however unintentional, in structures of oppression. We must articulate reflections on God that can imaginatively and faithfully portray the relevance of concepts of the divine in movements for global transformation. In theological practice we must concretely demonstrate the compatibility, and maybe even the synonymous identity, of mystics and prophets.

God and Religious Diversity: Toward a Theocentric Pluralism

Paul E. Capetz

For most Christians in the Western world at the dawn of the twenty-first century, the fact of religious diversity has assumed a new and historically unprecedented significance. There has always been a variety of human religious and moral outlooks, but in our time adherents of other traditions are no longer strangers living in remote lands on the other side of the world; rather, they have become our neighbors and workplace colleagues whose children are befriended by our own at school and on the playground. In recent decades Islam has come to the attention of Christians as a vital political and cultural force, just as in the middle years of the twentieth century the Holocaust and the founding of the state of Israel occasioned a new awareness of Judaism as a living tradition. And although Asian immigrants have resided in the West for centuries, the number of Hindus, Buddhists, and representatives of other Eastern religious groups has grown as more and more immigrants have sought a home in Western countries.

Christianity has always had to deal with the existence of a plurality of various interpretive frameworks for understanding what it means to be normatively human. Traditionally, however, this diversity has been evaluated negatively. But the new question is whether the de facto plurality of religions can and should be embraced in a spirit of pluralism, that is, whether an appreciation of human religious diversity is a good thing.

All of us, I contend, are faced with the challenge of affirming that we share a common humanity that admits of many variations. The task of building a humanly just and ecologically sustainable global community requires us to find ways of truly respecting differences while valuing and cultivating our own distinctive ways of being human. If we cannot find a way to live together in a spirit of pluralism, then the job of creating the necessary conditions for human life to be sustained will not be accomplished. As I see it, the survival of humanity itself is at stake in the call to embrace pluralism.

The problem of insiders versus outsiders, "us" versus "them," is deeply rooted in the Bible. Israel believed itself called by the one true God to be a chosen people and looked disdainfully upon the nations ("the Gentiles") as idolatrous worshippers of false gods. Within Israel the prerogative of being the chosen people was contested between Jews and Samaritans. Among the Jews there were the various sects of Pharisees, Sadducees, Essenes, and Christians, each claiming to represent the true Israel. Christians have viewed their own religion as the only true or valid religion on the supposition that it alone contains the fullness of truth revealed by God. The other religions were seen, at worst, as various forms of pagan idolatry (polytheism) or, at best, as incomplete (for example, Judaism) or degenerate (for example, Islam) forms of the true revelation of the one God. Nonetheless, theological controversy regarding how to interpret this one true religion was never absent from Christianity. First, there was the effort to distinguish orthodoxy from heresy (Gnosticism). Then other splits emerged. The Eastern Orthodox still consider the Western Augustinian heritage to be a deviation from the authentic apostolic tradition. Within the West until recent times, Catholics condemned Protestantism as heretical, whereas Protestants, for their part, rejected the Roman church as idolatrous. But even Protestantism itself has never been a unified movement. It has given rise to many denominations, each claiming for itself to have the correct interpretation of the Bible. Within these denominations, there have been and continue to be conflicts between liberals and fundamentalists. The list could go on and on.

My point in adducing these historical considerations is to suggest that our attitude toward religious diversity outside of Christianity is only one side of a larger question, the other side being the theological diversity within Christianity. Not only do we need a new way to think about the religious traditions of other people, but we need to learn to think about our own in a new way as well. I suspect that a pluralistic attitude toward non-Christians will be difficult for those Christians who believe there is only one authentic form of Christian faith and life. Hence, in my advocacy of religious pluralism I do not claim to speak for all Christians. Still, I do maintain that my reasons for affirming religious plurality are consonant with my central theological convictions as a Christian.

My theological perspective is rooted in a very particular strand of Christian theology that is constituted by four identifying markers: Western (Augustinian), Protestant, Reformed (Calvinist), and liberal. Let me briefly explain what these four labels mean for me. First, the Augustinian tradition understands religion primarily in terms of the affections (loves) of the heart. The ideal for religious and moral life consists in a proper love of God and of all things in appropriate relation to God. Doctrines are important as intellectual efforts to understand the affective dimensions of human religious and moral life (as in the motto "faith seeking understanding"[19]), but they are not the central thing. Second, Protestantism rejects the absolutizing of any and all human religious authorities and traditions. Human beings must not confuse their own perspectives with that of God. In their return to the Bible, the original Protestants believed that they were basing their theologies on the Word of God and not on any merely human opinions or traditions, since "popes and councils can err."[20] Third, in my interpretation of it, the Reformed tradition is fundamentally theocentric, rather than Christocentric. This means that Jesus is important because of the redemptive influence he has on Christians when their hearts are set free from misplaced objects of love and value, corrupted affections, and constricted perspectives in order to become free for a proper ordering of life in relation to God. This is what it means to call him "Christ." We call ourselves Christians because the encounter with Jesus has liberated us from bondage to self and reoriented our lives toward God. In this tradition, serving God is the primary concern; salvation, as usually understood, is subsidiary. Fourth, the liberal tradition affirms the insights from the modern sciences and the historical-critical study of the Bible that require us to understand the many ways in which classical Christianity was shaped by assumptions about reality that reflected the limitations and biases of ancient cultures and societies. These insights not only deepen our sense of the relativity of each religion but also lead to a new ethical awareness that scriptures and traditions are developed by finite, culturally bound human beings who are subject to the corrupting influences of sin. Since even the Bible is brought under the category of "tradition," it is no longer possible to affirm, with the original Reformers, that the Bible is exempt from the ambiguities and corruptions of human tradition. Hence, an absolutizing of the Bible as though it contained in some unambiguous sense the very words of God is idolatry. Again, I am aware that not all Christians share these presuppositions, but since the content of the term *Christian* is not self-evident given the internal plurality within the history of Christianity, it is important for me to be clear as to how I identify myself before addressing the issues before us.

In many discussions of religious pluralism, the theological issue that presents itself is the question of whether non-Christians can be saved. There are usually three options represented in this discussion: the exclusivist, the inclusivist, and the pluralist.[21] The exclusivist takes the traditional Christian viewpoint that "outside of the church there is no salvation."[22] Presumably this entails for non-Christians eternal damnation. The inclusivist affirms that Christ is the only savior of the world, but that non-Christians are saved through Christ whether they know him by name or not. This position does away with the threat of hell for those outside of the church while continuing to maintain that Christianity is, in fact, the one true religion. What is usually taken to be the pluralist position is that there are many roads leading to the same goal. Buddhism, Islam, Judaism, and Christianity are merely different ways to salvation. I reject the first (exclusivist) position entirely. I accept some aspects of the second (inclusivist) and third (pluralist) positions, albeit with qualifications.

In my view any religion that claims for itself to be absolute and unambiguously true is idolatrous. Such a view fails to acknowledge human finitude and the inevitable corruption of perspective that follows from absolutizing what is relative. For the exclusivist, unless one affirms that everything in one's own religion is true, then nothing is true. As I see it, there is much in traditional Christianity (not to mention the other religious traditions) that is false and bad. But this admission does not entail that there are no profound truths or examples of goodness to be found and cherished in the tradition. It is similar to saying that American history is filled with instances of injustice and betrayal of democratic ideals, but this does not mean that everything about America and what it stands for is to be rejected. The inclusivist teaches, I think, an important lesson: the Christian sees in representatives of other religions something like the salvation known in the church. For instance, I have known Jews who are more loving than many Christians I have met. So if love is a "fruit of the Spirit" (Gal. 5:22), then I infer that the Holy Spirit is at work in the lives of these non-Christians. Where the inclusivist is wrong, in my view, is in the implication that these non-Christians would fully understand themselves only if they named

Christ as the source of their love. There is still a hint of arrogance in this position, even though it tries to work against the traditional exclusivist viewpoint. In spite of its name, the third position is not really pluralistic, as I see it. The problem here is that not all religions teach the same things or hold out the same goal for their adherents. This superficial version of pluralism actually flattens out the differences among the religions that need to be faced honestly in our world today.[23] Moreover, I assume that the other religious traditions are just as internally complex and rife with controversy as is the Christian tradition. For that reason, it is dangerous to make sweeping generalizations about Islam or Buddhism or any other religion; instead, we need to ask about which form of Islam or which expression of Buddhism we are speaking.

One question that needs to be asked is what exactly we mean by salvation. For most Christians, it has usually been understood to involve some sort of life after death. But for many Christians today, this focus has subsided and made way for a new appreciation of this world as the context within which Christian existence has its meaning and purpose. I raise this issue because the question of the salvation of non-Christians may take on a completely different significance if life after death is not the sole or the primary meaning to be given to this concept. With respect to the question of life after death, I think it is wise for Christians to admit to some tentativeness about it (Eccles. 3:18–22). The surest thing we can and should say is that we entrust ourselves to God in death as in life (Rom. 14:7–9). Hence, I think that the usual question "Can non-Christians be saved?" presupposes something as certain (namely, life after death), which I would leave as open-ended. Salvation should be understood first and foremost as the appropriate relation of the human being, individually and collectively, to reality in its most comprehensive sense. This leads us immediately into the question of God as the name Christians give to this encompassing whole in which we find ourselves.

In a strictly formal sense, the word "God" involves both an objective pole and a subjective pole. The objective pole refers to reality in its most comprehensive or encompassing sense (sometimes spoken of as ultimate reality) in relation to which human life is situated. The subjective pole refers to the center or centers of value for the human person. The religious question is whether the center of value is considered to be reality in its widest, all-embracing sense. While both God and the world can be viewed as the largest realities with which human existence has to do, God should be considered as that reality which calls the world into being, whereas the world should be understood as that which has been called into being by God. In a material vein, we can say that, from a Christian perspective, God is identified as that power which bestows being (God as creator) and also bestows value on that which has being (God as redeemer). Hence, all of God's creatures (which, taken together, constitute the world) are valued by God simply as such, that is, by virtue of their participation in God's creation.

In this vision of God and the world, religion and morality are closely linked. The religious problem as viewed from a Christian perspective is idolatry: focusing the affections of the human heart around centers of value that are less than ultimate because they do not embrace the whole of being. Idolatry has the moral consequence of failing to bestow value on that which God values. Hence, our concern is only directed to those persons, communities, and objects that have value to us in relation to a limited sphere, such as the family, the nation, the race, Western civilization, and so forth. But a life oriented toward service of God finds itself constantly called out of narrow spheres of concern and preoccupation to participation in larger contexts and with a view to broader horizons. Such religious faith in God can lead, therefore, to an enlargement of our moral affections and sensibilities that is the necessary condition for the building of a humanly just and ecologically viable world community. It also leads us to appreciate ways of being human that have been shaped by other histories, cultures, and religious traditions than the ones in which we find ourselves thrown by accident of birth.

Some Christians might object to my ideas by replying that pluralism is merely a contemporary version of ancient polytheism. The ancients could worship many gods, including those of other cultures, because they did not serve the one true God. If they had, they could not have been so tolerant of these other religions. There is an important half-truth in this equation of polytheism and pluralism. Many forms of monotheism, including Jewish, Christian, and Islamic forms, have been notoriously intolerant. I am convinced that an intolerant monotheism is a greater danger in today's world than a tolerant polytheism. But the sort of pluralism I am advocating is not identical with polytheism as Jews and Christians opposed it in the ancient world. The crucial difference is this: the polytheist divinized the various powers that shape human life in the world, whether these powers work for good or ill, and believed that it is necessary to appease now this power and at other times that power. By contrast, the monotheist affirmed that, ultimately speaking, all of these diverse powers impinging upon human life are expressions of one power that transcends them. The powers of nature and history, culture and society are not to be divinized at all; they are God's good creatures and, as such, are to be appropriately valued and respected. But none of them is divine.

The similarity between this view of polytheism and the pluralism I advocate lies in their recognition that the human experience of living in the world is manifold. In my view, the problem with traditional monotheisms, beginning with that of ancient Israel, is the result of assuming that our group alone has the Word of God, or that we alone are the chosen people, or that outside of our church there is no salvation. The "earthen vessels" are mistaken for the "treasure" to which they point, and as a result God is denied the glory (see the admonition in 2 Cor. 4:7). Hence, monotheism cannot be opposed to polytheism in a simple and nondialectical fashion: a theocentric pluralism would embrace the openness of polytheism without abandoning the central insight of monotheism into the distinction between creator and creation or the One and the many.

Polytheism and Monotheism through History

A caveat needs to be inserted here about the concepts "polytheism" and "monotheism." It is possible that polytheism was originally an oppositional term that reflected the monotheistic critique of it. This means that a contemporary historian of religion should not take what Christians and Jews have said about polytheism in a polemical vein as necessarily reflecting an accurate understanding of how ancient polytheists understood their own religious experience of life in the world. What was of deep concern to ancient Jews and Christians was the deification of finite and relative powers as though these were of infinite and absolute significance. This was the reason behind the Christians' refusal to worship the Roman emperor as a god. But beyond this obvious difference in religious practice, there are a few things to note historically that complicate the radical dichotomy between polytheism and monotheism. First, there were tendencies toward a monotheistic viewpoint in some of the Greco-Roman philosophers who venerated the traditional gods as aspects of the one deity believed to lie behind these various manifestations of divinity. Second, the Christians also affirmed plurality in their apprehension of the divine, which led to the formulation of the doctrine of the trinity: God is one substance in three persons. Third, many Christians throughout history (for example, Roman Catholics) have believed that praying to saints is not incompatible with their faith in the oneness of God. These brief illustrations should caution us about an uncritical use of these terms.

It should be recalled that earliest Christianity arose out of the hope that faith in Christ could overcome the various divisions in the world that prevented humanity from realizing its unity: Jew and Gentile, slave and free, men and women, civilized and barbarian, philosophers and nonphilosophers (Rom. 1:14; Gal. 3:28). But the ideal was not realized. In fact, Christianity actually contributed to further divisions between people. In its long history it has persecuted Jews and instigated crusades against Islam, burned heretics and fought the advances of science, condoned European colonialism and provided divine sanction to the practice of enslaving Africans in America, oppressed women, and underwritten prejudice against gay people. This is, of course, not the whole story of Christianity, as I am fully aware. But it is not a minor aspect of our history either, and we have to come to grips with this demonic side of our inheritance. Christians today have to ask themselves to what extent we want to participate with others in building a humanly just and ecologically sustainable global community. We also have to consider whether inherited notions about other religions can be perpetuated if we are to engage in this task.

The appropriate response of Christians today should be one of repentance and humility: repentance for the sins that have been committed in the name of Christianity and humility in the face of the contemporary challenge posed by the actual religious diversity that more and more characterizes our daily life. Would we really have to abandon all of our most cherished religious convictions and moral values if we were to embrace such pluralism? I doubt it. Imagine, if you will, a Christian who can live ever more deeply and profoundly into the story of Jesus and yet listens gratefully to a Buddhist telling the story of the Buddha. Or a Christian who, on the basis of the biblical affirmation that persons are made in the image of God, not only works to uphold the dignity and basic human rights of all persons but learns to respect more than merely human life from a Hindu. Imagine a Christian studying the Bible with a Jew and learning to see both testaments from a Jewish perspective. A Christian who exemplified this sort of repentance and humility might actually do more to witness to the meaning of a Christ-shaped life of service to God than any sermon ever could. Let us leave the rest to God.

God beyond Racism and Sexism

Laurel C. Schneider

Feminist theologians have pointed out for decades that the God of Christians has been conceptualized in almost exclusively male terms. Black and womanist theologians have also pointed out for decades that the God of Christians has usually been conceptualized, at least since the invention of race as a "natural" category, in almost exclusively white and Euro-cultural terms. Both theological tendencies have contributed to male dominance and white supremacy in a world structured almost wholly by patriarchy and distorted by the systematic subordination of dark-skinned people. For those who take sexism, racism, heterosexism, and classism seriously as real evils and as barriers to faithful Christian living, the great theological challenge is to strip away the crud of patriarchy and white supremacy from our inherited concepts of divinity and to work toward language and images that bring the God of mercy, of justice, and of embodied engagement in the world more clearly into focus. Like all intellectual endeavors, the history of Christian theology is deeply embedded in the cultural norms and prejudices of its theologians. That fact is no less true now, although we are more aware of it and of the related fact that our concerns and norms are not the same as those of earlier generations.

As early feminist theologians like Mary Daly and Rosemary Radford Ruether (b. 1936) claim, gender and particularly maleness has always figured explicitly in Christian images and latently in Christian concepts of God, but only recently have they become a concern in constructive theology. Some of the principal theologians of the tradition such as Augustine, Thomas Aquinas, and Luther (among others) presupposed the superiority and so greater godliness of the male over the female and did so without apparent thought for the legitimation they were providing to a social and political norm that served only men. The generally subordinate status of women changed little throughout modernity until late in the twentieth century when the hard-won suffrage efforts of women in the industrialized countries began to yield legal and political gains for women in general. But the ideologies of gender hierarchy remain, deeply rooted in the cultural fabric of Western life and in theologically grounded and legitimated assumptions about the "natural order" of things.

The racist aspects of Christian concepts of God are more subtle to the extent that, unlike gender, race is not explicitly invoked in every Lord's Prayer and in almost all ritual references to God. But race ideology is no less present in the history of Christian theology, evident in symbolic developments of light and darkness, in racist interpretations of biblical stories about Ham, Hagar, and the Canaanites, and in popular artistic depictions of God and of Jesus as distinctly European in features (think of Michaelangelo's famous paintings of God in Sistine Chapel or the popular sentimental paintings of Jesus by Werner Sallman and Heinrich Hoffman). By the nineteenth century at least, this kind of racism was firmly embedded in Christian theological imagining. The flourishing of slavery in the Americas over hundreds of years infected an entire colonized world with a rationale of racial hierarchy. Even after the institution of slavery finally was legally abolished in the United States in the nineteenth century, its poisonous logic remained and remains in the vast economic structures that it spawned. The global legacy of racism persists like an inheritance that heirs cannot or will not dispose of, either because they believe it still provides wealth or because it is all they know. This legacy has even infected feminism to the extent that white feminists have often sustained fundamentally racist attitudes and practices in assumptions that white women's experiences adequately represent all women.

By the late-twentieth century some theologians committed to the overarching Enlightenment ideals of civil rights began gradually to realize that God "Himself" and Jesus the white-skinned, blue-eyed Son stand in the way of Christian redemption from the poisonous legacies of hierarchalized gender and race ideologies. Once sexism and racism are recognized as distortions of the good or as evils to be eradicated, God the source of goodness cannot be conceptualized in images and terms that serve to maintain either sexism or racism or any dominance of an elite class of beings at the expense of other, subordinated beings without throwing theology into profound contradiction. Elizabeth Cady Stanton (1815–1902), Malcolm X (1925–1965), Howard Thurman, Albert Cleage (1911–2000), Mary Daly, James Cone, Rosemary Radford Ruether, and Jacquelyn Grant are some of a growing number of scholars who have begun the difficult work of criticizing the myth of a God who looks (and behaves) like the dominant elite and reimagining divinity in ways consistent with their core beliefs in a God not of oppression but of liberation.

Constructing truly liberating concepts of divinity out of the texts and traditions of Christianity that make sense in this era of struggle against social structures of racist, sexist, and heterosexist domination is difficult. The triumphal, masculinist, and Eurocentric God of Christian rulers has been invoked for terrible ends against women, nondominant men, and the colonized. The answer is not to reverse the power and retain the structures, however. It is important that constructive theologians not reinscribe domination and exclusion in an attempt to correct the past. The last century has, in some sense, been a particularly stark object lesson in the capacity of human beings to believe anything, to embrace delusion, and to deploy theological ideas of divine superiority or vengeful wrath toward horrifically violent and brutal ends. But it has also been a century of object lessons in the confounding power of humility, of the possibilities that emerge from near hopelessness when God is understood to stand against no one but to confound the logic of domination and violence.

In addition to the challenge of avoiding simple reversals of power by imagining God as an avenging woman, for example, or as a triumphant African king, there is also the challenge of constructing concepts of God that do not dispense entirely with the tradition that produced us. The liberating constructive task requires that we search for ways to imagine and conceptualize divinity that do not reject entirely the long and rich tradition of images and concepts for God that we have inherited but that understand God as the healing and corrective answer, the very reality that stands against human tendencies toward destructive greed and violent domination of others. This very reality is perhaps best conceptualized as the face of the other, as the writer of Matt. 25:40 suggests and as both Christian and Jewish existential phenomenologists from Dietrich Bonhoeffer (1906–1945) to Levinas have argued.

The deep wisdom resident in ancient Jewish iconoclasm is a refusal to make images of the God of creation for fear of diminishing that God to a dangerous tool of human aggrandizement. The deep wisdom resident in the ancient Christian recognition of divinity imaged and embodied in a poor, colonized political prisoner is a claim that God is neither distant nor abstract but near and utterly invested in the world. While there is a tension between the two insights—one cautions against any recognition of divine presence and shape, while the other gives radical specificity to divine presence and shape—both provide a strong starting point for conceptualizing God in terms that not only make sense to those committed religiously to overcoming racist and sexist ideologies but also restore to us a capacity for communally affirming lives oriented toward this God.

What are the building blocks of a doctrine of God that confound the logic of gender and race domination and violence? Black and Latin American liberation theologians argue that it is through the teachings and ministry of Jesus that clues to this God can be obtained. To the extent that Jesus is divine, we see a clear preference for the company of children, of the ridiculed, of the subjugated. In other words, we see an image of God not only as friend and lover of the vulnerable or suffering but as the vulnerable and suffering themselves. In Jesus' own homeless birth and life under the yoke of colonial rule we have an image of divinity that stands in opposition to triumphal, militaristic models of power and instantiates the cost of those models. The God revealed in Jesus' actions and teachings is incompatible with imperialism and so, presumably, with racism and sexism.

If Jesus of Nazareth is the only source of information for God (as some theologians argue), his maleness is a stumbling block for thinking against the tradition that has so masculinized God. But some have suggested that, had Jesus been a woman, there would be no Christian story precisely because the subjugation of women would have silenced her before she could even call disciples. Others point to the remarkable relationship that Jesus had with women, his regard for their leadership and ministry, and his clear support of their dignity. But for many this is not enough, and while Jesus embodies the values and principles of solidarity with the subjugated, outcast, and vulnerable that we seek for a post-racist, post-sexist doctrine of God, Jesus himself can only provide part of the substance of what divinity is. And this claim of partiality is fully consistent with Christian traditional trinitarian thought that posits Jesus as one of three substantial aspects, or persons, of God.

Despite the partiality of Jesus as source of revelation for God, it is good to start with him in our effort to see and imagine the God who confounds our tendencies toward racist and sexist social worlds. Starting with Jesus establishes two critical requirements for any concept of God. The first is that God is incarnate, engaged, in and of the world, and the second is that God is invested in eschatological hope for the world, a hope focused on peace-making and peace-embodying relations. Incarnation and embodiment have tended, in the history of Christian thought, to be relegated only to one arm or person of the trinity and to reside in the doctrine of Christ but not in the doctrine of God or Spirit. Feminist theologians have done a great deal to debunk this separation, arguing that it is God's embodiment in all of the world that reflects the creative, engaged divine life so evident throughout the Bible. The fact that the earliest Christian theologians (Paul, Augustine, the church fathers) were mostly educated and formed by Greek assumptions of the utter superiority of disembodied ideas (or spirit) over matter (or body) has profoundly shaped all subsequent Christian imagining about God but should not have the final word.

Indeed, one of the traditional christological doctrines that has served male privilege well and that continues to serve it in those churches that continue to refuse the ordination and full priestly participation of women is the limitation of divine embodiment to the person of Jesus. The unnecessary interpretation of the line attributed to Jesus that "no one comes to the Father except through me" (John 14:6) as a claim for exclusive embodiment has led to a deep-rooted and triumphal exclusivism that ultimately serves to limit the freedom and abundance of divine creativity and activity in the world. I would argue that releasing God from the limitation of embodiment in one male person and recognizing that embodiment is the revelation of much more than the individual man/God of Jesus are large steps toward scraping away from God the sediment of sexist projections. While the importance of Jesus' embodiment of God as articulated by black and womanist theologians is much more complicated and nuanced, to the degree that Jesus has been imaged as a white European and exploited for racist purposes, my concern about notions of exclusive embodiment may also implicate racist projections and require further constructive exploration.

The Problem of Incarnation

It is interesting to note quickly a couple of parallels between my argument and those of Hegel, on the one hand, and H. Richard Niebuhr (1894–1962), on the other. Hegel believed that it was a mistake for traditional theology to identify the Holy Spirit with the third person of the trinity alone; instead, he proposed viewing God itself as Spirit. On account of this revision of the inherited tradition, he insisted that God as Spirit leads us to recognize that God is essentially self-revelatory. Niebuhr argued against various forms of "unitarianism" in the history of Christianity, by which he meant the one-sided identification of God with only one function, whether God is creator or God is redeemer. Niebuhr accused Karl Barth—who propounded the most radically Christocentric theology in Christian history—of perpetrating a "unitarianism of the second person." Like Niebuhr I am interested in pushing the envelope of uncritical monotheism that, in the end, collapses into henotheism through its creedal limitations of the incarnation to one event or, in the case of Barth, to one "gospel." Like them, I believe divinity to be ultimately free, but I argue that freedom, to mean anything, must be greater than traditional interpretations of an exclusive incarnation in Jesus Christ can abide, even if that exclusivity is expanded to an ontological principle of humanity since Jesus. My argument with Niebuhr, and with Tillich for that matter, is that while expanding divinity and incarnation both beyond theism and beyond a mythico-exclusive narrative, their attempts to rationalize the doctrine of God through a more universalized ground (Tillich) or principle (Niebuhr) of being-itself falls into the trap identified by Bonhoeffer, that is, such universalizing concepts lose the very point of incarnation altogether, its specificity in an actual body. The parallel could be strengthened by an assertion of essential (divine) embodiment, and the challenge is to do so without falling into the essentializing trap that loses sight of embodiment!

Traditionally feminists have also argued that one of the standard features of patriarchalism (rule of the Father) is the notion that true masculinity is expressed in domination and rule over women, children, male servants, and land. The truly insidious dimension of patriarchalism is that the masculinity and femininity it describes and demands need not be synonymous with maleness or femaleness per se. But in patriarchal cultures, as most men and women in the world today can attest, masculinity is defined in terms of domination in all aspects of life, profoundly affecting the psychological health of men and women raised in those cultures. So by extension, to the extent that God's being is understood to be exclusively or even nominally male, the cultural baggage of this association is the same for God as it is for men: to be successful is to be powerful; it is to be "on top" and dominant, and the evidence of success is in the subordination (or feminization) of others.

Along these lines, the truly masculine man or God displays dominance over as many groups of people, animals, and plots of earth as possible, including (and especially) other men. This expectation distorts and heavily burdens human men, and it feeds both racism and heterosexism because successful masculinity defined like this can be expressed in a myriad of ways. A man who cannot dominate in one area can still be a man by asserting dominance in another. And masculinity understood this way is also powerfully heterosexist and classist. If to be a man a person must dominate another, the dominated is, by definition, feminized. The right ordering of relationships that then support patriarchal masculinity is a heterosexual pairing (even if the partner is male, one of the pair must be more feminine, or "bottom," to the real man's masculine "top"). For a man to couple with a man is unthinkable in the logic of patriarchal masculinity, and women coupling with women only exists (that is, has relevance) when a man's claim to one or both is thereby compromised. When masculinity is synonymous with dominance and femininity with subordination as it is in patriarchal symbolism, God, according to this logic, *must* be understood as male in order to have any power to sustain, to govern, or to save. To be anything other than male, symbolically, would mean that God is subordinate to some other, more masculine power.

Despite the fact that Jesus' own life does not demonstrate tendencies toward dominance and could in fact be read as a feminization of God within a powerfully patriarchal cultural environment, the development of the doctrine of God by men clearly invested in maintaining their social privilege has, ironically, put Jesus' maleness to the service of patriarchal masculinity much more than it has subverted that construction of masculinity. It is clear that unlinking patriarchal masculinity from God is a serious ethical requirement of any theologian dedicated to the end of sexism, racism, heterosexism, classism, nationalism, colonialism, or any other expression of patriarchalized hubris. And one powerful way to unlink patriarchal masculinity from God is to free God from the limitations of a single, historical embodiment as male.

The revelation of divine incarnation in or as the world also leads to other liberating and compassion-building ways of understanding God that confound racist and sexist investments. White supremacy and male dominance both require constant vigilance and reaffirmation in a world that is mostly not white and largely not male. A God constructed in terms of eternity and immutability serves both white supremacist and masculinist efforts by casting into all time and space a construct of divinity that is unchangingly male and unchangingly disembodied (following the ascension of Jesus into heaven, that is).

To understand God as profoundly and excessively incarnate is both to affirm the Christian story of divine investment in the world and to cast judgment on all theological attempts to diffuse the radical solidarity of divinity with all of creation, with all the living. For one thing, bodies are always in motion, always changing even as they participate in a larger continuity over time and space. Bodies are vulnerable and adaptive, and no body is fully independent or disconnected from any other. Embodiment is not sameness; it is in some ways the opposite of sameness, but it is continuous and mutable. A static and unyielding divinity is truly incommensurate with the very fabric of existence and is not in fact supported by many biblical stories that indicate a relational God who weeps over a beloved people, a beloved earth, who anguishes and builds, who argues and responds, who watches over creation (like a mother eagle), and who is as steadfast as a rock.

A construction or constructions of God that dismantle the distortions of so many years of white supremacy and male privilege can start with embodiment in all of its rich, smelly, textured, noisy, colored, responsive, birthing-soft, and aging-tough variety. Several theologians have made significant contributions to this task. Process theologians like John Cobb have worked to overcome the static, immutable, and disembodied aspect of the Christian doctrine of God by making divinity the essence of actual existence, an existence that is always in motion. Conceived this way, God is a kind of principle of change and the *telos* (goal) toward which all change moves, and God's power is no longer one of dominance but one of persuasion. This is a remarkable and substantive move away from patriarchalism and so opens up a possibility for imagining the God who in fact does not instantiate supremacist constructs. God also must be more than a mechanism of evolution, albeit a mechanism of evolutionary hope for a better world. Sallie McFague finds the abstractions to which process thought can tend problematic and suggests that understanding the world as God's body should retain a more personalistic aspect to divinity a God to whom a person can pray which other attempts at construction can easily miss. And Karen Baker-Fletcher's work on divine courage to thrive links God clearly with embodied investment in the life of the world.

The cosmos *is* God's body, but it is more than that as well. Although Christian theologians who are working to reassert the importance of embodiment as a fundamental aspect of divinity tend to shy away from full associations of God with world lest God somehow be reduced in the equation, they tend to miss the growing scientific consensus that "body" is not appropriately relegated to the opposite of "spirit" any longer. As medical inquiry continues to chip away at Western inherited assumptions of essential differences between spirit and body, the possibility emerges that God is indeed the cosmos, is indeed the soul of the world as Emerson asserted in the nineteenth century, though soul is something much more "material" than he assumed.

If we think and imagine more deeply along these lines, we face the challenge of understanding divinity as less particular than the white-haired, European-featured patriarch of Michelangelo's Creation of Adam and much more varied and chaotic than Barth's pristine Absolute Other. God as the bodysoul of all that is cannot, as McFague has argued, be separated from anything that is. But the Christian story allows for even more than this still rather abstract notion of God as some sum or essence or heart or soul that is the body of the cosmos. The Christian story of incarnation allows for particular and immediate embodiments within the larger embodiment that is God. Jesus, fully divine and fully human, is a particular, immediate, and temporal presence of God. And the good news, especially for all of the non-men (meaning all who have been subjugated by the myth of patriarchal masculinity and white supremacy) is that Jesus is in fact of faith not the only one.

God the bodysoul of the cosmos creates the world, sustains it, and engages in all that is toward healing. God is ever emergent, responsive not only to our prayers but to our imaginings and concepts. The constructive task is one of attention to all that God is that confounds our tendencies to diminish life. As I have written elsewhere, "we experience the green-gold earth, the hard and unyielding tragedy of it, the vital and overwhelming life of it; we embrace the ordinary; we breathe; we stretch thought; we ask our questions. And sometimes here, in the smoky fabric of the world that makes us, like the rare vulnerability of a truth, divinity folds into the shape of what we imagined, and answers."[24]

2

Human Being

M. Shawn Copeland, Dwight N. Hopkins, Charles T. Mathewes,
Joy Ann McDougall, Ian A. McFarland (chapter editor), Michele Saracino

The Montgomery, Alabama, bus boycott began in 1955 with the arrest of Rosa Parks, an African American woman who refused to leave her seat for a white man. A citywide boycott of the buses by African Americans ensued, but as it continued into 1956, things began to get difficult for the protestors. The phenomenal success of the boycott frightened the white authorities, who began to disrupt the informal carpool and "taxi" services that the African American community had set up for those of its members who had depended on the buses to get around the city. For those who could not get a ride in a car and would not ride the bus, the only alternative was often a very long, exhausting walk. At one point, Sister Pollard, a seventy-year-old African American woman who had been an enthusiastic supporter of the boycott, was offered a ride by a sympathetic passer-by. She declined. "But aren't you tired?" she was then asked. "My feets is tired," she replied, "but my soul is rested."[1]

◆

It was Valentine's Day, and Mark had decided to surprise Rochelle with dinner at a new Italian place in town. As they soaked in the atmosphere, they saw a restaurant filled with other couples seeking a romantic night out, including two young men at the table right next to theirs. At several points during the evening Mark glanced in their direction with a furrowed brow and a vaguely disapproving stare. Finally, as Mark and Rochelle were ordering dessert, the two men got up, shared a kiss, and left the restaurant holding hands. As soon as they had gone, Mark shook his head and heaved an audible sigh of relief.

"I'm glad *that's* over with."

"What do you mean?" Michelle asked. "They didn't bother us any."

"Look," said Mark, "I'm no Nazi. As far as I'm concerned, what people do behind closed doors is their own business. But I don't see why *they* have to flaunt their affections in public."

"It didn't look like they were flaunting anything to me. I mean, they didn't do anything we don't do pretty regularly."

"But they're not like *us*. With them it's just not natural."

"Maybe it seems natural enough to them."

"That's not what I mean. It's not about feelings; it's about, well, plumbing! Men and women were made for each other. Anyone can see that. They complement each other physically that's how babies are made. Homosexuals just don't can't have that kind of relationship. It's just not how people are put together. It's not what bodies are for."

Rochelle thought for a minute.

"What I don't understand," she said finally, "is what makes you so sure that making babies is what bodies are for."

◆

"Simon Peter said to them, 'Let Mary leave us, for women are not worthy of Life'.

"Jesus said, 'I myself shall lead her in order to make her male, so that she too may become a living spirit resembling you males. For every woman who will make herself male will enter the Kingdom of Heaven'." (*Gospel of Thomas* 114)

◆

"I recently served on a ministerial search committee that was debating whether a woman should be hired as the next pastor. No specific candidate had yet been considered; the discussion was about hiring a woman 'in principle'. Should calling a woman be a priority since we had never had a female pastor? Or should we simply call the best candidate, male or female? As we debated these questions, revealing comments were made about what a woman minister is and is not.

"In support of hiring a woman, some members suggested that women ministers are more nurturing and pastoral than men; that women are good listeners and excellent teachers of children; and that a woman's more intuitive spirituality would bring a sense of God's 'feminine side' to our worship. Some members also argued that we needed female role models in the community, that the pastoral presence of a woman 'makes a difference'. On the other side, several members asserted that women have soft, high voices, which people in back pews cannot hear; that they usually do not have enough experience to be senior pastors; and that the congregation was simply not ready for such a radical change. A few committee members even argued that having a female minister 'makes a difference' in a negative way, although it was hard for them to say exactly how. One member put it succinctly: 'It's just not the same'."[2]

State of the Question

As technology advances, globalization expands, and intercontinental travel presents us with an ever-shrinking planet, Christians cannot ignore questions posed by culture even if they want to. Arguably, theology has always been connected to culture, for as a human endeavor, it necessarily approaches its subject from a material perspective. Still, the main focus of theological anthropology has tended to be the supernatural orientation of humankind as beings created (in the words of Gen. 1:27) "in the image of God" (*imago Dei*). As a result of this focus, the other, more material side of existence had been overshadowed, even obscured. Since being human involves both these trajectories reflecting the image of God and grappling with the burden of that reflection in everyday life it would be fruitful to explore the interplay and ambiguity surrounding these two dimensions of human life.

The issues that complicate Christian existence today are many; following are three examples. First, there are the traditional problems related to *freedom and responsibility*, both of which are becoming increasingly ambiguous because of a pervasive relativist ethic. Moreover, the fields of psychology and sociology, to name just two, are challenging the more conventional doctrinal approaches to human freedom and responsibility by stressing the contextual character of sin and evil. Second, thinking theologically about being human has become complicated by issues surrounding *identity and alterity* (otherness or difference) with respect both to individual and communal levels of existence. A third way in which the theological doctrine of the human person is challenged by culture is regarding the questions of *time and memory*. A marker of human finitude, a trace of past existence, and the matrix of future hope, human temporality is a significant factor in understanding what it means to be human from a theological perspective. Nevertheless, the cultural pressures for expediency have occluded time and undermined a sense of journey from human living. As a result, proper appreciation of the human significance of time is threatened in contemporary society.

Freedom and Responsibility

One of the greatest gifts God imparts to humanity is freedom: the potential to make decisions in the face of ambiguous situations. We are presented by Christian theology with a magnanimous image of God, a creator who gives to creation the opportunity to be human without restrictions. As promising as the patrimony of unbridled liberty is, like any inheritance it is beset with uncertainties. For one, even though being created with freedom is a theological axiom that underscores the human capacity for choosing and deciding what is good, much contemporary rhetoric around freedom has limited its significance to issues of rights and entitlements. Freedom has become conflated with democratic struggle for representative political power. By contrast, much of the Christian tradition has emphasized that the freedom given by God is meant for God and for others; accordingly, it is a liberty that finds its fullness in taking responsibility for justice. This connection between freedom and responsibility has been obstructed by secular culture and rendered almost anachronistic. The occlusion of obligation from freedom is only one tension in contemporary theological anthropology. A further consequence of disconnecting freedom from responsibility is that one overlooks the link between freedom and sin.

There are many ways of conceptualizing sin, ranging from humanity's break with covenant to refusing to live in the *imago Dei*. Whatever the rhetoric, the idea evoked is that sin subverts God's plan for humanity. However, today it is becoming more difficult to discern what this "plan" might be. Behaviors that were deemed deviant in the past are now being reconfigured as a product of social situations, and even viewed as normative. The development of the field of psychology in the twentieth century has reframed Christian ideas about human existence and the predicament of sin. In addition to rethinking what constitutes good behavior, those working within theological anthropology have become further stymied over the difficulty of discerning what is true in light of the widespread attitude of relativism that appears to pervade contemporary culture. On the one hand, relativism has the positive potential of acknowledging the specific, contextualized predicament of the other. Yet, on the other hand, relativism seemingly makes it difficult to make any absolute judgments of value. When grappling with the question of how to be human in relation to others, relativists answer that all options are viable, depending on the situation: there is no one right or just course of action. Relativism clearly complicates engaging freedom and agency by raising questions of perspective in assessing what it means to be human.

Identity and Alterity

The commitment to understanding self in relation to others is decisive for any theological anthropology today. The problem may be described as one of identity. Simply put, *identity* means sameness. Theologically, the sameness among human beings is in their being created in the *imago Dei*. In this way Christians confess that there is one human nature. This said, it must be noted that difference complicates and enriches this one human nature. The term *alterity* refers to those differences, either biological or social, that emerge within this species that shares one common human nature. The experience of alterity (or otherness) has meant that a central question in theological anthropology from the beginning of Christianity has been, "What role does alterity play in being human?" As the form of the question suggests, the fact of difference is not contested, but its impact on the *imago Dei* is open to question. As this chapter on the doctrine of the human person unfolds, two instances of alterity will be highlighted. Among the voices of the tradition, the implications of gender difference will be raised, while in Shawn Copeland's constructive theological essay, the implications of racial difference will be emphasized. Implicit in both discussions is the argument that difference is too often (and problematically) interpreted from an essentialist stance, in which difference is interpreted as inherent in people's biological makeup, and the social construction of difference is erased. Constructivist arguments maintain that difference is an effect of socialization, that is, of nurture. Alternatively, biological determinist or essentialist arguments claim that difference is a function of biology, that is, of nature.

Problems arise in theology when difference is located only in biology. For then people become prisoners of their specific corporeality stigmatized as "other" to the extent that biology determines their destiny. Throughout history, when difference became located in body, some bodies (especially male, white ones) were deemed more valuable than others. As our anxieties about difference easily become focused on our corporeality, it is not surprising that many of us go to great lengths to overcome bodily stigma through various, often painful regimens, such as plastic surgery, excessive dieting, and so on. It appears as if happiness, even salvation, can be attained if one overcomes the hindrance of being embodied. Theologically, this type of logic can lead to an anthropological dualism, in which the body (including feeling) is subordinated to the soul (identified with reason).

It is important to note that alterity takes many forms, the most obvious of which include gender, race, and class differences, though alterity extends to the level of national difference as well as to situations of religious pluralism. Within our everyday existence many of us encounter Baptists, Catholics, and Presbyterians, as well as Jews, Shiites, and Buddhists. As alterity rather than sameness becomes the norm in our perception of human existence, new ways of living with others need to be imagined. A typical way of dealing with others is through a minimalist attitude of tolerance, in which others or those deemed different are barely accepted or put up with within the community. Nevertheless, some theologians have argued that the message of the gospel transcends an attitude of tolerance to that of a posture of embrace. After all, Jesus does not simply put up with the marginalized; he engages them in their corporeality, as other. Taking the challenge of embracing others seriously would require Christians to rethink their attitudes toward other Christians as well as toward non-Christians.

Time and Memory

Being human involves a nuanced understanding of freedom as well as a critical sense of alterity; it also demands a comprehensive sense of time. Human beings are created in time and as a result are finite beings. The notion of finitude evokes many ideas and feelings related to the predicament of having limits and boundaries, a beginning and an end. Contemporary constructive theology has complicated a rather straightforward reading of time by engaging two important questions. How does time figure within our lives today? What is the role of memory and history in being human in relation to God?

The first query regarding time in everyday life is rather obvious. Ask any of your friends, family, or colleagues how time fits into their lives. The short answer will probably be that it does not. Hurried by life, we have no time to think beyond the moment at hand. Language about spiritual journey and struggling to live in the image of God seems strangely out of touch. As we struggle to survive within late capitalist societies, time is a precious resource that is squandered among several jobs, family responsibilities, and schemes that promise success and happiness. An elusive hope at best, happiness for many is never obtained, and many are left with feelings of loneliness and despair. They have forfeited time with others for the dream of achieving another's idea of success.

Aside from having no time, humanity is burdened by sorting out past times, that is, dealing with memories within both the personal and interpersonal realms. Being human for God and others means relating to others in peace and conflict by way of memory and story. Memory may become distorted by feelings of anger, grief, or fear. For being human to emerge, however, a concerted effort to retrieve memory and engage in truth telling must become a priority. Memory is already part of the Christian tradition, most obviously expressed within the ritual of communion. Still, memory becomes theologically relevant beyond fellowship as ritual to fellowship as community. How many of us have become alienated from one another or from a community in general because of distorted memories or bearing false witness? The early Christians were charged with witnessing to the message of the risen Christ. Human beings today are analogously encouraged to witness to the truth of their histories legacies that may hurt some and free others.

In conclusion, Christians tend to agree that being human means being created for a purpose for God and others. Nevertheless, to speak about a particular goal for humanity at this point seems premature. The goal of humanity is at best being aware and being committed to faith in everyday life—a journey tested by the limits of human agency, engaging the other *as* other, and being faithful to God in time and through memory. In what follows, each of these challenges will be shown to lurk in the shadow of the image of God and will be revealed as possible openings to a flourishing future with God and others.

Voices from the Tradition

Is there anything special or distinctive about what Christians have to say about human beings? From the very beginning Christians' beliefs about God distinguished them clearly from both pagans and Jews. Writing to the Emperor Trajan in the early second century, one Roman official reported that Christians sang to Christ "as though to a god"—a characterization that agrees with a roughly contemporary Christian sermon that exhorts believers "to think of Jesus Christ as of God" (see Pliny the Younger, *Epistulae* 10.96.7 and *2 Clement* 1:1). Though it took a long time for Christians to reach consensus on what these practices implied about God, there was no question that Jesus made a difference in how Christians talked and thought about God.

As important as these ideas were for the first Christian communities, however, it is not immediately clear that they reflect an understanding of human being significantly different from that of the surrounding culture. Christians continued to speak of human beings using many of the same terms (*body* and *soul*, for example) that non-Christians did. And while all early Christians may have agreed that showing partiality was incompatible with faith in Christ, the issue at stake was arguably less a new understanding of humanity than a claim that the boundaries of the human should be made more inclusive. Whereas formerly Jews may have viewed Gentiles as beyond the pale (as reflected in the rhetoric of Rom. 1:16–32, for instance), now it was claimed that "for neither circumcision nor uncircumcision is anything; but a new creation is everything" (Gal. 6:15; cf. Rev. 21:5).

By contrast, the effect Jesus had on Christian thinking about human beings was not so clear-cut. It certainly made some difference. Both the Book of Acts and the letters of Paul bear witness that the confession of Jesus had concrete effects on the relationships between Jews and Gentiles within the church (Acts 10:1 11:18; Gal. 2:1–14). These developments reflected a belief in divine impartiality (Acts 10:34; Rom. 2:11; 1 Pet. 1:17; cf. Matt. 5:45) that was justified in specifically christological terms. The reason why past exclusions are no longer valid is that the divisions between people have been overcome in Christ (Eph. 2:11–16), in whom all believers are equally children of Israel's God (Gal. 3:26; cf. Rom. 8:14–17). So fundamental was this perspective to the church that when Paul in the early 50s wrote, "There is no longer Jew or Greek, there is no longer slave or free, there is no longer male and female; for all of you are one in Christ Jesus" (Gal. 3:28), he appears to have been citing a formula that was already traditional.

And yet this contrast between old and new was itself more than capable of raising difficult questions in the church, as the debates over the proper relations between Jews and Gentiles bear witness. If the emphasis is placed on the contrast between the new humanity in Christ and the old, it becomes easy to wonder whether the differences of (for example) gender and race that are overcome in Christ are part of God's good creation or signs of some defect in the created order. On the other hand, if the abiding significance of these differences is affirmed, then it might seem to follow that social practices designed to reinforce them should be preserved.

In short, a central problem faced by the church in its reflection on human being was that of mapping out the contours of this "new creation" in Christ. One area where early Christians appear to have differed sharply with one another is over the status of women in the church. It was one thing to confess with Paul that in Christ there is no longer male and female, but quite another to specify what that meant in terms of concrete practice. Thus, while the writer of 1 Timothy enjoined women to "learn in silence with full submission" (1 Tim. 2:11), the noncanonical (but evidently very popular) *Acts of Paul and Thecla* paints a picture of life in Christ that includes a wholesale rejection of women's subordination to fathers, husbands, and established political authority. Far from remaining submissive, Thecla is prepared to claim in Christ's name just the kind of authority to teach publicly that is explicitly denied women in 1 Tim. 2:12. In this way, the two traditions diverge sharply when it comes to working out the ecclesiastical and wider sociopolitical implications of the confession of Christ as the one savior of women and men. By implicitly raising the question of what it means to be human, such debates set the stage for more explicit reflection on theological anthropology, or the Christian doctrine of human being by later generations.

Three Classic Perspectives on Human Being

Christian beliefs about humanity acquired more definite contours in the course of debate with various interpretations of human being encountered both inside and outside the church. One prominent example is the controversy over Gnostic interpretations of Christianity in the second century. The term *Gnostic* covers a wide range of teachings, so generalizations are difficult, but a number of Gnostic groups (evidently drawing on biblical passages like 1 Cor. 2:13–15) held that there were in fact different grades or types of human beings, including the "spiritual," the "psychic," and the "material." Only the first group possessed the spiritual essence that would permit them to rise to the realm of the divine; the psychics were at best capable of some lower state of salvation, while the material were destined for annihilation. This perspective was condemned by what eventually prevailed as "orthodox" (or "catholic") Christianity, whose proponents insisted that all human beings were both equally in need of salvation and equally salvageable.

1. Irenaeus of Lyons

A leading figure in the debate with Gnostics was Irenaeus of Lyons (c. 135–c. 200). In the course of his systematic attack on Gnostic belief in his book, *The Refutation and Overthrow of the "Knowledge" Falsely So-Called* (usually known by the shorter title *Against Heresies*), he outlined what would become some of the decisive features of the "catholic" or "orthodox" Christian understanding of human being.[3] In opposition to the Gnostic belief in distinct human types constitutionally predestined to different ends, Irenaeus insisted that all human beings were equal in that they possessed free will that made them responsible for their ultimate destiny (*Against Heresies* IV.37). Connected with this idea of equal human responsibility was an emphasis on the significance of time as the context for human growth and development toward God. While God could have made humankind perfect from the beginning, human beings' integrity as creatures was better preserved by their being allowed to grow toward perfection gradually through the exercise of their own powers (*Against Heresies* IV.38). This emphasis on human beings as creatures designed to grow and change is strikingly illustrated by Irenaeus's conviction that Adam and Eve were created as children rather than fully mature adults (*Against Heresies* III.22).

This emphasis on human responsibility and a correspondingly positive appraisal of change stood in sharp contrast to the determinism characteristic of Gnostic thought. Equally removed from the Gnostics' dualistic emphasis on the spirit as the only lasting reality is Irenaeus's insistence on the importance of the body as an integral dimension of human being. In line with the Christian belief in a final resurrection, Irenaeus insisted that salvation involved the whole person, including the body as well as the soul (*Against Heresies* V.6). Working from this perspective, Irenaeus argued that when Paul spoke of "spiritual" people in his letters, he was referring not to individuals whose identities were independent of their bodies, but rather to those who have subjected their bodily existence to the rule of God's Spirit.

All of these themes come together in what is probably the most influential aspect of Irenaeus's anthropology: his interpretation of human being in terms of humanity's creation in the image of God. Although the phrase is taken from the biblical creation narrative (Gen. 1:26–27), it does not function as a central anthropological category in either the Old Testament or the New. For Irenaeus, however, the search for a credible interpretation of the image of God (*imago Dei*) in human beings served as the central focus of theological anthropology and virtually every theologian who has written on the doctrine of human being since has followed his lead. In Irenaeus's case, the heart of the divine image lies in human free will (*Against Heresies* IV.37.4). At the same time, Irenaeus refused to limit the image to any one part of the individual, arguing that the divine image ultimately encompassed the whole human being in body, soul, and spirit.

Irenaeus's anthropology thus coalesces around several key ideas: a holistic view of human being as a composite of spirit, soul, and body; an emphasis on human freedom and responsibility; and an appreciation for the positive significance of time as the medium within which human life with God is realized. All three concepts contrast sharply with the more fatalistic perspective of Gnosticism. Yet despite the holism and inclusiveness of his anthropology, Irenaeus leaves important questions open. On the one hand (and in line with the perspective found in the *Acts of Paul and Thecla*), he insists that human beings are free and thus ultimately responsible for their fate; on the other (and corresponding more to the position of 1 Timothy), he views particular features of human bodily existence like gender as integral to our status as creatures made in the divine image even though these are clearly not a matter of choice. His perspective thus raises the question of the extent to which the possibilities of human life with God both now and in the future are constrained by the physical differences between people.

Were the Gnostics Really That Bad?

Irenaeus's criticism of Gnosticism achieved canonical status in later Christianity. The Gnostics were universally remembered as obscurantist, elitist, and individualistic, and their teachings as confusing and inconsistent. Yet it is clear that Irenaeus had his own agenda, and that his characterization of Gnosticism is not written from a sympathetic point of view. For much of Christian history, it was difficult to know how accurate his portrayal of Gnosticism was, for the simple reason that almost no Gnostic writings had survived. Since the mid-twentieth century, however, a significant (if still comparatively small) body of documents from communities like those Irenaeus engaged has been recovered, leading some scholars to venture a more attractive vision of Gnostic teaching than that found in Irenaeus's writings.

There seems little doubt from these writings that Gnostics did believe that there were deeper truths in the Bible that were not accessible to ordinary believers and, to this extent, were elitist. To find these truths they engaged in a strongly allegorical form of biblical interpretation that stressed the importance of the text's spiritual rather than historical meaning. Also, it seems clear that Gnostics were disposed to deny that freedom was a defining principle of human existence in the way that Irenaeus and other thinkers of the emerging "orthodox" strand of Christian thinking insisted it was.

On the other hand, a number of Gnostic texts are striking for one feature that suggests more egalitarian tendencies within the communities that produced them: the persistent use of feminine language to describe God. Given that Irenaeus at one point (*Against Heresies* III.13) suggests that women in particular were attracted to Gnostic teachers and that women in at least one such group were actually allowed to preside at the celebration of the Eucharist, it seems reasonable to conclude that such language had definite social consequences. Specifically, it appears certain that within at least some Gnostic circles women enjoyed a higher status than was typical of orthodox communities of the same period, by which time the very limited vision of women's role expressed in 1 Timothy 2 had become dominant.

2. Gregory of Nyssa

Writing around 200 years after Irenaeus, the Cappadocian theologian Gregory of Nyssa (331–c. 395) shared his predecessor's emphasis on free will as central to the divine image in human beings but was much less inclined to include the body (see *On the Making of Humankind* XVI). Noting an apparent inconsistency between Paul's insistence that in Christ "there is no longer male and female" (Gal. 3:28) and the creation narrative's claim that humanity created in God's image was made "male and female" (Gen. 1:27), Gregory explains sexual difference as a side-effect of humanity's creation in God's image. He reasons that no created image of God can share God's essential changelessness, since the very fact of coming into existence from nonexistence testifies to a creature's mutability, or vulnerability to change. According to Gregory, God knew ahead of time that this human openness to the possibility of change would take the form of disobedience to God's commands, and that the consequence of this disobedience (sin) would be death. In order to keep the human race from extinction, God made humanity male and female in order to provide a biological mechanism to preserve the human species under the conditions of sin. He concludes that in the absence of sin, there would have been no need for sexual difference and teaches that there will be no male and female after the final resurrection (see *On the Making of Humankind* XVII).

It is common (and not altogether unfair) to accuse Gregory of being captive to Greek philosophical ways of thinking that set the spiritual dimension of human life both above and against the physical, but his anthropology should not be dismissed too readily as symptomatic of a hatred of the body in general or of sexuality in particular. Unlike the Gnostics (whose fatalism he, like Irenaeus, was keen to oppose), he did not view physical existence as evil: our fleshy bodies were the gifts to us from a good God to preserve the human race from the threat of extinction. At the same time, however, he sees the differences between bodies as the bearers of those divisions between people that Jesus had overcome. Gregory's interpretation of physical (especially sexual) difference thus provided a framework that allowed him to acknowledge the divine origin of human difference while also maintaining that human beings were created equal in the beginning and will be equal again in the final consummation (*On the Making of Humankind* XVI.17). In this way Gregory is also able to give a positive significance to the temporal character of our existence, but because he interprets our lives in time as a means of transcending rather than fulfilling our embodiedness, it is difficult to overcome the impression that for him material existence is "good" only in a somewhat qualified sense.

The Eschatological Character of Gregory's Anthropology

The rigorously eschatological character of Gregory's thinking ruptured certain notions of the "existential career" of human beings that were current at the time he was writing. Most important, Gregory's notion of humanity's unending journey into God (*epektasis*) radically alters what it means for human nature to have a "goal" or "end." In this way Gregory's eschatological anthropology challenges the received notions of human nature in particular and created nature more generally. In order to understand the significance of Gregory's thinking here, however, some further explanation is required.

Traditionally, philosophers had imagined "nature" as a closed system, bounded temporally at both ends (as in Plato) or infinite temporally but having no escape from the rhythm of birth, life, and death (as in Aristotle). In these pictures humans were either fundamentally finite parts of the closed natural order (as, arguably, in Aristotle), or essentially not part of that natural order at all (as, arguably, in Plato). When Christian theologians began thinking about human destiny in a Greek context, these assumptions had a powerful gravitational effect on their reflections, and it was easy for them to imagine the eschaton as the "fulfillment" of humanity's "natural" end—that is, as the completion of human beings. While there is something to this language, it holds two problems for Christians. First, it allows "nature" to set the terms for our eschatological destiny and thus seems to call into question God's transcendence of nature and in particular the character of God's free grace (because it makes grace seem nothing more than an aid to nature). Second, it suggests that at the eschaton humans are completed, finished, in a way that gives them no further room to grow; so that, in the words of the Talking Heads song, heaven is "a place where nothing ever happens."

Gregory responded to this with a brilliant bit of philosophical theology. He argued that humans naturally think formally in terms of teleology (that is, in terms of a final, completed, and thereafter changeless state of being), but that the actual "end" we will realize is in fact an "endless end," a process of infinite journeying into God (*epektasis* in Greek). The model for this, Gregory thinks, is Moses, who, "as he was becoming ever greater, at no time stopped in his ascent," and whose example teaches us that in seeking God we should expect "never to be satisfied in the desire to see him. But one must always, by looking at what he can see, rekindle his desire to see more. Thus, no limit would interrupt growth in the ascent to God, since no limit to the good can be found nor is the increasing of desire for the good brought to an end because it is satisfied" (*Life of Moses*, §§227 and 240). Gregory's anthropology is inescapably eschatological: we are not yet our true selves; that will happen only at the eschaton. But to understand what it will mean for us to be our true selves, we must leave behind the logic of finite, self-enclosed reality and think instead of entering into the "endlessness" of God's infinite existence. As Gregory understands things, our "attainment" of full humanity has no end, but is rather a matter always of moving on to the genuinely new—not the novelties of contemporary consumer culture, but rather the newness of being born ever again, ever anew into an ever-renewed morning.

Without noting this point, we might underplay the way theological anthropology gains its distinctive shape in important part from other doctrines. Human embodiment is not the only thing worth noting in a discussion of human existence; another thing worth noting is the character of human destiny, typically discussed under the aegis of eschatology in Christian theology. The nature of our "perfecting" is as basic a part of theological anthropology as the nature of our created constitution. Here, as in so many other places, we see the way that these doctrines interrelate and are perhaps distorted when seen in isolation from one another.

3. Augustine of Hippo

Augustine (354–430), bishop of the North African city of Hippo, provides still a third ancient Christian perspective on human being. Early in his career Augustine had been a follower of the dualistic Manicheans, who believed that all matter was evil. When he became a Christian, Augustine reacted strongly against this position, affirming the inalienable goodness of the material world in general and of human bodies in particular. He therefore did not follow Gregory of Nyssa in interpreting human sexual difference as a temporary expedient that would be transcended in the resurrection. On the contrary, Augustine insisted that our sexually differentiated bodies were a positive good that would be preserved even in heaven, when they would no longer be needed for the purpose of reproduction (see *City of God* 22.17).

While in this respect Augustine recaptures something of the holism of Irenaeus's perspective, the emergence of another debating partner alongside the Manicheans led him to break with Irenaeus's and Gregory's shared tendency to identify the image of God in human beings with freedom of the will. This second influence on Augustine's thought was Pelagianism. Pelagius was a British ascetic who, evidently motivated by a desire to rekindle a sense of moral urgency in what he saw as a complacent Christian church, stressed the role of obedience in securing salvation. Augustine was himself a well-known proponent of the ascetic life and certainly no enemy of ethical rigor, but he was concerned that Pelagius's emphasis on human effort in achieving salvation came at the expense of a proper stress on the role of divine grace.

In Augustine's view the Pelagian position failed to take seriously the way in which the power of sin undermines the ability of human beings to direct their lives to its proper end in God. While Adam and Eve had been created with a free will capable of avoiding sin (in Augustine's Latin, *posse non peccare*), their act of disobedience resulted in a corruption of the will, after which neither they nor their posterity could avoid sinning (*non posse non peccare*). In disobeying the God who was the source of their creaturely freedom, humanity had chosen a state of bondage. Furthermore, no subsequent act of the will could undo this choice, since every such attempt only confirmed humanity's alienation by repeating Adam and Eve's attempt to secure their lives before God rather than trusting in God as the only trustworthy source of life.

In defending this position (which amounted to the first fully developed doctrine of original sin), Augustine argued that only his radical interpretation of human depravity could make sense of the practice (firmly established in Augustine's North African context) of administering baptism—a sign of divine forgiveness to infants. Furthermore, he insisted that the Pelagian position undermined the good news that human beings were saved by the free gift of God's grace by teaching that human beings saved themselves. In pressing home his point against his adversaries, Augustine held that the graciousness of God's redeeming grace depended on its being absolutely unconditional on human work or merit.

Augustine's views entailed a vision of human being that was to prove enormously influential among Western Christians (though not in the Orthodox churches of the East). In effect, he held that human beings' distinctiveness lay not in their having been empowered to *achieve* communion with God through the exercise of an autonomous will, but rather in their being able to *receive* such communion as a gift. Since Augustine shared the established belief that God was immaterial, he reasoned that this communion was spiritual rather than physical and thus tended to identify the image of God in human beings with the rational faculties of the mind. So while a belief in the goodness of the whole of the created order led Augustine to conclude that God's renewal of human nature included the body as well as the mind, the language of the divine image pertained to the latter only.

The anthropology that emerges from this two-pronged response to Manicheans and Pelagians raises its own set of questions. With Irenaeus,

Augustine affirms that bodies are good and destined to be preserved eternally as marks of individual identity. At the same time, however, he grants little significance to the body in structuring human communion with God: the image of God is realized in mind, which, though eternally associated with a body, does not appear to depend on the body for its function. By implicitly ruling out the possibility that the particular characteristics of people's bodies might limit their prospects for life with God, Augustine marks out an interpretation of the life to come that is broadly egalitarian, but his strategy raises questions about the contribution that one's physical existence in time and space makes to one's eternal destiny.

An Alternative Augustinian Anthropology

The Augustinian anthropology detailed here is certainly legitimate and has often been the "received" Augustinian anthropology, at least in the twentieth century. But it is not the only one. This anthropology relies on a certain canon of Augustinian texts, especially the *Confessions* and the anti-Manichean and anti-Pelagian writings, to the detriment of Augustine's sermons, scriptural commentaries, and magisterial treatise on the Christian doctrine of God, *On the Trinity* (*De trinitate*). Were one to begin from this set of texts, a significantly different anthropology would begin. For instance, the picture of true human being in *De trinitate* begins not from reason or will but from love—from the human's capacity to love. This immediately implicates other people in one's proper "being human" and dislodges the autonomous powers of the mind (at least as we moderns conceive of the mind). The human self is *ecstatic*—constituted in part by going outside of itself, in love—and *passionately valuational* governed by what it values,—by its loves.

By describing the human's relationship to the divine in the vernacular of love, Augustine in *De trinitate* complicates the question of whether we "achieve" or "receive" communion with God. This is because love is a complex reality, conjoining "active" and "passive" elements in equally primordial ways. Who among us can actively *choose* voluntarily to love another? Love is a bit more of a "happening" than that; we suffer love. Then again, no one will deny that our actions do not matter in loving another; and certainly how we respond to the impact of love in our lives greatly affects the future presence of such love. Human psychology is far more complex than a simple vocabulary of agency or passion will allow, and Augustine might suggest that Irenaeus's and Gregory's focus on freedom of the will leaves out the immense complexity of actual human persons.

These questions about the relationship of time and space to human destiny are magnified by Augustine's theology of grace. Unlike Gregory of Nyssa, Augustine did not view human bodies as ultimately dispensable, but his desire to affirm salvation by grace alone has seemed to some to run the risk of evacuating human decisions in time and space of any role in shaping human destiny. While Augustine is careful to affirm that human freedom and responsibility are not cancelled by God's decisions (see his *Treatise on Grace and Free Will*), his way of defending the character of salvation as gift has led critics to charge that he decouples our future existence from our present experience.

The Body, Time, and Eternity in Augustine

Many people wonder whether Augustine really valued human embodiment. Such worries are often connected to a parallel worry about whether Augustine really valued history. Both of these concerns stem from a certain interpretation of Augustine's thinking on the relationship between time and eternity. The interpretation goes like this: simply put, for Augustine time is simply a place of marking time, and everything that matters happens in eternity. Thus, predestination is understood as saying that history is determined in such a way that there is nothing we can do to change it.

There are several problems with reading Augustine in this way. Most important, it is unclear what it would mean for us to change history, given that we are the ones who (at least in one sense) make it. The picture here is of multiple paths history can take, multiple realities, but with human beings constrained to follow only one route as if we were tied down by God on a runaway rail car, with God throwing all the switches. But there is an alternate picture of predestination, namely that God genuinely wills what we authentically do; that somehow the two wills need not operate to conflict with one another, but work on different levels.

This account of divine sovereignty and providence implies a general picture of God's relation to creation and eternity's relation to time that most Christian theologians have affirmed. On this understanding, eternity's relation to time and thus God's relation to history is like the relation of the center of a wheel to the edge of the wheel. If the edge of the wheel is history (assuming beginning and end do not meet), the center is equally related to all "instants" of the edge, as if with an infinite number of spokes. God (as Creator and Sustainer) is simultaneously immanent (present) to all moments of time without being at all confined to any or all temporal moments. Far from being unrelated to history, God is present throughout it.

But our current world seems to have a hard time understanding this picture. Instead, we tend to imagine "time" and "eternity" as realities alongside one another as though heaven were simply another place within the realm of creation (high up on clouds, say) that goes on at the same temporal clip as our history (thus "right now" in eternity the angels are watching me type this and you read it). According to this picture, heaven is just as much within the temporal succession as everything else except that no one gets older there. And God, in heaven, foreknows eternally what is going to happen next as if he had seen the movie many times before. It is this last thought that generates the worry about determinism that is often raised in connection with Augustine's theology.

But in fact for Augustine this picture of heaven and earth as parallel realities will not do. First of all, Augustine's understanding of the relationship between time and eternity means that the whole idea of "eternal foreknowledge" is a contradiction in terms: eternity is not before history; it simply transcends it. Because of this, God's "predestination" does not precede our actions in time, like the work of a divine puppeteer. God's transcendence of history is far more radical than simply not being affected by the flow of time. God knows *all* times immediately and is actively willing their existence (in their moments). And yet God's relation to history is no less real because of God's transcendence. Indeed it is precisely God's absolute transcendence over creation that enables God to render Godself completely open to and completely vulnerable in creation. God's relation to creation is best understood not in the abstract categories of philosophical theology but in the Incarnation, in Christ. Similarly, heaven is fundamentally an eschatological concept: until the eschaton, all the dead are in a holding pattern, not hanging out with God.

All of this is joined in a very interesting and poignant question Augustine asks at the end of the *City of God* about the wounds on the bodies of the martyrs: Will the martyrs be resurrected with the wounds on their bodies, or will those wounds be effaced and thus the effects of history undone? Augustine is clear: the wounds, and by extension all the marks of time on creation, will remain though they will be transfigured into marks of glory. Time is part of creation, and its importance to creation is real. And creation's importance is real too, as God in Christ has shown. For Augustine there was no question of his valuing history or embodiment; God chose a body as the vehicle of redemption, and our eternal fate is to be embodied, as God created us to be, albeit in bodies far more glorious than our current ones are.

Conclusions: Retrospect and Prospect

It would be very misleading to suggest that the range of Christian reflection on human being is in any way exhausted by this very cursory review of three figures from the church's first centuries. Subsequent writings in the area of theological anthropology have revealed problems and perspectives beyond their horizon. In the modern period, for example, theologians have identified the image of God in human beings with the capacity for self-transcendence, or openness to the world in general and God in particular; defenders of this view include Reinhold Niebuhr, Karl Rahner, and Wolfhart Pannenberg. A still more radical departure from the classical tradition is represented by those theologians (for example, Karl Barth) who are wary of identifying the divine image with any sort of individualized capacity like freedom or rationality and argue instead that the divine image refers to the way in which human beings, like the persons of the Trinity, are defined by their relationships with each other and with God. Nevertheless, Irenaeus, Gregory, and Augustine raise a set of problems that remain central to the topic of theological anthropology to the present day. Three issues in particular can be identified as crucial points of debate and discussion for theologians struggling to say something coherent about what it means to be human from a Christian perspective.

First, *how do we relate to God as the specifically human creatures we are*? For Irenaeus and Gregory human being finds its center in the freedom by which individuals on whom the light of Christ has shone are empowered to follow the path to life with God. Although sin is real, it is a threat that we have been enabled to overcome by being joined to Christ in baptism. For Augustine, by contrast, the freedom with which we had been created has been lost. Acknowledging the reality of sin therefore means recognizing our inability to defeat it but also recognizing that in Christ God has stepped in to secure our existence in spite of our incapacity and unworthiness. Here a fundamental issue is the extent to which we are responsible for giving value and meaning to our lives. Does a proper estimation of the destiny of human life as communion with God and each other mean stressing human beings' responsibility for "press[ing] on toward the goal for the prize of the heavenly call of God in Christ Jesus" (Phil. 3:14)? Or should more emphasis be placed on the status of human life as a gift that is given independently of any activity on our part?

Second, *what is the relation of the body to human identity*? Is the body just a temporary expedient (and thus incidental to our identities before God), as Gregory believed? Or is it part and parcel of our being as creatures made in God's image, as Irenaeus held? Once again Augustine represents a third perspective, affirming with Irenaeus that embodiedness is an inalienable element of human existence, yet siding with Gregory in locating the essence of our humanity (the "image of God") in the mind. Given that our bodies are the bearers and markers of our differences from one another, it is likely that our attitude toward the body will say something about how we view human difference. Is difference (whether of gender, race, sexual orientation, physical ability, or some other factor) merely a surface phenomenon that is irrelevant to who we are before God, or is it a defining feature of human being? Also, since our bodies link us materially with the rest of the world, the status of the body will probably influence how humanity's relationship to the wider creation is understood. It is probably no accident, for example, that Irenaeus, who places such emphasis on the role of the body in defining human identity, has a far more robust account of the renewal of the whole creation than either Gregory or Augustine.

Third, *what is the relation between the "old" creation described in the first chapters of Genesis and the "new creation" in Christ*? Are the two related in terms of organic development, albeit one marred by human capitulation to the powers of sin as Irenaeus thought? According to this view, human beings were created to grow, change, and mature through time. By contrast, Gregory saw life in time and space as something of an unfortunate detour designed to overcome the effects of sin rather than an integral part of human existence. For him the end is more the restoration of the beginning than a genuinely new development. Different still is Augustine, whose stress on the sovereignty of grace suggests a radical newness to life in Christ that almost eclipses the old order. These different perspectives raise the question of the relevance of historical circumstances to our ultimate destiny and, more broadly, the relationship of the church as the sign of the new creation to the wider society. Reflection on the relationship between old and new raises the question of whether it makes sense for Christians to work to change the social circumstances in which they find themselves in light of their expectation of the final shape of the future.

The contemporary essay in theological anthropology that follows addresses all these questions by examining the relationship between church practice (specifically, the Lord's Supper or Eucharist) and race. Though written from a self-consciously black Catholic perspective, the relevance of Shawn Copeland's essay is not limited to any one racial or confessional constituency within the church. By addressing the relationship between the "new creation" that is the body of Christ and the experience of mutilation and death suffered by the bodies of black women and men within a self-confessedly Christian culture, the essay maps out an approach to theological anthropology very different from those of Irenaeus, Gregory, or Augustine. Especially characteristic of this contemporary approach is an emphasis on *the particularity of historical experience* as a reference point for theological reflection and *the inherently social character of human existence* both inside and outside of the church.

Constructive Proposal

Body, Race, and Being:

M. Shawn Copeland

The terms in the title of this essay orient us to issues as provocative and substantive as they are controversial and ungainly. The very word *Eucharist* is saturated with meaning. As religious ritual, the Eucharist (or mass or Holy Communion or the Lord's supper) has long been a topic of intense research, debate, and publication. More important, as David Ford reminds us, the Eucharist is "the principal act of worship of the majority of the billion and a half or so Christians in the world today."[4] Catholic teaching holds that the Eucharist is a sacrament, what Augustine identifies as "revealing sign" (*sacrum signum*). So a sacrament discloses or manifests something or someone that is hidden or opaque. That same teaching maintains that Christ is *really present* with us and to us in the Eucharist.

In Catholic teaching, Eucharist also relates to the concept of the *body*. To speak of the body is to signify, according to Jörg Splett, "the most immediate and proximate object of our experience."[5] The body is always with us; it is inseparable from us. It is the mediator of our engagement with the world. But the body is no mere object with which we are confronted: *the body is something that we ourselves are*. The immediate imperatives of hunger or thirst, pleasure or pain are not just the body's imperatives; they are *my* imperatives, *your* imperatives.[6] Yet there is a "more" to me, a "more" to you than the body, even as that "more" is mediated by means of the body.

Not only is the body individual, but it may be communal or corporate. When Paul writes to the Corinthians, "You are the body of Christ and individually members of it" (1 Cor. 12:27), he refers to a body raised up by Christ for himself within humanity, the "mystical body" through which the domain of Jesus' body is extended. In that same letter the apostle writes: "I received from the Lord what I handed on to you, namely, that the Lord Jesus on the night when he was betrayed took a loaf of bread, and when he had given thanks, he broke it and said, 'This is my body that is for you'" (1 Cor. 11:23–24).

Referents and meanings of body shift easily; where bodies count, race matters. To speak about *race* is to court controversy. What is race? Race may be considered a biological characteristic or physical descriptor—a term for inherited traits that characterize a group. Race is also illusion, fiction, modern social construction. The philosophers of Greek antiquity identified race as an "accidental" quite inessential. Yet race can and does function in ways that are all too essential; indeed, race can assume life-and-death proportions, particularly when bodies are red or brown or yellow or black. Scaling or evaluating the racialized body renders mere observation as judgment and reduces decision to preference. Those moments stain history and action, liberty and finitude, culture and religion; they point to a genealogy of the domination and reduction of human bodies. That process of domination and reduction is what is meant by racism.

Racism is structural; it goes beyond personal prejudice or even bigotry to join those feelings or attitudes to the exercise of legitimate power. As James Boggs, David Theo Goldberg, and Iris Marion Young have argued persuasively, racism does not rely on the choices or actions of a few isolated individuals; it is institutionalized. Racism is both an ideology, or biased way of thinking, and a set of practices. Racism justifies and maintains social oppression not only through the formulation of specious arguments but through poisoning human potential for authentic religious, moral, psychological, and spiritual growth. Racism is idolatry: it spoils the spirit. As such, it is an insult to Eucharist.

You may feel as queasy as I do in situating the words *racism* and *Eucharist* together in the same sentence. These words evoke two opposing domains of meaning—the one cannot but insinuate sin and evil, the other divine goodness and grace. While I want to emphasize the structural character of racism, precisely because it *is* structural it seeps, like an odorless, colorless gas, into our institutions even those charged with our human development and flourishing. There it deforms our ideas, attitudes, dispositions, and practices—even religious ones.

This essay is divided into four sections. The first reprises the relation of slavery to Christianity. Their entanglement bears a primary responsibility for the rebuffs black women and men encounter at the eucharistic table, as we shall see, even in the twenty-first century. The second section treats two forms of social oppression spawned by slavery and racism: the *objectification* of black bodies and black personhood and *lynching*. To uncover the objectification of black bodies, we draw on the freed peoples' memories of slavery. Although slave narratives, transcriptions of oral interviews conducted years after Emancipation, present difficulties for scholars, they remain an indispensable source for any history of the enslaved people as told from their perspective. These memories contest the "public transcripts" of the slaveholders and present a critical, even didactic counterdiscourse that recognizes and defends their humanity, spirituality, subjectivity, and agency. Historian James McGovern has observed that after 1865 "the American practice of *lynching* blacks became a systemic feature of race relations."[7] Between 1882 and 1903, 2,060 black men and women were lynched, roughly one person every other day for 20 years.[8] In 1892, lynching reached an all-time peak at 235.[9] Duration and intensity—*nearly 300 years in the English-speaking colonies and the Republic, in contrast to 136 years of black statutory freedom*—invest slavery and its legacy in lynching with *gravitas*. Although the enslavement and lynching of black men and women neither exhaust nor circumscribe African American or even American experience, we cannot ignore the trajectory of maldistributed, transgenerational oppression these vicious practices have set in motion.

Data from the first and second sections lead to a theological interrogation of the eucharistic community. This third section questions the precariousness of black belonging, the difficulty of incorporating blacks into the ecclesial body, and thus the structural impediments to the theological recognition of blacks as human persons within American Christianity. This section gives special attention to the generative, if paradoxical, *logos* of the cross, whose shadow falls across the eucharistic table.[10] From this analysis, we may be in the position to say something in the fourth section about solidarity, about what it might mean to be the body of Christ in our present-day context.

Slavery and Christianity

Slavery in the United States has murky beginnings; it was the offspring of greed and indentured servitude. When masters defaulted on time-bound contracts and attempted to extend their legal hold over men and women, white and black, it is not surprising that indentured servants rebelled. Historians cannot be precise, but sometime around 1640 in colonial America, slavery came to be associated almost exclusively and exhaustively with black bodies, and, correspondingly, black bodies came to signify enslavement, to be slaves.

Our contemporary American understanding of slavery has been shaped by popular cultural treatments like the film version of Margaret Mitchell's *Gone with the Wind*. However, in practice, slavery was neither romantic nor uniform. It was diverse and opportunistic; anyone who could own slaves did. Plantations and farms required overseers, drivers, field hands, cooks, housekeepers, nursemaids, weavers, domestic servants, blacksmiths, mechanics, carpenters, craftspersons, and artisans. Slaveholders made money on their human property by leasing slaves to other whites who owned small farms or operated businesses in urban centers. Furthermore, slavery was never confined to the South: at some time or another prior to Emancipation, men and women who lived in New York, Massachusetts, Rhode Island, Ohio, and Wisconsin engaged in slaveholding or slave trading. Slavery was a business and a way of life, but, most basically, it was a lie. Nearly everyone touched by slavery learned to live with it by learning to live with a lie—a monstrous moral fiction that insulted God and human nature.

Slavery was also deeply entangled with Christianity. When white Christians first confronted the logic of slavery, their understanding of baptism underwent syllogistic mutation: To be a baptized Christian was to be free; blacks, Africans, were natural slaves; therefore, blacks could not be baptized. Such logic had lethal doctrinal and pastoral, moral and ethical consequences. There were political and economic consequences as well. And when faced with the specter of slaves who were baptized, it was crucial for the slaveholding classes to break the link between being Christian and being free. Thus, in 1664 the lower legislative house of Maryland asked the upper house to "draw up an Act obliging Negroes to serve *durante vita* . . . for the prevention of the dammage Masters of such Slaves must susteyne by such slaves pretending to be Christened." It was intended that slavery should stand in perpetuity, and Christianity would be one means to that end.

This is not to suggest that there was uniformity of opinion on the relationship between Christianity and slavery. White planters and pastors sometimes clashed, sometimes shared the same opinions about the religious instruction of their slaves. Some planters insisted that the time needed for proper instruction interfered with work routines in the fields or other employments. Other planters maintained that the Africans were too "brutish," too savage for Christian initiation. These "opaque bodies" could not have been made in the image of God; rather, they were created inferior, natural slaves.[11] As historian Albert Raboteau has shown, in order to support their views, white planters drew on biblical passages and putative theological arguments as well as appeals to the superiority of European culture. Indeed, clergy (both Catholic and Protestant) as well as members of Catholic religious orders of men and women owned slaves.[12] At the same time there were pastors and missionaries who wanted to instruct and baptize the enslaved people and who defended their share in humanity. In Virginia the religious establishment often criticized slaveholders for their refusal to have slaves baptized. And during most of the seventeenth century, Anglican clergy preached either freedom from slavery as a by-product of baptism or the admonition that one Christian should not enslave another.

However, to the majority of slaveholders, the mere suggestion of common human nature insinuated the possibility that, as Christians, the enslaved people might make a claim of fellowship and thus threaten the power differential that sustained the positions of master and slave. Clerics therefore attempted to "build a wall" between the notions of equality as taught by Christianity and the master-slave hierarchy.[13] In this endeavor, the Bible served as a principal tool and was used both to legitimate and to sacralize the bondage of black bodies.

Election or Entitlement?

Part of the task of being human with others is relinquishing privilege. Slave masters maintained their position of power over the enslaved by taking refuge within an ideology of entitlement. Locating privilege in history, however, is a relatively easy task, especially when compared with trying to pinpoint the inequities of privilege in our everyday lives. This is particularly difficult in a culture that indoctrinates people into thinking they deserve this or that—that they are chosen and special. Before addressing the communal character of Eucharist, then, it is important to understand how one's understanding of self as special or chosen is always in relation to an "other." Put differently, the way in which chosenness is interpreted complicates the performance of being human.

Chosenness is a religious idiom that can be found in Scripture. Reading Torah, one quickly learns that Israel is the chosen people, elected by God from the rest of humanity for a special sense of being, as well as a sacred place to dwell. In Deut. 7:6 Moses explains, "For you are a people holy to the Lord your God; the Lord your God has chosen you out of all the peoples on earth to be his people, his treasured possession." This is only one illustration of the notion of chosenness, as the idea of election extends beyond Jewish identity to that of other religions and cultures. To be sure, divine election carries over to Christianity. It is known from Pauline literature that Gentile followers of Jesus longed to be part of this chosen category, wanted to be loved by God just as Jewish Christians were. Interestingly, whether read within a Jewish or Christian worldview, those elected are imbued with a sense of approval, prestige, and even authority.

Important as the notion of chosenness is for a religious sensibility, election can also be found in cultural myth. One needs only to read the propaganda of fascist or white supremacist movements to detect chosenness in the larger culture. In these cases, one group understands itself as privileged, special, and almost divinely moved for power and greatness. This feeling of specialness, along with other historical and social factors, led to the subversion of communion on the basis of race described above. Nevertheless, claims to specialness extend even further than racial propaganda. One only needs to think about how American privilege and specialness was employed in the second Gulf War of 2003. Specialness in this context is disclosed in spreading American values, including the ideals of freedom and choice as well as practices related to consumption. Instead of laying claims to the Holy Land under the name of God, as the Crusaders did, modern Americans lay claims to legitimacy through the spread of multinational capitalism. Framing oneself as chosen enables and even entitles a person and/or society to live without limits. Distortions of chosenness in these ways are obstacles to building communities of justice.

In addition to the theological and political manifestations of chosenness, claims to specialness occur on the interpersonal level as well, such as in family systems or professional environments. Here one can rethink how privilege is figured in more intimate relations, again complicated by gender, race, class, and so on. Whatever the context, once it is argued that a people is chosen, many complicated questions arise. Are there certain responsibilities with the privilege of election? Can you reject election? How does one's election relate to the destiny of another's nonelection? Does nonelection of the other translate into rejection of the other? Does chosenness lead to chauvinism? Is chauvinism necessarily problematic?

Without being able to answer all of these queries, it remains clear that chosenness in the religious imagination differs from the manifestation of chosenness in culture. Chosenness in the biblical context is an event of *obligation*. God elects a people for God and for others. This is a relationship of irrevocable responsibility and expectation. But in the contemporary societal context, culture calls humanity for itself rather than for others, with the result that all references to chosenness by God and for others are stripped away. The cultural stress on self over and against the other makes the call for solidarity all the more difficult and, at the same time, all the more poignant. This problematic relation of self over other can be summed up as an attitude of *entitlement*, which assumes that one deserves this or that at all costs, even to the detriment of others. Those entitled pose as if things are due to them, without any strings attached. With an emphasis on survival and self-preservation, the disposition of entitlement obscures the wants and the needs of others. Destroying one's capacity to be for others, the posture of entitlement beguiles the subject into believing in the commonsense logic that charity begins at home. Any sense of responsibility and obligation is erased from the conversation.

The detrimental effects of entitlement have not gone unnoticed, as sociologists, cultural theorists, and clinicians struggle with the rationale of the ideology of entitlement. Some psychological studies of entitlement attribute the modern inclination of entitlement to a deep sense of cultural narcissism. With narcissistic tendencies, the individual cannot distinguish between self and other to the extent that the confusion becomes pathological. Without differentiating between self and other, the self thinks all the world is under his or her control. She or he is entitled to it all, because there exists no other to contest his or her claims. Here, the boundaries that mark difference are completely ignored, allowing the subject to collapse him- or herself with the other, thereby undermining the unique gifts the other brings to the table. Clearly this cultural display of election as privilege is a complete subversion of the religious roots of chosenness, which demand a charitable component of being in relationship with others. When in a relationship of election, we are chosen to be for the other; we are in it for others. This is a radically different perspective from being in relationship for self, which is the effect of entitlement. In order to coexist and flourish with others in solidarity and in a pluralist world, we need to deconstruct this illusion of entitlement. As we proceed in remembering, that is, putting chosenness back in its charitable context, it is important to note that this process is not without risks, and may involve conflict.

The Wounded Body of a People

In order to consider ways in which black men and women have been wounded, let us first draw back the veil on the sacrilegious objectification of their bodies and persons. This reduction began in the seizure and theft of the body; the willful and violent severing of the captive body from community and personhood; imprisonment in dank places below ground; then, the agonizing physical confinement, psychic disorientation, and trauma of the Middle Passage. More lessons in chattel slavery's idiom of power followed: handling and seasoning, bartering and selling. Finally, the idolatrous attempt to unmake human being: as Hortense Spillers writes so movingly, "the captive body becomes the source of an irresistible, destructive sensuality… reduces to a thing, becoming being for the captor."[14] The captive *body* is no longer subject but object. Moreover, as object the captive body is not so much representation of *otherness* but, in physical and biological expression and in response to it, becomes an *other thing*. Thus slavery rendered objectified the black body as an object of *property*, an object of *production*.

THE BLACK BODY AS OBJECT OF PROPERTY

Chattel slavery was not just a kind of feudal system peculiar to Southern plantation agriculture. It was structured, sanctioned, interpreted, and enforced by the laws of the United States. In the putative legal system, the slave is defined as "one who is in the power of a master *to whom he belongs.* The master *may sell him, dispose of his person*, his industry and his labor" (emphasis added).[15] Slaves were "deemed, sold, taken, reputed and adjudged in law to be *chattels personal*, in the hands of their owners and possessors, and their executors, administrators, and assigns, *to all intents, constructions, and purposes whatsoever*" (emphasis added).[16] As Spillers observes, these laws aimed to "erase every feature of social and human differentiation" and reify African personality.[17]

Enslaved Africans were, according to William Goodell, "reputed and considered real estate; [and were], as such, subject to be mortgaged, according to the rules prescribed by law, and [could be] seized and sold as real estate."[18] By law, black bodies—black men, women, and children—could be put up for sale at whim or need. Slave traders, slave pens, and the slave market served this function. When interviewed about her experience of slavery, Katie Rowe, a former slave, described the way in which the Africans were handled and inspected like cattle: "De white men come up and look in de slave's mouth jes lak he was a mule or a hoss."[19] Free born in the United States, kidnapped as an adult, and sold into slavery, Solomon Northup confirmed this practice. Customers calling at the slave pen, he wrote, "would feel of our hands and arms and bodies, turn us about, ask us what we could do, make us open our mouths and show our teeth, precisely as a jockey examines a horse."[20] Buyers would tell slaves to roll up the legs of their pants or lift up their skirts in order to inspect for blisters, signs of disease, or scars from whippings that indicate evidence of a slave's disposition toward rebellion.

Moses Grandy tells of standing in the street when a slave train passed by with his wife in chains. Grandy pleaded with the trader, Mr. Rogerson, to learn why his wife had been sold. The trader replied that the slaveholder wanted money. Rogerson drew his pistol and threatened Grandy away from the wagon, but allowed him to stand at a distance and talk with his wife. Grandy said, "My heart was so full that I could say very little. . . . I have never seen or heard from her from that day to this. I loved her as I love my life."[21]

Delia Garlic was 100 years old when asked about her suffering under slavery. Emphatically she stated: "Slavery days was hell." She continued,

"Babies was snatched from deir mother's breast and sold to speculators. Chillens was separated from sisters and brothers and never saw each other again. 'Course dey cry. You think they not cry when dey was sold like cattle?"[22]

The Black Body as Object of Production

For the sake of the profits of the plantation, enslaved women and men were reduced to instruments of labor. Black women and men worked from sunup to sundown, usually 6 days each week, and sometimes for some hours on Sundays. On some plantations slaves were supervised in the fields by black drivers who, in turn, were under the direction of white overseers. On other estates they worked the fields under the immediate supervision of white overseers, the plantation owner, or a member of the owner's family.

There was little gender differentiation when it came to heavy labor in the field. Harriet Robinson pointed out that "women broke in mules, throwed 'em down, and roped 'em."[23] Interviewed in Asheville, North Carolina, Fannie Moore said that her mother would "work in the field all day and piece and quilt all night."[24] And Sarah Gruder recalled, "I never knowed what it was to rest. I just work all de time from mornin' till late at night. I had to do everythin' dey was to do on de outside. Work in de field, chop wood, hoe corn, till sometimes I feel like my back surely break. I done everythin' 'cept split rails."[25]

W. L. Bost recalled the brutal whipping of one enslaved man whom he described as "stubborn" and who would not do as much work as the plantation owner thought he should: [The man] been lashed lot before. So they take him to the whippin' post, and then they strip his clothes off and then the [overseer] stand off and cut him with the whip. His back was cut all to pieces. The cuts about half inch apart. Then after they whip him they tie him down and put salt on him. Then after he lie in the sun awhile they whip again. But when they finish with he, he was dead.[26]

Interviewed in a rural area outside of Houston, Richard Carruthers, who gave his age as one hundred, recalled a rough tempered overseer by the name of Tom Hill: "[Hill] used to whip me and the other [slaves] if we don't jump quick enough when he holler and he stake us out like you stake out a hide and whip till we bleed. . . . Sometime he take salt and rub on the [slave] so he smart and burn . . . and suffer misery."[27] Slavery aimed to sever black men, women, and children from their sacred humanity and control of their bodies; slavery sought to deprive them of personhood and identity. Lynching terrorized and traumatized black bodies and spirits.

LYNCHING: TERRORIZING BLACK BODY AND SPIRIT

Lynching was a capricious instrument of terror that Southern (and also Northern) whites used to deconstruct the new order of political and economic relations that the Union victory achieved and the subsequently amended Constitution affirmed. The motivations for lynching included attempted or alleged or actually committed arson, robbery, theft, assault, murder, the poisoning of well water, insulting whites or failing to show proper deference, disobeying an order, and sexual assault against white women. Lynching aimed to restore and then maintain white racial dominance, to monitor and control the boundaries of caste and class.[28] The spectacle of a castrated and burned black man (and sometimes a black woman) served to intimidate and pacify purportedly restive blacks. And, as McGovern argues, it put whites on notice that anyone "who balked at the caste system and attempted to initiate personal as against caste relationships with blacks ran the risk of severe social ostracism, especially in the small towns and rural areas."[29] Northerners may have found lynching revolting, but George Frederickson states, their "opposition to [it] was . . . a limited and ineffectual phenomenon."[30]

In Georgia in 1899 Sam Holt, a black farm laborer, was charged with killing his white employer in a quarrel over wages. In the presence of a crowd of more than two thousand people, Holt was first tortured before being doused with oil and burned. *The Springfield (Massachusetts) Weekly Republican* recorded these events:

> Before the torch was applied to the pyre, the [Negro] was deprived of his ears, fingers and genital parts of his body. He pleaded pitifully for his life while the mutilation was going on, but stood the ordeal of fire with surprising fortitude. Before the body was cool, it was cut to pieces, the bones crushed into small bits, and even the tree upon which the wretch met his fate was torn up and disposed of as "souvenirs." The Negro's heart was cut into several pieces, as was also his liver. Those unable to obtain the ghastly relics direct paid their more fortunate possessors extravagant sums for them. Small pieces of bones went for 25 cents, and a bit of liver crisply cooked sold for 10 cents.[31]

In Helena, Arkansas, in 1921 William Turner was alleged to have assaulted a white telephone operator. But the nineteen-year-old was never brought to trial. Instead, William Turner was lynched not once but twice: after one mob of whites had lynched him, a second mob cut down his body and burned it in a bonfire in front of city hall. The *St. Louis Argus* reported that Turner's body was hauled through Helena to provide a moving target for white men armed with pistols who lined the principal streets of this town. . . . Turner's corpse was roped to the rear end of an automobile and driven up and down the main streets of Helena at various speeds as white men hooted, yelled, and perfected their marksmanship by shooting at the almost disintegrating remains. No colored folks were allowed on the streets. When the celebrants had had their fill, the body was burned.[32]

To further demonstrate their supremacy, the white men of the town ordered William Turner's father, August Turner, to remove the battered and charred remains of his son's body.

In 1916 Jeff Brown was lynched by a mob in Cedar Bluff, Mississippi. Reportedly, Brown was walking on a street near train tracks when he spotted a moving freight going in his desired direction. The *Birmingham Voice of the People* reported that somehow in his run to board the moving train, Brown accidentally brushed against the daughter of a white farmer standing on the sidewalk. The girl screamed. "A gang quickly formed and ran after [Brown], jerking him off the moving train. He was beaten into insensibility and then hung to a tree. The sheriff has made no attempt to find out who the members of the mob were. Picture cards of the body are being sold on the streets at five cents apiece."[33]

Picture cards, photographs of lynched black bodies, were common. In 2000 James Allen released to selected museums around the country portions of his extensive collection of these postcards. The catalogue for the exhibition, *Without Sanctuary: Lynching Photographs in America*,[34] widens the aperture on social sin. With seeming nonchalance, "the celebrants" sent these grim "souvenirs" to friends and relatives, siblings and parents by way of the U.S. mail. These photographs reveal as much about the racist, orgiastic behavior of a white mob bent on consuming black (male) bodies as they do about the terror and anguish of lynch victims. These images strain credulity; we do not know where to direct our eyes. It is difficult to look at the tortured man or woman and just as unnerving to linger on faces twisted with glee as they preside over what Orlando Patterson has so rightly called a "feast of blood."[35] Slavery, lynching, and their extension in white racist supremacy aimed to desecrate black humanity and occlude black bodies from signifying the sacred reality of *being human*. These vicious practices denigrated the black body as a site of divine revelation, as a basic human sacramental capable of making visible the divine.

Can the Body Be Revelatory?

What exactly are the theological implications of the claim that desecrated bodies of black human beings are "a site of divine revelation?" What does the revelation claim mean for whites? For blacks? How does it affect the self-definition of white and black (as well as brown, yellow, red) folk as Christians, both as individual "races" and as a collective North American citizenry? What is the impact of the idea of the revelatory human body on Christian witness and ethics? How does this assertion change the Christian view of and participation in the Eucharist within the context of a highly racialized United States? Finally, the issues of repentance, reparations, and reconciliation are probably worth looking at in this context, especially in the light of the Jubilee traditions recorded in Leviticus 25. For instance, Jesus' words in Matt. 5:23–26 (and parallels) suggest that before we come to him and the table of the Lord's Supper, we should first make amends with our sisters and brothers whom we have injured.

A broken and tortured body—the body of Jesus of Nazareth—is the most powerful mediating symbol of Eucharist. In their endurance of whippings, lacerations, abuse, rape, torture, and lynching, the bodies of black women and men form the site of other stigmata. It is no wonder that the most well-known Negro spirituals reflect on the crucifixion of Jesus; in *their* flesh, black women and men made themselves available for a deeper grasp of the suffering of *his* body. As idolatrous practices, slavery, lynching, and their extension in white racist supremacy not only violate black bodies but also blaspheme against God, against the body of Jesus of Nazareth, against the Body of Christ.

Performing and Subverting Eucharist

The word *Eucharist*, as we noted earlier, is saturated with meaning: Eucharist evokes the dangerous memory of Jesus of Nazareth, who insisted that unless you eat the [his] flesh . . . and drink his blood, you have no [eternal] life . . . for my flesh is true food and my blood is true drink" (John 6:53, 55). The significance of Eucharist rises from the table words and gestures of Jesus on the night before he died. That ritual meal and its bloody aftermath *embody* the etymology of the Greek verb *eucharistein* that denotes the "proper conduct of one who is the object of a gift." The embodied and performed meaning that radiates from Jesus' last preresurrection meal goes well beyond ordinary attitudes or gestures of thankfulness.[36]

The sacramental meal of the church grows from this more comprehensive notion of thanksgiving. With care and prudence the church sets a table around which we gather to encounter Christ. Here we are formed in and for discipleship. Here we learn to recognize and cherish the face of Christ revealed in our eating and drinking; here we learn to befriend, to treasure others as he treasured them in compassion and solidarity. *Eucharist* presses for outward evidence of a gratitude that indicates the gift has been received and has effected a proper response, but an *improper* response may come forth as well.

Conflict as a Prelude to Fellowship

There is implied both a proper and an improper response to the eucharistic invitation to fellowship. The proper response might be seen as struggling fiercely against the social sin of racism and imagining human solidarity in light of Jesus' call for communion with all, especially those who are stigmatized in society. Conversely, the improper response would seem to be engaging in conflict with those who are different. Unfortunately, sidestepping conflict is not always feasible or productive. Moreover, Jesus offers no practical insights as how to deal with the messiness of the diverse banquet called life. Once we are seated at the table, what are we to do with the feelings evoked by different cultures and traditions? This situation constitutes an undoubtedly uncomfortable and awkward predicament. Being human here requires being open to the feelings of fear, messiness, awkwardness, anger, hope, and even conflict such a setting might bring. In this sense conflict may be a proper way of working toward fellowship.

In our everyday lives many of us are most comfortable with people, places, and things with which we are familiar. Whether a favorite coffee shop or an old friend from the neighborhood, sameness has a way of making humanity feel grounded. It is not surprising, then, that the opposite of the same—namely difference (or otherness)—evokes feelings that cause pause, question, and even concern. An elusive notion at best, difference is often maintained by borders (often intangible and largely social in origin) erected to demarcate where self ends and another begins. By way of these borders, otherness can be framed not only in terms of race but also into questions of class, gender, sexual orientation, religion, national origin, abilities, and so on.

Reactions to difference are far from uncomplicated. In spirit, Christianity presents as open to difference, cutting across boundaries that divide communities. Indeed, the message of Jesus is based in Jewish piety, a hospitality that extends to others beyond borders. This open tradition within Christianity is found in Luke 14, in the parable of the great banquet. Jesus commands those marginalized in the community to be brought to the table into fellowship. One of the underlying messages is the importance of embracing otherness. Nevertheless, the presence of many others at the dinner table is the ideal, and arguably the reality might be much less sanguine. Others at the table disrupt the status quo, the usual. Others bring to the table different appetites, various tastes some of which may offend. Being human in such a situation demands that those at the table not merely embrace the face of otherness, but embrace the conflict that such alterity courts. This may seem a strange statement to make—being human means being open to conflict. Nonetheless, conflict is a given in human relations. Disagreements, divergence, and dialectic can be found in all forms of human relationship. Openness to that reality offers the chance to avoid the violence accompanying conflict that is ignored, unheard, or erased.

To make this point clearer, it may help to move beyond Jesus' parable, locating the "great banquets" in everyday life. For instance, the pluralist context in the United States might be read as a great banquet in which many cultures and many religions are present. In America it is not too strong to suggest that difference binds people together, that difference is the occasion for solidarity. But that ideal has not yet been realized in America. As noted above, the United States was built, quite literally and crudely, on racial difference in a way that testifies to a peculiarly American struggle with otherness. Because racism in a variety of manifestations continues to alienate people from one another, the United States would appear to be only at a very early stage in developing a culture of accepting others.

Many feel as if the only viable options when faced with the "other" are avoidance and violence. Avoidance can range from disassociating with those deemed other to neutralizing their difference through politically correct language. On the other hand, violence subverts difference by erasing it through random attacks or even genocide. Obviously any move toward being human with others in solidarity requires another option, namely, having the courage to deal with the conflict that difference brings. Conflict here is not gratuitous violence, but an openness to the ambiguity, risk, fear, and danger that interpersonal encounter yields. An embrace of the liminal space, of the boundary between self and other is the positive side of conflict. Before solidarity, then, there is a witnessing to boundaries, the risk of danger, and the hope of fellowship. Such witnessing can be performed in racially charged social situations but also in one's personal relationships. Whatever the situation, effectively managing conflict in all relationships is part of the performance of being human and moving toward justice.

THE PRECARIOUSNESS OF BELONGING OR BEING IN-CORPORATED

Two instances will illustrate the precariousness of black belonging to (or at least attempting to belong) to the body of Christ. First: Not long ago, one of our African American students at the Institute for Black Catholic Studies spoke of an encounter at Eucharist. A mature woman and daily communicant in a small Texas town that still maintains segregated Catholic churches, the woman traveled on alternate days to the church set aside for white parishioners. At the greeting of peace, she extended her hand to a white woman nearby who took it limply, then reached for tissues to wipe her hands. This gesture of cleaning was performed in relation to no other person except this black woman. Second: Last year, a Nigerian priest recounted to me the shock and hurt of an African woman religious in habit at Eucharist in a white parish in the Milwaukee area. The first time this sister, the only black worshiper, approached the cup, the Eucharistic minister refused to extend it. Thinking the cup empty, she simply returned to her pew. But by the third time this happened, the sister had begun to notice that (white) others immediately behind her were offered the cup. Without any further analysis or argument, we would agree that such behavior subverts the gratuitous gift of the *body* of Christ whose being and work effect for us the very condition of the possibility to claim the gift of his body through his Spirit.

Eucharist is at the heart of the Christian community. Participation (*koinonia*) in the body and blood of Christ is communion with the whole Christ: the suffering Christ, the Risen Lord, the body of believers. These two poignant vignettes disclose the hunger of black members of the body. In these situations the food is not unclean (see Jesus' discussion of the division between clean and unclean foods in Mark 7:14–23), but those who come to the table are so marked by race, by racism. The trajectory set afoot by slavery and lynching spoils not only ordinary, face-to-face interaction but sacred time and activity as well. Race assumes an essential and ontological importance that excludes black participation and incorporation into the body, and thus subverts the gift Eucharist is.

Two Kinds of Ritual

Today what does it mean for us to eat and drink the body and blood of Christ ritually as compared to white Christian mobs ritually eating and drinking (metaphorically) the lynched bodies of black folk? In this context, it is important to remember that Sunday after church is when many of the lynchings occurred. This meant that after eating and drinking Christ's body and blood in church, these same white Christians immediately left church and brought their children and picnic baskets to view a lynching of black women and men on another wooden cross.

But there is a double exclusion here: These instances illustrate denial of Eucharist—denying the actual elements of communion to someone and falsifying the ritual sharing of peace that precedes eating and drinking. Such denial of Eucharist equates as refusal of Eucharist. The Host at the table who feeds us with his own body and blood is rebuffed. Such subversion is sacrilege. But such refusal also deprives other (white) members of the whole Christ. To paraphrase Miroslav Volf, such refusal promotes a false purity through which some (white) women and men set themselves apart from so-called (black) defiled persons in hypocritical white purity and exclude "the boundary breaking (black) other from [their] heart[s] and [their] world."[37] In such instances of denial and exclusion from the table, despite the propriety of word and gesture, Eucharist is rendered empty ritual. *Christ cannot yet be fully present and, I dare say, will not come.* Exclusion from and denial and refusal of Eucharist, as David Ford says, undermines the intrinsic and "pivotal locus of Christian identity" and dislocates the power of the sacrament (grace).[38] All are left hungry.

THE CROSS AND THE TABLE

To come to the table, one must be a disciple. The "way" of discipleship is the way Jesus is, and the way Jesus walks leads to the cross. "Whoever does not carry the cross and follow me cannot be my disciple" (Luke 14:27). In order to eat the bread of life, to realize ourselves as the body of Christ, Christians must walk the way of the cross to reach the eucharistic table.

The Lukan Jesus, like the Jesus of the other Synoptic Gospels, blesses, breaks, and identifies bread with himself before he completes his way to the cross. In this Gospel the breaking of bread is the gesture that clears the eyes of those forlorn disciples who met a stranger on their way to Emmaus (Luke 24:30–31). Marianne Sawicki comments in her book, *Seeing the Lord*, on Luke's association of hunger with the possibility of understanding resurrection life and of recognizing the resurrected Lord.[39] How will we know him when he appears? The resurrected Lord seems often to be at table or on the beach with a grill.

But here I am interested in preresurrection texts. In Luke 14 we find Jesus on a Sabbath at table, a dinner guest of a Pharisee. Jesus bluntly tells his host: "When you give a banquet, invite the poor, the crippled, the lame, and the blind. And you will be blessed, because they cannot repay you, for you will be repaid at the resurrection of the righteous" (14:13–14). In other words, make space in your hearts, at your table, in your communities, in your lives for the marginalized. Perhaps to ensure that the Pharisees and those gathered at table have got the point, Jesus reiterates this lesson in the parable of the great banquet. Someone invites guests to a wonderful meal. The host sends a servant to summon the guests, but they retort with excuses and rebuff his hospitality. They are "filled" with their own preoccupations and privilege. Angry, the householder tells a servant, "Go out at once into the streets and lanes of the town and bring in the poor, the crippled, the blind, and the lame." The servant does so and returns to report that there is still room at table. Again the host sends the servant "out into the roads and lanes, and compel people to come in, so that my house may be filled. For I tell you, none of those who were invited will taste my dinner" (14:23–24).

To come hungry to his table, to experience and recognize hunger seems to constitute a possibility for discipleship. If we would be disciples of Jesus, we must be willing to recognize and alleviate hungers whether for Eucharist or food or truth or justice, whether our own hungers or those of others.[40] We cannot overlook his appearance in the least, in those whom we do not expect to approach the table. The parable of the great banquet reiterates a warning thrown down earlier by the Lukan Jesus: "Woe to you who are full now, for you will be hungry" (Luke 6:25). Surely, this saying is meant for those of us who have the luxury to watch hungry women and men standing in line at a soup kitchen, those of us who have the power to withhold Eucharist.

The cross rises between the meal the Lukan Jesus shares with his disciples before he dies and the bit of grilled fish that he eats with them in Jerusalem (Luke 24:41–43). At the Passover meal, Jesus declares to his friends that he shall not eat or drink again until the kingdom of God comes (Luke 22:16–18). He promises them that when the kingdom does come, they shall sit with him at his table in places set specially for them, eating and drinking with joy (Luke 22:28–30). Thus, to be his disciple means to eat and share eucharistic food, to feed others, to eat and drink with them the food that lasts.

Charity as Exposure

Humanity can only reveal itself as a site of God's presence when it enters into the final act of being human: sharing with and for others, or charity (*caritas*). Even as cultural pressures of entitlement and narcissism create the illusion of moving humanity closer to the image of God, their promises fall short. Worldly gifts never nourish spiritual hunger—an appetite that will only be satiated by being human beyond self, for God and others. Charitable relations give meaning to human existence. Still, pinning down the meaning of charity is not easy. Charity is often thought of in terms of kindness, or events of giving. However, the meaning of charity transcends reflection and action, incorporating affect as well. *Affect* refers to the feelings and emotions that ground human interaction. This affective dimension of charity needs to be underscored, given that the negative feelings surrounding difference often divide humanity. By dealing with the feeling the other evokes, whether it is love, compassion, anger, or jealously, the subject exposes himself or herself for the other, thus becoming charitable.

Theologically, the Christian notion of charity is exemplified in the incarnation. God becomes human in Jesus Christ, taking on pain and suffering for the other humanity. Limiting charity to the Christian tradition is not feasible, however. Long before Christianity emerged as an institutionalized religion, charity was part of the Jewish tradition and usually framed within the rubric of hospitality or generosity for the well-being of another. Hospitality, for Jews, emanates in the memory of being in exile, being others in a strange land. One merely needs to heed Torah to be reminded how Yahweh commands Israel to be hospitable to those in need, for Israel was once in need, once in exile, and once a stranger. Similar to Judaism and Christianity, Islam has a strong sense of charity embedded in its worldview. Indeed, charity is one of the five pillars of faith to which Muslims adhere. Moreover, in the contemporary context charity cannot remain solely within the religious imagination, as economic status and political agenda also influence how one reads charity. In addition to issues concerning the allocation of capital, charity can be demonstrated in basic human affinities for companionship and compassion.

It is important to note that in all acts of charity, there is an openness to go beyond giving, to being open to receiving. Being receptive to charity is difficult because accepting charity marks one as exposed, dependent, and vulnerable. Charity as exposure in modern, consumerist societies, vulnerability is interpreted as a weakness. We are encouraged to buy products in order to gain control over our lives and to make ourselves self-sufficient. Interestingly, clinicians and sociologists claim that this need for control is another symptom of our narcissistic culture, and in actuality, we become alienated from control through exorbitant consumption. Against this cultural claim that dependence on another is a sin, the Christian worldview maintains that being human emerges precisely in one's need for another. Notice how dependence within the religious imagination is evidence of right-relationship with others, rather than a scar of shame.

In response to the malignant legacy of racism, charity would involve not just inviting all people to the table but also embracing their particularity as well as sameness. Only when chosenness is remembered as charity is humanity able to repair social sins, such as racism. Charity in this instance would demand a relinquishing of privilege, such as leadership and ownership, both of the table and at the table—an undoubtedly risky task. Furthermore, charity here would involve a willingness of all parties for change. Too often, claims of victimization thwart possible points of conversion, as most obviously illustrated in the conflict between the Israelis and the Palestinians. Among the many initiatives between these two communities, arguments about which community has been hurt more undermine peace. There needs to be a commitment to relationship through charity for being human to emerge authentically. Again, instances of charity need not be limited to the more politicized issues of racism and Zionism. It would be worthwhile for Christians to examine potential points for charity within their own traditions. Why are some Christian tables too full for the participation of other Christians? Is not Jesus' invitation for communion an offer that transcends religious denominations?

All of these seemingly disparate situations, which are in need of charity, have one clear message in common. Being human in relations with those who are different from us within the context of our everyday lives is a process that demands considerable openness and gamble of all parties. While openness and ensuing conflict in most predicaments are rarely life threatening, they do cause us to reveal things about ourselves that make us very uncomfortable. This is all part of the drama of being human with others in solidarity. One could ask, What is the incentive for charity? The only response is meaning and life, for the alternative is alienation and death—messages present in the gospel as well as in our ordinary lives.

Embodying Christ and Transformation of the Social Order

On more than one occasion, Augustine reminds us that the Eucharist is "the symbol of what we are."[41] What does it mean to *em-body* Christ, to reveal in our words and deeds his abiding but hidden presence in our world? Because of our social context, in which "otherness" shifts constantly to our (or another's) advantage, what is at stake here is the very realization of the body of Christ. And love in deed—compassionate solidarity—meets denial and exclusion.

Solidarity is a task realized by human subjects through, with, and in community. This community is not founded on personal preference; socially constructed prerogatives of history, creed, culture, race, gender, social condition, or sexual orientation are dismantled. The resurrected Lord sends us into streets and alleys, shelters and schools, homes and hospices to find and feed those who are despised, abused, and marginalized. These children, women, and men are the only sure sign of his presence among us in our efforts to be whom we receive at the table. Or to paraphrase Sawicki's wry observation: Jesus turns up in bodies other than his own.[42] Sitting at table, breaking and eating the bread, and drinking from the one cup with these women and men involve an encounter with the presence of the crucified and risen Lord. We recognize him in those around the table, we repent our collusion and complicity in their suffering and oppression, we ask his and their forgiveness, we share the body of the Lord, we *become* the body of the Lord. These despised and brutalized women and men are our companions in the work of justice; they are our partners with whom we must struggle to find out what it means to live the way of Jesus; standing beside them, working with them, we glimpse the promised Parousia.

Conclusion

In any black Catholic theology of Eucharist, at least three dynamics ought to be operating. First, signification of the absolute and complete 'otherness' of God, even as that God seeks and embraces humanity with passion and compassion. At the same time, this theology ought to nurture love for Eucharist and the One who is present in it. Second, the disclosure and disruption of human hegemony and power. The black Catholic theological project entails a spiritual-political project: it attends to a suffering world. Despite its marginality, black Catholic theology and its theologians enjoy a measure of privilege, albeit small, through our experience of *eucharistic hunger*. Eucharist obliges that we nurture the least. For love of the crucified Jesus, black theology and its theologians are compelled (2 Cor. 5:14) to an openness that imitates his openness to bodies *othered* by differences of history, creed, culture, race, gender, social condition, or sexual orientation. Third, insistence that the body of Christ is no metaphor: at bottom, this is a yearning for a metaphysics that recognizes and thematizes (even in the black underground) the reality and luminosity of being. The phrase "body of Christ" is not mere metaphor because it denotes a way of being in the world and with one another with Christ through the Spirit to the glory of the Father. I can do no better than close with Augustine's forceful admonition: "Because you are the body of Christ and his members, it is your own mystery that lies on the altar, it is your own mystery that you receive. . . . Be what you see [there], and receive what you are."[43]

3

Sin and Evil

Margaret D. Kamitsuka, Kris Kvam, Sallie McFague,
Linda Mercadante, Darby Kathleen Ray (chapter editor),
Stephen G. Ray, John E. Thiel, Tatha Wiley

"Departing from Bigoraj around 2:00 a.m., the truck convoy arrived in Józefów just as the sky was beginning to lighten. Trapp assembled the men in a half-circle and addressed them. After explaining the battalion's murderous assignment, he made his extraordinary offer: any of the older men who did not feel up to the task that lay before them could step out. Trapp paused, and after some moments one man from Third Company, Otto-Julius Schimke, stepped forward....When the first truckload of thirty-five to forty Jews arrived, an equal number of policemen came forward and, *face to face*, were paired off with their victims. Led by Kammer, the policemen and Jews marched down the forest path. They turned off into the woods at the point indicated by Captain Wohlauf, who busied himself throughout the day selecting execution sites. Kammer then ordered the Jews to lie down in a row. The policemen stepped up behind them, placed their bayonets on the backbone above the shoulder blades as earlier instructed, and on Kammer's orders fired in unison."[1]

◆

"Not far from us, flames were leaping up from a ditch, gigantic flames. They were burning something. A lorry drew up at the pit and delivered its load—little children. Babies! Yes, I saw it saw it with my own eyes...those children in the flames. . . . Never shall I forget that night in camp, which has turned my life into one long night, seven times cursed and seven times sealed. Never shall I forget that smoke. Never shall I forget the little faces of the children, whose bodies I saw turned into wreaths of smoke beneath a silent blue sky."[2]

◆

"[We urge the] severest measures against the Jews be adopted and that they be banished from German lands." Protestant Evangelical Church, December 17, 1941[3]

State of the Question

The preceding narratives seem more like pages from a ghastly psychological thriller than pages from history. Yet we know too well that these scenes that were enfleshed over and over again during the Holocaust have been repeated in Bosnia, Cambodia, Rwanda, and many other places before and since the Nazis' descent into their particular hellish madness. How does one describe human doings so heinous as to be nearly unfathomable, yet so frequently committed as to be banal? While the word *evil* immediately comes to mind, it seems almost ludicrous to believe that one word can bear the weight of such malevolence. Even when one adds the word *sin*, it may still seem that language fails to appreciate and convey the enormity of what is confronted in the preceding vignettes. Be that as it may, a core belief of the Christian faith is that there is no human phenomenon, no matter its horrendous complexity, that is finally unnameable and indescribable using the categories of our scripture and faith. So then the question arises: How do the categories of sin and evil help us make sense of the narratives that opened this chapter? How do they help us name and understand the lesser known experiences of perversion and diminishment that unsettle and often rupture our daily lives?

The categories of sin and evil are descriptive, not analytic ways of talking about "presence" or actions that bring about destruction and suffering. In other words, these are naming categories. Their usefulness is predicated on the conviction that once named, sin and evil lose the power of mystification and become phenomena to which people of faith may respond in fitting ways. These categories are not mutually exclusive; rather, they signify vantage points from which to talk about suffering and destruction. The relationship between sin and evil renders them not fully intelligible without reference of one to the other. Finally, these categories provide a somewhat equivocal, yet nonetheless useful, means of talking about individual and "extrapersonal" forces and agents that are the culprits and victims of destruction.[4] In other words, the terms provide a way to talk about trespass and violation in both personal and corporate terms.

The account that opens this chapter, which is drawn from a description of the activities of a Nazi police battalion that participated in the extermination of the Jews of Poland, narrates the experiences of the active agents of evil. It is evil conceived in the hearts of human beings and wrought at their hands. It is the experience of evil that has everything to do with volition—people choosing to do the morally questionable: in this case, remaining in a troop formation, thereby ensuring one's participation in murder. This narrative is one about choices and their consequences. Human free will is at center stage forcefully represented by the differing choices that men made on that dreadful day. This has most often been the vantage point from which Christian reflection on sin and evil has proceeded.

From Paul through Augustine and on to the Protestant Reformers, as well as throughout the classical Roman Catholic tradition, the primary locus of reflection on sin and evil has been through the eyes of the sinner. That is, the preponderance of Christian reflection on happenings that entail moral culpability (sin) has been a backward glance from the event of evil to the interiority of the culpable sinner. This both follows from and reinforces the fundamental presumption that sin leads to evil. Consequently, if evil is present in any form, other than natural disaster, the deduction is made that sin must be afoot. There is a parallel assumption within the tradition that the experience of evil is somehow the punishment for sin. For example, in the Gospel of John the disciples ask Jesus, "Rabbi, who sinned, this man or his parents, that he was born blind?" (9:2). Together these assumptions represent a matrix within which reflection on sin and evil is carried out using the category of will. That matrix is one that presumes the interior life of motive and predisposition to be the appropriate one for interpreting sin. While certainly this has been the primary focus of the tradition, the question may be raised: Is this the only perspective from which to talk about evil? The second vignette offers a resounding answer to this question: *no!*

It is also possible, perhaps necessary, to interpret evil from the perspective of ones whose experience is that of being "sinned against." They find themselves thrust into a world of evil, which they had no hand in making. The phrase *world of evil* is used here to symbolize those situations and conditions in which the experience of evil characterizes the very terms of the existence of the violated, yet can in no meaningful way be attributed to the autonomous actions of the sufferers. This is the thrust of the second vignette. This narration of evil, which is drawn from the experience of Elie Wiesel on his first night in a Nazi death camp, evokes evil as tragic circumstance. The question of the culpability of the sufferer is not one that occurs to us. Who dares ask, "Who sinned, these babies or their parents, that their ashes should fill the evening sky?" It is here that the second interpretation of evil evil as tragic, unchangeable circumstance becomes a helpful device, for even a cursory glance at this vignette, or any of a myriad of such accounts, confronts us with the sense that those preyed upon by evil are dealing here with more than the sum of their persecutor's bad decisions. Moreover, we intuit that there must be some power beyond mundane volition that can explain how it is that "blameless people" can experience such evil at the hands of "ordinary men."

While this malevolent surplus of experience has been interpreted in various ways, Christian reflection on evil has traditionally concluded that a tragic confluence of factors conspire to inflict pain and annihilation upon human persons and creation. Human hands play a role, yet the enormity of the brutal reality in which they participate cannot be captured by the word *sin*, no matter the inflection given to the word. This surplus of annihilating experience may be understood as the intersection of sin and evil or, put another way, the experience of sin as evil. This is perhaps what Paul had in mind in his thinking about sin as a power unleashed upon the world (Rom. 5:10–17; Eph. 6:12).

Notice of this idea of a malevolent surplus of experience can help us to understand how the ideas of sin and evil, and their relationship to each other, have been interpreted by much of the Christian tradition. If sin is the term with which we designate culpable ways of being in the world, then evil points to the reality that every sin carries with it a surplus of malevolence. This surplus of malevolence can, and frequently does, coalesce with other contingencies in such a way that a reality is created that can only be termed a *world of evil.* Because this world of evil is understood as a confluence of contingencies, with perhaps only one of them being the surplus of malevolence, we are not here dealing with a fundamentally dualistic interpretation of evil. Rather, we recognize that a helpful interpretation of sin and evil must deal with both individual and corporate culpability understood as sin *and* the experience of evil that is a consequence of that sin.

History

The horrendous accounts of evil that introduce this chapter would stir feelings of indignation, anger, and empathy on the part of any compassionate person. The most ordinary moral sensibility would judge these events to be scandalous affronts to justice, to diminish human dignity, and to pose a serious challenge to the view that human beings are basically good and virtuous. Much of the meaning that is created in human cultures—from the support structures of the family, to the formation of personal conscience, to systems of law—works to restrain evil where it begins, to resist its insidious effects, or to offer comfort before its seemingly irresistible power. The world's classical religious traditions are particularly devoted to this business of restraining, resisting, and offering comfort in the face of evil. Of all the forms of culture they are especially articulate in giving expression to the belief that evil, however prevalent, has no lasting hold in the order of things, that the death and deathliness it causes in human lives and in history is not the way the world should be.

Christianity contributes its own distinctive voice to this choir of world religions singing the song of evil's demise. Christian faith strives to offer hope and meaning in the face of evils great and small that human beings do and that human beings suffer. The particular claims that Christianity makes about God and creation, the saving work of Jesus Christ, and the abiding presence of the divine Spirit to the church and the world are all, in one way or another, judgments about evil's corrupting power and about God's restoration of humanity and nature before evil's terrible consequences.

Traditionally, the task of writing a Christian systematic theology has begun with some aspect of the doctrine of God—with an exposition of the divine nature, or God's creation of the universe, or God's revelation. But if the task of writing a systematic theology began explicitly with the most fundamental emotional concerns of Christian faith, it would address the ways that evil insidiously creeps into every human life, and only then, out of the physical and emotional suffering that accompanies encounters with evil, it would speak of the overcoming of evil through God's energies and human initiative. In this chapter we attend to these emotional concerns by exploring the symbolism of evil in the classical tradition of Christian theology and by considering how contemporary interpreters of that tradition have both appreciated and struggled with its claims. In this investigation, as in all the topics at stake in a Christian systematic theology, our success will be measured by the extent to which our words capture both the tradition's time-honored wisdom about evil and its truthfulness about the ways evil manifests itself in our own historical moment.

A Classical Christian Explanation of Evil

Speaking articulately and carefully about evil is a difficult thing to do, regardless of the tradition in which this speaking takes place. Elaine Scarry has insightfully observed that we have an extraordinarily small vocabulary when it comes to giving expression to the body's physical pain—one of the most basic symptoms of the human encounter with evil.[5] One might very well say the same about the body in emotional pain. Words often fail us when we try to express the suffering we experience either directly or as witnesses to evil in the lives of others. The philosopher Paul Ricoeur has argued that ancient people fill up this void of personal inexpressibility with communal stories that "narrate" evil.[6] These stories or myths plot the origin of evil in order to explain the persistence of evil in everyday life. The myth's symbolic language offers its believers a "surplus of meaning," Ricoeur's phrase to describe the story's rich capacity to disclose hidden meanings within human experience and to do so with a frequency that keeps pace with the newness of experience. Ricoeur is particularly interested in the symbolism of evil in Western culture, which, he argues, has produced two powerful ways of narrating the human encounter with evil: the Adamic myth and the tragic myth. In this chapter these categories provide a template for understanding the Christian symbolism of evil.

The Adamic myth is Hebrew in origin; its source is the Genesis story of the sin of Adam and Eve, the first parents. Sin, Ricoeur claims, is the symbol at the heart of the myth and relates a very particular understanding of evil. According to the story, evil issues from the human will's subversion of God's good creation, an act stirred by aberrant desire on the part of the creature to be the Creator, to stand in the place of God. This sinful deviation from the divine will is more than disobedience. It is a corruption of the gifted nature of all that exists, especially the extraordinary gift of human free choice that arrogantly chooses sin over the divine will. The Adamic myth, Ricoeur observes, is thoroughly anthropological; it makes humanity "a *beginning* of evil in the bosom of a creation which has already had its absolute *beginning* in the creative act of God."[7] Read historically and critically, the story narrates the particular experience of ancient Israelites who believed themselves to be covenantally bound to their God and for whom the story explained the motivation and consequences of unfaithfulness to the covenant. Ricoeur, however, argues that the symbolic power of the story lies in its universalism, which represents the sin of Adam and Eve as the sin of every human being.[8] According to the Adamic myth, evil is not primordial or imposed but breaks into the world through a free choice against God's will, a sin that dashes the created innocence of humanity with the palpable guilt of human suffering that sin causes.

A Critique of Adamic Language

Where is Eve in the so-called Adamic myth? Eve has a peculiar place in Christian notions of evil and sin because she stands at both the margin and the center of Christian understandings of the origins and consequences of sin and evil. The term *Adamic myth* and the more commonplace phrase *the Fall of Adam* each display Eve's marginal location. Christians rarely speak of "the Fall of Adam and Eve." The phrase "the Fall of Eve and Adam" is unheard in Christian communities, even though this rendering follows the narrative ordering of the Genesis story.

The erasure of Eve's name is not a sign of honor. She is known and blamed for being the first human being to sin. Yet she is ignored because, as a woman, her sinning has an inadequacy, and it takes the man, Adam, to complete the sin. This position is influenced by Paul's assertion that "sin came into the world through one man" (Rom. 5:12), in a passage that develops a parallel between Adam and Christ. Significantly, this passages uses the Greek *anthropos*—a gender-inclusive term that could be translated into English as "human being" for both Adam and Christ. Yet even recent translations like the NRSV retain the rendering as "man," conveying associations with the maleness of Jesus and Adam.

Thomas Aquinas also illustrates Eve's marginality when he considers the question, Would the children of Eve and Adam have contracted original sin if Eve had sinned and Adam had not? Thomas makes solely fathers rather than fathers and mothers together or solely mothers responsible for transmitting original sin. Premises gleaned from Aristotelian biology concerning male activity and female passivity are at work in Thomas's answer. But Thomas's position also is shaped by Paul's teaching. In his *Summa Theologiae* (Part 2–1, Question 81), Thomas writes: "If the woman would have transmitted original sin to her children, [Paul] should have said that it entered by two, since both of them sinned, or rather that it entered by a woman, since she sinned first."

Christian understandings of sin and evil not only overlook Eve but also place her on center stage. The opening chapters of Genesis position Eve at the center, both by presenting her as the first human being to sin and by presenting her as the first human being to occasion the sin of another human being. Christian scripture underscores her central position when 1 Tim. 2:14 declares, "Adam was not deceived, but the woman was deceived and became a transgressor." This text has had a crucial role in constructing Christian readings of the Genesis story. Its stress that Eve was the first to become a transgressor as well as its appeal to her deed as the reason why no woman "should have authority over a man" but rather should "learn in silence with full submission" has provided interpretive lenses that shape what Christians have seen conveyed by the Genesis text. In this way patriarchal structures and norms have been grounded by the doctrine of creation.

The Christian theological tradition develops Eve's centrality in ways that blame not only her but also the women who come later for the presence of sin and its effects in the world. For example, in the second century Theophilus describes Eve as "the author of sin." A few years later, Tertullian exhorts the women in his congregation to dress as if they were going to a funeral because, as daughters of Eve, "*you* are the Devil's gateway" and "*you* are she who persuaded him whom the Devil was not valiant enough to attack." Tertullian further insists that women bear a distinctive responsibility for the death of Christ Jesus: "On account of *your* desert that is death even the Son of God had to die."

The repercussions of Eve's ambiguous location reverberate to this day. One of the most important aspects concerns the ways Eve's associations with sin and evil play into notions that women are particularly untrustworthy. Eve's central role in the primordial story finds its echo in associating women with danger and seduction. First Timothy's injunction for women not to have authority over men continues to shape the practices of many Christian homes, churches, and denominations. Eve's marginal place also finds echoes in notions of the irresponsibility and secondary status of women. Either way—from the margins or from the center—the lesson is gleaned: do not trust the "daughters of Eve" because they either are so cunning that they will lead you into harm through deception or are so subordinate that they cannot be held accountable for their decisions and actions. Although academic theologians currently tend to desist from such positions, the associations of Eve and her daughters with enticement and guilt, frailty and weakness as well as blame and shame are legion in popular piety, Internet humor, and advertising. Clearly, the logo for Apple Computer, with its display of an apple with one bite taken out of it, conjures up not only knowledge but also temptation and enticement.

The tragic myth can be found in many cultures but can be exemplified most clearly in the plays of the ancient Greek tragedians such as Aeschylus and Sophocles. In the Greek tragic worldview, evil is rooted in the finite conditions of human existence itself. Fault lies not in human action; rather, the burden of evil, according to Ricoeur, "is part of a complex of misfortunes, to which death and birth contribute a note of contingency and ineluctability that contaminates human action, so to speak, with their fatality." Free will does not account for the origin of evil. Humanity enters the world powerless, and no act of choice can avoid the miseries that the ordinary course of events brings to life. "Thus," Ricoeur observes, "the fatality of death and of birth haunts all our acts, which are thereby rendered impotent and irresponsible."[9] This tragic narrative typically portrays the inevitable and overwhelming power of evil as the impersonal forces of fate, the "malevolent surplus" that latches onto human lives and directs them inexorably toward their demise. Ricoeur describes this dramatic plot as a spectacle intending to evoke sympathy in the audience. At times the events of the spectacle can be explained through a theology that makes God or the "gods" the agency of both good and evil, a causality that insists on human powerlessness before evil by affirming "the nondistinction between the divine and the diabolical."[10]

Ricoeur acknowledges that there are other ways of narrating evil but regards the Adamic and tragic myths as enduring stories in Western culture that give voice to the encounter with evil. The Adamic myth, by making much of free choice, accounts for evil as guilty wrongdoing, as sin. It bespeaks a rhetoric of blame that locates the origin of evil in human deeds. The tragic myth, by making much of human powerlessness, accounts for evil as the passivity of undeserved suffering. It bespeaks a rhetoric of lament that locates the origin of evil beyond human agency, in a world of evil. Whereas the Adamic myth looks for evil in the perpetrator, the tragic myth looks at the effects of evil in the victim. As different as these perspectives on evil may be, Ricoeur insightfully calls attention to the surprising ways in which each myth incorporates elements of the other, even to the point of their mutual conflation.[11] It is interesting to note that the choices of Adam and Eve unfold against the backdrop of the serpent's alluring temptation that they will find a benefit in their disobedience (Gen. 3:1–5), creating a tragic resonance in a world created good and in which the evil of sinful choice has yet to appear. This same mythic mixture surfaces in the way the Greek chorus or soothsayers offer alternative courses of action to the tragic hero's fatalistic march to destruction, an Adamic resonance in a world overwhelmed by the force of bad luck. This blending of mythic perspectives testifies to the complexity of the human encounter with evil, to the ways in which the evil perpetrator can also be a victim to some extent, and the innocent victim of a particular evil may be guilty of evil in other respects. Blame and lament can both voice the suffering that is symptomatic of the human encounter with evil.

Ricoeur's categories provide narrative confirmation of Scarry's judgment that we have a surprisingly narrow range for expressing our encounter with evil. Nonetheless, these categories can be a helpful resource in representing the Christian symbolism of evil, perhaps for the reflexive reason that Ricoeur draws to a great degree on Christian reflection in defining his categories.

The Adamic myth has served as a touchstone for the Christian symbolism of evil for several reasons. The Genesis story of the first sin stands within the Jewish sacred writings that Christians embraced as their own and that they too regarded as God's inspired word. The typological thinking of ancient people could find in the figures of Adam and Eve the prototypes of all that their descendents might have been and of all that their descendents actually have become. But, most important, the story's insistence on human responsibility before God in freely willing evil and virtue was an extraordinarily attractive belief in the early Christian movement. The first Jewish Christians understood themselves to be a people bound in covenantal relationship to God and, like all Jews, were firmly committed to the value of human responsibility before God. Evil, they maintained, has no standing in the universe

God has created thoroughly good. Rather, evil issues from the betrayal of God's will by the misuse of the divine gift of free choice, a guilty act that implicated the sinner in the same rebellion against God perpetrated by Adam and Eve.

This belief in human responsibility for evil through free choice, and thus in the resistibility of evil through free choice, was an appealing view in the context of the persecution that the Christian movement faced throughout much of the first three centuries of its history. During this time of persecution, Christians encountered the evil of the world as the violence of the Roman empire that could be wielded in their enslavement, physical torture, or even death. Living a Christian life during these times entailed the acceptance of an extraordinary standard of discipleship expressed in the high ethical expectations of Jesus in the Sermon on the Mount (Matthew 5–7 and Luke 6), and exemplified most dramatically by the martyr's heroic choice. By contrast, the evil of human sin is portrayed in this Adamic symbolism as the choice for perdition through the rejection of Jesus and the path he offers to the coming kingdom of God.

Sin as Disobedience and as Personal

The centrality of the story of Adam and Eve in the Christian account of evil cannot be overstated. Two underlying points of the story are deeply embedded in the Christian religious imagination. The first is that the distortion of creation by evil lay not in God's intent, but in human choice. The second answers the story's implicit question, What is sin? The narrative clearly dramatizes how human beings become estranged from God: taking and eating unnamed fruit, Adam and Eve violated the single command God had given to them that they *not* eat of the tree of the knowledge of good and evil. They *knew* the command and freely *disobeyed* it. It is this conception of sin, as a freely chosen *act* that violates God's law, that dominates the Christian tradition.

Early Christian theologians reinforced this notion of sin as disobedience by appropriating Roman law and Stoic ideas of natural law in their theology of sin. They grounded an objective moral order in God's eternal plan for the order of the universe. It was thought that human reason can discover the order that God intends for the social world. These discovered truths are called the natural law. Morality is defined in terms of compliance with the natural law, while immorality, or sin, is noncompliance or disobedience to that law.

In identifying morality with law, Christian theologians evaluated all human acts on whether they conformed to law. The development of private confession in the early tradition further focused the attention of confessors on acts. They determined the "crime" committed, the defendant's culpability, and appropriate penalties: the sin, the penitent, the penance. Augustine's definition of sin as "anything done, said, or desired against the eternal law" reflects his appropriation of a juridical and privatized concept of sin already shaped by the theological tradition. Summing up the character of this theology, moral theologian John Mahoney writes that it shows "a preoccupation with sin; a concentration on the individual; and an obsession with the law."

This Adamic understanding of evil was not the only symbolism that flourished in first-century Christianity. Early in the tradition Paul interpreted the Adamic myth in a way that transformed the story into a Christian version of tragedy. In his letter to the Christian community at Rome, written in the late 50s C.E., Paul presents the sinful consequence of Adam's free choice as a tragic burden borne by all of Adam's descendents. "Therefore," Paul asserts, ". . . sin came into the world through one man [Adam], and death came through sin, and so death spread to all because all have sinned" (Rom. 5:12). Sin causes death in Paul's influential reading of the Genesis story. Death is God's just punishment for the sinful rebellion of the first parents, an evil act replicated in every human life and proved by the inevitability of everyone's death. Sin, like the death it brings, is irresistible. Paul conceives of the inescapability of evil as the compelling power of the first sin to corrupt every subsequent human will. Unlike later Christians, who would convey their belief in the strength of sin by the doctrine of original sin, Paul does not believe that human persons are born in sin. Rather, he seems to hold that all the descendents of the first parents stand under the sway of their terrible example. Although Adam and Eve had free choice, their children through the ages do not. Sin, for Paul, is a kind of compulsion by which the human will is enslaved (Rom. 7:14). In a striking passage, he affirms his tragic style of faith by denying the ability of free choice to resist evil at all: "For I know that nothing good dwells within me, that is, in my flesh. I can will what is right, but I cannot do it. For I do not do the good I want, but the evil I do not want is what I do" (Rom. 7:18–19).

If we use the Ricoeurian category of tragedy to represent Paul's views, it is important to distinguish Paul's Christian version of tragedy from the ancient Greek tragic sensibility. Whereas classical Greek tragedy unfolds in a world permeated by the impersonal power of fate or bad luck, Paul's Christian tragedy presupposes a world created by a personal God providentially at work in bringing the universe to its redemption through the grace of Christ

(Rom. 8:18–25). Whereas classical Greek tragedy does not recognize a pre-tragic state of human freedom, Paul's account of human fallenness presupposes a primordial state in which the first parents incur responsibility for evil through free choice. What makes Paul's account tragic, in spite of these differences from classical Greek tragedy, is that he conceives of the first sin and its deathly consequences as a ravaging power in history before which humanity stands powerless. And yet the Adamic resonance of the first evil choice ripples throughout tragic history in the Pauline assumption that, though powerless before evil, human persons are still strangely guilty as the descendents of the original perpetrators. That this tragic vision of Christian life could coexist in first-century Christianity with the Christian appropriation of the Adamic myth testifies to the diversity of Christian belief and the desire at work in this fledgling tradition to account for the broader range of the existential encounter with evil.

The process of canon-formation in the early Christian centuries solidified the Adamic and tragic options in the Christian symbolism of evil, since the Gospels, with their largely Adamic perspective, and the letters of Paul, with their largely tragic perspective, were both incorporated into the New Testament collection of writings that Christians came to regard as God's inspired word. Ever since the circulation of these texts in the early communities and throughout the subsequent history of the Bible, Christians have tended to find one or the other of these myths to be a more compelling account of evil and have adjudicated the biblical diversity of symbolism by reading the favored perspective into the other, an interpretive practice that denies scriptural diversity by claiming that either the Adamic or the tragic symbolism truly captures the nature of evil. It is not surprising that one of these interpretive approaches achieves dominance in a certain style of Christian faith, whether in the life of a particular believer or in the shared faith of a community. Far more unusual is the circumstance in which a believer's style of faith shifts from one symbolism to the other. It is remarkable that this kind of change in allegiance took place in the life of a believer who, of all Christian thinkers, had the greatest influence on the tradition's thinking on sin and evil before God—Augustine.[12]

Soon after his conversion to Christianity in 386, Augustine began to write treatises against Manicheism, a Gnostic religious sect he had joined as a young man and abandoned on his spiritual journey to Christianity. In typical Gnostic fashion, Manicheism portrayed reality as a dualism, as a cosmic conflict between good and evil forms of existence. For the Manicheans, all material existence is evil, the work of an evil god who is the lord of the physical universe. Lost in this realm of darkness are bits of divine spirit, the very being of the true and good God who presides over a spiritual realm utterly disconnected from the evil universe. Manicheans, like the young Augustine, believed their inner self to be divine spirit tragically entrapped in a body subject to the suffering of an evil world. Manicheans understood their salvation to be assured by their self-divinity. Death allowed the divine spirit to escape the body and return to the spiritual world above, its eternal home beyond the evil universe.

Augustine's early writings attack Gnostic dualism by highlighting Christian belief in the goodness of a creation willed into existence by the one and true creator God. All that has being, Augustine insists, is good because its origin lies in the goodness of God's own divine being. Evil has no status in being. It is rather a privation—the absence of being—and so the absence of the goodness that all being shares. In order to present an utterly nondualistic account of evil against the Gnostics, Augustine argues that evil is nothing. This explanation does not mean that evil is not rampant in the world. Even though Augustine's early writings exude a real confidence in human virtue, they clearly assume that evil is pervasive. The description of evil as nothing means that evil has no standing in existence but is instead the vitiation of the divinely created and hence thoroughly good character of existence.

Augustine's anti-Manichean writings are strongly Adamic in their account of the origins of evil. Evil, Augustine maintains, lies finally in an aberrant act of a creaturely will, in its sinful choice against the divinely willed order of things. Summarizing the argument he developed in his early work *On Free Choice of the Will* (388–395), Augustine states:

> So it follows that . . . neither the goods desired by sinners, nor the free will itself which we found to have been numbered among certain intermediate goods, are evil in any way, and that...evil is a turning away from immutable goods and a turning toward changeable goods. This turning away [*aversio*] and turning toward [*conversio*] result in the just punishment of unhappiness, because they are committed, not under compulsion, but voluntarily.[13]

Evil does not dwell in creaturely things, the "intermediate goods," that the sinner invests with idolatrous importance. Nor does evil lie in the being of the sinner or more particularly in the power of free choice, also intermediate goods created by the good God. Evil issues from an empty desire that Augustine calls "lust" (*libido*),[14] a label Augustine is willing to apply to all sinful motivation. As evil, lust may be considered a privation in two ways. First, lust is a desire for what does not fully exist, since intermediate good—the object of all sinful desire—are not the supreme good. Second, this lustful conversion or "turning away" from God and "turning toward" temporal things is itself a privation of moral conversion, the absence of the authentic "turning toward" God's unchangeable will that makes for every virtuous act.

This account of evil was an effective argument against the Manicheans. It rejected dualism as a coherent explanation of evil. And by placing the origin of evil in aberrant free choice, Augustine undercut the Gnostic belief in the predestination of all matter to death and the predestination of the spiritual self to eternal life. The young Augustine insists that human persons bear responsibility for evil, for their will is able to resist evil by conforming itself to God's will. Augustine considers humanity to be so completely responsible for evil that he includes both moral evil (the evil that humans do) and natural or physical evil (the evil that humans suffer through natural causes) within the scope of that responsibility. For Augustine, physical evil, such as suffering from disease, accident, or death from natural causes, is a consequence of the way the Adamic fall continues to be enacted in every life. Although the suffering of victimization may seem to be evil from the perspective of the sufferer, it is actually God's just punishment for the moral evil that every person does,[15] a claim that places responsibility for all evil squarely on the shoulders of human free choice.

Moral Evil versus Natural Evil

We can think of moral evil in terms of "simple" and "complex" sin. Simple sin is what most people think of as "sin"—the lie you told, the food someone stole, sexual misconduct, and so forth. It is what Catholics confess to a priest and what Protestants carry around as guilt! It is probably an overrated category in terms of importance. Much more important is complex sin, which covers a number of different human activities:

- the sins of omission rather than commission: the silent sins of indifference and neglect;
- habitual sin: patterns of sinning that eventually define who we are;
- communal sin: doing what everyone else is doing—for example, conspicuous consumption by first-world people;
- systemic or institutional sin: the most serious and deceptive sin—for example, slavery, sexism, racism, classism, heterosexism—when a form of sin becomes an accepted interpretation of who we are so that we no longer even realize we are "living a lie."

Natural evil is the dark side of the complex universe in which everything occurs: the mutations that do not please us—deformed babies, swarms of killer bees, AIDS, and so forth—but it is the same process that gives us joy and pleasure—healthy babies, the beauty of butterflies, our self-reflective minds, and so on.

Natural evil is the dark side of the process that produces everything we value. It is at the heart of the amazing, complex, extraordinary planet that is our home. If we cannot accept this, then we cannot accept who we are and what the world is. Hence, it is not really "evil"; rather, it is the way things are.

Another category of events usually included under natural evil is accidents—hurricanes, floods, plane crashes, and so forth. Some of these are just that chance accidents (Mary was on the plane that went down; John missed the plane due to traffic). But other so-called natural disasters are increasingly aided by human sin: hurricanes, poverty, starvation, unclean water, desertification of arable land, floods, and droughts caused by global warming, bad environmental practices, and human greed.

Hence the category called "natural evil" is perhaps a misnomer: it is not really "evil" in that much that falls under this rubric is due to the way an evolutionary, ecological reality works, while some of it is purely accidental. Moreover, a good deal of it is due to human sin or moral evil.

The young Augustine's strong confidence in the resistibility of evil through free choice is all but lost in his later writings against the British monk Pelagius and his followers that date from the year 411 to Augustine's death in 430.[16] Pelagius believed that heroic discipleship was the calling of every Christian and that the highest ethical standards taught by Jesus could be attained by the created power of the will. Against Pelagius's moral optimism, Augustine now argued that the sin of Adam and Eve had so viciously corrupted the will that it possesses no effective power to will the good through its own natural ability. The older Augustine understood sin to be a tragic heritage for which humanity bore corporate responsibility. Like Paul, Augustine regarded death as a punishment for sin. But to this terminal bodily marker for sin's irresistibility, Augustine added a bodily marker at life's beginning by claiming that all are born in sin as inescapable sharers in Adam's guilt. It was Augustine who, more than any other theologian, developed this particular symbolism of evil that was embraced by the subsequent tradition as the doctrine of original sin. Moreover, Augustine appealed to the struggles of his own ascetical lifestyle in order to identify another bodily marker for sin's irresistibility throughout the course of life in the persistence of sexual desire. Just as sexual passion wells up in experience contrary to the dictates of reason and, as passion, is irresistible, so too sin, as this very desire, is beyond the power of the will.[17]

Original Sin

Christians often think of *original* sin as the *first* sin. After all, the primary biblical warrant for the doctrine is the story of humankind's first sin. But it was actually the question of redemption, not of sin, that generated the doctrine. Christians proclaimed that everyone required Christ's redeeming grace, and it was the question of the universality of sin that prompted early Christian theologians to turn to Adam and Eve. In the Genesis story they found the explanatory principle they sought: sin is universal because all *inherit* Adam and Eve's sin. *Original sin*, then, means "inherited sin."

By illuminating the reason for the universality of sin and the need for redemption, the doctrine of original sin answered the question, "Why the incarnation?" It answered others as well—why human beings, not God, are responsible for evil; why they face death; and why women are subject to the rule of men.

If the doctrine clarified so much, why is it problematic? Even early in the tradition, some Christians were troubled by the idea that sin could be *inherited*. Sin is a failure on the level of human freedom and decision. How can a bad decision or an evil orientation be inherited? The proposal that original sin is transmitted through procreation invites a question about sexual relations: If sexual relations transmit sin, are *they* sinful? We raise further questions today. The doctrine asserts the necessity of Christ's grace and the necessity of the church for the mediation of Christ's grace. Does this exclusivity of Christ preclude the mediation of salvation by other religious traditions? The doctrine also provided the theological tradition with the position that Eve's punishment—her subjugation to the rule of her husband—is applicable to all women. But does the biblical writer's depiction of God's authorization of male domination reflect *God's* position or, perhaps, the *patriarchal culture* that provides the horizon within which the biblical writer thinks and lives? The doctrine of original sin has been useful in providing centuries of Christians with an answer to a cardinal human question: Why are we not good? But it has also contributed to Christian religious exclusivism, to a punitive sexual ethics, and to the historical victimization of women.

Through this significant shift from Adamic to tragic symbolism, Augustine sought to convey not only the power of evil in a fallen world but also the power of God's love to bring the gift of eternal life to an undeserving humanity. The later Augustine espouses a kind of Christian belief that accords all salvational power to God and all guilty responsibility for evil to humanity, an adjudication of divine and creaturely power that leads him to modify the understanding of free choice developed in his early work. In *On Grace and Free Will* (426–427) Augustine writes:

> There is, however, always within us a free will, but it is not always good; for it is either free from righteousness when it serves sin, and then it is evil, or else it is free from sin when it serves righteousness, and then it is good. But the grace of God is always good; and by it it comes to pass that a [person] is of a good will, though he [or she] was before of an evil one.[18]

Whereas the young Augustine ascribed the power of both good and evil choices to the natural activity of the will, the older Augustine saw the will's natural power exercised only in evil choice. Virtuous choice, he now claimed, is not accomplished through the efforts of our own nature but only in and through the power of divine grace. Without grace, free will has no effective choice and is only "free" to sin. The consequences of Adam's sin have been so devastating that all of humanity stands under a sentence of eternal death whose fittingness is only further assured by every natural and so sinful act.

Such a tragic account of human powerlessness before evil consistently leads Augustine to speak of humanity's comparable powerlessness before God's saving grace. A strong doctrine of predestination is the only logical conclusion to which Augustine's tragic symbolism of evil can lead:

> Not only . . . good wills [of the graced], which God . . . converts from bad ones, and, when converted, . . . directs to good actions and to eternal life, but also those which follow the world are so entirely at the disposal of God, that [God] turns them whithersoever [God] wills, and whensoever [God] wills, to bestow kindness on some, and to heap punishment on others, as [God] judges right by a counsel most secret to [Godself], indeed, but beyond all doubt most righteous.

Both sin and grace, evil and goodness lie beyond human power, even though humanity is guilty before the powerlessness of sin. Every human person enters the world in sin and can do nothing through natural power but increase guilt by every deed. However virtuous a given act may be, apart from grace it remains a deadly reenactment of Adam's betrayal of the Creator. Divine grace, like sin, is irresistible. Its unyielding power is God's merciful response to the nearly unyielding power of sin. Grace cannot be embraced by human choice but only be bestowed on some by God's eternal election. Augustine's later, tragic understanding of the depths of sinfulness moves him to relinquish any heroic understanding of Christian discipleship. The saints are the saints by virtue of God's eternal predestination and not through meritorious deeds of their own. And as Augustine affirms pointedly in the passage quoted above, God's eternal predestination of the saved and the damned can only be judged righteous since God's will is the very measure of such a value.

Augustine's career-long change of mind on the nature of evil charted the principal biblical options on the origin and effects of evil. But Augustine's authority throughout the subsequent Christian tradition also conveyed those same options to later Christians who could find confirmation in his different positions for their own symbolic sensibilities on evil.

Sin as Social or Structural

Augustine's writings on sin bequeathed to subsequent theologians an influential structure for sin-talk that locates the root of sin in the individual's will. Whether one sees the will as free (early Augustine) or as bound by the forces of evil (late Augustine), sin involves evil choices by an individual who is guilty before God. Theologians in the twentieth century, such as Reinhold Niebuhr, Paul Tillich, and Karl Rahner, spoke of sin in terms of the self inevitably succumbing to existential anxiety in distorted ways and gave increasing attention to the effects of sin in unjust social, political, and economic systems. Nevertheless, these theologians continued to echo the Augustinian paradigm of sin because their analysis of the root of humanity's sin implies that structural evil is a powerful ripple effect of a distorted individual will—a ripple effect that could systemically influence subsequent individual choices. In other words, according to the dominant voices in Christian thought through the centuries, sin is primarily about individual choices.

Liberation theologian criticize this view of the relationship between individual and collective evil. They emphasize even more than their existentialist predecessors the social forces shaping human consciousness and material existence. Liberationists call the hegemonic forces of evil that disempower and ravage whole communities of people "structural" or "social" sin. These evil forces cannot be meaningfully reduced to the effects of the sinful choices of some set of perpetrators or to the individual guilt that even the victims carry to some extent. They are, rather, the powerful sedimentation, institutionalization, and "normalization" of perverse choices choices that metastasize without apparent provocation. Hence liberationist writings often refer to the "innocent" or "undeserved" suffering of the oppressed. This politically strategic rhetoric of powerless and undeserved suffering goes hand in hand with the liberation-theological call for solidarity with and justice for the oppressed. These theologians believe that the category of structural or social sin gets at the pervasive, systemic, and ongoing nature of massive evil better than an Augustinian or existentialist paradigm can alone. This contemporary approach to sin thus exemplifies a tragic symbolism of (to some extent) powerless and undeserved suffering, of a "world of evil," within a Christian belief system.

The teachings of the Council of Trent (1545–1563) reinforced the main themes of the medieval Catholic tradition that strongly supported the early Augustine's Adamic account of the resistibility of evil through personal responsibility and free choice. And yet, like nearly all post-Augustinian forms of Christianity, Tridentine Catholicism affirmed the doctrine of original sin and the traditional notion of suffering and death as divine punishment for sin. The Lutheran and Reformed traditions were strongly attracted to the later Augustine's tragic account of the irresistibility of evil after the first Adamic choice, even to the point of ascribing personal sinfulness and guilt to the mysterious workings of the divine will. As different as these Adamic and tragic symbolisms are, it is important to note their shared commitment to a nondualistic view of evil that finally has its origin in the human will. This commonly Christian stance means that even Pauline and late-Augustinian versions of the tragic myth finally remain glosses on the Adamic myth, however particular, influential, and abiding these glosses may be. This final centrality of the Adamic myth voices the Christian belief that God does no evil, even when the power of suffering and death lies within God's infinite power.

Constructive Proposals

Tracking the Tragic: Augustine, Global Capitalism, and a Theology of Struggle

Darby Ray

To be a middle-class North American Christian in the twenty-first century is to enjoy unprecedented power and privilege. It is also to participate in structures of evil so subtle and complex, so intertwined with commonly held assumptions about human nature and the good life, as to be nearly invisible. To open our eyes to the presuppositions and consequences of global capitalism, which is surely the dominant discourse of our time, is to be stared down by our own complicity in evil. It is to feel the unbearable weight of our culture's privilege, of our individual guilt. It is to hear an unmistakable summons to repentance and conversion.

Confession of Sin

Sunday after Sunday, Christians gather in congregations in which part of the liturgy includes a confession of sin. In many congregations the wording of the confession includes: "Most merciful God, we confess that we have sinned against you in thought, word, and deed, by what we have done, and by what we have left undone," and "We have not loved you with our whole heart; we have not loved our neighbors as ourselves."

What meaning can we glean from this common practice? When Christians make a confession of sin, whose sins are they confessing? When they state, "we have sinned," are they speaking only as individuals, or are they also speaking as a corporate body?

Many Christians understand the meaning of the practice solely in personal terms. Understanding themselves as confessing their own personal participation in sin, they see themselves as speaking of how each of them has not loved God or neighbor as he or she ought. Other Christians understand the practice to involve not only their personal confession. Understanding the use of "we" to signify the corporate body, they see themselves confessing the sins of those gathered in the congregation. They also may understand themselves as confessing the sins of the wider Christian community.

Does the confession of sin also involve confessing the church's own sinfulness? This question is controversial ecumenically. Several Christian churches speak only of the sinfulness of individual human beings, not of the church itself. Stressing the church's holiness, they find it irreverent to say that the church participates in sin. Other Christians, however, maintain the importance of recognizing that the confession of sins includes confessing the church's own participation in sin. For them the notion of "social sin" not only applies to individual persons but also infects the life and work of the whole church—the decisions and actions of congregations, denominations, and worldwide communions.

There are important reasons to explore ways to speak and think about the church's own participation in sin through its practices and policies, its translations and liturgies, its beliefs and actions. Uncovering ways that congregations, denominations, and worldwide communions participate in sin would provide fruitful grounds for self-examination by these communities. Their examinations would urge their confession for the church's seduction by evil principalities as well as for silence in the face of injustice. Confessing "what we have done, and what we have left undone" as Christian communities would form a strong basis for corporate acts of repentance.

Yet any such conversion requires that we understand how we got where we are—how it is that we find ourselves so thoroughly saturated and intimately involved with a way of seeing and being whose destructive consequences are increasingly impossible to deny. What insights from Christian theology can serve this analytical task? Are we guilty of rebellion against God? Or have we been swept helplessly away by forces about which we knew nothing and over which we had little or no control? Both the language of blame and the language of lament are helpful as tools of expression and understanding. While Adamic symbolism highlights free choice and blameworthiness and is particularly helpful in describing the culpability of the middle and upper classes in the death-dealing march of global capitalism, the tragic myth underscores the anguish of the sinned-against—their undeserved suffering and despair, the degree to which their freedom is constrained and their agency mitigated by forces largely beyond their control.

Neither of these theological discourses as summarized above can articulate the subtlety and interplay of sin and evil to my satisfaction. They mark the boundaries, the options at each extreme, but they fail to give voice to the vast expanse in the middle, the grey moral terrain where most people live. Thus, I propose to push these categories a bit further, to test their flexibility and efficacy in relation to real, lived experiences of sin and evil. Eventually I want to move boldly in the direction of the tragic, even the dualistic, to see what insights into the character of sin and evil and their undoing might be found there.

The first step in this direction is a return to Augustine. There can be little doubt that his earliest writings reflect an Adamic standpoint and his later writings a tragic perspective. However, Augustine's most compelling account of sin and evil, and the one best able to hold together the truths of both symbolic extremes as well as to shed light on the complexity of sin and evil for both perpetrators and victims, is nestled within Books VII and VIII of his *Confessions*. Here, we encounter a phenomenology of evil that insists that although evil has no metaphysical standing, it nevertheless can and does take on a life of its own and accrue a power that rivals God and the good. Thus, there is a sense in which we humans are responsible for our evil and at the same time swept away and bound by its power. How can both these things be true?

Reiterating the anti-Manichean convictions of his youth, the mature Augustine of the *Confessions* insists that the starting point for understanding human evil must be the goodness of God and, by extension, the goodness of everything God created. Insofar as beings *have* being, thought Augustine, they get their being from God and hence are good. There is no evil being, substance, or force; there is merely an infinite array of goods, some more reflective of God's immutability and perfection than others, but all good because they are products of the Good. From whence, then, comes evil? In addition to *being* good, says Augustine, we humans *desire* the good. At root, we are lovers, creatures of desire. The trick is that we cannot seem to keep our priorities straight—we forget that God is the one lover who can fully satisfy our desire, and we turn instead toward lesser loves. These loves are *good*, but they are what Augustine calls "intermediate" goods. They reflect God's being and goodness, hence pointing us toward their Creator, mediating our relationship to God, but if exalted and loved as terminal goods, they become obstacles to us. When treated as ends in themselves, proposes Augustine, lesser goods actually function as evil—yet it is not *they* that are evil but our will that perverts them, that turns them into something they are not, that loves them inordinately. Thus, evil results from what Augustine calls "the swerving of the will" toward lesser goods and away from God.[19] It is this twofold movement that is the essence of sin, and yet it is crucial to note that this "swerving" is not usually a willful act of disobedience or rebellion against God, an intentional idolizing of the ungodly that is easily congruent with the sharp edges of the Adamic myth; rather, it is a crime of passion, a case of misplaced desire, an errant infatuation mistaken for true love.

This dynamic of misplaced desire is the root assumption of capitalism and constitutes the sinister beauty of its allure. In order to have continual economic growth and gain the generally unquestioned *telos* of twenty-first-century human existence and society we must spend more, consume more, and produce more. In order for any of that to occur, we must *desire* more. Indeed, our desire must be insatiable, *and* it must be directed toward what Augustine knew as lesser goods. Capitalism depends upon and actively cultivates misdirected desire, and it is so successful precisely because, as Augustine knew so acutely, we *are* creatures of desire who seek out relationship and intimacy and are hence vulnerable to perversions of that desire. To spend, purchase, and consume is not in and of itself evil, but when we do these things inordinately, beyond all need and reason and to the detriment of those in need around us—when we "swell greedily for outward things" and so ignore higher goods such as love of God and neighbor—then we participate in and are responsible for evil.[20]

Such inordinate "swelling" of desire is no doubt a choice to which culpability may be assigned, and yet to understand it fully requires a recognition that this choice is rarely driven by active malevolence or intentional self-aggrandizement. Rather, it is most often motivated by a desire for some good—perhaps the good of financial security in an age of systematic outsourcing and downsizing, the good of a more comfortable life for ourselves and our family, or the good of social acceptability and inclusion. None of these "goods" are evil, but when they are sought outside the context of the ultimate good of love of God and neighbor without the limits that such love imposes, then they function for us as evil because they pull us away from higher goods and toward lesser ones. This pull is often subtle, even indiscernible to the one caught in its current, yet relinquishing to the pull is fully the action of our untamed will, our misdirected desire, and for it, insists Augustine, we are responsible. Here, then, is a sophisticated rendering of the Adamic myth, one that softens its edges by emphasizing the subtlety of human evil, the way it is at one and the same time fully our own creation and responsibility and yet somehow also an almost inevitable outgrowth of who we are as creatures destined for love but often confused about where to find it and hence continually missing the mark.

How do we get from this relatively sanguine picture of human evil to the ravages of poverty, war, and environmental annihilation that characterize our world today? We move, with Augustine, away from the Adamic and toward the tragic, yet without forsaking the convictions of the former. What starts out as innocuous confusion and misdirected passion becomes before long an all-out addiction in relation to which we are pathetically impotent. In Book VIII of *Confessions*, Augustine uses the image of a chain to explain the dynamic. Our desire for lesser goods seems harmless enough, but with each decision to love the intermediate more than the ultimate, we add a link to the chain of our own bondage to sin. Before we know it, our desire for security or comfort or social inclusion has turned into habit. Now, without thinking or realizing it, we automatically grasp for lesser goods, fooling ourselves into thinking they can satisfy our desire. Gradually, says Augustine, the force of habit turns to necessity, to addiction. We cannot live without those lesser goods; desire for them dominates our consciousness; we are incomplete without them; we *must* have them. Anyone who has lived at any proximity to addiction can appreciate Augustine's insight into the dynamic of human evil—its subtle beginnings in human freedom and its too-fast spiral into obsession and helplessness. Addicts are no longer free; their will is not their own; they are bound "hand and foot," as was Augustine, by the power of what was once a voluntary trifle.[21]

Augustine's Ambivalent Legacy

Augustine apprehended the world through the lens of his social class, ethnicity, political status, religious loyalties, and gender. The fact that his culture was patriarchal and that he took its social institutions and values as normative influence the way he thought about sin and evil. His insights into the personal perversions alienating human beings from God were matched by his oversights about sin. In various ways, we could argue, Augustine's theology validates a morally objectionable world, a sinful world.

For example, Augustine took for granted the androcentric projection of male nature as normative, the reduction of female nature to biology, women's subjugation to male rule, and the legal and religious status of women as nonpersons. He reinforced the cultural view of women as the moral, intellectual, and ontological inferior of the male through his assertion, contrary to Gen. 1:27, that women do not possess the image of God fully themselves, as do males, but only through their relation to a male: "the woman, together with her husband, is the image of God," but separate from him, "she is not the image of God" (*The Trinity* 7.7.10). In this way Augustine sustained separate and unequal gender spheres. Lacking the image of God, he thought, woman is more prone to sin. These views remain influential in the Roman Catholic argument against the ordination of women, as well as in the subordination of women in Protestant churches. Clearly, Augustine's theological anthropology functions to perpetuate the systemic evil of sexism. As such, his theology of sin not only defines sin but also manifests sin.

A second example of Augustine's ambivalent legacy to Christian thought and practice is the sexual ethics he bequeathed, undoubtedly grounded in his struggle to understand and control his own sexual desires, which he experienced as sin. His pessimism about the place of sexuality in creation, his ambivalence about the value of marriage, and his shame of the irrational character of the sexual drive are powerfully present in his theology. The purpose of marriage is procreative, he insisted. Even in marriage, Augustine saw sexual desire as lust and lust as sin. Marital sex is moral only if it is open to procreation; it is a "tolerable sin" because children are needed. Nonprocreative sex is, quite simply and without exception, immoral. Augustine's sexual ethics remain embedded in Christian thinking. The 1968 Catholic encyclical *Humane Vitae*, prohibiting birth control and naming nonprocreative sex as sin, is Augustinian through and through. By contrast, many contemporary theologians argue that Augustine named sexual evil wrongly: it is *coercive* sex that is evil, not nonprocreative sex.

While Augustine's definitions contribute to our understanding of the dynamics of sin, this larger web of ideas is deeply problematic. Acknowledging the insights of the theological tradition while at the same time working to identify and root out the elements of tradition that perpetuate diminishment and destruction is an ongoing task of theological interpretation.

How else can we explain the inhumanity of corporate greed, the depravity of first-world consumerism in the face of the destitution of the masses, and the unflinching destruction of ecosystems and habitats than with a typology of human evil that pinpoints both the undeniable role of human freedom and responsibility *and* the way in which these free choices often spiral out of control, putting even the perpetrators of evil at the mercy of its relentless unfolding? The truth about evil is that it is both Adamic and tragic, both chosen and imposed. Clearly, there are perpetrators and victims, the former best described in Adamic terms and the latter in tragic terms—perpetrators using their power recklessly, unthinkingly, inordinately, and victims suffering the anguish of such abuse. But in each case the major dynamic is tempered by the minor one, frustrating attempts at absolute moral clarity, at simple designations of good and evil, innocence and blame. If our goal is to understand sin and evil, the Adamic and the tragic cannot be separated.

Thanks to technologies of communication, transportation, and commerce, the world of the twenty-first century is more deeply interconnected than ever before, and it is increasingly clear that the unifying logic or discourse is the language of capitalism. Not everyone chooses to recognize the primacy of that language, and some speak defiantly in other tongues, but there can be little argument that it has become the global discourse with which all others must contend. It *is* the defining myth of our time. While we each have choices to make about the degree to which we will "buy into" the myth, practically no one on earth has the freedom to opt out altogether. It is that pervasive and that powerful. And at the heart of capitalism, I have argued, is the exact dynamic of freedom and bondage narrated by Augustine's phenomenology of evil as set forth in Books VII and VIII of *Confessions*. Capitalism assumes that we are creatures of desire, and it stokes our desire for "lesser goods" to the point of addiction, finally rendering us powerless to opt out of its dynamic. What would it mean, after all, to get "outside" of capitalism in today's world? Even those who want nothing to do with it, who view it as the pinnacle of Western corruption or imperialism, or whose minds and bodies bear the scars of its excesses and exclusions, are nevertheless pulled inexorably into its captivating cadence.

The Adamic myth helps us analyze and address capitalism. It lets us identify the inordinate desire of some nations, classes, and individuals, and call those entities to account for their sin of rebellion against God, neighbor, and nature. But it is the tragic myth that offers the more compelling account of how whole peoples and generations can become seduced by a world of evil, addicted to destructive ways of seeing and being, enslaved by the cumulative effect of our misguided free choices. Surely it is this powerful sense of our own incapacitation that prompts so many Christians to embrace a notion of metaphysical evil. "The Devil made me do it" may signal a trite attempt to shirk responsibility, to forsake this world of hard moral choices in favor of some cosmic battlefield where we are merely passive spectators of a metaphysical duel between the forces of good and evil. But there may also be in this talk of the Devil a profound insight into the intransigency and pervasiveness of human evil, a sober recognition that evil *does* seem to metastasize and take over, destroying everything in its path.

I am fascinated by the trope of a battle between God and Satan because it spoke so powerfully to many early Christians, Augustine included, and continues to spark the imagination of the enormously influential religious right today. Instead of dismissing the idea as theologically primitive or offensively dualistic, I wonder what truths it might have to offer about human nature and the evil we perpetrate and experience.[22] Rather than locate the battle in an otherworldly time or place, I suggest that we use the trope of struggle to help us understand the nature of Christian existence in relation to the seductive lure of capitalism. According to a favorite narrative of the early church, God defeated the powers of evil personified as the Devil by deliberately choosing *not* to embrace their logic. Rather than crush the Devil by force or coercion in other words, rather than fight violence with violence, God chose instead to use the "power" of weakness; that is, God relinquished the power of omnipotence, transcendence, and infinitude in favor of incarnation, finitude, and compassion. In so doing, God took the Devil by surprise, exposing his avarice and the carnage of his misdirected desire and igniting among those who had ears to hear a moral outrage against evil understood as inordinate desire and indefatigable consumption.

To live with integrity in the midst of the evils of global capitalism requires first that we *see* the clash of values and desires that is underfoot, that we open our eyes to a struggle of cosmic proportions—a battle between compassion and consumption, between love of God and neighbor and love of mammon. The next step is to *join* the struggle to try, moment by moment in our ordinary lives, to curb our inordinate desires and redirect our passion toward *com-passion*, "feeling with." For Christians, the knowledge and experience of a God who engaged in this very struggle in the life and work of Jesus opens up for us a novel option for seeing and existing even in the midst of great evil. Salvation does not wipe evil magically away but instead changes our relationship to it, liberating us from bondage to its consuming logic and freeing us for authentic love of God and neighbor.

Anguish and Victimization

Linda Mercadante

The undeserved victimization of Jesus is at the core of Christian tradition. Our scriptures show a God who clearly sides with the victimized and oppressed. It is ironic, then, that theology has spent so little energy understanding and treating the issue of victimization. Instead, Christian theology has focused more attention on sin and sinners. Christian tradition stands squarely on the fact that "all have sinned and fall short of the glory of God." This universality of sin has been a pivotal recognition throughout Christian history.

Of course, it has never been a secret that sin also has its repercussions on others. The various liberation theologies, among others, focus much attention on systemic sin, such as structural injustice and the various "isms"—sexism, racism, ageism, for example—that can dominate a whole society. Yet theology has given the bulk of its attention to the individual sinner. Of course, the focus on the sinner has a clear mission. First, it helps exonerate God from responsibility for evil, and second, it preserves some measure of human responsibility. Without this, it would be more difficult to understand how we can receive grace, turn toward God, accept salvation, or at least recognize our bondage.

Because of these important goals, Christianity has spent relatively less theological energy on those whose only fault has been to be in the wrong place at the wrong time, the archetypal "innocent bystander." Even though the tragic aspect of sin and evil is part of our heritage, it has become habitual for many to view human dysfunction from the well-worn groove of individual sin, the Adamic side emphasizing human responsibility.

This is an easy step to make when trying to help victims who manifest the symptoms of trauma: despair, anger, listlessness, self-blame, and self-pity. On the cultural level, these behaviors grate on our Western upbeat "isms": optimism, activism, and positivism. A victim's plight reminds us uncomfortably of our own human vulnerability and our potential complicity. Yet there is also a problem of blaming the victim, for from the "seven deadly sins" tradition through Kierkegaard and some contemporary interpreters, unappealing behaviors have long been categorized within our definitions of sin.

It is time for Christian theology to add a focus on victimization. Such a move will not, contrary to popular belief, allow sinners to escape sanction and victims to claim they are sinless. Instead, this focus will make clearer the dangerous temptation many victims face to replicate the sin that has been perpetrated against them. It is a fact that the movement from innocent victim to guilty perpetrator is a temptingly easy one to make. Yet we need to avoid slipping into the sinner groove too soon in our assessment of these behaviors. To this end, we need to carve out a theological space for the condition of being-sinned-against. A focus on victims will reveal the dynamics of the victimization/sin cycle, how it can be avoided, and how communities can help direct the healing process.

This work is necessary because it otherwise may seem natural to categorize the sin/victimization problem as a zero-sum game. In other words, if we can find even one percent of complicity, the temptation is to claim a person has not been "truly" victimized. But this does not help victims, who often blame themselves anyway and so need the reality of their victimization confirmed first before focusing on genuine responsibility and right action. If this is not done, related issues get drawn into this nexus, and the focus moves too quickly to such things as forgiveness and God's role. When victims hear blame in efforts to apply Christian theology to victimization, the trauma is exacerbated, not helped.

Both domestic violence and addiction, although quite different on the surface, present particularly interesting theological tests. Although many would like to categorize addiction as a case of personal sin and domestic violence a case of victimization, to the sufferers it is not clear how much of the problem lies with human choice and how much with social, familial, biological, or other largely unchosen factors. We need to make sense, theologically, of their claims to be in bondage to a disease or process yet in some ways responsible at the same time.

Having a specific label for this nexus is helpful. Thus, I propose that the term *anguish* be used to describe the condition that takes hold of a person who has been sinned against and rendered powerless by it.[23] In this usage, anguish does not simply mean "being sinned against." All have been sinned against. But anguish occurs when there is no way to deflect or productively address one's being caught in another's sin. The defining moment comes when the person is rendered, however briefly, powerless. This is an objective condition in which agency is stolen and help does not arrive in time. Normal self-protective strategies break down; resources are not adequate.

Like Reinhold Niebuhr's well-known proposal of "anxiety," anguish is "pre-sin." It is an aspect of the human condition. However, it is unlike anxiety in another way, for anxiety involves an improper personal response to the tension caused by being both finite and free—whether that is an overreaching of one's freedom or a self-indulgent sinking into one's inherent limitations (which Niebuhr labels "sensuality").

Anguish is not constitutive of the human condition in the same way as anxiety. Rather than focusing on the inner tension between a person's inherent finitude and freedom, a more individualistic schema, here the person has experienced constraint from outside, by the misuse of someone else's freedom, the working out of someone else's anxiety. Thus, anguish is a more interpersonal category than anxiety has traditionally been. With anguish, a different form of unquiet results from choices being inordinately narrowed from the outside. It is a distress in the face of what should be rather than anxiety in the face of what could be. As such, it more closely resembles despair rather than hubris or self-indulgence.

Anguish should not be seen as synonymous with finitude. It is not just a gloss on the tragic view of the human condition, although it does take the tragic element seriously. Anguish refers specifically to humanly imposed harm as the downside of human relationality. We are all beings-in-relation, and that vulnerable relationality is as likely to produce negative as positive results.[24] To ignore this and to focus primarily on self-actualization as the locus of sin are too limited. Our constitutive relationality is the receptive side of the human condition. But harm can come when someone else's agency is used to rob us of ours.

Anguish is a state anyone can enter, since everyone has been rendered powerless by another's sin even if only briefly, such as in childhood. But the observation that all have felt anguish because of others' sins against them is not to claim that we are all, in some way, victims. We may have all experienced anguish, but we have not all come into bondage to it. Whether we have depends largely upon one's inner and outer resources.

One can become in bondage to anguish as the condition hardens and becomes intractable in cases of especially traumatic or prolonged victimization. Then the personal repercussions of anguish take hold of a person, as though the sin that was perpetrated against them has taken them prisoner.

Victimization involves some form of life-changing unfairness, such that one's perceptions, beliefs, trust level, feelings, and patterns are irrevocably affected. In such a situation, feelings of despair and hopelessness are reactions commensurate with the situation.

Many have seen despair or hopelessness as ultimately a lack of faith and trust, thus inevitably leading to or already being a form of sin. But in this usage I am proposing, the despair of anguish is not always and already an aspect of sin. The condition of anguish springs from one's human predicament when inordinately constrained. As such it is a constituent part of the situated human predicament. In other words, anguish is a realistic desperation. This is not to say that victims cannot sin; only that anguish is a reaction to another's sin.

This is a somewhat different approach from the now-classic feminist reinterpretations of sin. In these explanations, problems such as lack of initiative, lack of focus, trivialization, distraction, or other refusals of one's own agency are violations of the self as God intended it to be.[25] But anguish is not simply an alternative side of sin. Instead, this condition is not volitional at its outset, at least when volition is considered a key component of sin, as it is by many today.

Anguish is also somewhat different from, although connected to, the more situational Korean Minjung theological category *han*, which speaks of the hard knot of oppression that can reside in a person or group. Unlike *han*, anguish focuses attention on the human condition per se. But anguish is like *han* in that it describes what one can see in victims, that is, the sense of being trapped, pressed down, and hemmed in on all sides. It speaks of the hopelessness, muteness, isolation, and pain that can result from being victimized.

Adding the term *anguish* to our theological vocabulary can help by reframing the issues of victimization and sin, thus allowing victims to make distinctions that will allow them to move forward and heal. This is necessary since victims often see their bondage to anguish and the resulting despair, passivity, pessimism, fear, meaninglessness, and self-hate as inappropriate, wrong, avoidable. The behaviors can be labeled "sin" in the sense of estrangement from God, self, and others. But such linkage is probably a counterproductive discussion-starter when speaking about victimization or to victims. It is problematic because it can imply that at the outset there was a self-destructive determination or a choosing to become a victim. Instead, a victim has often been caught in a surprise, incapacitating attack that rendered his or her will to resist severely damaged.

Of course, the idea of sin can be broached once victims understand that they often absorb the evil perpetrated against them. As such, it becomes a perpetual self-judgment and captivity. Yet that self-loathing, alienation, and distrust is really the long-term aftermath of victimization that has been implanted rather than chosen. In the end, victimization is no less destructive than sin in its effects. But recognizing the source of this particular bondage is crucial. In the case of bondage to anguish, it is the imposed consequences of others' sin that we see and experience. Opportunities for choice, reaction, and use do exist, but the range of options is necessarily colored and limited by the trauma inflicted. The victim's temptation to answer sin with sin, to cooperate with the evil forced upon her, or to turn away from even a pin-prick of graced light, is where she may interact with anguish to produce her own sin.

Acknowledging the state of anguish can help victims differentiate their condition from the choices that they may unknowingly be making in response. If the choices have become self-destructive—even though they may have begun as coping devices—victims have the possibility of recognizing that they have internalized the evil perpetrated against them. This recognition is the first step in returning a measure of freedom, a renewed hope in the reality of grace, and the real possibility of healing.

Sin, Evil, and Economics

Sallie McFague

> *"Probably the most challenging task facing humanity today is the creation of a shared vision of a sustainable and desirable society, one that can provide permanent prosperity within the biophysical constraints of the real world in a way that is fair and equitable to all of humanity, to other species, and to future generations."*
>
> Robert Costanza et al.,
> *An Introduction to Ecological Economics*

This one-sentence vision of life on planet earth is chilling in its combination of simplicity and impossibility. It is a planetary economic, ecological picture of what might be in contrast to what is. "What is" is very different: a world controlled by market capitalism where sustainability and justice for all inhabitants are not central goals. Rather, this worldview is based on the satisfaction of individual human monetary desires, which are seen as more important than fulfilling the basic needs of all creatures both now and in the future.

Each of these two visions of the good life rests on an anthropology—an understanding of who we are in the scheme of things and what we should and should not do. Each has an implied view of sin and evil. In market capitalism, sin is understood solely within the Adamic myth: sin is against God—the focus is on the individual in relation to divine commandments. Its view of sin is narrow and superficial: sin is basically avoiding immoral, unethical acts in personal and professional life. Hence, salvation within this view is seeking divine forgiveness for discrete lapses. Salvation is for individual sins. Evil, as the consequences of sin, does not appear; those sinned against and the enormity of evil do not enter the picture. Since this model of sin and evil eliminates such issues from view, those who live within market capitalism (and increasingly, that includes most of us) can bracket out all issues of sin and evil except the narrow one of personal and professional morality in relation to God.

Strangely, while market capitalism began with a classic Christian anthropology of selfish greed—the basis for the allocation of scarce resources and the eventual "trickle down" of prosperity for all in the twenty-first century—it has eventuated in a näive, optimistic, narrow, and undifferentiated view of sin and evil. Neoclassical economic theory, based on Adam Smith's ideas, claims that the very core of who we are—individuals motivated by insatiable desire for more and more goods—is the basis from which to build the good life for all. From the selfish desires of billions of human beings turning the earth's resources into goods for sale, prosperity for all will presumably come eventually. This vision of the good life, however, neglects two huge facts: the just distribution of the earth's resources as well as the limits of these resources. We now know that these matters are not mysteriously taken care of by the "invisible hand" of economics; on the contrary, the insatiable greed of billions of human beings causes horrendous injustice to other creatures, human and nonhuman, as well as undermining the sustainability of the planet itself. But market capitalism does not deal with the tragic dimensions of sin and evil; its view of sin is narrow and curiously unrelated to its anthropology—sin is only against God, even though its anthropology implies that unregulated greed results in sin against neighbor and nature. By bracketing sin within Adamic limits, it eliminates from view the massive evil that our individual choices have created for others on planet Earth.

The ecological, economic planetary picture implies a very different view of sin and evil. It rests on an anthropology that underscores the intrinsic links between the Adamic and tragic dimensions of sin and evil. Basically, profoundly, and thoroughly, human beings are interrelated and interdependent with everything else on the planet, all animate and inanimate realities, from microorganisms, worms, and plants to water, land, and air. We may be basically greedy (as market capitalism rightly claims), but we are even more needy. We depend on these others absolutely and from minute to minute. We are not essential to the earth's ecosystem; they are. Within this picture, the Adamic myth certainly functions, for we have a "challenging task"—"the creation of a shared vision" of how to live justly and sustainably. In other words, our peculiar distinctiveness in the great interdependent network of life is *choice*: we know how to help the planet thrive, and we know how to destroy it. Sin is still in our hands: in this picture we are the partners with God who have the freedom to choose life or to choose death. In this view, salvation is working with God for the flourishing of creation. As Irenaeus suggests, "The glory of God is every creature fully alive."

There are some crucial differences, though, between this view of sin and evil and that of capitalism. Here sin is not primarily against God, nor is it mainly immoral personal failings; rather, it is against neighbors (all of them, both human and others residing on earth), and it is a failure at the level of life as lived on a daily basis. Sin is refusing to be *part* of this incredibly complex, rich web: refusing to share with other needy creatures and refusing to assume our special role as caretakers of the rest. Moreover, in this view, billions of people living this way create institutions, attitudes, practices, and policies that constitute "evil"—a malevolent surplus of pain, deprivation, deterioration, starvation, and death way beyond anything we can imagine. And there is a third difference: while we who are the main perpetrators of this evil cannot imagine such suffering, others can and do. While *all* have sinned, we do not all sin equally, nor do we all experience the effects of sin equally. We first-world privileged people—those wherever they live who enjoy the fruits of market capitalism—are greater sinners than those who experience the evil that comes from our sins. In this picture, we do not sin directly against God but against our neighbors. Our sight moves from heaven to earth, from the vertical to the horizontal, from the spiritual to the physical. In order to learn the consequences of our sin—its tragic dimensions in detail and to a degree that might change us—we must pay attention deep, prolonged, and intense attention to those "sinned against."

In market capitalism, sin is seen "religiously" (against God), and evil disappears from view. In the ecological vision, sin is seen "biophysically" (against life and its needs) with evil very present in the starving, dying bodies of others. For our time (whatever may have been the case in other times), sin needs to be understood in a sociocultural, planetary context. Moreover, distinctions need to be made between greater and lesser sinners. For middle-class North American Christians, sin is not primarily sexual (the issue that almost all Christian churches have focused on for the last few decades), but monetary: refusing to share with those others with whom we live and on whom we depend, so that all may have the basics and the planet may be healthy. This is a far greater sin and a much more difficult one to overcome than the lesser sins we prefer to dwell on.

Implicated Resistance

It is a common fallacy to believe that our relative privilege or participation in an unjust social system renders us powerless to work authentically on behalf of the victims of that system. Quite the contrary, there are none better suited to work at wresting justice from the beast than those who live in its head and not its stomach.

It is a reality that by accident of birth, by dint of learning, or by simple chance, many people of goodwill find themselves embedded within sinful social systems in a privileged way. Oftentimes, even though they are able to see the wrong that is being done to their neighbor, they believe their privilege robs them of the ability to challenge the system on that neighbor's behalf. They are confirmed in this belief by the system itself—How can someone strategize at Starbucks on behalf of the poor? and frequently by those on whose behalf the struggle is waged—Why is a suburban "soccer mom" at the demonstration against police brutality? This belief is, however, mistaken. The Christian tradition is replete with stories of those who used their positions of relative privilege to struggle on behalf of their suffering neighbor (for example, Dietrich Bonhoeffer).

The term *implicated resistance* is helpful because it recognizes that persons of good will can and must struggle on behalf of their neighbors from exactly the place they find themselves. Persons of good faith do not stop being educated, stop being affluent, or stop bearing the particular privileged racial or ethnic identity granted them by the unjust system in which they live. Rather, they interpret these historical "accidents" as means by which to engage and even transform systems of dehumanization and domination. This call to privileged resistance is not, however, a license to accept gradualism. It is a call to work tirelessly for social transformation because we recognize that the systems of oppression that damn the bodies of the marginalized likewise damn the souls of the privileged (Matt. 25:31–46).

Quite simply, sin for privileged people is taking more than our share. It is, at one level, as plain and direct as if we said to a hungry person, "There is no room for you at the table." It is, in other words, a rejection of Jesus' parable of the feast, in which *all* are invited to the table, regardless of who they are. It is a refusal to attend to the basic, bodily needs of earth's creatures while we adorn ourselves with luxuries. At an individual level, it means amassing goods one does not need when others—humans and other life-forms—are going hungry, deteriorating, and dying. It begins with millions of individuals making daily and often implicit or unconscious decisions to be selfish. These decisions, multiplied by the millions (billions?) over centuries, create a worldview—a set of assumptions supported by institutions and policies—that results in the way of life we call market capitalism. From the base of human greed a system has developed that is so pervasive, so "natural," so conventional, that it is now without critique or question. It is not sinful to be selfish; rather, it is the way everyone lives. Yet, it is precisely the privileging of selfish individualism over the well-being of other creatures and the planet that has resulted in the enormity of evil our planet is presently experiencing from the effects of rapid climate change to billions of people living on a few dollars a day. The tragic dimensions of an economics for the planet built on human selfishness certainly approaches the level of a "malevolent surplus"—consequences so enormous, so horrendous, that apocalyptic images come to mind. Are we human beings, especially the privileged ones, living in such a way as to bring about the end of the world? We have created a world in which evil is so deep, widespread, systemic, and overwhelming that nothing less than cosmic status for it seems appropriate. Is it a "power" over against us? Is the battle between the forces of good and evil, between God and the Devil?

Some would like to see it this way because it moves the finger of blame away from us. The example of economics—of two pictures of how we should live on our planet—suggests otherwise. It suggests that the Adamic wisdom is right when it tells us that we are at the heart of the problem: the finger of blame points to our ability to choose selfishly or for others, for death or for life, for a just and sustainable planet or for the short-term gain of a few of us. *We* are central to the enormity of evil in our time; we should focus *on ourselves* and our contribution to the evil in the world. While natural disasters (some not entirely "natural") as well as many other factors contribute to the tragic dimension of sin and evil, our actions certainly do as well. Our denial is deep, as is our need for repentance and change of heart. We need to take a hard look at ourselves as sinners complicit in an economic system that is causing enormous damage to our planet. We are contributing to a world of evil simply by continuing to live within a worldwide economic system that is neither just nor sustainable.

Theology as Action

If the problem of human sin and evil is so dire and our participation in it so undeniable, then why spend time on theology? Shouldn't we focus our energy on things that can make a real difference, instead of wasting time pondering the nature of God and other big but impractical realities? In a world racked by human suffering and ecological deterioration, isn't theology a luxury only the privileged few can afford?

While the popular media sounded the death knell for religion only a few years ago—claiming that the forces of secularization were fast eclipsing the need for religion today—we recognize the enduring strength and importance of the phenomenon. Far from disappearing quietly into the night, religion is a vital presence in the contemporary world, a powerful motivator of human action, both individual and corporate.

Given the significant role of religion in shaping everything from worldviews and national politics to personal piety and fashion, the task of understanding, interrogating, and continually rethinking religion takes on new importance. Theology is the attempt to bring the resources and insights of the religious past into fruitful conversation with the challenges of the present. In other words, theology is all about problem solving, about asking how the wisdom of the ever-unfolding tradition might help us address the contemporary situation. If we are to bring the considerable resources of religious institutions and people to bear on the needs of today's world—the need for a sustainable, life-affirming economics, for instance; or the need for peaceful transformations of violence and oppression—then theology is a must. There must be people whose priority is to look critically at the interplay between theological ideas and everyday practices; to listen carefully to the voices and experiences of suffering and ask how religion has contributed to that suffering as well as how it might offer words of hope and healing.

The Adamic and tragic myths are well illustrated in economic worldviews. From individual beginnings—each of us taking more than our share, each of us wanting it all—emerges an unjust, unsustainable model for the distribution of the necessities that all creatures need. The consequences of sin are clearly illustrated in the sad state of our planet and its inhabitants. The end is indeed tragic, but it is principally from the Adamic beginnings—the choice of each of us to refuse a place at the table to the others. *Can* we live differently? Is a different world *possible*? There are many answers to that question; for Christians, the kingdom of God—the invitation to all to share in the banquet—is our hope and our encouragement to work for such a world.

Sin and Power: Poststructuralist and Post-colonial Theories

Margaret Kamitsuka

Structural sin and *social sin* are two common terms used in contemporary theological accounts of evil that focus on its widespread and systemic nature. There are at least three important objectives at work explicitly or implicitly in theological accounts referring to sin and evil using these categories. One objective is to *correct the individualistic orientation* that historically has characterized the tradition's formulations of sin. Sin has often been spoken of as originating in the individual's willful turning from the good, with social evil seen as a cumulative, collective ripple effect of individual evil choices. Religious confessional discourse is imbued with this inward and private focus on the soul's struggle with temptation and sin. This suggests how ingrained the discourse of privatized sin is in the Christian tradition and how intentional the theologian has to be to expose the structural workings of dominating power. A second objective of theological discussions of structural or social sin is *pastoral and political*: to give voice to the voiceless suffering of various underclasses and marginalized groups, trying to empower them to resist while spurring others to be in solidarity with them. This pastoral and political objective leads to a third, what I will call *a critical-ethical objective*: to name evil and assess moral culpability, given oppressive structures and individual collusion with those structures by sins of commission or omission. The second and third objectives have received powerful expression in numerous early twentieth-century social gospel, late twentieth-century liberation, and more recent post-colonial theological texts. If an account of social sin is to meet these three objectives adequately, it must understand the function of power in oppressive societal structures. Social theories that have been widely used for this purpose in past decades (such as class, race, and gender analysis) lie outside the discipline of theology, traditionally understood. This essay discusses two more recent theories of power—poststructuralist and post-colonial—that can be especially helpful in accomplishing these three theological objectives (and can be used to supplement other social theories already in use).

I suggest applying the theory of power drawn from poststructuralist philosopher Michel Foucault's writings as one way of avoiding an individualistic approach to sin. A poststructuralist approach situates selves in their socially embodied discursive relations. *Discursive* is a technical term Foucault uses to describe the linguistic conventions shaping bodies of knowledge that a given society uses to structure and regulate itself. For example, the discourse of medicine classifies disease, and the discourse of sexual morality separates deviancy from normalcy. Discourse is thus socially situated. It develops over time in ways that make the rules of language use seem self-evident to members of society who have accepted those modes of discourse as conveying truth. That is, one might disagree with a doctor's bedside manner but most people (in the West) accept as truth modern, secular medical science's understanding of bodies and their pathologies. Poststructuralism analyzes the ways in which the individual is constituted as a subject by being "subjected to" the regulating power of a particular society's truth-conveying discourses—what Foucault calls "power/knowledge."[26] According to poststructuralism, there is no avoiding these discursive relations; there is no stable place where one can definitively transcend power/knowledge effects and find a "pre-given entity" prior to or apart from these cultural and linguistic structures.[27] Given that the individual is seen as constituted within a nexus of societal discursive conventions, even so-called private or personal sin is linked to collective structures. The sinfulness that the believer may, for many reasons, perceive and speak of in a highly internalized and individual way can be analyzed poststructurally to expose its culturally constructed character. A Foucauldian approach to sin, therefore, militates against an individualistic and privatized theological formulation by virtue of the way it situates moral agency in terms of the discursive construction of identity.

This poststructuralist approach can contribute to the pastoral and political objective of fostering empowerment of and solidarity with those who are oppressed because of the way it analyzes how resistance to domination arises. Much of Foucault's historical work investigates how individuals and whole communities have been disciplined and regulated in a myriad of ways by institutional mechanisms (penal systems, psychiatric medicine, education, religion). These investigations support his theory that power, even when it seems monolithic and centralized, turns out upon closer analysis to be a network of widely extended apparatuses. There is rarely a direct route from the peripheral, local authority mechanisms back to some centralized hub of institutional power. Power structures are variously disseminated and marked by "faults, fissures and heterogeneous layers."[28] An example of this is Roman Catholicism in the sixteenth century, which presented itself (and may have been experienced at the time) as a tightly regulated and highly centralized institutional power structure. The historian, however, can identify the ecclesial and political gaps and fissures that allowed Protestant Reformation movements to emerge and survive.[29] Foucault's historical approach to structures of power bears the technical name of "genealogy." Genealogical investigation uncovers not only the instabilities within extended power systems but also how marginalized discourses of history emerge and resist dominating power. Foucault calls the latter phenomenon the "insurrection of subjugated knowledges"—that is, the breaking forth of local or popular protest movements present (even if very repressed) within most dominating and seemingly monolithic power/knowledge regimes.[30] From a genealogical perspective, power "must be analysed as something that circulates. . . . It is never localised here or there, never in anybody's hands" in any exclusive sort of way.[31] Power is not just what my oppressor possesses. It is always a power relation—a relation that may have subjugating effects but also creates subjects. For example, capitalism creates a proletariat; patriarchy creates subservient women. These groups acquire their identity in relation to the structures that discipline them. While that power is repressive, it can and does entail levels of what Foucault calls "pleasure" for the subjects under its control. As Foucault explains: "If power were never anything but repressive . . . do you really think one would be brought to obey it?" Hence, power "induces pleasure" and compliance (for example, the docile worker, the happy housewife) but also "produces discourse"—including discourses and practices of resistance, ranging from subtle noncompliance to overt challenges to dominating power.[32]

This approach to power has the potential to correct a tendency in some liberation theological writings to employ more or less static oppressor-oppressed categories that view the sinned-against primarily as victims in relation to some totalizing domination. Such categories are meant to express compassion for the downtrodden and outrage against injustice, but these categories sit somewhat paradoxically with calls for liberation requiring that one envision agency on the part of the victimized. Thus, even within a tragic model of sin that foregrounds powerless suffering in the face of massive evil, one needs to theorize the possibility of a praxis of resistance. Adopting a view of power such as Foucault's highlights the role of agency amid oppression, hence fostering empowerment. Foucault's approach exposes the local gaps in centralized forms of domination where resistances can emerge. This philosophical approach does not negate the reality of tragic victimization but carves out theoretical space for agency and activism, especially when combined with the Christian notions of empowering and transformative grace and prophetic justice. Because this theory explores how power circulates (nearly) everywhere, it avoids essentializing people as simply victims of various subjugating "isms." Even in the midst of a subjugating process, an agential subject is being produced and, hence, there follows the possibility, if not the actuality, of an insurrection of subjugated knowledge and transgressive practices.

Poststructuralism carves out a theoretical space for agency viewed through a very particular conceptual lens. It is a discursively constructed agent whose identity is constantly negotiated and renegotiated at the nexus of multiple cultural discourses. Some find this philosophical approach to agency too deconstructive, especially for liberation movements where communal identity is just coalescing in resistance to oppression (see related box, "Critiques of Poststructuralism"). Religious scholars from the two-thirds world have been suspicious of imperialist ideologies imbedded in first-world postmodern philosophy and in first-world academy-based secular and theological accounts of global oppression. Many two-thirds-world theologians have turned to post-colonial theory as a more indigenous theoretical way of addressing the sinful effects of colonialism in its various manifestations. These theologians employ, in particular, the post-colonial concept of "hybridity" as a way of accounting for the complicated political agency of the "subaltern" (oppressed) subject. This concept emerged out of the post-colonial experience to describe the ways in which subaltern subjects sometimes both embrace and confront the "master's tools" (the writer Audre Lorde's term) when constructing a new post-colonial identity.[33] What could look like complicity with the oppressor may in fact be a complex, seemingly paradoxical, process of formulating and activating subaltern agency in relation to colonialist as well as indigenous cultural practices, languages, attitudes, and religions. For example, two-thirds-world women might employ Western feminist frames of reference to combat indigenous forms of sexism, on the one hand, while concurrently using women's precolonial cultural practices to confront the presence of colonialist attitudes destructive of women's and men's indigenous identity, including some Euro-American feminist attitudes. Botswana theologian Musa Dube describes hybridity as "the right to reap from both fields, from that of the colonized as well as the colonizer, and [to] use whatever they find life affirming."[34] One Native American (Cherokee) Christian theologian, Andrea Smith, calls this "walking in balance," which can encompass many tasks: revitalizing precontact indigenous traditions; speaking critically to post-contact unjust structures in Native communities; attacking non-Native appropriation and commodification of Indian spiritualities; and affirming parts of the Christian tradition that some

Native people deem to be harmonious with Native religions.[35] What post-colonial theorists call hybridity is thus a pragmatic exercise of power and agency, reflecting a very grassroots and contextualized approach to cultural, economic, and political survival in contexts of pervasive structural evil.

The critical-ethical objective of naming and assesing evil requires the ability to highlight differences in the material effects of social and interpersonal sin and to name oppressive sociopolitical structures as evil. Interpersonal wrongs (ranging from gossiping to adultery) affect a limited circle of people and can be traced, in theory, to a sinful instigator, whereas social sin multiplies and extends far beyond the evil actions or intentions of one person or set of persons. Theologians increasingly want to name those sinful effects as structural evil. For this task of naming evil, one would need to invoke something like Gayatri Chakravorty Spivak's notion of "strategic essentialization." Speaking originally to the Subaltern Studies group of post-colonial historians in India, Spivak describes their approach as one of reading back into the Indian historical narrative an identifiable collective consciousness of revolutionary resistance to colonialist oppression. She suggests that this notion of a revolutionary consciousness is a distillation or essentialization of a much more complex and ambiguous situation. The notion functions as a kind of "theoretical fiction" invoked for "strategic use . . . in a scrupulously visible political interest."[36] That is, the essentialization is used strategically in order to mobilize political resistance to a specific tyranny—in this case, British colonization. It is necessary to essentialize community identity strategically in this way when oppression creates a group for whom the circulation of power has been effectively cut off. This approach to power allows the theorist to name evil definitively within specific political contexts. (Spivak cautions against any essentializing move that obscures the strategic nature of this naming of oppressor and oppressed.)

Strategic essentialization and hybridity are complementary post-colonial concepts that can be used in tandem. The former provides a means to assess the moral culpability of the oppressor; the latter creates empathetic understanding for the complex and ambiguous negotiations required in real-life processes of cultural and political transformation.

Taken together, theories of power, such as the poststructuralist and post-colonial ones I have outlined, could contribute importantly to the theologian's analysis of structural sin. Without theoretical resources such as these, theological accounts of sin and evil—whether the model is Adamic or tragic—risk failing to fulfill all three of the objectives noted above.

Sin and Evil as Social Constructs

> *"Nothing is intelligible outside its history."*
>
> Teilhard de Chardin

For Christians, the Hebrew Bible and New Testament are foundational texts for theological reflection on sin and evil. Yet these texts do not themselves stand outside the context of human sin. Inevitably, they bear the imprint of our limited understanding and vision, our perversions and distortions. Thus it is that in scripture we find ambiguous, sometimes conflicting, articulations of sin and evil—articulations that some of us identify as doing more damage than good and hence as themselves sinful.

The prophetic proclamation of God's desire for human freedom and justice, for example, clearly depicts exploitation of others as sin. In numerous biblical texts, God expresses deep concern for those who suffer the evil of oppression. Yet other texts—also biblical—function to legitimate unjust forms of authority and servitude by affirming and generating class stratification and unequal participation of persons in the social order. Witness this proclamation from 1 Timothy, for instance: "Let all who are under the yoke of slavery regard their masters as worthy of all honor, so that the name of God and the teaching may not be blasphemed" (6:1). Or this, from Ephesians: "Slaves, obey your earthly masters with fear and trembling, in singleness of heart, as you obey Christ: . . . doing the will of God from the heart" (6:5–6). Thus, biblical texts effectively sanction and even "Christianize" the oppressive relation of master to slave and the exploitative economics of slave holding. Similarly, exploitation of women is positively depicted and even dictated as part of faithful living in other biblical texts. While one text proclaims that "for freedom Christ has set us free" (Gal. 5:1), another admonishes, "Wives, be subject to your husbands, as is fitting in the Lord" (Col. 3:18), and "Let a woman learn in . . . full submission. I permit no woman to teach or to have authority over a man; she is to keep silent" (1 Tim. 2:11-12). Clearly, biblical concepts of sin and evil can function to challenge an oppressive status quo, but they can also be used to sustain that very order.

Just as biblical texts inevitably reflect the limitations and perversions, along with the faithfulness and integrity, of their authors, so do later theological texts. Indeed, no text is free from bias. All are products of particular times and are designed to serve particular interests. The question, then, is, Whose interests will our theology serve? Whose interests do the interpretations of sin and evil presented in this chapter serve?

Critiques of Poststructuralism

Various scholars today are voicing criticisms of the postmodern turn. Catherine Keller issues a warning against an uncritical appropriation of postmodern theory for feminist theology. She worries that interest in postmodernism may represent an antifeminist turn because the major proponents of postmodern thought have been mostly (French) men: "we nurture ourselves from *les papas* Derrida, Foucault, Lacan," whose engagement with feminist issues is often peripheral.[37] Many scholars of color are suspicious that postmodern philosophy in general represents another domain "dominated primarily by the voices of white . . . academic elites who speak to and about one another with coded familiarity,"[38] as bell hooks comments. Others, like Cherríe Moraga, claim that postmodern theory has attained a "hegemonic influence" in North American academe that suppresses or distorts the distinctive modes of thinking emerging from communities of people of color by labeling their appeals to experience essentializing or "naive."[39]

Although many scholars of color and those from the two-thirds world have embraced post-colonial theory, others voice criticisms of it that echo many of the concerns about postmodernism. Cherokee scholar Jace Weaver argues that post-colonial discourses, like postmodern ones, are too "depoliticized," and that as long as colonization (religious, economic, and so forth) continues in Native communities, "the post-colonial moment for Native Americans will not yet have arrived."[40]

4

Jesus Christ

Karen Baker-Fletcher, Michelle A. Gonzalez, David H. Jensen,
Joerg Rieger, Cynthia L. Rigby, Deanna A. Thompson (chapter editor)

"I haven't talked to anyone about this for a while," she began, the smile fading, and sadness deepening in her eyes. "But I'm worried for my kids now. The problem is my husband. He beats me sometimes. Mostly he is a good man. But sometimes he becomes very angry and he hits me. He knocks me down. One time he broke my arm and I had to go to the hospital. But I didn't tell them how my arm got broken."

I nodded. She took a deep breath and went on. "I went to my priest twenty years ago. I've been trying to follow his advice. The priest said I should rejoice in my sufferings because they bring me closer to Jesus. He said, 'Jesus suffered because he loved us'. He said, 'If you love Jesus, accept the beatings and bear them gladly, as Jesus bore the cross'. I've tried, but I'm not sure anymore. My husband is turning on the kids now. Tell me, is what the priest told me true?"[1]

◆

For 3 months Hatuey led guerilla warfare in Cuba against the Spaniards, until he was captured in 1511. Hatuey was condemned to death. Right before he was burned at the stake, a Franciscan attempted to convert him, promising him the glories of heaven. Hatuey then asked if Christians went to heaven. When the Franciscan affirmed this, Hatuey answered that he did not want to go to a place where he would find such inhuman, cruel people.[2]

◆

The crowd gathers outside the cathedral and in the streets of San Antonio. The plaza in front of the cathedral is full, and crowds line the surrounding streets. Dolores sees a dark-haired man dressed in a small sheet. He is carrying a heavy cross, the weight a clear strain on him. She watches as the man is tortured and tormented. The crowd yells and screams, taunting him to continue his journey. A man who looks like her uncle is dressed in Roman military garb. As he lashes out at the man, Dolores realizes that it is her uncle, yet he is not acting at all like he usually does. He is someone else.

"Es Jesús," her mother whispers in her ear, as the man walks by them. "El está sufriendo por nosotros y con nosotros." ("It's Jesus. He is suffering for us and with us.") They follow him through the streets of downtown. Dolores is confused; she thought they only celebrated Jesus in the church building and at home. Now it seems as if the city has become a church—all the traffic is stopped, and they process through the streets freely. She watches the monseñor take the cross from Jesus and carry it for him. He seems so humble, so unlike the daunting man preaching at the front of the church every Sunday.

Dolores is overwhelmed by the screams, the sobs, and the passion of the moment. As the soldiers nail Jesus to the cross (they are actually fake, her mother assures her, but to Dolores it looks so real), tears well in her eyes. She sees the pain Jesus experiences. She hears the pain in the people around her: a mother lamenting a son murdered in a gang-fight last year, a man muttering about his lost job, a young woman praying her boyfriend will return. Dolores realizes that since they are all with him, Jesus is not suffering alone. She also realizes that because he suffered, they do not suffer alone. He accompanies them all in the daily sufferings of the struggle that is life.

◆

"I want to believe God understands me," Betty said, her eyes tearing with frustration, "but I don't see how Jesus tells me this." "You mean," I asked knowingly, "he couldn't have known what it is to be a woman?" "Oh, that—yes. I've struggled with that since I was thirteen. I remember feeling so alone, when my parents told me Jesus was with me no matter what. How could he know what it was like to have a period? But I got over that. Now, it's something else, something harder." She shook her head, embarrassed to go further. "Cindy, every morning I stare into the mirror and wonder who that old woman is staring back. I'm simply not the person I see. And I'm sick of people treating me like a frail old lady. I'm not. Just this morning, some kid in the check-out line in the grocery store started talking to me as though I didn't know how to sign a credit card receipt. Some days I just can't take it. I reassure myself that God is somehow with me in this, but I really don't believe it. Jesus died when he was only thirty-three, right? How did he know what it was like to be old?"

State of the Question

Almost 2,000 years ago Jesus asked, "Who do you say that I am?" (Matt. 16:15), a question that Christians have attempted to answer and continue to contemplate. Answers to this question, as the opening vignettes demonstrate, are tied to the life and death issues that shape Christian faith and theology at any historical moment. There is a deep ambiguity and a lived tension in articulating who Jesus was and who he continues to be for Christians across the globe. Whether it is his suffering on the cross, his uniqueness as a historical human being, the soteriological implications of his ministry, death, and resurrection, or the exclusivism often implied in the Christian message, defining Jesus is of utmost concern for Christians.

The life, ministry, death, and resurrection of a first-century man named Jesus has inspired, challenged, and mystified humanity. The quest to understand who Jesus was and his significance for us today continues to plague Christians and non-Christians alike. This search is especially important for Christians, those followers of Jesus who through the centuries have proclaimed him as the Son of God and the Savior of humanity. This belief is central to Christianity, the linchpin of Christians' distinctive worldviews and beliefs. Jesus' mediation of God's revelation stands as the foundation of Christian faith.

Within the field of theology, the study of Jesus' history, context, nature, and significance fall under the heading of Christology. Christology is the subdiscipline in theology that studies the identity and meaning of Jesus Christ, with special attention to his historical identity, his salvific impact, and his significance for Christians. Historical christological studies emphasize the creation of the doctrine of Jesus Christ within the history of Christian theology. For every generation of Christians, the significance of Jesus as the Christ is constantly being reinterpreted based on one's sociocultural, historical, and political context. There is therefore not one unified Christology, but various Christologies that are shaped by the diverse communities that struggle to interpret God's revelation through God's son Jesus. The historical, the theological, and the constructive are tightly connected.

To speak of Jesus as the Christ is to make a *theological* statement. On one level, Jesus is the name of a first-century Jew who lived in Palestine 2,000 years ago. He became a public figure in the last few years of his life, which ended tragically and violently around the age of thirty. These claims are based on *historical* understandings of this man, whom we know very little about today, in spite of the fact that his life and message transformed the very course of human history. In the past few decades there has been an explosion of materials, both academic and popular, that seek to uncover his "true" nature and biography. These historical questions, which have permeated modern scholarship, emphasize Jesus' humanity. This modern emphasis on Jesus' historical existence often comes at the expense of Jesus' divinity. Claiming Jesus as the Christ, however, is to make a theological statement about the religious nature of Jesus' identity and ministry. This has implications for how we understand Jesus' soteriological (salvific) role in human history. The word *Christ* literally means "anointed," one who is blessed with oil. At first glance, this characterization appears insignificant. However, in light of Jewish Messianic hope for the coming of their Savior (the Anointed One),

Jesus understood as the Christ casts him as the fulfillment of Jewish prophecy, the Savior of humanity.

Beginning in the eighteenth century a movement called the "Quest of the Historical Jesus" sought to reveal the true Jesus, who, scholars claimed, was radically different from the Jesus constructed by Christian faith communities. In the mid-twentieth century two new waves in this quest for a historically accurate depiction of Jesus emerged, the most recent drawing extensively from nonbiblical sources to illuminate modern understandings of Jesus. Of central concern for modern historical scholars is understanding the implications of Jesus' message for the here and now. Was Jesus proclaiming a future kingdom of God? Or has it begun here on earth? In addition, what is humanity's role in this endeavor? While scholars may claim to provide a historically accurate portrait of Jesus, we must always remember that the scholar's culture and hermeneutic always influence his or her historical reconstruction.

One cannot divorce Jesus' ministry from his pivotal role in salvation history. In more classical theological terms, Christology and soteriology (the doctrine of salvation) are intimately interconnected. Ultimately, efforts throughout history to name and understand Jesus' identity are grounded in soteriological concerns. Even Christologies that emphasize Jesus' ministry and its moral implications are elaborating a vision of how Jesus' life is a model for humanity to emulate and follow. In a similar vein, one cannot have a full vision of Jesus' life and ministry without addressing the horror of his public crucifixion and the joy of his resurrection. The cross is not the last word. Jesus' crucifixion is not what makes him exceptional. What distinguishes Jesus is the promise of forgiveness, love, and saving grace found in his resurrection. The resurrected Jesus, who continues to bear the marks of his crucifixion, teaches us that the ever-present promise of rebirth is organically tied to his ministry. The redemptive import of the resurrection constantly revives and renews humanity through the Spirit. However, the cross teaches us that Christian discipleship has a price; to follow Jesus is to embark on a dangerous ministry.

The heart of this chapter is found in two major sections: historical and constructive. The historical section outlines major developments in Christology throughout the history of Christianity. This section closes with the challenges posed by the twentieth century for contemporary theology, which serve as a springboard for the constructive pieces. The constructive section is a four-part exploration of the above-mentioned perennial issues within Christology: the scandal of particularity, the question of redemptive suffering, soteriology, and triumphalism. The final section of this chapter links Christology with other loci in the book, demonstrating the interrelationship of the theological task.

There is no one Christology but several Christologies that are shaped by the context and culture from which they emerge, including the Gospel portraits. The Christology in this chapter approaches the significance of Jesus Christ in light of the life-and-death issues that characterize the contemporary era. Whether it is the continuing exploitation of third-world peoples, the growing feminization of poverty, or the militarization of the world around us, this chapter asks what Jesus' life, ministry, and salvific presence have to tell us in light of these pressing concerns. What is the significance of Christology in light of the sufferings of peoples? Breaking from the model of classical Christologies that often emphasized ahistorical, abstract understandings of Jesus Christ, this Christology engages the concrete, gritty issues that characterize the contemporary era.

Historical Developments

Since Jesus of Nazareth walked the face of the earth, Christian believers have tried to discern and articulate who he is and why he matters to the way we live. How he has been understood and the implications of these understandings have varied greatly. In the name of Jesus, people have been condemned and people have been forgiven; people have been enslaved and people have been liberated; women have been ordained and women have been denied ordination; nature has been destroyed and nature has been valued and protected. It makes a difference who we understand Jesus to be and what we understand him to have taught and accomplished.

New Testament Developments

Already in the Gospels we see the development of varying Christologies. The Gospel of Mark portrays Jesus as enigmatic: his true identity is known by the demons but not by others. There is no birth narrative in Mark; Jesus is seemingly "adopted" by God the Father at the time of his baptism. The original ending of the book is cryptic, telling us that the women are so terrorized by Jesus' resurrection that they say "nothing to anyone" about it (Mark 16:8). Instead of telling us who Jesus is, Mark seems to ask us how we will respond to this powerful, disturbing figure.

Matthew and Luke, by contrast, are very interested in telling us who Jesus is. Matthew, writing to a largely Jewish audience, presents Jesus as one who fulfils the Old Testament prophecies about the coming Messiah (see, for example, Matt. 1:23; 4:6–10, 15–16; 12:17–21; 13:14–15). Luke, writing for a Gentile audience, insists that Jesus is one who reaches out to marginalized persons (see, for example, Luke 13:10–17; 14:16–24; 15:11–32; 19:1–9). Both Matthew and Luke include birth narratives and descriptions of how the church responds to Christ's resurrection. But these accounts are developed in ways that shape different Christologies. For example, Matthew, wishing to emphasize Jesus' descendency from David, develops a genealogy that traces Jesus' father Joseph back to Abraham (see Matt. 1:1–17). Luke, eager to present Jesus as the brother of all humanity, tracks Jesus' line back to the first human being, Adam (see Luke 3:23–38). Matthew responds to the resurrection and ascension by arguing that we should "go therefore and make disciples of all nations" (Matt. 28:19). Luke, on the other hand, segues his Gospel into a sequel (the Book of Acts of the Apostles) that describes the church's ministry to the marginalized. The church, for Luke, is clearly called to follow in Christ's footsteps.

The Christology of the Gospel of John is different still. While John does not begin with birth narratives, he has clearly moved far away from Mark's adoption motif. Like Matthew and Luke, John seeks to tell us who Jesus is. But he does not begin with a genealogy. Instead, John's Christology centers on the notion that Christ is the Word (Greek: *logos*) that existed with God in the beginning, the Word that became flesh (John 1:1, 14). This idea is often known as "*logos* Christology." Christology in the Gospel of John emphasizes Jesus' close relationship with the Father and the disciples' intimate relationship with him. "Abide in me as I abide in you," Jesus urges (John 15:4). The salvific work of Christ is to make us "one" with him and with one another, even as he is one with the Father (see John 17).

The Pauline letters, the earliest writings of the New Testament, portray Jesus as the one crucified, risen, and returning soon. Paul emphasizes that Jesus frees us from the confines of the Law (see, for example, Romans 6–8). He urges Christians to pattern their behavior after the Christ who showed great love and compassion (Eph. 5:1–2), emptied himself in order to serve (Phil. 2:1–13), and reached out to include the marginalized as members of his body (1 Cor. 12; Gal. 3:28).

These varying understandings of who Christ is and what impact he has on our lives continued to be developed in the early centuries of the church.

Some of the major christological decisions and changes were noted in the early church councils, including Nicaea and Chalcedon.

The Early Councils

A major christological decision was made in 325, at the Council of Nicaea. Jesus Christ is *homoousios* with the Father, it was declared of the "same substance . . . very God of very God."[3] This statement was made in direct refutation of the teachings of Arius, a theologian who tried to address the conundrum of Jesus' relationship to God by arguing that Jesus Christ is of "like substance," but not the "same substance," as God the Father. With this proposal, Arius was trying simultaneously to honor both the oneness of God (monotheism) and the unique status of Christ in the developing faith system of the early Christian community.

In confessing that Jesus was *homoousios* with the Father, the early church was making the claim that Jesus is equally God with the Father. This idea, that the man Jesus was also fully divine, continued to be developed. 125 years after the Council of Nicaea, at the Council of Chalcedon (451), leading Christian scholars came together to reaffirm the *homoousios* and to consider how the humanity and the divinity of Jesus Christ are related. Two schools of thinking—one based in Alexandria, the other in Antioch—took conflicting positions in the debate. While the Antiochians (led by Theodore of Mopsuestia and Diodore of Tarsus) attended to the distinction of the two natures of Christ (the human and the divine), the Alexandrian school (led by Athanasius and Apollinaris) emphasized their unity. Both schools had soteriological concerns in mind in putting forward their arguments. Both wanted to honor the classic insight of Gregory of Nazianzus: "that which is not assumed is not redeemed." The Antiochians explained Christ's assumption of our humanity by emphasizing that the divine nature indwelled the human nature without the attributes of the two natures affecting one another (Word-man Christology). Their concern, in maintaining a clear distinction between the divinity and the humanity, was to honor their conviction that the divinity is in no way compromised by the humanity. It is one thing to say that Jesus Christ suffered *as a human being*, they argued; it is unacceptable to say that, in the suffering of Jesus Christ, God also suffered. The Antiochenes rejected the idea that Mary is *theotokos*, "God-bearer," for similar reasons: they thought it preposterous to think that the immutable God would be born of a human woman. The Alexandrians, by contrast, emphasized the unity of the divine and human natures to the point where they mutually affected one another (*communicatio idiomatum*). Developing what has become known as Word-flesh Christology, they held that the Word suffers in the person of the incarnate one. It is because God is born of Mary and entered into suffering with us, they believed, that suffering creatures are redeemed.

The Significance of Mary

The figure of Miriam of Nazareth, mother of Jesus, has a complex and rich history within Christianity. The theological significance and prominence of *theotokos* has varied throughout the historical eras and in multiple geographical contexts. As early as the Gospel narratives, we find differing interpretations of the role and presence of Mary in Jesus' ministry and in the early Christian community. Luke's narrative, for example, depicts her as a grace-filled collaborator in salvation history; John's narrative symbolically positions her at the foot of the cross, the moment the church is born. The image of Mary is often evoked to affirm Jesus' preferential option for the poor and marginalized. She is seen as sister and *compañera*, especially for poor women. Whether it is her Magnificat or her apparition before the indigenous man Juan Diego on the hills of Tepeyac in 1531, Mary is often characterized by her solidarity with the poor. She has been symbolic of many things, including the perfect disciple, the idealized church, Christian obedience, and the maternal dimension of God. Thus, her image has functioned in both liberating and oppressive ways for women—in solidarity with women's struggles and as an impossible ideal for everyday women.

Unlike the focus of the Quest of the Historical Jesus, the historical Mary is not often the subject of study. In fact, many scholars would argue that the various apparitions of Mary that have been reported throughout the world have little to do with the first-century Jewish woman who gave birth to Jesus of Nazareth. Whether it is the Mary of history or the Mary of faith, one thing is clear: she remains the most important female figure in Christianity, inspiring Christian imagination.

The debate at Chalcedon ended with the formulation of a statement that honored the positions of both schools, while guarding against heretical extremes. It was declared that Jesus Christ is "fully human and fully divine . . . one *prosopon* and one *hypostasis* ["person"] . . . existing in two natures . . . without confusion, without change, without division, without separation."[4] "Without confusion and without change" warned the Alexandrians that to think of Jesus as having one nature—a "mixture" of divinity and humanity—is problematic. Such a being is neither fully human nor fully divine and therefore cannot be "God with us." "Without division and without separation" advised the Antiochians not to "compartmentalize" the two natures of Christ, as though they had nothing to do with one another. Such extreme separation could only render impossible the believers' shared hope that God has assumed the human condition in the person of Jesus Christ.

The Problems with Nicaea and Chalcedon

Nicaea's affirmation of the essence shared by Son and Father (*homoousios*) and Chalcedon's depiction of the divine and human nature united in the one person Jesus Christ are hallmarks of Western Christology. At times they appear as a theological litmus test, where acceptance of their terms designates orthodoxy and questioning them signals heresy. The language of the statements, however, resists reduction to a definition of Jesus Christ. Indeed, they are strikingly indirect, excluding some interpretations of Christ (such as Docetism), but specifying rather little. The statements delineate, then, the space within which appropriate speech about him may take place. Yet ambiguities within these classic statements abound, rendering them problematic as Christianity faces its third millennium.

One problem that has been widely discussed in the modern era is the obscurity of the statements' language. The categories that Nicaea and Chalcedon employ—*prosopon, hypostasis, ousia*—are difficult to communicate in our time. Modern presuppositions about nature, person, and essence differ significantly from the meaning of these terms in the fifth-century Mediterranean world. Translation often results in theological anachronism remote from contemporary Christian faith. In light of these difficulties, we might consider moving away from these ancient Greek philosophical categories and instead use language that is more directly connected to the saving work of Jesus Christ and the experience of redemption through him.

A second, related difficulty concerns the relationship between ontology and discipleship. If one issue of Nicaea and Chalcedon is captured by the question "Who is Jesus Christ?" that question has often been answered apart from what it means to *follow* Jesus Christ. Nowhere do the classic documents connect the person of Christ to his ministry of healing, reconciliation, and peace and only marginally does Nicaea connect his person to the cross. Reading these statements in our day, one easily gets the impression that the ontology of Jesus, his metaphysical make-up, is paramount, while his ministry and call to discipleship are ancillary. Though the ontology of Chalcedon and Nicaea certainly serves a soteriological purpose, pointing the way to the salvation of humankind, one wonders whether some readings of the statements unwittingly distance Jesus from the kingdom of God that he proclaimed. Finally, and perhaps most significant, the connections between the statements and their imperialistic context are problematic. Nicaea and Chalcedon are inextricably connected to movements of empire that sought to expand, unify, and trample dissent. Then, as now, the pen of Christian confession can fit snugly into the fist of imperial consolidation. Defining the limits of Christian belief, then, becomes a guise for preserving present arrangements of power. In interpreting these statements, a healthy hermeneutic of suspicion, or critical thinking and questioning of assumptions, is warranted: How do they serve the interests of the current American empire? How do they smother the spirit of dissent? How do they foist an inappropriate mask of uniformity on the One who proclaimed much on behalf of others and little on behalf of himself?

Development of Atonement Theories

In the eleventh and twelfth centuries there emerged a great interest in understanding, in more detail, how it is that Jesus Christ's life, death, and resurrection work to accomplish salvation for us. Soteriological concerns shifted from a focus on the incarnation to a focus on the purpose of the cross. Traditionally, three major theories of atonement are highlighted.

In his classic work, *Cur Deus Homo* ("Why God Became Human"), Anselm explains what is now commonly known as the satisfaction theory of atonement. Anselm argued that, if estranged human beings were to share fellowship with God once again, God's honor would first need to be satisfied. It is inconsistent with God's perfectly righteous character, Anselm thought, to tolerate sin. Because God desires to be in fellowship, and because we (who are sinful) are incapable of satisfying God's honor, God became human. In the person of Jesus Christ, the gap between our unrighteousness and God's righteousness is bridged. With his death on the cross, Christ took upon himself the penalty for our sins and made restoration possible.

Debate about Anselm's theory did not wait until the twentieth century. About 30 years after Anselm's publication, Peter Abelard wrote that he did not even recognize Anselm's God as the God Christian believers love and serve. He further held that Anselm's logic was faulty: "How did the death of his innocent Son so please God the Father that through it he should be reconciled to us?"[5] Abelard proposed an alternative way of understanding how Jesus Christ accomplishes salvation that has since become known as the moral exemplar theory. According to Abelard, Christ's love, demonstrated to us in the Gospels, compels us to respond in kind. Contemplation of Christ's love for God, submission to the Father's will, concern for others, and death on the cross (an act, Abelard thought, of "perfect love") will itself inspire us to live as Christ lived.

A third approach to atonement theory is difficult to attribute to any single figure. *Christus victor* theory is identified with several theologians throughout the ages, including Irenaeus (second century), Martin Luther (sixteenth century), and C. S. Lewis (twentieth century). It was developed, in the twentieth century, in Gustaf Aulén's *Christus Victor*. This theory presumes that God and the forces of Satan are in battle with one another and that Jesus Christ will, ultimately, be victorious in this battle. *Christus victor* holds that, while Satan and Satan's demons are no real rivals to God (who will inevitably conquer them in Jesus Christ), they nonetheless exercise real power along the way to the coming of the kingdom. In the event of the cross, Jesus is temporarily defeated by these evil powers. In the resurrection, he overcomes them. Living with an awareness of Christ's ultimate victory, Christian believers are called boldly to name sin and evil, working for the promised reign of God.

Stumbling over the Cross: Suffering, Atonement, and Redemption

Amidst the numerous theories over the meaning of Jesus' death, the cross remains a "stumbling block" (1 Cor. 1:23) for contemporary Christians, most pointedly for women, children, and men whose lives bear the marks of crucifixion. Questions over traditional interpretations of Jesus' suffering and self-sacrifice related to the violence of the cross come to the fore in our global context, where sacrifice on the part of millions serves a privileged few. Wary of the cross, many wonder how the suffering of an innocent man brings about healing for others. Heeding the claim of Holocaust survivor Elie Wiesel, who said that a religion that glorifies suffering will always find someone to suffer, feminist theologians in particular have mounted scathing critiques of how traditional models of atonement glorify suffering, praise debilitating forms of self-sacrifice, and valorize passive acquiescence to sinful structures that harm women, children, and men.

The Anselmian satisfaction model of God's redeeming work highlights the gravity of sin and the costliness of redemption, but it also causes feminists to stumble over its portrayal of God. Here God's grace seems to be made conditional upon satisfaction, and justice appears more important to God than mercy. As Rebecca Parker asks, "Do we really believe that God is appeased by cruelty?"[6] Standing alone, this model also bears an ahistorical quality: we learn *why* God became human but fail to hear that the character of Jesus' living matters at all. What matters is his death rather than his embodiment of God's reign.

In the Abelardian model, the focus on a subjective change within human consciousness can encourage an examination of the sinful webs of illusion and self-deception in which we find ourselves entangled. Serious concern arises, however, when the Jesus of the Gospels emerges primarily as a model for Christians to emulate. Here feminists stumble over the model's abusive potential. Jesus is exalted for his choice to become a victim, suggesting that becoming Christ-like involves becoming a victim, too.

The cosmic battle imagery of the *Christus Victor* model—especially if taken literally—seems archaic to modern ears. Feminists critique the dualism embedded in the imagery, the apparent trickery by God in the overcoming of the devil, and the seeming lack of material evidence that God actually overcame the devil decisively. Today, however, this model is also being mined by some feminist and other contemporary theologians for its subversive potential to bear the good news of God's reconciling love to broken humanity. In this model God is not seen as orchestrating the death of Jesus; rather the forces of evil carry Jesus to the cross. The apparent victory of evil is ultimately confounded through the resurrection by the mysterious, life-giving work of God. For those Christians across the globe whose existence is framed by life and death battles against the demonic forces manifest in global economic and political structures, this model may offer a way to understand God's atoning work as that which defies those structures and claims decisive victory for the loving kingdom of God.

Medieval Catholic Christology

Thomas Aquinas captures the synthetic sensibility of the high Middle Ages. Using Aristotelian metaphysics as an interpretive key, his Christology bears the traces of Chalcedon, Anselmian atonement theory, and a rearticulation of the humanity of Jesus. Thomas's conception of the person of Jesus restates the orthodoxy of Christ's two natures. Fully human and fully divine, Jesus Christ is both the culmination of God's saving intention for creation and the means by which humanity is returned to God, its source. The primary purpose of the incarnation is to repair the damage wrought by human sin, to provide satisfaction, and to restore the broken relationship between humanity and God. As much as Thomas relies on Anselm, he expands his predecessor's understanding of atonement with a commensurate emphasis on the resurrection: "As Christ destroyed our death by his death, so he restored our life by his resurrection."[7] Thomas also dwells on the humanity of Jesus more than many of his medieval contemporaries; though Jesus possessed beatific knowledge of God and his Sonship, he, like all other human beings, had to rely on his senses, experience, and human mind in gaining knowledge of the empirical world. No single image captures this synthetic Christology; indeed, Thomas multiplies the names of Christ in several of his writings to include Jesus and teacher, brother, food, and defender.

This expansion of traditional titles reaches even greater prominence in Julian of Norwich's *Showings*, which display an undercurrent of maternal imagery. In a series of visions, Jesus appears to Julian as Mother, the One to whom we owe our being. The Motherhood of Jesus includes providential care, forgiving mercy, and restorative love. Julian invokes childbirth to describe the anguish and joy of this care: Jesus "is in labor until the time has fully come for him to suffer the sharpest pangs and the most appalling pain possible."[8] In birthing, sustaining, and forgiving humanity, Jesus Christ nourishes us as a mother feeds her child.

Reformation Christologies

The sixteenth century brought renewed interest both in the classical christological statements (Nicaea and Chalcedon) and in the nature of the atonement. One of the primary goals of the Reformers was to clarify the relationship between Christology and soteriology. They criticized the Roman church for teaching that salvation was accomplished, in part, through the mediation of the church. They disagreed that confessing to a priest, engaging in acts of penitence, praying to the saints, and purchasing indulgences could help ensure that souls would ultimately find rest in God.

Martin Luther and John Calvin were among those who emphasized that Christ is the one Mediator between God and humanity. "*Solus christus*!" the Reformers cried—"By Christ alone!" (*not* by Christ plus the church). In his *Ninety-five Theses* (1517), Luther condemned the church for falsely teaching that salvation is works-driven rather than a gift of grace. In paying attention to ourselves and our own condition and trying to "reach Christ," he later argued, "we lose sight of Christ, who alone is our righteousness and life."[9] John Calvin wrote extensively on Christ's role as Mediator, exploring the meaning and implications of the Chalcedonian formula. He emphasized that the point of the union between the fully human nature and the fully divine nature was to benefit us: "Only he who was true God and true [human] could bridge the gulf between God and ourselves,"[10] Calvin wrote in his *Institutes of the Christian Religion*. "The sole purpose of Christ's incarnation was our redemption. . . . It is too presumptuous to imagine another reason or another end."

The emergence of Protestant Christologies can be seen especially in Luther and Calvin's understanding of what happens in the Eucharist. Believing, in good Chalcedonian fashion, that Christ is fully human and fully divine, Luther argued that the body and blood are also fully human and divine. *Consubstantiation* is the idea that the actual body and blood of Christ are literally "in, with, and under" the bread. Calvin did not believe, as Luther did, that the property of ubiquity was shared by Christ's divinity with Christ's humanity. Christ's humanity, he thought, was physically located in heaven and could therefore not be located in the bread and the wine. His understanding of the "real presence" of Christ was that the body and blood of Christ (which are in heaven) are joined to the bread and the wine by the "vivifying work of the Holy Spirit."

What was important to the Reformers was that the Eucharist be celebrated not as a work to attain salvation but as a reminder that Christ is the basis of our salvation. It was for christological reasons, then, that the Reformers did not want to privilege the role of the priest, but argued for "the priesthood of all believers." The idea that the vocation of every Christian believer is equally important is grounded in the convictions that it is Christ who has accomplished salvation for us and that we are living in faithful recognition of our redemption in Christ.

In order to better articulate the breadth and benefits of our salvation in Christ, the Reformers revisited the atonement theories in light of the three offices of Christ. Christ as prophet shows us the way to God, by his love forging a path on which we are called to follow behind (Abelardian atonement). Christ as priest bears the penalty for that which we cannot carry, taking upon himself the consequences for our sin (Anselmian atonement). Christ as king has won the battle over Satan, uplifting us to do good works in the kingdom of God (*Christus victor*).

Radical Reformation

For the dissenting voices of the Radical Reformation, Jesus Christ is best expressed as the Prince of Peace. These early Anabaptist Christians wishing to restore "New Testament Christianity" were inspired by their belief in a Christ whose lordship stood in direct opposition to temporal authorities who extended rule by the sword. Jesus Christ is the one who submits to the world's violence and exposes its idolatry and ephemeral nature through his cross and resurrection. He thus calls his followers to a fundamental reorientation in life away from false powers that enforce belief and subservience through violence, toward the power of peacemaking and reconciliation made real in Jesus' flesh. The tragedy of "establishment" Christology, in the eyes of the Radical Reformers, is that the One who rejected the sword becomes a tool for the Empire's self-aggrandizement. Violent atonement theories (such as Anselm's) can readily be twisted into justification for the state's ruthless extension of power. Indeed, Anabaptist dissent with the politico-theological establishment often resulted in martyrdom. Between 1525 and 1528 most of the movement's early leaders had been tortured and executed. Their enduring witness compels us to ask in what ways the Prince of Peace has been twisted into a Lord of Empire in our time.

Conquest, Colonialization, and Slavery

During the Reformation period, Europeans continued settling in the Americas. Along with their Western way of life, they brought with them their Christian faith and their desire to win converts. Roman Catholics and Protestants alike made positive contributions to the establishment of the global church that are still celebrated today by indigenous Christian communities. But the contributions were not without ambiguity. Bolstered, in particular, by their conviction that they were "victorious" in Christ, European settlers mistakenly conflated their desire for land and material wealth with their conviction that, as followers of Jesus Christ, God was on their side. The results were disastrous. It became impossible, at times, to differentiate between missionary efforts grounded in the sincere intention to "save souls" and the determination of conquerors to overtake other peoples for their own material gain. The conquerors were unwilling to compromise on the truth of their convictions, particularly their convictions about Jesus Christ. As Adolf von Harnack explains, "It is a gruesome story. On the question of 'Christology' [people] beat their religious doctrines into terrible weapons, and spread fear and intimidation everywhere."[11]

Even when extreme acts of violence were not in evidence, the spread of Christianity was often accomplished in paternalistic ways. The mission system, established by the Roman Catholic Jesuits in Central and South America beginning in the mid-sixteenth century, for centuries not only worked to transplant Christianity to countries such as Brazil, Columbia, Peru, Mexico, Ecuador, Bolivia, and Chile, but also worked, as a decidedly hierarchical system, to establish *Spanish* Christianity. Protestants, in the centuries following the Reformation, could be just as tyrannous. This is evident, for example, in the machinations of the Puritan church in seventeenth-century New England, a church infamous for its witch hunts, attempts to convert disinterested Native Americans, and intolerance of Baptists.

Shared by all of the zealots of the sixteenth to eighteenth centuries was the desire to establish homogenous Christian communities, rather than an appreciation of diversity. This desire was, in part, grounded in their unfortunate christological understanding that to claim Jesus as Lord is tantamount to being converted to a European way of life.

A corollary to colonialism is slavery, also justified by appeal to triumphalistic Christologies. In the United States the enslavement of Native American peoples by the Spaniards was argued on the grounds that they would be "better off" guided by Christian masters than by living lives marked by pagan rituals. The importation and exploitation of African peoples in the eighteenth and nineteenth centuries employed a similar rationale. The analogies of Christ as Master and human beings as Christ's servants were applied to the white master–black slave hierarchy. Slaves were told that, by being obedient to their masters, they were serving Christ. Remarkably, African American slaves turned this faulty Christology on its head, laying claim to a Jesus who would "come soon" and liberate them from their oppression. Recognizing that Jesus was God, as Jacquelyn Grant points out, "meant that White people were not God."[12]

Spanish Conquest of the Americas

On December 21, 1511, Dominican Fray Anton Montesinos preached a sermon denouncing the cruelty, tyranny, and abuse of indigenous peoples in the Americas. Montesinos critiqued the *encomienda* system, in which indigenous peoples were supposedly given basic necessities and education in exchange for hard labor. Standing in the tradition of his Dominican brother, Bartolomé de Las Casas, he was horrified by the unjust deaths of the Indians in Hispaniola and Cuba. The abuse of the *encomienda* system, in addition to his firsthand witness of the slaughter of the indigenous, is what led Las Casas to denounce the Spanish treatment of the indigenous and later the trans-Atlantic slave trade.

The prophetic words of Las Casas, who saw the poor of Jesus Christ in the suffering of the indigenous, can be contrasted to another prominent figure during the *Conquista*, Hernan de Cortes. Cortes was a zealot, and he concretely linked the political and religious dimensions of the *Conquista*. While other conquistadors described their military actions in terms of service to God, no one did so as enthusiastically as Cortes. Cortes conquered in the name of the cross. He interpreted the conquest as a Holy Crusade to free the natives of Mexico from the devil, and he saw himself as God's agent in this endeavor. For Cortes the cross was an emblem of Jesus' suffering for our salvation. He justified the conquest of the Indians as done for the benefit of their own salvation. Cortes saw himself as directed, protected, and aided by the Christian God. He showed great interest in converting the indigenous peoples because they envisaged the establishment of a Christian kingdom to replace the Aztec empire.

Las Casas was deeply troubled by the relationship between the greed of the Spanish and the death of the Indians. Las Casas came to believe that in the Indian, as the poor and oppressed, Christ is present. Cortes, while believing his violent military conquest was sanctioned by divine providence, was blind to the humanity and rationality of the indigenous. In this violent, unequal encounter of civilizations, the worldview of the indigenous of the Americas was shattered. In the name of Christianity the Spaniards ruptured the Indians' cultural and religious ties. Not only their lands but also their political and sociocultural structures were conquered.

Enlightenment Responses

The Enlightenment commitment to the powers and benefits of reason generally led christologists of the eighteenth and nineteenth centuries to think about Jesus Christ from the vantage point of history and logic rather than by beginning with the creedal claims of Nicaea and Chalcedon. G. W. F. Hegel reasoned that the notion of incarnation "made sense," rationally—an infinite God would eventually realize Godself as finite, otherwise that God would be limited to being infinite, and would therefore be limited (and *not* God). David Strauss, determined to discover what we can really know about this man from Nazareth, explored the Jesus of history, publishing *The Life of Jesus* in 1835. (Today, the Jesus Seminar follows in the spirit of Strauss's efforts). While pre-Enlightenment theologians tended to answer the question "Who is Jesus Christ?" by beginning with faith convictions they believed were gifts of the Spirit, Enlightenment theologians tended to think "from below to above," developing claims about Jesus on the basis of empirical evidence. During this period of christological development, it became common to differentiate between the person and work of Jesus Christ. This was because, while it was difficult historically to account for Christ's work, it was almost impossible to say anything empirically verifiable about Christ's person.

One strength of Enlightenment approaches to Christology was that they provided a guard against fideism (fervent belief that claims to be self-evident to those "in the know," refusing discussion or debate). The weakness was that they could not go as far as they wanted to, given that it is impossible to reason one's way to faith claims such as, for example, the *homoousios*. As noted early on in Kant's *The Critique of Pure Reason* (1781), even reason has its limits. While it can enable us to *describe* some things about Jesus of Nazareth (applying empirical and historical standards), it cannot itself lead to faith *in* Jesus Christ.

Enlightenment theologians John Wesley and Friedrich Schleiermacher, aware of the benefits and limits of reason-based Christologies, developed understandings of Jesus Christ that drew from resources from both "below" and "above." Wesley's soteriological emphasis, aiming to improve upon the insights of the Reformers, emphasized human agency as well as divine agency in relationship to Christ's salvific work. While Wesley affirmed *solus Christus*, he argued that human reason and effort did come into play in the completion of our salvation, the process of sanctification. "If [we] remain unrighteous, the righteousness of Christ will profit [us] nothing!" he insisted, encouraging attentiveness to spiritual disciplines and good works.[13]

Schleiermacher, often called the pioneer of modern theology, challenged the Enlightenment split between the "person" and "work" of Christ. Who Jesus is and what Jesus does are mutually informative, he argued, reasoning that we know who Jesus is not only on the basis of historical data but also because we, like him, are human beings who share in some level of God-consciousness. "What we celebrate [at Christmas] is nothing other than ourselves as whole beings—that is, human nature . . . viewed and known from the perspective of the divine,"[14] Schleiermacher insisted. All of us experience what Schleiermacher identifies as "the feeling of absolute dependence"; to be Christlike is to live in deeper recognition of this dependence. Christ himself manifested "fully actualized God-consciousness," according to Schleiermacher.

Schleiermacher thought that Christologies founded in supernaturalism and Christologies founded in empirical verifiability were equally faulty. For Schleiermacher, it was not important to say either that God broke the rules of nature in raising Jesus from the dead or that it is possible to prove, historically, that Jesus rose from the dead. Believing that the supernatural is evident in the workings of the natural, he argued that the important thing about Jesus' resurrection is that Jesus showed us who he really is and therefore who we really are in him.

Schleiermacher and Colonialism

In a section on Christ and miracles in his work *The Christian Faith*, Schleiermacher concludes that "even if it cannot be strictly proved that the Church's power of working miracles has died out, . . . yet in general it is undeniable that, in view of the great advantage in power and civilization which the Christian peoples possess over the non-Christian, . . . the preachers of to-day do not need such signs."[15] A statement like this gives a rare and deep glimpse into the assumptions of modern Christology and what is usually overlooked by its critics—the roots of modernity in colonialist attitudes.

Christ's power of working miracles and even the power of the church to continue those miracles do not need to be questioned per se. No rationalistic shortcut is necessary. It is simply that the achievements and the influence of the colonialist nations make miracles and other supernatural inventions unnecessary. Christology fits right in with the powers that be—Christ mirrors them to such a degree as to become identical with them. This self-congratulatory attitude of the self-proclaimed "civilized" nations seems out of date today. We have become more aware of others and their differences. Our prejudices are not quite as strong any more. Many of the remaining Christian missionaries proclaim dialogue and "inculturation."

Is it possible, however, that Christology in the self-proclaimed "first world," which considers itself postmodern and post-colonial, still proceeds in a similar spirit to that of the old colonialists? Many Christians still display a similar—even if more hidden—confidence that their political, economic, and religious systems are in tune with Christ's own power. Who would dare to question that view?

Challenges of the Twentieth Century

Theologians of the twentieth century were both heavily invested in Enlightenment ideals and profoundly aware of their limitations. Commitment to a rediscovery and analysis of history led to the recognition of the many crimes that have been perpetrated in the name of Christ. The capabilities of reason continued to be honored, but a growing awareness that reason could be utilized for destruction as well as good fed an eagerness for new methodological approaches.

The most pronounced twentieth-century example of the misuse of human reason is the Holocaust and its associated christological exclusionism. The heinous murder of six million Jewish people was justified christologically. Consider this statement, made by the German Christian Church of the

1930s: "Christ, as God the helper and saviour, has, through Hitler, become mighty among us. . . . Hitler [National Socialism] is now the way of the Spirit and Will of God for the church of Christ among the German nation."[16] Challenging the association of Hitler with Jesus Christ, a countercultural Christian movement that self-identified as the Confessing Church issued a theological statement that insisted there is one Lord and that Lord is Christ, not Hitler. Signed by members of the Lutheran, Reformed, and United churches, the Barmen Declaration (1934) "rejected the false doctrine" that Hitler's person and ideology were revelatory, standing alongside the "Word of God" we know in Jesus Christ.[17]

The Holocaust was not the only event of the twentieth century marked by injustice. Here we consider four twentieth-century movements that strove to correct various destructive or passive social forces: the Social Gospel movement, the modern Catholic Incarnational movement, the Neoorthodoxy movement, and the Liberationist Movement. Each of these had a Christocentric focus.

1. *The Social Gospel Movement.* This United States–based movement began late in the nineteenth century and was committed to correcting pervasive social injustices, including child labor abuses, domestic violence, alcoholism, and class inequalities. Many of the suffragettes, including Susan B. Anthony and Elizabeth Cady Stanton, were advocates of this movement because of their shared concerns for social equality and overcoming abuses. Walter Rauschenbusch, a Baptist minister and leading spokesperson of the movement, argued that serving Christ and not money meant that we must work for the equality and happiness of all persons. Exegeting the teachings of Christ, he argued against a strictly capitalistic economy of production. "Christ spoke of the difference between the hireling shepherd who flees and the owner who loves the sheep," he noted, insisting that we cease treating workers as "mere hirelings."[18] Rauschenbusch wondered if, by 3000 C.E., someone would write a book titled *The Decline and Fall of the Christian Empire.* What would the twentieth century be known for? he wondered. His hope was that it would be seen retrospectively as "the real adolescence of humanity, the great emancipation from barbarism and from the paralysis of injustice, and the beginning of a progress in the intellectual, social, and moral life of [humankind] to which all past history has no parallel."[19] And he thought that "social religion," grounded in the teachings and example of Christ, was the key to success.

   Charles Sheldon, a novelist, agreed with Rauschenbusch's remedy to the situation. His book, *In His Steps* (1896), describes the transformation of a town whose community members follow their pastor's suggestion to ask "What would Jesus do?" before each of their actions.

Sheldon's conviction that social behaviors founded in the person and teachings of Christ can actually improve society continues to reverberate in today's popular "What Would Jesus Do?" ("WWJD") movement.

2. *Modern Catholic Incarnational Theology.* Karl Rahner anchors his understanding of Jesus Christ within a rich purview of God's self-communication in history and creation. God wills to reveal Godself to the world in self-giving love, animating the world's response at every moment. From creation to eschaton, God wills to save. The incarnation of Jesus of Nazareth, who is both "the absolute promise of God" and the acceptance of God's self-communication, does not reveal itself in alienating otherness but as creation's own fulfillment. This approach is both evolutionary, as it grounds Christology in a prior understanding of creation and God's self-communication to humanity, and eschatological, as creation reaches its climax in Christ. This modern Roman Catholic sensibility, which is skeptical of any Christology that distances the creature from the Redeemer, is also echoed in the work of Pierre Teilhard de Chardin, who, through dialogue with contemporary science, suggests that the movement of the universe anticipates mystical communion in Christ.
3. *Neoorthodoxy.* This movement emerged largely in response to the crisis in Western culture following the two World Wars. As Langdon Gilkey explains, the "liberal theology" of the nineteenth century was so strongly "wedded" to cultural optimism about humanity's capacity to improve the future that "sensitive Christian leaders" attempted to find a way to locate "the Christian message . . . beyond a culture in crisis."[20] Karl Barth, Emil Brunner, Dietrich Bonhoeffer, and Reinhold and H. Richard Niebuhr are among those identified with Neoorthodoxy. Counteracting the prevailing optimism with regard to natural theology and human reason, these theologians emphasized both the transcendence of God and the impact of sinfulness on creaturely existence. Most importantly, Neoorthodox theologians revived the Reformation principle of Christocentrism, upholding the centrality of Christ to Christian belief and to the work of systematic theology. What God is up to in the world cannot be ascertained on the basis of reason and persuasive argument, they insisted, but is known on the basis of God's self-revelation in Jesus Christ. Emphasizing divine transcendence, sinfulness, and the centrality of Christ, they believed, would counteract the tendency of their contemporary religious and political leaders to project an understanding of God founded in their own image and preferences. The charge to discern who God is by looking to Jesus Christ was used by Barth and Bonhoeffer (leaders in the Confessing Church movement) to condemn the German Christians for treating Hitler as a messiah-figure. Bonhoeffer was executed by the Third Reich due to his commitments, which included his involvement in a plot to assassinate Hitler.

4. *The Liberationist Movement.* Liberation theologies drew from the insights of both modern Catholic thought and the spirit of Vatican II and Neoorthodoxy while at the same time being deeply critical of certain aspects of these developments. In his classic text, *A Theology of Liberation* (original Spanish edition, 1971), Gustavo Gutiérrez presents Jesus Christ as Liberator. Christologies developed from the vantage point of the marginalized, he argues, understand Christ to redeem us from sinfulness that is more than a personal problem. Sin is, rather, a systemic problem that "demands a radical liberation, which in turn . . . implies a political liberation . . . [which] is the gift which Christ offers us."[21] Leonardo Boff, in *Jesus Christ Liberator*, argues that liberation Christology participates in the "messianic task" of "freeing all human beings and bringing them to complete fulfillment." This is "what Jesus wanted more than anything else in this world," according to Boff.[22] The Christologies of Gutiérrez, Boff, and other Latin American liberation theologians sought, in part, to challenge European and North American privilege, exhorting wealthy Christians across the globe to repent of their excesses and join in solidarity with the poor.

   Other liberation theologies have emerged in the last 25 years to present understandings of Christ that challenge the status quo. African American liberation theologians, including James Cone, hold that "Jesus is Black," arguing that we know God is the "God of the Oppressed" because Jesus, a Jew, understood what it means to be marginalized.[23] Similarly, feminist theologians, including Rosemary Radford Ruether and Elizabeth Johnson, argue that Jesus Christ challenges patriarchal presumptions about the character of God's power. The incarnation itself represents the "*kenosis* of the Father" the emptying of the patriarchal throne,[24] the condemnation of oppressive hierarchies. Christ's death on the cross is an expression not of how God's honor is satisfied but of "God's Compassion Poured Out" in the person of Christ, who, again, enters fully into the suffering of the marginalized.[25] With Christian theologians from every time and place, liberationists hold that who Jesus Christ is makes a difference to how we live in relationship to God and each other.

Asian Christologies

Asian theologies are marked by their efforts to articulate Christian theology that is *of* Asia versus merely *in* Asia. In the words of Sri Lankan theologian Aloysius Pieris, an authentic Asian theology emerges only if Christianity is baptized in the "Jordan of Asian religion" and the "Calvary of Asian poverty." This double and nonexclusive concern for inculturation and liberation mark many of the theological developments emerging from Asia in the late twentieth and early twenty-first centuries. In the area of Christology, this double baptism has resulted in various constructive proposals.

For Pieris, an authentic Christology must speak to the poverty of the Asian peoples and the religiousness of non-Christian religions. In a continent where less than 3 percent of the population is Christian, Asian theology must recognize and take seriously the soteriological implications of non-Christian religions. Asian theology must also speak of the masses of poor people in Asia. Pieris understands a central feature of Jesus' ministry as his struggle against mammon, wealth, and greed. The poverty of the cross is a direct denunciation of the mammon of the elite classes.

The feminist theology of Chung Hyun Kyung uses Asian women's experiences as a starting point for the theological task. Women's narratives and popular religious practices are a central source. Chung is critical of the traditional christological images of Jesus as Suffering Servant, Lord, and Emmanuel, for they disempower and marginalize women. The Suffering Servant image, while allowing for Asian women to understand Jesus as accompanying them in their own suffering, reinforces humility and subservience in women, oppressive values in a patriarchal society. Jesus' Lordship becomes a means of perpetuating patriarchal lordship. Jesus as Emmanuel shows, once again, God's accompaniment. This image has been distorted, however, to become a means of emphasizing Jesus' maleness and consequently male ecclesial authority. Chung offers the images of Jesus as shaman and woman as an alternative to these patriarchal models. These offer contemporary, creative ways of conceiving Jesus' accompaniment and salvific presence in the lives of Asian women. In a similar vein to Pieris, Chung stresses the masses of oppressed Asian peoples (the *minjung*) as central to christological formulations. Jesus as the *minjung* within the *minjung* is a liberative model that highlights an inculturated and liberationist Christology. The unity of these two strands is a hallmark of Asian Christologies.

Constructive Proposals

Who is Jesus Christ today? How does the significance of his ministry, life, death, and resurrection speak to Christians in the contemporary world? While the constructive proposals presented here to answer these questions do not cover the entire scope and nature of christological reflection, they do address concerns that are especially pressing today. The first proposal tackles the question of Jesus' uniqueness, often referred to as the scandal of particularity. This proposal examines the scandalous claim that God became incarnate in one human being, with all the limits, gifts, and flaws of humanity, and what significance that reality has for Christians. The second proposal addresses the significance of Jesus' suffering humanity, especially how it is used as the interpretive lens through which our suffering and the groaning of all creation is viewed. Underlying this section is the question of redemptive suffering: the significance of Jesus' suffering in light of the suffering of the entire creation. The third proposal is soteriologically focused, addressing Jesus' salvific role in human history. This section explores the understanding of Jesus as Prophet, Priest, and King. Special attention is given to the marketplace co-option of Christology, and how, if revisited, these offices can work to reclaim the Christ of scripture. The last proposal attends to Christian triumphalism and exclusivism. This proposal raises the question of whether confessing Jesus as the Way automatically invalidates the truth-claims of other religious traditions. Although divergent in focus, the authors of these four proposals share a common commitment to doing Christology from the points of pressure, where death threatens to overwhelm life. For each author, Jesus as the Christ brings good news to the spaces of life most in need of healing.

The Scandal of Particularity

Cynthia L. Rigby

A popular song asks what it would be like if God were really "one of us."[26] Christian believers through the ages have claimed that God *is* one of us, in the person of Jesus Christ. But how can it be that the infinite God is known to us in one particular and limited person? Such an idea is scandalous! It throws into question some of our common conceptions about what God is like, challenging us to rethink who we are in relationship to this God.

Søren Kierkegaard explains it this way. He argues that most people are "offended" by the idea that God became incarnate as a real, particular, limited human being. We are offended because we think we know what God is like: God is holy, infinite, and all-powerful. This, we conclude, means that God is *not* a person struggling with temptation, a man who dies as a criminal, or a baby squirming in a manger. But Kierkegaard thinks the notion of the incarnation tugs at a much deeper nerve than our perceptions of God. Anxious to promote our own piety, he explains, we might *think* we are offended by what the incarnation tells us about God. What really offends us, however, is what the incarnation says about *us*. If God *has* entered into our particular, limited existence, this means that we are, indeed, truly known and unconditionally accepted by God. It is easier to hide behind offense than it is to bear grace, according to Kierkegaard. It is easier to believe that Jesus never failed a math test than it is to live into God's embrace of all that we are.[27]

An Encounter with Jesus

The importance of the scandal of particularity is seen in the story of Jesus' baptism by John as told in Matthew 3. John is not planning to baptize Jesus. Just before Jesus approaches him, John is lecturing on the difference between the baptism he offers and the baptism the Coming One would offer. "I baptize you with water for repentance," John explains, "but one who is more powerful than I is coming after me; I am not worthy to carry his sandals. He will baptize you with the Holy Spirit and fire" (v. 11).

Perhaps it doesn't surprise us that, just as John is giving a speech about the miraculous things the Messiah will do, Jesus approaches as the living fulfillment of John's words. Certainly it makes sense that, if Jesus is the one the nation of Israel has been waiting for, he is worthy of a grand entrance. But in between John's dramatic words and the seeming imprimatur of the Trinity, there is something that doesn't seem to fit: Jesus asks to be baptized. Why is John taken aback—even scandalized—by this request?

There are several reasons for John's reaction. First, John understands his own importance to pale in comparison with that of Jesus. He has just been explaining to the crowds that he is not worthy, even, of carrying Jesus' sandals. He must have been shocked when Jesus asked him not only to carry his shoes but to act in a priestly and prophetic role toward him, baptizing him as a mark of repentance.

Second, John does not seem to think that Jesus needs to be baptized. After all, Jesus is the one who is coming to judge hypocrisy and unfruitfulness (see vv. 7–12). He is the one who will judge; he is not among those who should repent in preparation for the coming judgment.

Third, John is scandalized by Jesus' request because he believes the Coming One will be extraordinary; to baptize Jesus is, in some sense, to place him alongside all of the other ordinary people whom John has baptized.

John finally agrees to do the baptism after Jesus explains that his baptism is, indeed, consistent with the "fulfill[ment of] all righteousness" (v. 15). Often this verse is interpreted as though Jesus is assuring John that it "couldn't hurt" to be baptized, as though the baptism itself is incidental to Jesus' person and ministry one way or the other. On the contrary, Jesus seems to convince John that his baptism is indispensable to his spiritual state.

In his encounter with Jesus, John bore his weight on his arms, lowered him into the water, and raised him up. Looking at his face for a split second through the mottled water of the Jordan, did John wonder just for a moment whether his prophetic words concerning Jesus were wrong? Could this frail, dependent human being really be holding a winnowing fork and ready to begin baptizing with the Holy Spirit and with fire?

John is scandalized because Jesus is not what he expected. The Messiah, sent by God, should not need pastoral care and should not need to repent. John is scandalized because he expects his work to be replaced by the more complete work of Christ. On the contrary, however, John is asked to make a genuine contribution to the life and spiritual identity of the Messiah. How can this be?[28]

The Church's Question

Christian believers have always wondered how it can be that God has entered into the ordinariness and limitation of human existence. In the early centuries of the church, debates raged over whether and how we can say that Jesus Christ is human and divine at the same time. If Jesus is an ordinary human being who needs a mother to rock him to sleep and who actually feels the pain of the cross, how can we at the same time say that he is the omnipotent Creator of the universe, the Word made flesh? In the third century, Arius tried to avoid making scandalous claims about God by saying that Jesus is not exactly the same as God (*homoousios*), but that he is *like* God (*homoiousios*). In 325 at the Council of Nicaea, the church declared that Arius was wrong, upholding the surprising claim that this particular human being—the one who was, as the Apostles' Creed testifies, born of Mary and suffered under Pontius Pilate—was, indeed, of the "same stuff" as God. In the fourth century several theologians tried to avoid ascribing the suffering of Jesus to the being of God by arguing that God dwelled only in the mind of Christ (the *nous*) but not in his body. Along the same lines, theologians such as Nestorius did not want to call Mary the "bearer of God" because they thought it was incomprehensible to imagine that the infinite God could be born as a particular baby to a particular woman. Notice that those who resisted the suffering of God and an understanding of Mary as God-bearer were all trying to avoid the scandal of saying that this particular historical figure, a man who was born of Mary and died on the cross, was and is God.

Remarkably, the church again affirmed these scandalous ideas in 451, when at the Council of Chalcedon the statement was made that Jesus Christ is "one person in two natures, fully human and fully divine, without confusion and without change, without separation and without division." Also affirmed at Chalcedon was Mary's identity as *theotokos*, the bearer of God. It is important to note that Christian believers who embraced these statements did not claim to understand how it was, exactly, that Jesus Christ could be human and divine at the same time, without being half human and half divine. They did not pretend to comprehend how God could enter into the womb of a woman and be born a creature. But they thought it was important to affirm these scandalous claims because, in part, they believed they made for a stronger soteriology.

One of the most universally agreed-upon statements, in the course of the christological debates, was commonly attributed to the great fourth-century theologian, Gregory of Nazianzus. "That which is not assumed is not saved," these early believers agreed. If God has not assumed our humanity *really*, in all of its frailty and creatureliness, then we cannot rightly say that God is with us. At Nicaea and Chalcedon, the church committed to living with the scandalous questions raised by the confession that God is with us in the particular event and person of Jesus of Nazareth. In short, to live with the scandal is to lay claim to the hope that we are, indeed, redeemed. It is not only to resist complacency in relation to what Jesus Christ reveals about God (and God's relationship to us), but to engage continuously what the incarnation says about us (and our relationship to God).

Scandalous Challenges

Nervous about facing the scandal head-on, human beings historically have too often assigned Jesus' particularities a privileged status rather than recognizing that the divine attributes might need to be rethought. Instead of marveling that God has entered into historical existence with us, we have elevated the details of this existence in ways that avoid their scandalous implications.

This has been done at great expense to all, but especially to those who share fewer of the particularities of Jesus of Nazareth. Clearly, none of us is a first-century Palestinian Jew. Fortunately, we do not know much about Jesus' physical appearance. But we do know he was a human being, which has led us to claim humanity as superior to other forms of creatureliness and to justify our anthropocentrism. And, certainly, he was male. As Daphne Hampson has pointed out, since the time of Nicaea, Jesus' maleness as God-in-the-flesh has been used to promote male humanity as normative humanity. Females have been seen, consequently, as less human. The historical fact of Jesus' maleness has been used to justify the corporeal punishment of wives by their husbands, barring women from ordained ministry (for example, the Roman Catholic Church prohibits women's ordination because they do not bear physical resemblance to Christ), and the use of exclusive language.

These abuses of the fact of Jesus' particular gender surely overlook the significance of the scandal itself. The fundamental claim of the incarnational event is not that some should be privileged over others but that God has entered into existence with, and included, all. The God known to be infinite entered into the limitation of creaturely existence as a particular, limited creature and asked to be baptized. In doing this, God in Jesus Christ showed us not only that God is with us but that we as particular, limited beings are included in the life and work of God.

God with Us in the Dust

Karen Baker-Fletcher

Christians today still struggle with the concept of the incarnation of God and the notion that the historical Jesus is the Son of God. It is easy for Christians in an increasingly scientific age to take an adoptionist stance in which Jesus *becomes* the Son of God. This makes sense to those who want to avoid questions of divine conception and virgin births. Jesus becomes a unique human being, prophet, and rabbi in this rubric. But this is not satisfactory to those in the Jewish tradition who argue that Jesus was not such a unique rabbi and prophet, that there were other rabbis, such as Hillel, who taught a similar message.

Then there is the question of the impassibility of God that asks whether or not God can suffer or be harmed in any way. If, according to scripture, Jesus is "Emmanuel," God with us in the flesh and therefore God "as one of us," it does not make biblical sense to say that God is impassible, unfeeling. Neoclassical philosophers and process theologians give particular attention to the writings of the early church fathers, who described God as distant, removed, unfeeling. Feminists, womanists, and liberationists join with process thinkers, pointing to the God of the Hebrew and Christian scriptures as responsive and even able to change God's mind. God responds to prayer, to joy, to pain and suffering. Jesus, Emmanuel, God with us, embodies an empathic God.

But recently theologians have wanted to move beyond an anthropocentric understanding of God and reality. Eco-theologians note that a literal translation of Gen. 2:7 reads that God created *adam*, which means "earth creature," from the dust of *adamah*, which means earth. Like contemporary science, Gen. 2:7 suggests that humanity is made from matter, from dust. Some theologians then argue that if God is incarnate in Jesus, and if human beings are made from the dust of the earth, then Jesus is not only "flesh and spirit" or "human and divine," but Jesus is also *earthy* and *divine*. A womanist theologian might employ Alice Walker's term *earthling* to describe what it means to be an earth creature. The point is that Jesus is not only of the flesh and of God, but of the earth and of God. If Jesus is God with us, then Jesus is God with us in the very elements—dust, water, air, and energy—that make up our bodies.[29]

What, then, is the difference between Jesus and other humans? It is not that we are like Jesus in the suffering we humans endure. It is the other way around; Jesus is like us, relates to us, identifies with us, having experienced the violent consequences of human sin. Jesus is like us because Jesus has been sinned against. He therefore can identify with human suffering. Jesus is like us because Jesus also feasts and rejoices with us. But we are not Christs. Jesus does not sin but is sinned against. Jesus is unlike us because Jesus is the Christ, the anointed one, one with God. God alone in Christ can promise restoration, redemption, salvation. As human beings we may participate in this activity, but we do not initiate it.

If Christ feels with us and suffers with us, what does this mean as we consider the classical understanding that God sacrifices his only son on the cross? Delores Williams, a womanist theologian, suggests that popular understandings of "sacrifice" all too often misrepresent the meaning of the cross. What is most important about Jesus is his life and ministry.[30] Doctrines of atonement that represent Jesus as God's ransom to Satan or as a substitution sacrifice raise questions of theodicy—God's responsibility for evil. Further, historically women have been placed in the role of sacrificial victim, frequently encouraged to stay in abusive domestic relationships in the name of redemptive suffering. In certain misrepresentations Jesus comes across as suicidal, and God comes across as an abusive father. Women, in too many instances, have played the role of sacrificial lamb.

This is a problem. Some feminist and womanist theologians reinterpret Jesus' willingness to die for his teachings as (in Sharon Welch's words) an "ethic of risk."[31] That is, Jesus knew the consequences of his actions; nevertheless, he willingly engaged in a ministry of healing, salvation, and liberation. He entered this ministry fully aware that some would be against him. An ethic of risk does not have to *replace* life-affirming, carefully delineated interpretations of sacrifice. However, an ethic of risk offers a viable alternative for those who experience the word *sacrifice* as misused and abused and void of positive meaning and power. Viewing Jesus' life as an ethic of risk helps clarify that God does not crucify his son; rather human beings commit the violent act of crucifixion. The cross then becomes a symbol of human sinfulness and not a symbol of an abusive God.

The cross is also a symbol of Christ's love and willingness for his body to endure death in order to affirm the truth of the victory of life over death, good over evil, righteousness over unrighteousness, divine justice over human justice. Because of the resurrection, the cross is not victorious; Christ is victorious. While the cross cannot be the *only* symbol of Christ, it also cannot be eliminated from Christian God-talk. We do need to remember it to repent of violence. But it is not the crucifixion that makes Christ unique. Others were crucified before Jesus, with Jesus, and after Jesus. What makes the story of Jesus the Christ distinctive is the resurrection, which is not victory over mortality but victory over evil. The ministry of Jesus of Nazareth continues in the risen Christ. In his ministry of healing, forgiving, and saving grace Jesus uniquely reveals the power of abundant life.

Jesus is willing to lose his life for the sake of life. Jesus can do this because Jesus, the Word of God at creation, is life and the very power of life is in Jesus. The Word that was with God at Creation, who heals and delivers in Mark, recreates through the power of the Spirit in the love of God the Creator. The redemption and restoration available to creation in the resurrection is an act of continuous, life-affirming, creative activity. God is revealed in the life and ministry of Jesus as well as in ongoing processes of renewal. Christ is Emmanuel, God with us, embodied and incarnate creation that is restored and redeemed by grace. Through God who is with us we experience divine love in and with creation.

For those who claim to be followers of Jesus, if Jesus exemplifies our full humanity in flesh and spirit, then Jesus is dust and spirit. To imitate the life of Jesus, then, requires loving and just relationship with the earth and one another. It means that we need to remember that the very dust of the earth is of intrinsic value to God, who creates something out of seeming nothingness. According to Matthew 25, Jesus calls humankind to love the least of these and the stranger. Through the will to power, human beings proudly make excuses to continue oppressing the least of these. Many of us who are affected by ecological injustice have awakened to participate in grassroots movements for nontoxic environments. But many of us have also failed to wake up to the realities of our deteriorating environment. Some of us would become active if we were more informed. But some of us have chosen not to listen or give conscious effort to these problems. When we are reluctant to listen, we reinforce not only the earth's oppression but our own, because it is from the dust of the earth that we are created and it is the earth that sustains the earth creatures that we are, creatures called into restored relationship through Jesus the Christ, who has dwelt and dwells among us.

Christ's Offices Reconsidered

Joerg Rieger

"If Jesus saves, I want to know where he shops." This piece of graffiti seen on a bathroom wall some time ago is of course a deliberate misreading of the verb "to save" and the related noun, "salvation," but it raises deeper questions. Are we still able to think about Jesus Christ and salvation without being pulled into the vortex of the capitalist economy, which surrounds us from all sides and determines more and more who we are? Our lives are increasingly shaped by the flow of capital, both positively and negatively. This is true not only in business and industry where one would expect it, but increasingly also in the academy and the churches. As a result, even some of our most cherished visions of Christ and salvation do not escape the fact that money and matters of the economy control much of our lives and shape the way we think.

Theology, whether consciously or unconsciously, is easily plugged into the market and its support structures. Notions like Christ's love and charity are reconceived in terms of the economic principles of compassionate conservatism, Christ's justice in terms of the expanding "war on terrorism" and the expansion of free-market economics, Christ's redemption in terms of the freedom of the market from challenges like the starvation of millions of children each year, and salvation through Christ in terms of success or, as stated above, savings in the (super)market. If these sorts of things are not addressed, they will continue to reshape our images of Christ from below the surface and thus pose a greater danger than most openly pronounced heresies. Can theological reflection on the work of Christ in salvation help us to see through these distortions and develop an alternative vision?

Salvation in Christ has often been understood in terms of three functions or "offices" of Christ. But how can the language of Christ as king (or as ruler, to use a more gender-inclusive term), as priest, or as prophet resist the lurings of the market and the kinds of distortions that we never notice? The reflections of John Calvin, sixteenth-century father of Reformed theology, and of Friedrich Schleiermacher, nineteenth-century father of liberal Protestant theology, can help us recognize the problem and push us to pursue new perspectives.

In our globalizing late capitalist economy, the image of Christ as ruler is no longer seen in terms of the feudalist monarch or the powerful politician of the modern state. Christ as ruler is now more easily confused with the image of the manager or the C.E.O. In this case, Christ is the one who "gets the job done no matter what," who stands for those who believe that they have pulled themselves up by their own bootstraps, and who advocates the survival of the fittest when economic times are tough. In this context Calvin's insistence that Christ's reign is "not earthly or carnal . . . but spiritual" and "lifts us up even to eternal life" might provide some resistance to the capitalist value system. Clearly, Christ is not about money. But Calvin still works with the (social) images of "up" and "down," and he promotes Christ's "wealth" and "benefits" in a way that can easily be misread today.[32] After all, the transactions of wealth itself are increasingly relegated to the virtual realm, and the meaning of life in late capitalism is not determined by sheer "earthly" monetary wealth but by the "spiritual" things one can do with it. Our capitalist values include the "spiritual values" of happiness, fun, and entertainment. As Karl Marx and some of the other critics of capitalism made us realize, one of the prime challenges of capitalism has to do with the ways in which it influences and reshapes the spiritual realm, and so Calvin's emphasis on the spiritual does not automatically provide us with an alternative to late capitalism.

Schleiermacher's interpretation of Christ as ruler/king displays a reading that picks up Calvin's insights but is better adapted to the requirements of the fledgling capitalism of his own time: "His kingly power is not immediately concerned with the disposal and arrangement of the things of this world which means that nothing remains as the immediate sphere of His kingship but the inner life of men individually and in their relation to each other."[33] In other words, Schleiermacher argues that Christ's work of salvation is effective "in a purely inward way," related to "sanctification" and "edification," in effect providing strength to those entrepreneurial spirits of early capitalism—the members of the middle class.[34] In addition to the fact that neither Calvin nor Schleiermacher sees Christ as ruler over "worldly" affairs or the public domain and thus they leave plenty of room for the economy to run its own course, both offer little resistance and no alternatives to the top-down perspectives of the global economy.

What would happen, however, if we took a look at these things not from the top down but from the bottom up and without playing off against each other categories like "worldly" and "spiritual"—a perspective that is more faithful to Jesus' own ministry and self-understanding (see, for example, Luke 4:18–19)? If we view the global situation not from the top but from the bottom of real life—for instance, from the perspective of the pain inflicted by economic disparities—another image emerges. Christ as ruler does not join forces with the powers that be—this point appears to be certain, despite all other questions that might need to be raised about the shape of Jesus' life. On the contrary, Christ initiates subversion at all levels—for instance, by healing people on the Sabbath, which is why the powerful (both the "spiritual" Pharisees and the "worldly" Herodians) conspire to kill him very early on in his ministry (Mark 3:6). This strange view of Christ as ruler is validated also by the images of Christ after Good Friday and Easter. Christ as ruler, who sits at the right hand of God the Father (as we confess in the Apostles' Creed), is none other than the crucified Christ who shares the fate of the marginalized not only in his life but also in his death on a cross: the marks on his hands and his side do not go away, not even after the resurrection (John 20:24-29). This Christ, validated by a resurrection that does not allow for Christian triumphalism, redefines what we mean by the terms *ruler* and *power*. What a challenge to the status quo!

The second image of Christ as priest is easily adapted to the spirit of the age by conjuring up images of all kinds of healers, pop-psychology redeemers, and lifestyle coaches who ride the waves of the market by promising us happiness and life without conflict if we make use of their services. Calvin's interpretation of Christ as priest who "obtain(s) God's favor for us and appease(s) his wrath" and who furthermore enables us to become "companions in this great office,"[35] is concerned with metaphysical truths but is now easily co-opted by these contemporary healers and redeemers and provides little resistance to them since it does not touch the life-and-death conflicts on the ground. Schleiermacher's efforts to conform Christ's priestly office to the commonly acknowledged moral standards of his day open the door even wider to the logic of late capitalism in all its forms. He argues that we must not ascribe to Christ as priest "any other rules of conduct than such as we have to recognize as valid for us all"[36] and thus rejects an understanding of Christ's death as voluntary, since this would go against common sense and be immoral. Christ, therefore, cannot go against the grain. Common to both Calvin and Schleiermacher is the concern to restore harmony "at the top." Calvin is concerned with metaphysical dimensions, Schleiermacher with social ones. These particular concerns for harmony display little interest in the tensions that remain on the underside.

Viewed from the underside, however, the role of Christ as priest appears in broader perspective. Here the ongoing tensions of everyday life and the tensions that erupt as our various moral standards clash can no longer be overlooked. Christ as priest does not heal and redeem by a band-aid approach to suffering (John 8:36), by explaining it away like other religious characters (John 9:2), or by appeasing the powers that be (see Jesus' temptations, in which he resists power as offered by the status quo, Luke 4:5–8). No opiate and no sedatives are involved. Christ as priest redeems by activating the resistance factor of suffering and pain. This is the "stumbling block of the cross" and "God's foolishness" that the apostle Paul mentions, things that are incomprehensible to those in power (1 Cor. 1:22–25). It is precisely as the "suffering servant" (Jesus himself was no doubt familiar with the passages in Isaiah 53; see, for example, Luke 24:13–27) and as the one who loses his life because he does not give in that Christ resists the powers that be, moves to overcome suffering by breaking the vicious cycle of violence, and promotes a different sort of life (Mark 8:35).

The final image of Christ as prophet seems to hold more promise for a view of salvation that presents a real alternative and resists the late capitalist status quo. Yet even this image tends to get pulled into the vortex of the free-market economy. Here the prophet becomes the professional advocate, for example, who (having friends in high places) seeks to address injustice by calling for charity or by developing new social programs to help the victims. Unfortunately, both charity and social programs often end up with a mere reintegration of the marginalized into the status quo (neither is designed to challenge the system) and thus prevent real change and transformation—the things for which true prophets call. Calvin's interpretation goes in a somewhat different direction. For Calvin, Christ is prophet when he communicates doctrine and wisdom to us. As prophet, Christ has indeed a critical edge, since he critiques all other wisdom: "Outside Christ there is nothing worth knowing." Yet there is once again talk about *benefits*—the word that makes late capitalists listen up: "All who by faith perceive what he is like have grasped the whole immensity of heavenly benefits."[37] What prevents classical passages like these from being used in support of another group of prophets like the self-improvement prophets of New Age? There is now a spiritual market that runs hand in hand with the late capitalist market, and doctrine and wisdom are among the commodities sold to those who can afford them. How do we discern true doctrine in this situation? Schleiermacher's interpretation of Christ as prophet (who teaches, prophesies, and works miracles) takes the problem to the next level. There are areas where the economic and political successes of the modern world have been so impressive, he believes, that Christians take over significant parts of the role of Christ. One example is the working of miracles. Schleiermacher reasons that "even if it cannot be strictly proved that the Church's power of working miracles has died out, . . . yet in general it is undeniable that, in view of the great advantage in power and civilization which the Christian peoples possess over the non-Christian, . . . the preachers of today do not need such signs."[38] Christ's power is reflected in the power of modern Christianity and its economic and political advances. While few people today would phrase things in such a blatant way, does Schleiermacher's statement not reflect an attitude that is still with us and that drives our prophetic commitment for "outreach" to the various "disadvantaged" places around the globe?

Viewed from the places where the pressure is greatest, however, our image of Christ as prophet changes. Christ as prophet forces us to face the deep roots of actual tensions and sufferings in the present and how they are produced by the powers that be (Mark 12:1–12). The critical function of Christ as prophet, indicated in Calvin's work, might force us to start over. Christ as prophet points out the real tensions and pain of life (this is the difference between Jesus and the Pharisees and other religious leaders, Matt. 23:23–26; Luke 13:10–17). Christ as prophet leads to a self-critical attitude that lays open the ways in which we are all part of the system and encourages repentance and a new start (Luke 13:1–5). In this spirit, Christ as prophet brings liberation from the powers that be and helps us develop alternative ways of living that include new doctrine and new vision in organic fashion (John 8:31–32).

Christ's work of salvation, therefore, is complex and takes place on various levels. It cannot be co-opted by the powers that be, and it opens new ways of living that, as Calvin reminds us, cannot be confined within the limits of the current age but push forward into eternity. Precisely in this way it makes a tremendous difference here and now.

Christology and Triumphalism

David Jensen

Throughout the Gospels, Jesus asks questions of his audience: questions about riches, about discipleship, about the reign of God, about himself. The rabbi Jesus, particularly in the Synoptic Gospels, poses more questions than he answers; when he asks questions about himself, moreover, he invites others to respond. These responses have varied throughout the conflicted ages of the church: he is the Son of God, teacher of Wisdom, Messiah, sacrificial Lamb, bearer of perfect God-consciousness, New Being, Liberator, the

Word. Abundant answers to Jesus' question are in some ways indispensable: no single formulation can do justice to the One whom Christians proclaim as Savior and to the new life he brings.

Jesus Christ forms the center of Christian vision. To proclaim Jesus as the Christ is to claim that he reveals not a vague pattern discernible elsewhere in the universe, but the decisive inbreaking of God. Theologians often dub this the scandal of particularity—that the universal God encounters us in the life, death, and resurrection of an itinerant Jewish preacher from Nazareth. To encounter him is not to encounter any person, but God's self-revelation. Who is this Jesus? Though there is much that we cannot recover about his person, there is much about him that is strikingly different from the places where he is often proclaimed: he calls our attention to the others whom Christology has generally ignored.

Jesus of Nazareth is a human being, a first-century Palestinian Jew who lived under the rule of Caesar. To claim Jesus as human is to question any theological approach that denies his humanity, such as Docetism, or that sees his body as a sordid prelude to full revelation. The *human being* Jesus is the revelation of God. Second, to claim him as a Jew is to deny Christian supercessionism. If Christians claim that Jesus replaces Israel's covenant, we reject the One we call Savior, for his person and message cannot be understood apart from that covenant. Finally, to claim him as a subject of Rome is to recognize that Jesus lived and died under the yoke of a military regime: Jesus is a colonized Jew who proclaims a reign that flies in the face of all systems that would destroy otherness for the sake of uniformity. Jesus confronts the empire of his time *and* our time; in the United States, he confronts us.

As Jesus begins his public ministry, he reiterates the promise of Israel's covenant, particularly as it relates to the poor, stranger, and outcast. Torah grants privilege to the vulnerable in the land, in part because it recalls the vulnerability of Israel's own experience of being held captive slaves in a foreign land: "When an alien resides with you in your land, you shall not oppress the alien. The alien who resides with you shall be to you as the citizen among you; you shall love the alien as yourself, for you were aliens in the land of Egypt: I am the LORD your God" (Lev. 19:33–34). Echoing these strands, the Gospels focus on occasions when Jesus breaks bread with the despised and rejected. He shares meals with the prostitutes and tax collectors, who defy the bounds of respectability. Jesus' table fellowship embodies the privilege Torah grants strangers, demanding that an embrace of others is indispensable to living out the covenant.

To encounter Jesus is also to come face-to-face with a subject of Roman imperial rule, a colonized Jew. Like most colonial systems, the prosperity of the heralded *Pax Romana* was made possible by the relentless extraction of money, labor, and duty from the colonized. If peace benefited a few in Rome, it broke the backs of thousands. Jesus lived under the yoke of an empire that exploited non-Romans for the benefit of Rome; as the church proclaims him alive today, he calls our attention to all peoples who struggle under the boot of globalization and the grinding wheels of American neo-colonialism. When "others" labor in sweatshops on behalf of the cheap goods that we devour, only cheap grace ignores those others or pretends that they, too, benefit from the New World Order. As we come to grips with Jesus' question, "Who do you say that I am?" we come face-to-face with the Jew Jesus, a colonized subject who drew renewed attention to the covenant of Israel, especially in relation to the vulnerable in his midst. The identity of Jesus is bound up with communities that Christians have often maligned and neglected: the poor, the stranger, the Jew. To confess him as the Christ is to be drawn toward the life of communities not necessarily our own.

Jesus' question, however, does not rest in a consideration of his ministry alone—it also points to God's presence in Christ. This affirmation of Christ's divinity is perhaps the best example of a cosmic sensibility in Christianity. Captured in biblical resources as diverse as the prologue to the Gospel of John and the Letter to the Colossians, Christ is the point at which God's embrace of the world is made flesh. When Christians affirm the divinity of Christ, his revelation of God's fullness, however, an odd reversal occurs. God's presence in Christ is characterized more by vulnerability, interconnection, and relationship with others than it is by invincibility, aseity (absolute autonomy), and triumph. To claim God as *revealed* in Jesus Christ is to claim God's presence not only in the glorious events of his life but also in moments of defeat and his scandalous association with outcasts. The story of Jesus, the story of God's revelation in him, is less about triumph than it is about dining with nobodies, healing the ostracized, rejection, crucifixion, and an empty tomb. Jesus is the revelation of God because he calls us to new relation with the God of covenant—a God who is revealed not in the triumph of theology or marketplace but in the vulnerable, human connections that Jesus makes with others, even unto death. Jesus incarnates, makes real in the flesh, the relationships into which we are called as human beings: our relationship with God, with others, and with the cosmos itself. The God of incarnation reveals Godself not in suffocating sameness, but in the varied, pulsing life of the universe itself: a life that is lived constantly with *others*.

This is the God of Covenant, who exists not solely in Godself, but in vulnerable relationship with a people. This is a God who relentlessly seeks others, even when those others turn away. To claim Christ as the revelation of God is also to be drawn out of a life that seeks only its own.

Even in the quintessential moment of Christian triumph this eccentric dynamic becomes visible. When Christians proclaim Christ as risen, we recall that the God revealed in Christ is a God of life, that whatever death-dealing forces threaten and overwhelm, life abides in Christ. Not far from Golgotha lies the empty tomb and the resurrection story. As Mark's narration reminds us, the Risen Christ cannot be contained but goes on ahead of Mary the mother of James, Mary Magdalene, and Salome: "He has been raised; he is not here. . . . But go, tell his disciples and Peter that *he is going ahead of you* to Galilee" (Mark 16:6–7). The Risen Christ eludes the grasp of those who expect to find him; he goes on ahead to Galilee, at the threshold of the Gentile world. Here the restless movement of otherness in the Christian imagination surfaces again. The Risen Christ returns to Galilee, to the birth of Jesus' ministry, but also to the edge of a world of difference. The resurrection involves both a return of sorts to the place where Jesus' Jewish ministry began and a launching of his movement in a non-Jewish world. Many are the faces who will be confronted by the question, "Who do you say that I am?" Many, too, are the responses. In the midst of these voices, Christians are open to new life in the surprising contexts that it arises. To nourish that life in the company of others is to respond to the God revealed in Christ.

To encounter Jesus, to come face-to-face with the vulnerable Palestinian Jew of the Gospels, is also to come face-to-face with difference: with a man different from ourselves, with communities radically different from the church, with faces whom many would rather ignore. In a North American context dominated by marketplace ideology, moreover, the different others to whom Christ calls us can be reduced to commodities for the Empire. Yet the Good News itself struggles to resist commodification. Difference is writ large over the story of Jesus; sameness is prized little. What scandal it is when the figure of Christ is twisted into a mask for homogeneity. The distinctiveness of Christian confession is that this *particular* human being embodies the God of creation, the God whose creative life is in the glory of all things, fully alive. Christians look to Christ for the revelation of God, and this revelation spills over into the world.

Jesus Christ invites us to welcome the world—this vulnerable, humorous, painful, tragic, joyous world—as our home. To proclaim Jesus as

Messiah is to locate Christian confession in the midst of a world where others *do not* make this proclamation. Coming face-to-face with the Christian scandal of particularity Jesus Christ opens Christians to an immeasurably wider world, to abundant life with others. Of course, to stress this encounter is also to resist the death-dealing horrors that have always seen otherness as a scandal. To proclaim Christ is not only to say "yes" to a world of difference but also to say "no" to those powers in the world such as racism, anti-Semitism, sexism, consumerism, and militarism that would destroy difference under a religious banner. For Christians, Jesus Christ is Savior precisely because he releases us for new life: he saves us from a prison of sin that sees the self as the center and for abundant life with others, with God, and with creation. The God revealed in Christ is not chiefly a God of triumph but a God of vulnerable relationship with particular human beings. To live the Christian life, to follow Christ, is not to live to oneself but with others. Confessing Christ releases us to fuller life, hearing others' voices and challenges, responding to the ways in which Christ's question addresses them. Without them, we stand alone.

5

Church

James H. Evans, Mary McClintock Fulkerson, Roger Haight, Bradford E. Hinze, Leonard M. Hummel, Paul Lakeland, M. Douglas Meeks, Amy Platinga Pauw (chapter editor), Jamie T. Phelps, Kathleen M. Sands, Craig Stein, Kathryn Tanner

A Southern Baptist church has been expelled from a regional group of churches after its pastor baptized two gay men and welcomed them into the congregation. Delegates to a closed meeting of the Cabarrus Baptist Association in Concord, N.C., voted 250 to 11 on Monday to withdraw McGill Baptist Church's membership. The regional group of about 80 churches is affiliated with the Southern Baptist Convention. The Rev. Randy Wadford, missions director for the association, read a statement after the vote in which he said, "The homosexual lifestyle is contrary to God's will and plan for mankind. . . . To allow individuals into the membership of a local church without evidence or testimony of true repentance is to condone the old lifestyle."

The Rev. Steve Ayers, pastor of the 800-member church, responded: "The kingdom of God is about love, about God's grace and mercy. When a church becomes so judgmental that it won't accept people into their fellowship, it is a sad, sad day."[1]

◆

Gerald, the Bahamian minister of Good Samaritan United Methodist Church, welcomes his congregation in booming, rich tones as they enter for the Thursday night service, calling each member by name. Some wander into the sanctuary as if by accident; some walk in haltingly, slowly. Some of the congregants are wheeled in by attendants and parked near the pulpit. Here comes Cathy, striding in with her arms stretched straight out. She heads right for me and I give her a hug, meeting her delighted face with a big smile of my own. Here comes Marcy, screaming loudly. Two women attendants sit to either side of her, restraining her arms throughout the service. Philip ambles in grinning and sits next to me. About thirty people gather to worship here as the room fills with sounds of delight mixed with other, harder to identify noises.

Gerald starts the announcements by asking, "What's new?" Bill has been to Virginia Beach, or so translates Johnny, the only one who can understand him. "Beach" sets off a reaction; the delighted cry "beach!" is heard from several places in the room. Gerald calls for a round of applause for Bill. As everyone claps, Bill's face is split with smiles. New people are introduced and get a hand, too. Bob, an elderly white man dressed in coveralls with fourteen pens in the front bib pocket, comes in late and walks straight to the pulpit. He hands a folder to Gerald, who reads aloud the enclosed certificate of merit Bob has received for "supporting literacy." At Gerald's urging we clap for Bob, who takes a bow and sits down. Gerald intones a familiar call to worship, and the community echoes each line back. Some say it, some say something like it; the sound is chaotic and rich, more textured than the clear, etched noise of a group speaking in unison.

One of the highlights of the service is music. Instruments are handed out, and the energy level rises visibly with the start of hymn singing. Philip pops up out of his seat, walks to the front, and takes the microphone. Ignoring Gerald's attempt to turn him to face the community, Philip sings the entire hymn with his back to us. As we clap for Philip after the hymn, he raises his arms in a victory salute, then flexes his muscles as he strikes a body-builder pose.

Pastor Gerald reads the scripture lesson about God's giving of the Ten Commandments to Moses (Exod. 20:1–20). Engaging folks as he walks around, Gerald uses a large erase board to solicit responses to the story. "Who is afraid of thunder? Raise your hand." Some raise hands. "Who's afraid of lightning?" More hands. Bob volunteers commentary: "and lying on your back, the clouds above roll by." Mary, a tiny woman sitting frozen in a wheelchair, begins to squeal very loudly. An attendant begins to rub her forehead in a soothing way. Gerald draws stone tablets to represent the commandments on the board and asks for the community to name the commandments, one by one. Laughing and cajoling and chiding, he gets all manner of responses. A couple look at their Bibles, but the job of enumerating the commands is taken very seriously, as can be seen by the several fingers raised triumphantly in the air. "First!" "Two!" "Second," call out several of the men. Getting the "next number" seems as important as getting the content of the commandment. Gerald writes them down, and Bob adds, "love me as you love your neighbor." Gerald chuckles and holds him off to get others to speak. Concluding that love of God is summed up with Jesus' commandment to love our neighbor as ourselves, Gerald asks, "Who is my neighbor?" Marcy, a young woman with Down's syndrome, calls out, "ME!!" Gerald roars, "Yes, Marcy!" and begins to name people to the group: "Marcy is your neighbor. Bill is your neighbor. Philip and Ralph are your neighbors. And we can do it because God loves us; God helps us. We couldn't do it without God." A couple of attendants say "Amen!" This highly cognitive part of the service is relieved by "Jesus Loves Me," the most boisterous hymn of the service. Its familiarity rouses those who have been gazing off into space; they respond clapping, sometimes waving their arms. Tim sits curved, thin, and curled in his wheelchair; his body trembles a bit. His smile tells us that his guttural noises are sounds of joy. The Lord's Prayer is another familiar litany, and the resonance of voices echoing (if not repeating) fills the room. Philip is asked to blow out the candles; he stops in the middle of his task, looks up, and starts talking. Waiting, Gerald lets him pray, and Philip repeats the same sound over and over. When he finally sits down, Philip gets a round of applause.

◆

Ruth is a thirty-five-year-old divorced businesswoman with an eight-year-old son and two-year-old daughter. The daughter of an African American, Baptist father and a German, Lutheran mother, Ruth sometimes refers to herself as an "Afro-Saxon." Her divorce came about primarily because "the marriage had been quite abusive. As a result of my husband's persistent pattern of physical abuse I was at first unable to finish my course work at a very prestigious university." Ruth reports that she has feared the "punishment of God" for having filed for a divorce, and that this fear took on the very specific form of her belief that God had punished her through the proceedings and verdict of the divorce court.

> And, I'm not getting any money and I'm risking my job being here with this idiotic lawyer and this wicked man. And now the judge says to me, "I'm going to force you to have your children visit with this very wicked man because he took the time to come here and tell me that that's what he wants." Lord, what is this? And I cried and I said, "Lord, can you give me some faith?"

Abandoned by her husband, Ruth also felt abandoned by God.

> I get to the point where I say, "OK, Lord, you know you've brought me this far and we're out here in the wilderness and instead of giving me the extra money that I need to take care of these children, I'm going further into debt."

In addition to feeling abandoned by both her husband and God, Ruth relates her fear of the former to her fear of the latter. Furthermore, she identifies Luther's refrain throughout his commentary on the Ten Commandments in his Small Catechism that the faithful are to "fear, love, and trust God" as something that binds those fears together.

> I love and fear God. And you can't have that tension in a relationship. You can't be afraid of someone and also trust them deeply. You can accept discipline from someone that you love, and be in fear of their anger and their wrath, and not also really, really trust them. Because if they're just random in their anger, it makes you crazy. It can make you nuts. That's what abused women go through. They love this man who any Friday night could come home with flowers or a gun.

Later, Ruth calmly remarks, "I'm such a Lutheran. . . . I love the liturgy and I love Bach. I love the way the catechism contemplates God because it is exactly my experience."[2]

State of the Question

The Graced Problems and Problematic Graces of the Church

For every problem facing the Christian churches, for every trouble or limitation that threatens its existence and effectiveness, there can be found, in these very struggles themselves, occasions of grace and invitations to healing.

Yet even the most profound graces, the very gifts of God, received by a community of faith that has specified its identity and mission, can easily become problematic and distorted because of the incompetent and sinful character of the church and of its individual members. Given this complexity and opaqueness in the church's reality, how is one to describe the church? As paradox? As *simul iustus et peccator* (both holy and sinful)? As a broken sign and instrument of the resurrected Lord and indwelling Spirit? What is this church, its identity and mission, and what is it becoming?

When Christians in whatever context around the world speak and think about the church, the discussion inevitably turns to a consideration of certain basic metaphors. The church is spoken of as the body of Christ, the temple of the Holy Spirit, the people of God, and the household of God to name but a few. These and many other motifs are found in the Christian scriptures. In every age, as well, Christians have wrestled with a basic conflict between an idealized vision of the church and the harsh realities of the church in history, between pure image and everyday messy reality, between the visible and the invisible church. And in every age people have found in these metaphors ways to think and measure church, ways to describe the church, its identity and mission, and its failings, not only what it is, but what it is still becoming.

The Body of Christ and the Problematic of (Dis)embodiment: Race, Class, Gender

Paul the apostle introduced the metaphor of the community as the body of Christ in order to confront several conflictual situations in the nascent church. In Corinth the community wrestled with all kinds of gifted individuals, women and men, who made claims to communal authority, and with the communities' need for order in their assemblies. In Antioch, Galatia, and Rome there were culturally charged tensions between Jews and Christians, and between Jewish Christians and Gentile Christians about the practical requirements of membership; these tensions have reverberated in ethnic and racial conflicts ever since. In every community Paul dealt with he confronted situations of slavery, economic hardship, and inequalities. And those situations in which scandal and shame were associated with sexuality and gender, as these influenced personal and social practices, were topics that Paul did not hesitate to speak out on. Paul addressed these vexing problems. Some of the cultural differences he addressed are prized or celebrated today. Others, such as poverty or racism, evoke a moral consensus, even if there are still disagreements about policies to address them. Others, such as sexuality and gender issues, still evoke contention and strife. He deals with all of them by focusing on the transforming reality of Jesus Christ as the new Adam who forms all into one body. "Just as the body is one and has many members, and all the members of the body, though many, are one body, so it is with Christ. For in the one Spirit we were all baptized into one body—Jews or Greeks, slaves or free" (1 Cor. 12:12–13). This is a living body incorporated into the resurrected Lord: "For as all die in Adam, so all will be made alive in Christ" (1 Cor. 15:22). "As many of you as were baptized into Christ have clothed yourselves with Christ. There is no longer Jew or Greek, there is no longer slave or free, there is no longer male and female; for all of you are one in Christ Jesus" (Gal. 3:27–28; cf. Col. 3:9–11). Through baptism and sharing in the Lord's Supper, the scriptures attest, Christians become one in the body of Christ. This Pauline trope is extended in the epistle to the Ephesians, which speaks of the union of husband and wife in marriage in terms of the passage from Genesis, "and the two will become one flesh," which is applied to Christ and the church, Christ as husband, wife as bride (Eph. 5:31, 32).

The notion of a corporeal unity and interaction among the many members of the church is by no means a dead metaphor, but it is an ambiguous one. By affirming the bodily unity of the church as the physical extension of the risen Lord in the world, have differences been erased? Has the distinction between Jew and Greek been transcended into a "third race" that elides racial differences? Has the distinction between male and female been reproduced on one level within the church (portrayed as the bride of Christ) and elaborated in a social stratification often based on gender (ordained as male and non-ordained as female; headship with the family limited to males), even as the distinction has been denied on another level by the intimation of a belief in a new unity (or equality) of male and female, beyond gender, an androgynous body? Have heteronomous social and economic distinctions been maintained in the interest of ecclesial and civil harmony? The challenge facing the church is to rethink Paul's metaphor of the body of Christ not only in terms of the diversity of charismatic gifts but also in terms of the variety of physical and social bodies that offer gifts needed to enrich and bring to completion the fullness of the body of Christ.

The People of God and the Problematic of Divisions

The notion of the people of God is the oldest and most influential description of Israel and the Christian church. As the story of the tower of Babel was often interpreted, the ill-conceived efforts to construct their own way to God had profound consequences; the one people of God who had one language was scattered to the four corners of the world, creating many peoples with many different languages (Gen. 11:6, 8). Abraham is called to lead the chosen people of God (Gen. 12:1–3) into a promised land. And after the promise of prosperity is violated by acts of bondage, a bondage that in turn is vanquished by liberation, God instructs the many freed tribes that "I will take you as my people, and I will be your God" (Exod. 6:7). Whatever it is that unites the people of God in ancient Israel—blood, covenant, or both—their sinfulness, their idolatry, their acts of injustice threaten and destroy the relationship of this people with God: "you are not my people and I am not your God" (Hos. 1:9). The prophets keep alive the hope of recreating the people of God anew (Jer. 31:33). In this prophetic tradition, John the Baptist rails against presumption and announces new prospects: "'Do not presume to say to yourselves, "We have Abraham as our ancestor"; for I tell you, God is able from these stones to raise up children to Abraham'" (Matt. 3:9). "Once you were not a people, but now you are God's people" (1 Pet. 2:10). All nations are called to be disciples of Jesus and so become God's chosen people (Matt. 28:19–20). Herein lies a profound challenge: if people of all nations are to become the people of God by becoming followers of Jesus, what of all those other children of Abraham? The followers of Moses? The followers of Mohammed? The three Abrahamic traditions all lay claim to being the chosen people of God, and yet they have warred against each other in the name of that election. Pogroms, crusades, holy wars, holocausts have been the bitter and poisonous fruit of the encounters among these chosen ones of God. Can the three Abraham traditions learn from their histories of hatred and bloodshed a new way to repudiate their restricted vision of being a people of God? Even more challenging, how can the followers of the ancient traditions of the Vedas, of the Buddha, of Lao Tzu, of Confucius, and of the many indigenous religious traditions around the world, be honored and respected as peoples of faith and traditions of wisdom by the Abrahamic peoples for the light they shed on the diversity of God's people?

Temple of the Spirit, Priestly People, and the Problematic of Authority

Every Christian is through baptism and by the gifts of the Spirit to contribute to the building up of the church and to share responsibility for fulfilling the life and mission of the church. At the same time, Christians have always looked to individuals within the community to exercise leadership, people who have received gifts and cultivated talents of leadership needed to sustain the life of the community and to foster the participation of all the baptized in ministry and mission. Whether these leaders are identified with the offices of bishops, presbyters, and deacons, or with the positions of ministers, pastors, and elders, these roles have their deepest rationale in the gospel, in the apostolic tradition, and in the messianic anointing of Jesus Christ as priest, prophet, and king.

In ancient Israel, the temple in Jerusalem was the place where people and priests offered sacrifices to express gratitude and praise to God, to voice contrition and loving communion. In the Christian era, after the destruction of the temple in Jerusalem at the hands of the Romans, the people called church became identified with the temple and with the priests associated with the temple. "Do you not know that you are God's temple and that God's Spirit dwells in you?" (1 Cor. 3:16; cf. 2 Cor. 6:16). "You are a chosen race, a royal priesthood, a holy nation, God's own people, in order that you may proclaim the mighty acts of him who called you out of darkness into his marvelous light" (1 Pet. 2:9).

The church is the temple of the Spirit and a holy priesthood when the gift of authority given to the entire community is exercised authentically and received in various ways by all the members of the church. But the church, as temple and priesthood, becomes corrupt when either the charismatic gifts of the faithful or the gifts of leadership and office are not ordered to the good of the community but are turned into the goods of the individual or selected groups within the community. The graces of the charism and leadership become problematic when the authority of one is pitted against the authority of the other. The powers associated with charismatic gifts and offices can be corrupted by egoism and sectarianism as well as by the tyranny of the mob or the majority.

The Household of God, the Economy of Communion, and the Problematic of Globalization

The Christian community became church in households. Women, men, and families invited the followers of Jesus into their houses to break bread, share a cup of wine, and so enter into a fellowship, a communion with one another and with God. Much like the vagabonds and strangers who ate and drank with Jesus and became a community of friends, a new extended family, so too the people who gathered in homes came to form a church that was known as the household of God.

> So then you are no longer strangers and aliens, but you are citizens with the saints and also members of the household of God, built upon the foundation of the apostles and prophets, with Christ Jesus himself as the cornerstone. In him the whole structure is joined together and grows into a holy temple in the Lord; in whom you also are built into a dwelling place for God.
>
> (Eph. 2:19–22)

The household of God is based on an economy of communion. This communion is special because it is created by people partaking of the body and blood of Christ (1 Cor. 10:16) and by receiving the gift of God's Spirit in baptism (Acts 8:20; Romans 8). Individual members are said to participate in the divine life itself (2 Pet. 1:4). The economy of communion that characterizes the household of God is distinguished by a surplus of gift and gratitude, rooted in the divine source of communion and its appropriate response, each person giving to excess because of the excess they have received, each one living a life of gratitude for the abundance given. This economy is a dynamic communion of diverse individuals with diverse gifts, as communion is the relational matrix within which individuation is made possible. The divine fullness (*pleroma*) breaks in and through the shining forth of the individual gifts and callings of the cosmos, ecospheres, continents, nations, cultures, tribes, clans, communities, and each person. This economy of communion requires a commitment to living in solidarity with all the members of the community, but especially with those in need, and working for the common good of all, for justice in the world. The economy of communion is based on the principle of subsidiarity, in which human needs and problems are addressed by varying smaller and more local communities and institutions, but not without the support, and when necessary intervention and involvement, of neighboring local communities and sometime larger national and international networks and institutions.

The household of God with its economy of communion must confront the problems caused by false economic orders that violate the surplus of gift giving and gratitude and that obscure differences into an oppressive global uniformity. Solidarity and the struggle for justice are replaced by market-driven forces that privilege individuals and elite groups in a utilitarian doctrine of election. The powers of the market militate against subsidiarity by working against both local self-determination and the appropriate use of larger institutional involvement in the cause of the common good and justice for all. The household of God is called to be "the pillar and bulwark of the truth" (1 Tim. 3:15) against an oppressive economy of globalization that offers an alien and false order.

But it is not only alien economies that threaten the household of God. It is also the case that the grace that funds the household of God and the economy of communion can itself become corrupted and problematic. Family wounds inflicted by members of the household can be covered up, repressed, and denied by a code of family secrets, feeding an insidious culture of false communion. Every house has rules that are given for the individual and the group to flourish in and through communion, and often these rules serve this purpose. But the church can be corrupted, and individuals and groups within it harmed, by house rules that violate the diversity of gifts and callings or that hinder the authentic individuation processes that reflect the ongoing manifestations of the *pleroma* of God.

The church communicates the promise of the coming reign of God. The church is not the realization of God's reign on earth, but it does offer fragmentary signs of its coming. The problems that the church faces in every age require that the church is at its truest when it witnesses to the mystery of Christ's death and resurrection, when the Spirit is present in the ongoing conversion and repentance of the church from all that is sinful and false within it.

Historical Development

In this brief discussion of the history of ecclesiology, or the study of the self-understanding of the church, we will use the word *church* to mean the entire Christian movement; one might say "the great church," and not any one of its communions or denominations. We will focus on its development in the West. We also understand the church to be constituted in or by two relationships: it stands in relation to the world, or the history and society in which it exists, and in relation to God. This second relationship, more than the former, accounts for the church's unity: the whole church is sustained internally by one Christ, one revelation, one faith, and one Spirit. But externally shared bonds of unity also hold it together: one scripture, one baptism, one Eucharist. These two relationships cannot be separated; they mutually influence each other. For example, the historical form of the church influences the way the church relates to God; reciprocally, the way the church interacts with the world should, and ideally does, flow from the energy received from its relation to God.

This simultaneous double relationship that constitutes the church leads us to study it in particular ways. One can say that the church is one reality understood in two languages, the language of history and sociology and the language of faith and doctrine. A balanced ecclesiology will strive to understand the church not just in the doctrinal language with which it describes itself, nor merely through a social-scientific account of its actual behavior, but through a mutually critical combination of the two languages. The church, moreover, always possesses the dual character of what it actually is and what it is called to be.

A thorough knowledge of any historical organization requires study of its historical origins, its purpose, its trajectory across the times and territories of its constituents. But to represent such a history in a few pages from the perspective of the church as it is today inevitably communicates a false teleology and blinds the reader to the contingency of each critical stage of the passage from the past. Such a synopsis cannot communicate the unknown character of the future that formed the horizon of every community-forming decision. Recognizing these limitations and ambiguities we nevertheless propose to divide the history of the church into six broad stages, highlighting certain events and individuals in each stage for the light they shed on the development of the Christian church.

Origins: First and Second Centuries

Over the centuries the church has consistently appealed to the metaphors of the New Testament for its doctrinal self-understanding: the people of God, the body of Christ, the temple of the Spirit, the household of God. More recently advances have been made in understanding the historical and sociological dynamics of the gradual development of the church. The mutually critical merging of these two kinds of investigation has generated a much more nuanced understanding of the origin of the church.

A good example of this is the traditional doctrine that Jesus founded the church. Jesus research and historical examination of the development of the church during the first century offer little evidence that Jesus intended or actually did set up a body of followers distinct or separated off from the pluralistic Judaism of his day. Jesus' aim was to renew Judaism, and thus he did not intend what became the Christian church. But it is entirely evident that Jesus provided the very foundation of what went forward in his name. Jesus is the foundation of the church, both historically in the group of followers he left behind and theologically as the Resurrected One. Jesus lies at the very center of the Christian church; the church rests on its foundation in Jesus.

That Jesus did not set up the church means that its organizational structure developed historically. Among the many landmarks in the gradual separation from Judaism and assumption of an autonomous identity, the decision taken related to the congregation in Antioch around the year 48 carried great significance, namely, that circumcision was not a requirement for conversion to the Jesus movement. The shift from being a sect within Judaism to an autonomous Christian church unfolded gradually over the course of the first century and at different paces in different places. Some churches were influenced more by the Jewish synagogue; others had a looser structure of leadership. Some of those who exercised leadership were apostles or missionaries, bishops or overseers, presbyters or elders, teachers, deacons, prophets. It is difficult to distinguish how and when these functions were routinized into offices in the various churches. In short, the New Testament provides no single pattern of church order.

It was not until the second century that closure came to the process by which the church was founded. Two developments brought this about. The first was the emergence of the monarchical episcopacy, and the second was the formation of the scriptures into a canon, which provided in a loose sense a kind of constitution for the whole movement and the classic, inspired, statement of its faith. During the course of the second century the ministerial and organizational structure of the church was solidified in the offices of bishop, presbyter, and deacon; the churches were also animated by prophets and teachers. This basic structure, despite many variations within the ministries themselves, remained intact until the sixteenth century.

Post-Constantinian Christianity: Differentiation of Eastern and Western Churches

The church developed considerably during the second and third centuries: numerical growth, expansion of territories, the overflow from cities into surrounding rural areas, solidification of offices and liturgical patterns, corporate internalization of values and ethical norms. Tertullian's writings at the turn of the second century and in the third century show a Christian community in Carthage in an ambiguous and tense relationship with an "idolatrous" society and culture. Hippolytus's *The Apostolic Tradition* shows the organizational structure of the church in Rome and its patterns of liturgy and sacrament. Cyprian's treatises and letters provide a view of a fairly stable Christian church in Carthage undergoing persecution in the mid-third century. (Throughout this period Christians lived in relation to imperial persecution like Californians to earthquakes: though only occasional, they could be devastating.)

While for many people the peace of Constantine may have changed little, for the whole church it transformed everything. In the course of the fourth century Christianity became the established religion of the Roman Empire. In the wake of this, two contrasting Christian and ecclesiological ideals, reflecting the horizontal and vertical relationships that define the church, began to flourish in the fourth century: political theology and monasticism. Political theology, not to be confused with a twentieth-century title, saw the church as the new kingdom of God in history. Eusebius of Caesaria thought of Constantine as the new Moses at the head of a Christian empire. This idea springs up again and again in the course of church history and self-understanding. By contrast, monasticism, which has origins much earlier in various forms of Christian asceticism, flourished in Asia Minor and Egypt before spreading to Europe in the late fourth and early fifth centuries. The writings of John Cassian contain psychological and spiritual insights that inform monastic life to the present time; they stress a kind of serious, contemplative Christianity that finds expression in retreat from the world of public life, prayer, surrender of the will in obedience to God in a rule of life. Monastic ideals filled the void of the martyr-heroes from the time of persecution.

The office of the papacy in the Western church began to take visible form when the bishop of Rome began to exercise his authority in what in effect became a Western patriarchate. Pope Damasus in the fourth century consolidated the authority of the Roman church within Rome's sphere of influence, and Pope Leo I in the fifth century and Pope Gregory I at the end of the sixth were outstanding church leaders in the West who solidified the symbolic authority of the papacy.

Augustine's major contribution to Western ecclesiology came in reaction against the Donatist demand for holy ministers; his thought combines a practical realism with a Platonic symbolic idealism. This is seen in both his conception of the church and his sacramental theology. In fact, far from being an existentially holy community, the ever-expanding real-life church of the empire was riddled with sin and filled with sinners. But within the sinful church one finds those who are graced and destined for final salvation: this is the inner, spiritual, true church within the church. This important distinction will take on many new and different nuances in new situations in subsequent church history. In any case, ministers too were no more holy or morally pure than anyone else, and if the power of the sacraments depended on their virtue, one would never be sure of God's saving grace. The sacraments, then, are this-worldly empirical signs of God's transcendent and always efficacious grace, whether or not the minister is worthy. This objectification of the church's holiness corresponded with the new post-Constantinian sociology of the church.

Finally, Constantine's establishing the new capital of his empire in the East begins the gradual politicization and territorial separation between two extended families within the church already distinguished by language and culture. In the sixth century the Eastern church flourished in every way under the long reign of Justinian, and the Western church gradually spread to the North and West.

Eleventh-Century Gregorian Reform: Western Christendom

How could one possibly summarize the development of the church during the middle ages? The formation of Christendom, one Europe/one church, was contained within the continent but massive in complexity, solid institutionally but constantly challenged by secular rulers, the creator of a theology both critical and sophisticated but increasingly detached from real life, spiritually energized with Franciscan ideals but wealthy and worldly, rich in religious art and liturgical symbolism but plagued by mechanism and superstition. A list of institutions distinctive of the medieval church will symbolize its totalizing significance: popes, cardinals, emperors, kings, prince-bishops, and Lateran Councils; cathedral schools, Aristotle, universities, scholastic theology, and canon law; crusades and inquisitions; Dominicans, Franciscans, abbots, abbesses, third orders of men and women; confraternities and the feast of Corpus Christi; mystics, nominalists, and the *devotio moderna*; schism, conciliarism, renaissance, and papal corruption. And then note the people who left a permanent legacy: Hildebrand (Gregory VII), Anselm, Bernard of Clairvaux, Dominic, Francis, Clare, Thomas Aquinas, Bonaventure, Bridget of Sweden, Meister Eckhart, Marsilius of Padua, John Wyclif, Catherine of Siena, Gabriel Biel, Thomas à Kempis, Jean Gerson, Juan de Torquemada, Erasmus.

From this deep and lasting tradition we can isolate some dominant developments. One is the Gregorian Reform, which was named after Gregory VII but extended through the last half of the eleventh century. Its stated aim was to rescue the church from the control of secular rulers and its clergy and churches from lay ownership. Through monastic inspiration, newly gained political power, and the spiritual power of excommunication, the papacy gradually gained moral and legislative authority throughout Christendom. Conciliarist theory also ranks among the major contributions of the middle ages to ecclesiology. Conciliarism was a movement of thought, consisting of various theories of how the fundamental religious authority of the church was mediated to office holders through the whole community, or *congregatio fidelium*, especially when it was gathered in a general council. Medieval mysticism also contributed to what became a fundamental spirituality for clerics, religious, and lay people and came to classical expression in the *Imitation of Christ* of Thomas à Kempis. For centuries thereafter no book, after the Bible, was read more than *Imitation*. This spirituality also animated the confraternities—voluntary organizations or guilds—many with explicitly religious and benevolent goals. These organizations and the spirituality they embodied and nurtured form a positive bridge between the Middle Ages and the sixteenth century. The Reformation was not pure reaction but built upon a persistent late medieval spiritual desire for reform of the church in head and members.

Sixteenth-Century Protestant Reformation: Ecclesiological Pluralism

In ecclesiological terms, the sixteenth century was revolutionary; no century ushered in changes of a more radical and permanent kind. After it, the broad church would become a pluralism of churches in a wholly new sense. To illustrate this, it will be enough to name and represent briefly five significantly different ecclesiologies.

Martin Luther's ecclesiology focused on the congregation and unfolded within the imaginative framework of a local district or principality. That is, the whole or universal church is not institutionally or juridically organized. The church is defined as the assembly of saints or the congregation of the faithful; its central institution is ministry of the word; a true church is the congregation in which the gospel is taught purely and the sacraments administered rightly; each congregation has the divine right of appointing its ministers. Luther dismantled clerical structure with a doctrine of the priesthood of all believers. He did not lay down an organizational structure for the regional church; such structures were of secondary importance to the life of faith of the congregation. In fact, the Lutheran churches were organized regionally within the context of secular rule.

John Calvin's ecclesiology presented the church as God's historical instrument for mediating the salvation achieved by Jesus Christ. He developed an explicit organizational model for the church, with a definite institutional structure for the local congregation and the immediate region. The four offices of the church are drawn from the New Testament: pastors, teachers, elders, and deacons. A larger synod of ministers regulates the churches of a region. Authority in the church comes from the Word of God but is exercised in the community through a system of checks and balances. The four offices of ministry each has its sphere of authority that influences the others, but the consistory of elders has a final word.

Richard Hooker summarized the ecclesiology of the Church of England at the end of the sixteenth century. Theologically, the church is the body of Christ on earth. Hooker explicitly recognized the principle of ecclesiological pluralism, that is, the validity of various forms of church organization for different regions of the church. The three pillars of this ecclesiology define its distinctiveness. First, it is a national church, and the monarch serves as the supreme administrator or governor reminiscent of Constantine. Second, *The Book of Common Prayer* renders the standard forms of worship—the Eucharist, litanies, and other prayers, rites, and rituals—into comely English. This provides the whole national church with a common intelligible pattern of prayer and devotion. Third, *The Thirty-Nine Articles of Religion* defined in this initial reformation period the standard articles of faith. These articles strove to be both open to the Reformation movements on the continent and conservative of the Catholic tradition.

Menno Simons in the Netherlands and John Smyth, a charismatic Englishman who emigrated to Amsterdam in what turned out to be the last years of his life, can represent a "free church" tradition in ecclesiology.[3] This is a congregationally based ecclesiology, but not hostile to a larger association with oversight of like-minded churches. Two distinctive features of this ecclesiology might be called the principle of voluntary association and the principle of interiority. Regarding the first, these churches were founded on the conviction that the other Reformers did not go far enough; these churches thus stand over against both the Roman Church and other Protestant churches. The principle of voluntary association is reinforced by lack of social support and even persecution. As a result this ecclesiology insists on intense personal faith, which is emphasized by the rejection of infant baptism. The church also explicitly strives to be an existentially holy community as witnessed by a moral or upright life, and this is structurally supported by a common use of the ban or excommunication. The orders of ministry are simplified, with the two main offices being that of preaching and teaching on the one hand and oversight or governance on the other. This ecclesiology is also significant in mediating the idea of a separation of church and civil government and religious pluralism within a single civic or political unity.

Finally, the Roman Church's ecclesiology, which did not significantly develop in the course of the sixteenth century,[4] despite major reform measures still stands structurally in continuity with the church of the late fifteenth and early sixteenth centuries and in rather bold contrast with the free church. In contrast with the principle of personal faith, the church is an objective society into which one is baptized as an infant; in contrast to the principle of voluntary association, membership in this church is necessary for one's salvation; in contrast to the principle of spiritual interiority, the Augustinian principle of the objectivity of sacrament and the holiness of hierarchical institution as historical mediators of God's grace are emphasized; in contrast with an existentially holy community, this ecclesiology, again following Augustine, admits itself as a church of sinners; and in contrast to being over against the world and society, it is an integral part and public player in both.

In sum, by the end of the sixteenth century, a monolithic Christendom had disappeared, and in its place the Western church was a pluralistic patchwork of different churches displaying a wide variety of ecclesiologies. But pluralism within a particular society or political realm was not yet a commonly held value or principle.

Modern Ecclesiology and a Renewed Missionary Movement

We jump to the nineteenth century in order to note a distinctive development in ecclesiology in the thought of Friedrich Schleiermacher. He introduced experience as the basis of theology, while recognizing scripture, the witness to originating Christian consciousness, as its source. His view of the church rests most firmly on theological principles and bears an intrinsic relationship to the redemptive work of Christ. The salvific work of Christ consists in releasing into history Christian faith, a form of God-consciousness that is mediated through the Christian community. The church thus embodies God's presence as Spirit, and its mission is to spread this faith consciousness to all of history. Schleiermacher also converted his historical consciousness into a scheme whereby he discerned two levels in the defining structures of any given church: the church is made up of invariant and variable elements. Invariant elements hold a formal, constitutive place in the church as such. They are scripture, the ministry of the word, baptism, the Lord's Supper, the power of the keys or discipline of excommunication, and prayer in the name of Jesus. But more important for the discipline of ecclesiology and more indicative of its modernity are the mutable elements of the church. Schleiermacher recognized the church as a mixture of divine and human forces, the latter making it always defective in unity and mixed with error. The divine element or Spirit, however, is a constant pressure for unity, truth, and reform. Thus Schleiermacher expected pluralism among the churches, but every true church contains within itself a dynamism toward unity, so that no Christian church should completely break communion with another.

The ecclesiology of Schleiermacher had a rough Roman Catholic parallel in some respects in the early work of Johann Adam Möhler. Möhler did not develop an integral ecclesiology but outlined an ecclesiological vision of a Spirit-centered organic community that developed across history. The principle of development allowed for genuine difference across time and could function analogously among churches in different cultures at any given time. Communion ecclesiology provided an opening to a pluralistic ecclesiology. Unfortunately, Möhler did not develop this line of thinking further but seemed to reverse direction toward denominationalism. Moreover, the Roman Catholic Church, reacting against modernity and laicism in the mid-nineteenth century, developed an increasingly narrow ecclesiology that, strengthened by Vatican I's definition of papal infallibility, was disseminated to the whole church through the manuals written by the Roman School of ecclesiology at the Gregorian University right up to Vatican II.[5]

Landmarks in Twentieth-Century Ecclesiology

One can discern two broad reactions to the historical consciousness that gradually developed in the course of the nineteenth century. Some Christian churches turned to forms of authoritarianism. Various forms of evangelical fundamentalism sought protection in the inerrancy of scripture; dogmatic fundamentalism characterized the Roman Catholic Church's assertion of pure authority against modernism. More generally, however, the mainline churches gradually adjusted to the demands of historicity.

An Ecumenical Statement on the Notes of the Church

Being the creature of God's own Word and Spirit the Church of God is one, holy, catholic, and apostolic. These essential attributes of the Church are not its own qualities but are fully rooted in its dependence upon God through his Word and Spirit. It is one because the God who binds it to himself by Word and Spirit is the one creator and redeemer making the Church a foretaste and instrument for the redemption of all created reality. It is holy because God is the holy one who in Jesus Christ has overcome all unholiness, sanctifying the Church by his word of forgiveness in the Holy Spirit and making it his own, the body of Christ. It is catholic because God is the fullness of life who through Word and Spirit makes the Church the place and instrument of his saving, life-giving, fulfilling presence wherever it is, thereby offering the fullness of the revealed Word, all the means of salvation to people of every nation, race, class, sex and culture. It is apostolic because the Word of God that creates and sustains the Church is the Gospel primarily and normatively borne witness to by the apostles, making the communion of the faithful a community that lives in, and is responsible for, the succession of the apostolic truth throughout the ages.

The Church is that part of humanity which already participates in the communion of God, in faith, hope, and glorification of God's name, and lives as a communion of redeemed persons. . . . Yet at the same time the Church in its human dimension, insofar as it is made up of human beings who though being members of the body of Christ are still subject to the conditions of this world, is itself affected by these conditions.

The oneness which belongs to the very nature of the Church and is already given to it in Jesus Christ stands in contrast to the actual divisions between the churches. . . . The essential holiness of the Church stands in contrast to sin, individual as well as communal, which in the course of the Church's history again and again has disfigured its witness and run counter to its true nature and vocation. . . . The essential catholicity of the Church is confronted with a fragmentation of its life, a contradictory preaching of the truth. The consequence is that the integrity of the Gospel is not adequately preached to all. . . . The essential apostolicity of the Church stands in contrast to shortcomings and errors of the churches in their proclamation of the Word of God.[6]

Five positive ecclesiological developments in the course of the twentieth century build constructively on the premises of modernity. The first is the ecumenical movement and the formation of the World Council of Churches. The desire and actual movement of the churches to come together in some form of unity emerged in the twentieth century out of the great missionary expansion of the previous century and are also a product of modernity. A second major Christian event of the twentieth century is the Second Vatican Council (1962–1965). Internally, the council addressed the place and functions of bishops in the church, an issue that had never really been addressed by the Roman Church. But more importantly the Catholic Church reversed its stance of utter hostility to modernity, and in a constructive statement of the church's relation to the modern world it signaled at the same time a more positive and less defensive relationship to other Christian churches and to other religions. Third, the rise of women in official positions of leadership in the church constitutes a protracted ecclesiological event spearheaded by the American church. Women in the church directed the energy of the feminist movement, which has deeply affected American society and academy, toward reform of patriarchal and sexist church structures across the board. Fourth, in 1982 the World Council of Churches produced a document entitled "Baptism, Eucharist, and Ministry," which is a virtual outline for an ecumenical ecclesiology that seeks normativity and recognition by the broad spectrum of churches. This is not an ecclesiology for a specific church; the document presupposes a pluralism of churches. It is scripturally based, historically conscious, displays a sense of the historical development of diverse ecclesial institutions, and is sensitive to different traditions. Finally, the last development during the course of the twentieth century with ecclesiological import is globalization, the movement toward a more explicit and intentional interdependence of peoples in the world, with its accompanying demand for cultural and national identity. This has been absorbed by the churches of the non-Western world, whose members now outnumber the churches of the West, as a spontaneous post-colonial demand for the inculturation of the Christian church into indigenous cultures. In the future the church will become increasingly pluralistic, and it is incumbent upon the whole church to develop ecclesiological principles that will enable it to strengthen its unity in the context of this diversity. Globalization also places the whole Christian church in a new forceful way into a situation of explicit dialogue with other world religions. This is happening on the ground, among the faithful, in the urban centers of the world. When the Christian churches enter into this dialogue seriously, their own differences will be dramatically relativized, opening up new forms of critical ecclesiological questioning.

Constructive Proposals

Race, Body, Space, and Time: Ecclesiological Reflections

James H. Evans Jr.

One of the problems in understanding the church today is the attempt to ignore either the "treasure" or the "earthen vessel." In reality, the human character and the divine purpose of the church are distinct but inseparable. The human character of the church is the focus of the burgeoning interest in church growth. Here, experts analyze social trends and trajectories in order to maximize the appeal of churches to a somewhat jaded and skeptical public. The divine purpose of the church is the focus of the growing influence of "Word" churches. These churches advance something akin to a new

Gnosticism, a saving knowledge that cannot be challenged by knowledge from other arenas of life. These types and their derivatives have superseded the older traditional framework of liberal, conservative, or evangelical. Each takes from the older models whatever it needs to advance its purpose, but its purpose is not found in substance in any of the older models.

A curious but not altogether unexpected development in contemporary ecclesiology is the growing popularity of the patina, if not the essence, of the traditional African American church. Historically, the African American church has been in touch with the culture and political lives of its adherents. It could not escape the deep social trends within the black community. It understood itself as a fully human agency. At the same time, the African American church has always seen within its humanness a divine purpose at work. That divine purpose is the material essence of the ongoing revelation of God in the world. The formal aspects of that revelation include the scriptures but also involves the writing of God upon the human heart, on the slate of human history, on the tablets of human experience. This is why ecstasy, dance, and speaking in tongues often signal God's continual self-revelation in the church.

The treasure that constitutes the church is more than its form. It is this *more* that I want to articulate, in brief, for our consideration. Traditionally, the nature of this treasure in earthen vessels has been expressed in the classic formula of "one, catholic, holy and apostolic." These marks or notes of the church have endured as indicators of both the humanity and the divinity resident in the churches. Traditionally, the church has not only marks but mandates. Those mandates are to center its life around the *kerygma* (message), to manifest *koinonia* (fellowship) in its communal forms, to engage in *diakonia* (service) as it moves beyond itself, and to perpetuate its life through the *didache* (teaching). While these marks and mandates have provided the grammar for ecclesiological discourse, the African American church has provided an improvisational language based on but not tied to this grammar. Within the African American church these marks and mandates have been "morphed," so to speak, into the tropes of race, body, space, and time.

Post-Denominationalism

Do we live in a post-denominational age, that is, a period in which the identity of North American Christians is not so strongly influenced by the beliefs and practices of particular church bodies as it once was? Some say that we do because they believe that the numbers cannot be read as saying anything else. That is, numerous statistics seem witness to the experience of many of these Christians that the various ethnic, socioeconomic, and theological glues that once bound most of the faithful to a single tradition have loosened their grip. Furthermore, in response to perceived post-denominationalism, a number of theologians and church leaders have issued a strong call for mainline Protestant seminaries to train their students in the traditions of their denomination, so that they, in turn, may be empowered to "tradition" their congregations. On the other hand, others argue that, even in this new age, some congregations and churches persist in—and some persist—by highlighting their denominational distinctiveness. Nor can one overlook the fact that many North American Roman Catholic and Orthodox Christians who may or may not regard themselves as members of denominations identify themselves closely with those church bodies.

Race and the Church as One

The claim to oneness in the church has been important to understanding its life and mission from the beginning. It was the oneness of the church that distinguished it from the myriad of religious cults and societies among which it was born. Yet from the very beginning evidence that the church was not one was also present. The claim to oneness in the church has been challenged by the dispute between the apostle Paul and the Jewish Christian church at Jerusalem, by the emerging dissident movements of the third and fourth centuries, and most notably by the Protestant Reformers. The oneness or the unity of the church has been challenged on every hand. Schisms, denominational splits, realignments along class, ideological, and political lines give loud testimony to the fact that the church is not one. I want to suggest that in the United States the notion of race is both the stumbling block to and the cornerstone for an understanding of the oneness of the church.

It is a fact that in the United States every major denomination split over the issue of slavery in the nineteenth century. (A possible exception to this would be the Protestant Episcopal Church in America, for reasons that are somewhat complex). The Baptists, the Presbyterians, and the Methodists were all fractured by the economic power of slavery and the cultural power of patriarchy. Recently, efforts have been made to overcome these divisions. Conferences centered around reconciliation have been held for the purpose of reunification. Beyond the possibility that such reunification may be more a response to the decline of denominational influence and the rise of secularism than a genuine manifestation of the spirit of unity, whether of the North or the South, these churches have not included African American worshiping communities within their understanding of the oneness they seek. In other words, this quest for oneness says nothing about the ongoing influence of racism as a divisive influence in the life of the church.

What then is the basis for this quest for oneness? Traditionally it is the *kerygma* of Jesus Christ. As John MacQuarrie puts it, "The basic unity [of the church] has as its center Jesus Christ himself."[7] The Good News of the life, death, and resurrection of Jesus Christ ought to be enough to guarantee the unity of the church. Yet it must be remembered that this *kerygma* was originally presented within a definite context. The second chapter of the Acts of the Apostles describes the paradigmatic articulation of the gospel. It occurred within the context of racial and cultural diversity. The persons who heard that first sermon each heard it in their own dialect, idiom, and language. The fact that each heard the gospel in his or her own language is more important than the language in which it was preached. It highlights the fact that one cannot understand or appreciate the gospel outside of the racial and cultural context in which it is made manifest. It is within this notion of *kerygma* and race that we must attempt to understand what it means to say that the church is one.

The issue of race has, almost from the very beginning, influenced and perhaps shaped public discourse in this nation. Its potential for divisiveness was eloquently stated by W. E. B. DuBois when he noted that "the problem of the twentieth century is the problem of the color line." This observation made a century ago still rings too true. It has also been the problem of the church, shaping its organization and directing its mission. Race can be viewed as a superficial social construction, as some theorists maintain, with no basis in science. Others view race as biologically determined and part of the natural, or in some cases religious, order. DuBois viewed race, as understood within the African American experience, to be connected with the effort to be true to oneself. The racial complexity of the African American made that effort the more strenuous. The *kerygma* upon which the Christian faith is based is centered upon Jesus Christ as the Risen Son of God. The Good News of the resurrection and its revolutionary impact on human history are certainly central. However, the *kerygma* does not simply tell of something new and wonderful that has happened in the history of humankind. The *kerygma* calls for a response. It calls for obedience. That is, the church has to be true to its center or core. Race and *kerygma* call the church to be true to its core, to be obedient to the center of its existence. The oneness implied by race, as understood here, is not a racist hegemony but a way to connect with the whole human race in all of its diversity.

Race

Further pursuit of the relevance of race to ecclesiology would reflect the view that race matters even when it goes unmentioned. This is because race is an unstable category for identity and needs to be complicated in a variety of ways. Even as "scientific" theories of the inferiority of non-white races dominated Western thinking in previous centuries, many argue now that race is not a scientifically credible category for significant biological human differences. As socially constructed orderings of subjects, races are inventions that come and go. The category "Hispanic" emerged in the Census Bureau classifications with the deluge of immigrant poor from Latin America. In the early twentieth century, Jews, Irish, and Italians were all considered different races. Some groups (the Irish) become "white" and stay white. Others (Mexicans) were "white" in 1940 and more recently are not.

Taking racial instability seriously is important in debates over its usefulness in the project of liberation, and scholars differ over the importance of claiming racial identity for historically marginalized groups. However, race is also of importance to those deemed to be without it. Attribution of race is about power. The dominant group, "whites," has not been understood to have race, thus it has been taken as exemplary of human being. The development of "whiteness studies" is, then, not only the exploration of various "cultural" realities that constitute whiteness, but also the discovery that becoming white is a social accomplishment in relation to and won at the expense of the other. Whiteness is valuable property.

Recognition that race is everywhere necessitates a revisiting of all aspects of ecclesiology, for race is not simply a topic for ethics. Nor is its relevance confined to the history of the black or brown church. Race, a process of ascribing difference, is part of the history of the ostensibly "universal" church. It is embedded in the discursive construction of all subjects and not simply an issue of explicit exclusions. Subjects previously treated as generic or universal must be looked at again. (Who counted as fully human in various periods and what kind of subjects served as the "neutral" model of humanity from which to formulate Christology before modern notions of race?) Not seeing race is the privilege of those whose lives are not visibly harmed and constrained by it. A challenge remains: when is the claim not to see color support for an unjust status quo, and when is such a claim an appropriate reference to the human community in an attempt to advance some common emancipatory project? Appeals to unity, so important to the life and reflection of the church, require attention to the effects of racialization, along with other social markers of marginalization such as class, gender, and ethnicity. Premature appeals to our sameness can reinforce the disparities that still permeate our social lives, disparities that are not only residual from a long legacy of racism but also reinvented from contemporary mistrust and hostilities.

Body and the Church as Holy

The claim to holiness has always been paradoxical in the life of the Christian community. The church has always claimed a kind of holiness that was not always evident in its life. In fact, more times than not, the church has betrayed this claim. The church has manifested within its internal life and its external mission the full array of social shortcomings and failures. In essence, the church is sinful. Yet it claims holiness for itself. Part of the problem is that the claim to holiness has too often been identified with the notion of purity and simplicity. A holy church will always be an oxymoron as long as this is the case. The church is made up of persons who are at various stages of moral and faith development, people who are themselves struggling with competing passions and urges; that is, the church is made up of persons who are neither pure nor simple in their motives, desires, or existential makeup. How, then, does the church continue to claim holiness as a fundamental mark of its identity? I want to suggest that the notion of the church as "a body" is both a stumbling block to and the cornerstone for an understanding of the holiness of the church.

The Church and Sin

All churches agree that there is sin—individual as well as corporate—in the Church's history. They also agree that sin cannot affect the Church as a divine reality, whereas sin can affect the human reality and structure of the Church. Yet they differ in where they see the Church's divine reality, and thus in their understanding of the way the Church is affected by sin.

For some it is impossible to say "the Church sins" because they see the Church as a gift of God, and as such marked by God's holiness. . . . This gift of the Church is lived out in fragile human beings who are liable to sin, but the sin of the members of the Church are not sins of the Church. The Church is rather the locus of salvation and healing, and not the subject of sin.

Others, while they too state that the Church as the creature of God's Word and Spirit, the body of Christ, etc., is holy and without sin, at the same time say that it does sin, because they define the Church as the communion of its members, who at the same time as being believers created by the Spirit and Christ's own body, in this world are still sinful beings.

Thus some hold that one cannot speak of the sin of the Church, but one can and must speak of the sin of the members and groups within the Church, a situation described by the parable of the wheat and the chaff, and by the Augustinian formula of *corpus permixtum*. For others, sin in the Church can become systemic and also affect the institution. Some teach that it is impossible to single out individual points and items in the Church's life which can be affected by sin and others which cannot, but that this problem can only be tackled in a dialectical way: the Church itself is sinful insofar as it is a communion of those who although sanctified by God are never without sin, but is holy insofar as it is called into being and kept in communion with God through his holy Word and the Holy Spirit.[8]

The holiness of the church is traditionally expressed in the affirmation that the church is the "body of Christ." In much of Christian discourse this notion of the church as the body of Christ evokes a sense of mysticism, heightened spiritual awareness, and a contemplative mood. The notion of the church as a body, in this sense, has the ironic consequence of turning our gaze away from the corporeal nature of the church and toward its "holiness." Indeed, the New Testament does speak of the church as the body of Christ (Eph. 1:22–23; 1 Cor. 12:27). What is often lost is the quite obvious connection being drawn between the human body and the body of Christ. Yet Christian thought, from its Platonic through its Puritan manifestations, has never been at ease with the notion of connecting the holy with the human body. Thus, the notion of the church as the body of Christ has normally been construed as referring to the church's spiritual nature. This leaves unexamined the relationship between holiness and the church as a physical body.

What then is the basis for the church's claim to holiness? Traditionally, it is the *koinonia*, or fellowship, to which it is called. This fellowship is not simply a human association. It is also fellowship with Christ. These two aspects of *koinonia* are inseparable. One cannot be in fellowship with Christ and be alienated from one's brothers and sisters. The reverse is also true. Authentic fellowship with one's neighbors will lead to an understanding that they too are loved by Christ. The essence of this fellowship is sharing and participation. The ultimate symbol of this sharing and participation is communion as expressed in the Lord's Supper. In this sharing and participation the community identifies with Christ by symbolically sharing in his suffering and in the hope of the resurrection. The question that remains is "How far does this sharing go and to what extent does the church really participate in the suffering and hope evident in the body of Christ?"

African American churches have had to reconcile two seemingly opposed affirmations regarding the nature of the body; that is, the claim of their African religious sensibility, which affirms the goodness of the human body while connecting it to the divine, and the claim of Western Christianity, which denigrates the human body while using the idea of the body as an expression of Christ's indwelling presence. In the midst of these competing claims, African American Christianity has developed understandings of the body and holiness that place them in a unique perspective. The relationship between the suffering, broken, and bruised body of Christ and the tortured, burned, and lynched bodies of black people has never been lost on African American Christians. This reality forms the backdrop for understanding what it means to be the body of Christ. The body of Christ, in this sense, is not the neat, clean, symbolic invitation to contemplation. Rather, it is the disturbing, repulsive reality of living in a sinful world. But as disturbing and repulsive as these bodies were, they were also the incarnation of hope for the world. The church as the body of Christ and the *koinonia* must be seen as expressive of the physical nature of the church, and holiness must be seen as related to that physical nature.

One cannot love the body of Christ and hate human flesh. If the church is truly the body of Christ it must be a fellowship of the flesh and find its claim to holiness therein. As it subsists within the kingdom of God, the church must be "a fellowship of righteousness," as Walter Rauschenbusch insists.[9] The church must be both to be holy, *koinonia*, and the body of Christ because holiness must be thought of, like health in both social and physical bodies, in terms of balance and harmony.

Space and the Church as Catholic

The traditional claim of the church to catholicity has always been controversial. Within this claim lies both the promise and the peril of the Christian faith. Catholicity asserts that the church to be truly the church must be both universal and authentic. The claim to universality in the church is rooted in the Old Testament notion of a portable God and the New Testament notion of a missionary faith. The claim of the church to authenticity is rooted in the Old Testament quest for faithfulness to the One True and Living God (monotheism) and the New Testament claim to "One Lord, One Faith, and One Baptism" (unity). In an era when the catholicity of the church, in both the sense of its geographical expanse and its hold on authentic expression of the holy, is called into question, what sense does it make to continue to make this claim? I want to suggest that catholicity understood as the church's "space" is both a stepping stone and a stumbling block to a helpful understanding of this mark of the church.

The search for a place was endemic to the experience of the ancient Israelites. They were constantly displaced, either through their disobedience or through the providential will of God. They were constantly in exodus, exile, or wilderness, searching for the Promised Land. Indeed, a mark of

God's favor was the expanse of Israel and their influence into other lands. Yet it was, and is, often difficult to distinguish between the expansion of Israel as the will of God and the naked political conquests of other peoples and lands. The early church was essentially a missionary movement. Expanding its circle of influence was its *raison d'être*. The apostolic mission of Paul gave the impetus to spread the gospel abroad. The conversion of Emperor Constantine to Christianity made possible an alliance that gave Christian missions an imperial tint. Here, as well, it became difficult, if not impossible, to distinguish between mission and conquest. The church's understanding of catholicity included not only an expansionary dimension but a regulatory one. Missionary movements were almost always accompanied by the desire that the faith be practiced authentically. The expansionary spirit and orthodoxy go hand in hand. It matters little whether the orthodoxy in question is that of belief or practice. Because the notion of catholicity was shaped by these political factors, it became closely associated with the idea of ownership. The catholicity of the church could be measured by how much space to which it could lay claim.

What then is the basis for the church's claim to catholicity? Traditionally, it has been based on the notion of totality; that is, the church that is truly catholic must embrace all. This understanding of the catholicity of the church has resulted in endless and rancorous debate. Moreover, it has subtlely permitted the notion of catholicity to become a geographical idea. In essence, catholicity became conveniently connected with conquest. It was this connection that blinded the church to the dangers of imperial religion and missionary endeavors that were nothing more than mercenary raids. For the church, its catholicity cannot be based on an all-embracing ego or religious conquest; its catholicity must be rooted in the mandate of *diakonia*, or service.

The *diakonia* of the church is part of its essence. It is not just the work of those appointed to the diaconate, but is what the church as church does. This service is exemplified in the care for the poor and destitute, the marginalized and downtrodden, or, in biblical terms, "widows and orphans." The *diakonia* is the movement of the Christian community. This movement requires freedom. The connection between the *diakonia* movement and freedom can be seen in the impetus, often overlooked, behind the exodus of the Israelites. Their initial demands to Pharaoh were not for political power but for the freedom to serve their God. African American Christians during slavery experienced a similar dilemma. In the North, sanctuaries were often segregated spaces where white people and black people were separated. This was true of St. George's Methodist Episcopal Church in Philadelphia in 1789, where Richard Allen and Absalom Jones, two African Americans, were pulled from their knees while in prayer because their devotions were being held in white space. The two men left that church in search of a place where they could serve God without restriction. The connection between their desire to live in the catholicity of their faith and their desire to carry out the mandate for *diakonia* is clearly seen in the fact that their first act was not the establishment of a black church or a separate racial space for adoration but the establishment of the Free African Society, an organization dedicated to serving the population of Philadelphia, both black and white. Only later did Allen establish the African Methodist Episcopal Church. Segregation and service are incompatible. *Diakonia* requires catholicity. In the South, African American Christians during slavery lived with the reality that segregation was an affront to the catholicity of the faith, for segregation was interested only in establishing boundaries. That is why they worshiped in brush arbors and backwoods, creating sanctuaries wherever they encountered Jesus Christ, the center of the faith. The preeminent symbol of the claim of these slave churches to catholicity was the conscious identification with Africa. Many of these early churches included Africa in their names, not simply out of racial pride but out of a deep conviction that even in the throes of slavery, they were still part of a larger whole. These were, in spite of social dislocation, expressions of the catholicity of the faith. African American churches continue to claim authenticity in spite of ridicule, universality in spite of marginalization; they claim space without resorting to segregation (whites are welcomed into almost any black church while the reverse is often not true); and they live in freedom, in spite of evidence to the contrary.

Time and the Church as Apostolic

The claim of the church to *apostolicity* has always been subject to the question of relevance. The notion of the apostolicity of the church begs the question of the meaning of a community founded on a historical person and event for the pressing issues of the day. Apostolicity raises the question of continuity with the past and practical connection with the present. Many different Christian communities explicitly claim to be heirs to an apostolic succession, that is, an unbroken link with the original eyewitnesses to the ministry of Jesus. All churches do so, at least implicitly. The contention, often heated, is centered around the ways in which that succession is understood. The notion of apostolic succession, while not a biblical concept, arose when disputes around the meaning of the faith emerged after the death of the last eyewitness to Christ. John MacQuarrie notes that "the authentic Christian community had to distinguish itself and its message from the heterodox groups, and it sought to do this by establishing its continuity with the apostles."[10] However, the appeal to apostolic continuity actually raised more questions than it answered. The problem now was the relationship of the Christian community to its own past. Today, what sense does it make to speak of the Christian community as the manifestation of an apostolic succession? I want to suggest that *time* must be understood as that which both enables and inhibits the claim of the church to apostolicity.

The apostolicity of the church is related to the place of the church in time. The passage of time that brought the death of the original apostles made the issue of continuity with the past an urgent one in the life of the church. In addition, the delayed Parousia, meant that the early church had to, for the first time, contemplate an extended future for itself. In a very short period, the church moved from being a transitory, threshold community living on the cusp of a new age, to a thoroughly, though perhaps reluctant, historically situated institution. The New Testament epistolary writings chronicle this shift in the life of the Christian community. The church had to find a way to deal with its new *historical* character. How could it ground itself in a usable past and, at the same time, address the question of its relevance for future generations? How could it maintain the diachronic dimension of its identity? The answer was to claim an unbroken line of succession between itself and the apostolic ministry out of which it rose. This claim to apostolicity has often been specious in the life of the church. The succession is thought at times to be spiritual, as in the case of some Pentecostal churches, and in other instances to be physical, as is sometimes thought of in reference to the Roman Catholic Church. Whether spiritual or physical, as long as the church exists in time, the issue of succession will be critical.

What then is the basis of the church's claim to apostolicity? Traditionally, it is the *didache*, or the teaching function of the church. The apostolic character of the church is most clearly seen in its nature as a didactic community. Here teaching is more than simply the conveying of information. It includes a practical element. In essence, the church is apostolic to the extent that its *didache*, or teaching and practice, is continuous with that of the apostles through the ages.

Through Western eyes the claim to apostolicity in the African American churches has always been suspect. The subtle racism that continues to infect Western Christianity has made it difficult to see and affirm the continuity of the African American Christian witness with that of the apostles. True apostolicity, however, has nothing to do with an empty progression of formal connections within the history of the church. It has to do with the faithfulness of its teaching and practice. In its didactic function the church expresses its faithfulness to the gospel through time. In the African American church the didactic ministry occurs through intergenerational education. Within the African religious sensibility, the faithful witness is passed from one generation to the next through oral histories and stories. The historian (or the griot) has the responsibility for remembering, retelling, and reenacting the message (*kerygma*) that holds the community together. The didactic ministry of the African American church involves faithfulness, and faithfulness implies connection with what has gone before; through that connection the *then* becomes the *now*. The apostolicity of the African American church is not found in the formal continuity with the ecclesial manifestations of the past. The apostolicity of the African American churches is found in their spiritual and faithful continuity with teaching and practice of the apostles.

Conclusion

The marks or notes of the church have traditionally been described as "one, holy, catholic, and apostolic." From these marks have emerged the mandates of the church to proclaim the *kerygma*, to manifest *koinonia*, to engage in *diakonia*, and to ensure the continuity of the faith through the *didache*. For the African American church these marks and mandates have been given expression through the modalities of *race, body, space, and time*. From these modalities the church especially the African American church has received the mission to be *obedient, righteous, free*, and *faithful*. This seismic shift within the ecclesial landscape in the twenty-first century demands that we think ever faithfully and critically about what it means to be the church of Christ.

The Mission of the Church

Paul Lakeland

Mission means "sending" or "being sent." The mission of the church is thus that for which it is sent, those purposes for which Christ commissioned it. To understand the full complexity of the term *mission*, however, we have to approach it from at least three different perspectives. First, *who* is sent? Second, *to whom* is the church sent? Third, *what* is the church sent to do? In actual fact, the questions need to be asked in reverse order. That being said, there is a preliminary question that we need to address: What is the relationship between the mission of the church and the larger question of the *missio dei*, "God's mission," or what we might better understand as the divine purpose or creative will of God? These four questions will guide our examination of the mission of the church.

God's Mission and the Mission of the Church

God's purposes in and for the world are revealed to us through the Bible, but also through looking around us at the world. The world, in its goodness, is the expression of God's creative will, filled with the Spirit and offering glory to its Creator. Of course, there is abounding sin, suffering, and evil in this world, but the person of faith cannot see these as God's responsibility. In the Book of Genesis, God looks upon the creation and sees that it is good. As the early chapters of Genesis unfold, it becomes clear that God's purpose for the world is precisely that it shall be itself, a created reflection of divine goodness. God wills that all creatures, including human beings, be fully what they are—no more and no less. In the case of human beings, being fully what they are, made in the image of God, is made clear in God's commission of Adam and Eve for stewardship. On God's behalf, human beings will cherish creation. In a sense, they are commissioned as "cocreators" and "copreservers" of God's handiwork. Their tragedy, and that of creation, of course, is that they are not equal to the task. Moreover, it is apparent from the very beginning that their principal failure is their inability to recognize that their freedom does not mean autonomy. Their success in carrying out their mission is directly connected to their awareness that they depend on God, not on themselves, for their achievements.

From the beginning, then, God's mission and human purposes are closely intertwined, though there is tension between them. God's commission to human beings to share in the divine creativity is addressed, too, to the whole human race. Adam and Eve are not Hebrews, still less Christians. They represent all humankind. Their failure is our failure. Their task is our task. The Hebrew scriptures tell the story of God's continuing faithfulness to the task of creation and the new initiative that God takes with the covenant people. It is as if God is trying again to enlist human beings in the task of cocreation, this time choosing Abraham and his descendents. Once again, as in the Genesis account, human beings take up the task and are unequal to it. Time after time, the heroes of the Hebrew scriptures reveal their prideful egos; Moses, Saul, and David are good examples of the failure to do what God has called them to do, while Israel itself is another.

Christian scripture sees God's initiative in and through Jesus Christ to be a further effort to engage the human race in God's mission. Jesus is sent into the world to show the way in which a human being can conform his or her life to God's mission. The way of the cross is the way of conformity to the will of God. Jesus Christ is the perfect instrument of God's mission. He proclaims the kingdom of God. But he is also the perfect exemplar of the one who is called to mission. Discipleship, then, is mission, but only because discipleship is, like Christ, outwardly directed in response to God's call to share in God's mission. Discipleship, in other words, is commitment to the mission of Christ, which is in its turn carrying out God's mission. And God's mission is expressed in the creative will as it shows itself in the world. Thus, to complete the circle, the divine creative will is to a degree dependent on the faithfulness of human beings to the divine purpose. For Christians, this means faithfulness to their discipleship of Christ.

What Is the Church Sent to Do?

Given that God invites all human beings to cooperate in the work of cocreation, what is the specific mission of the disciples of Christ, the community called church? Formally, of course, there is no difference. That is, all human beings take up their mission insofar as they live out lives that respect and foster the integrity of God's creation, whether they know it or not, whether they know God or not. Through revelation, all the children of Abraham know more about God's purposes and are aware of their call to mission in ways that others are not. This is both a privilege and an enormous responsibility. However, there is a material specificity to the call of Christ to his church, one that historically Christians have understood as a more perfect revelation of truth but that might better be expressed as a clearer call to participation in the mission of God. When Jesus commissions the disciples to go out like sheep among wolves, when he calls his apostles, when he charges his followers to "preach the gospel to all nations," his commission to them is to spread the Good News of the gospel, to proclaim the imminence of the reign of God.

To talk of the mission of the Christian community, then, is to talk about being called to further the reign of God. But this calling is one that is always subject to historical conditioning and that must be asked and answered anew for every generation. Alongside the scriptural message that we have so far focused upon, there is also the need to "read the signs of the times." Reading the signs of the times is a vital dimension of contemporary religious reflection. It is a kind of *lectio divina* that focuses not upon the text of scripture but upon creation and human history as texts, in which the call of God and the challenges of meeting that call are always there to be seen. It is also a hazardous enterprise, since it requires an attention to the prejudices and ideology that we may bring to the reading through our own social location, gender, race, and so on, and that may distort our reading or lead us to find exactly what we are looking for. But it is a necessary activity, since without this prayerful and spirit-filled act of divination, the mission of the Christian community will be pursued näively, and thus ineffectually.

The Christian tradition, like other religions, cherishes a specific vision of what it is to be a human being and, since "ought" follows "is," sees itself as called to foster and protect that vision. To read the signs of the times, then, is to search our moment in history for all that seems to threaten the human and for those special people and places where the defense of the human and the world in which we live has been especially promoted. The anti-human will be the challenge that defines mission today. People and movements that struggle against the anti-human are our resources and our guides in the struggle.

There are many candidates for the label of "anti-human" in our world today: world poverty, disease, malnutrition, drugs, violence, terrorism, military and corporate greed, environmental collapse, and so on and so on. These are all signs of the anti-human. Reading these signs is a challenge, but one very persuasive contemporary reading of them unifies the problems under the heading of globalization. Readings of the phenomenon of globalization range from canonizing it to demonizing it, with many shades between. But there can be little doubt that the phenomenon of globalization offers the possibility of ameliorating the condition of the world's hopeless masses on the one hand, while apparently exacerbating their misery on the other. It may very well be the case that globalization is an unstoppable social force, if we mean by it the collapse of distance and the homogenization of values, which seem to follow inexorably in the wake of the miniaturization of the world brought about by the communications explosion in general and the World Wide Web in particular. But if we simply acquiesce in its inexorable advance, we abandon the Good News of the gospel. The gospel, of course, stands against evil, not against globalization. But it must stand today against those antihuman forces that gain power and momentum through the communications explosion, whether they be "savage" capitalism, power politics, or the contempt for the human that all forms of violence evince.

Mission and Christian Universalism

Based on Christianity's own experience with universalism, Christians can discern both graces and problems that globalism entails. Throughout the ages, universalism has led many Christians to the insight that what deserves their ultimate loyalty is not any nation, ideology, race, culture, or other "local" affiliation, but only God's creation as a whole. Christian faith in a universal God has nurtured radical ideas of human dignity and equality; today, that same faith helps to define and defend human rights internationally. Christian universalism can have salutary effects on the advancement of knowledge. If the truth of the gospel knows no limits, then the gospel can and must be reconciled with the best science and most profound thinking available.

Unfortunately, Christian universalism also has produced the opposite effects. Rather than a basis for equality, Christianity more often has built hierarchies of domination and submission. In relation to non-Christians, universalism has been a rationale for conquest and persecution. Confidence in the universality of the gospel too often has produced not open-mindedness but a lethal combination of ignorance about and arrogance toward knowledge that comes from other sources.

Universalism, then, can be emancipatory and redemptive. But it also can be destructive and imperialist. For Christian mission, both *ad intra* and *ad extra*, a great deal depends on telling the difference. If Christian mission is nothing more (or less) than the restoration of creation, criteria for discerning emancipatory universalism can be found in four features that the Bible ascribes to the world as God's creation: the world is good, free, historical, and participatory.

The goodness of creation implies, first and foremost, the material goodness of these bodies and this planet designed by God. Universalism can only be emancipatory if, first and foremost, it protects and promotes the physical well-being of humans, other life-forms, and the earth itself. An emancipatory globalization must create worldwide standards for wages, health care, and environmental protection. When globalization refuses these standards it shows the oppressive face of universalism.

The freedom of creation is the divine intention for each being and each community to be themselves. An emancipatory globalization can lead the peoples of the world to unprecedented levels of appreciation, encounter, and engagement with each other. But when globalization results in the homogenization or "Coca-colonization" of the world, this is cultural imperialism, not emancipatory universalism.

As a historical phenomenon, creation does not end "in the beginning." It continues through time, blending into the process of redemption. The *process* of redemption in history is not to be mistaken for the myth of *progress*, in which "developed" cultures are superior in every way to traditional cultures. A redemptive globalization will not impose the values of the modern West on other cultures but will emerge from multisided dialogue and sometimes struggle among the peoples of the world.

Finally, creation is participatory; all of humanity has both the right and the responsibility to be creatures who create. As globalization weaves information into a single web and economies into a single market, it can enable more and more people to take substantive part in the decisions that shape their lives. When globalization expands everyone's access to information and ideas, when it includes and empowers, then it is functioning as an emancipatory force. But when globalization takes decisions that ought be public and gives them over to the hands of private interests, then it becomes not a grace but a problem, a destructive expression of universalism.

Mission will never stop being partially about little things, binding up the wounds of those close to hand, comforting the dying, visiting the sick. But in face of globalization we also need to be aware that so much of what we are called to attend to close at hand is occasioned or intensified by much grander and less visible forces. The "wretched of the earth" and the "masters of the universe" are linked together. In the gospel vision, the linkage is one of a love that does justice. What are the concrete changes to which we must be committed if that relationship is to be marked by love, justice, and solidarity? Answering that question is a way of defining the face of mission today, not the whole of mission, perhaps, but that part of the mission of the church that is distinctive of our moment in history.

To Whom Is the Church Sent?

This question can be answered in fairly traditional terms. The church is sent to "all the nations," to preach the Good News. But given the nature of the contemporary mission as we have determined it above, the way in which it is sent differs remarkably from past understandings. In traditional understandings of mission, the church is the body that possesses the truth, and it is divinely commissioned to preach that truth to the ignorant of all other religions and none. This work of evangelization is successful when those who hear the message are moved to accept it and to become part of the body that proclaims it. The conversion of the world to Christ is the objective of Christian mission traditionally understood. In our contemporary approach, these assumptions have to be challenged.

Post-colonial Critiques of Mission

Although it is a call to spread good news, the "Great Commission" of Matthew's Gospel has done considerable damage. This is the judgment of post-colonial criticisms, which interrogate the effects of the past 500 years of Western expansion, in which Western values, including Christianity, were brought to every corner of the globe. Christian mission was woven into mercantile trading routes and imperial expansion from the very beginning. However, post-colonialists focus on the medium of Western colonialism, an economic and political relation between nations in which the sovereignty of one was dependent upon the power of the other "empire" nation. Emerging in the mercantile imperialism of the late 1400s to 1800s and accompanying missionary movements, colonialist forms of Western power were later enhanced through the force of monopoly capitalism in the late nineteenth through the mid-twentieth century.

Post-colonialist criticism reveals that missionary expansion has been inextricably complicit with forces of expanding power and the inevitable complexities of dominance and submission that attend them. Missionary literature of these centuries unabashedly brands the objects of mission as inferior in status. They were "the Heathen," according to a 1792 pamphlet. Africans were "savages" or "barbarians" practicing "primitive" religion. Even the "affirmation" in the 1537 papal announcement that Amerindians were human was rooted in an economy of Western superiority. Paradoxically founded in ostensibly well-intentioned desire to share good news, Christian mission's imaginaries for the Other and the practices that accompanied them effectively obliterated the dignity and agency of many populations in colonized territories.

Although the "Colonial period" has passed, the "post" of post-colonial criticism is not a chronological indicator, signaling that Christianity and the world have moved beyond the problems of Western dominance. Even with the coming of political independence for most colonized nations and the end of official colonial relationships by mid-twentieth century, new forms of global economic, military, and cultural dominance associated with global capitalism have emerged, frequently termed *neocolonialism*. Coinage of such terms as *coloniality* to refer to the continued residual effects of colonialism also reminds us that grave problems persist.

Despite universal renunciation of the dehumanizing terms of the past, what is problematic in continuing forms of coloniality remains unresolved. Some would argue that the more egregious treatments of "natives" as barbarian or pagan are corrected by recognizing the legitimacy of indigenous cultures. The missionary task is to *adapt* the gospel to a local culture—a process known as indigenization for Protestants and inculturation for Roman Catholics. The problem of colonized consciousness is, for example, solved by a recovery of traditional African religion, or at least by empowering indigenous African theologians. Others, however, insist that not only is a search for pure origins impossible, but inculturation and its terms (for example, culture as "clothing" or "soil" for the gospel) are themselves a species of post-colonialist Western discourse. However it is understood, post-colonialist discourse about mission constitutes a formidable search for the power of gospel as God's justice and will be vital to ecclesiology in the new millennium.

If the core of the Christian gospel is the message that God loves and cares for the divine creation and wills human fulfillment, then the church is called to proclaim this truth and to struggle against everything in our world that militates against it. However, the other great world religions also maintain this same truth in their different ways, and while Christians find Jesus Christ to be the exemplar and guarantor of God's love of the world, Jews and Buddhists and Hindus have other ways of expressing their commitments to the project of human liberation from all forms of bondage. The need for mission to be effective would suggest, then, that in addressing those of other faiths, it is the message *of* Jesus rather than Jesus as the message that ought to be stressed. In the end, the Christian claim that Jesus is savior means that through discipleship of Jesus, the church is led to faithfulness to God's call. Successful mission needs to be measured by its effectiveness in leading people to faithfulness to the call of God as they hear it in their lives, not by its success in persuading people to abandon their own faiths and choose Jesus as the one who is exemplar and guarantor of God's love. Thus is the mission of the church fulfilled, while the integrity of the great world religions is respected.

If Christian mission can be conducted in an atmosphere of respect for the wisdom of the world's religions, then a posture of solidarity and indeed of listening can and should be adopted. Mission today has to be collaborative and humble. In face of globalization, a solidarity of those who will work to protect the human race and our world is a necessity. But once we understand that God wills the salvation of human beings more than God wills the worldly success of Christ's church, it is also a theological responsibility. If the mission of the church is to succeed through alliances that lessen the sense that the church is privileged, and through a humble posture of listening to the wisdom of the world that is not the church, it can only conform the church more fully to Christ, who is its head, the one who was faithful to God in and through apparent human failure.

Who Is Called to Mission?

Different branches of the Christian church have answered this question in different ways, some stressing that mission is primarily the responsibility of ministers or clergy, others seeing mission at least as witness as a responsibility of the whole church. Typically, however, across the denominational divides, Christians have tended to distinguish between mission narrowly understood, which is conducted primarily through preaching the gospel, and mission more broadly construed as the exemplary lives of Christians in the world. Today we have to rethink this division of responsibilities.

If mission is primarily conducted through the church's active concern for God's world and in a struggle against the forces of the antihuman, then "preaching the gospel" in the narrow sense is more properly to be understood as a responsibility of "internal mission." Preaching the gospel is above all the way that Christians are reminded of their responsibility to mission and inspired to the cost of discipleship. The work of priests and ministers, in other words, is instrumental to the mission of the church, but not itself the mission of the church. The mission of the church is the work of the whole community, as it engages in a praxis of defense of the human, the contemporary proclamation of the Good News. In traditional categories we could call this "witness." But it is not so much witness to discipleship as it is witness that discipleship entails solidarity with suffering humanity, in the cause of faithfulness to God's love for the world. In the ancient world, those outside the young Christian community marveled at their praxis, exclaiming, "See how those Christians love one another." In our world, our mission will be successful if the world beyond the church looks at us and says, "See how those Christians love us!"

6

Spirit

Ada María Isasi-Díaz, Barbara A. Holmes, Serene Jones, Catherine Keller, Walter J. Lowe, Jim Perkinson, Mark I. Wallace (chapter editor), Sharon D. Welch

Sarah's daughter, Melanie, a reservist in the military, has just been called to service in Baghdad. Sitting in her pew on Sunday morning, after receiving the news, Sarah tries to keep on her staid and proper New England "church face." But when her friend Eleanor, the lay reader, begins to read the morning scripture, she dissolves into tears: ". . . until a spirit from on high is poured out on us, and the wilderness becomes a fruitful field, and the fruitful field is deemed a forest. Then justice will dwell in the wilderness, and righteousness abide in the fruitful field. The effect of righteousness will be peace" (Isa. 32:15–17).

◆

On the occasion of his eightieth birthday, Nelson Mandela celebrated with orphans and then married Graca Machel of Mozambique. Waving his assurance to the crowds, he offered a smile that was a balm to his wounded country, and then he danced. His feet were planted solidly; his arms were akimbo and in motion. Even though he hardly moved at all it was a dance of the Spirit. His dance was not the buck wild dance of praise that embarrassed David's wife. It was a Lazarus dance from death to life, the unlikely celebration of one who has been "dead" and now is alive. When Mandela was released from confinement, he moved like Lazarus. The sway was hypnotic. The body rocked with feet close together to celebrate being loosed and let go. There was so much to celebrate on this day of union. And so, with Graca close by his side, he swayed to the sounds and rhythms of the universe. At the end of my life, I want to dance this dance, a surprised jig, a modest boogie in celebration of the journey, the cycles of freedom and imprisonment, and the blessings accrued. Glory Hallelujah!

◆

Paco owns a shoe repair shop in Mexico just across the increasingly unfriendly border with the United States. He repairs shoes and makes meals for the workers in the *maquialdoras*. Then at night, instead of sleeping, he rescues. Crawling through viaducts he feeds, shelters, and clothes the homeless children who live under the city streets. Paco has never been on CNN; he is not associated with any group or organization. There are no books written about his exploits. When asked why he does this work, he says, "I read the Gospel and believed in the power of the Spirit."

◆

A videotape of a black North American Pentecostal preacher is shown to a number of *Candombles* in Bahia, Brazil. The Bahians watch the video with mute interest until the preacher moves from "warm-up" to "takeoff" in his delivery, shifting from simple communication to searing incantation, from quietude to incandescence. Suddenly, they lurch into agitated outburst, "Xango! Xango! Xango!" They do not speak English, nor do they know anything of Pentecostal worship. They simply know the arrival gestures of this *orixa* in the flesh of human "being," and the body language is all the eloquence they need.[1]

◆

A tired black woman, Effie, heads home along the railroad tracks at night after working since dawn for a white lady and is suddenly confronted with the Ku Klux Klan. She falls to her knees in prayer: "My Lord, my Lord, please help me!" There on the tracks is a huge white dog. The Klansmen are near. As she stares at the dog, a soothing warmth envelops her. From within the silence comes "Effie, keep walking." She glances back in wonder at the dog and feels the thought, "Walk, Effie, I am with you." Effie passes within inches of the white-shrouded figures, between them, in front of them. They do not see her. Effie slowly smiles and whispers, "Thank you, dear Lord."[2]

State of the Question

Strangely, when it comes to Spirit as a theological topic, we find that a shift of style—a different mood and motivation of our theological work—seems to take place. The cadence of our writing changes as a surprising rhythm and rapture of language begin to tug at our propositions and tease our dogmas. Our reflections on the Spirit thus have a feeling of freshness, the refreshment of life itself—yet not of life in its familiar rounds so much as a new song, a new creation that turns those rounds into a dance.

As the vignettes show, each in their own way, our experiences of the Spirit are often most obvious in times of dizzying transition, when we are searching for new vision and new hope. Long ago, in ancient Israel, Spirit-talk burst forth from the Hebrew prophetic tradition, generating a social movement aimed at creating an egalitarian community in which all things would be shared. Again, at Pentecost, after an austere gestation period, an ecstatic, multilingual Spirit gave birth to the church in the midst of crisis. Yet again, 1,000 years later, in a Europe rent by war, crusades, and plague, the prophecies of Joachim of Fiore announced a New Age of the Spirit, a third eon to correspond to the third person of the trinity. Again, 1,000 years later, after two World Wars and amid growing awareness of our failed stewardship of our planet and its resources, in a time we call "postmodern" because we sense that the hopes of modernity for universal progress have failed us, a new discourse of the Spirit (new, always new again!) is beginning to emerge.

What does this emerging discourse look like? It displays a broad spectrum of theological faces: feminists, evangelical Pentecostals, Western ecumenists have all turned to the doctrine of the Spirit as a resource for renewing their particular understanding of faith. For all those searching for renewal, the Spirit provides boundary-crossing space where outdated and dead ideas about one's religious beliefs can be challenged and new energy for faithful living can be found. For each searcher, however, that space looks quite different.

Three Sites of Spirit-Talk

> *I learned both what is secret and what is manifest, for wisdom, the fashioner of all things, taught me. There is in her a spirit that is intelligent, holy, unique, manifold . . . penetrating through all spirits.*
>
> (Wis. of Sol. 7:21–23)

Although the question of the gender of God has been discussed in feminist circles for decades, in recent years the Spirit has been the place where these explorations have been most fruitfully and provocatively answered. Throughout scripture and the tradition, the Spirit, as God's indwelling, corporeal presence within the created order, has been variously identified with the feminine and the maternal.

In the Bible the Spirit is envisioned as God's helping, nurturing, inspiring, and birthing presence in creation. The mother Spirit bird in the opening creation song of Genesis, like a giant hen sitting on her cosmic nest egg, broods over the earth and brings all things into life and fruition: "In the beginning when God created the heavens and the earth . . . while a wind from God swept over the face of the waters" (Gen. 1:1–2). In turn, this same hovering Spirit bird, as a dove that alights on Jesus coming up through the waters of his baptism, appears in all four of the Gospels to signal God's approval of his public work. The maternal, aviary Spirit of Genesis and the Gospels is the nursing mother of creation and Jesus' ministry who protects and sustains the well-being of all things in the cosmic web of life. Early Christian communities in the Middle East consistently spoke of the Spirit as the motherly, regenerative breath and power of God within creation. These early Christians believed that the Hebrew feminine grammatical name of the Spirit *rûach* was a linguistic clue to certain woman-specific characteristics of God as Spirit. As these early Christians rightly understood that God transcends sex and gender, their point was not that God was a female deity but that it is appropriate to refer to God's mystery, love, and power in male *and* female terms. In this chapter we will take the liberty of referring to the Spirit as "she" in order to capture something of the biblical understanding of God as feminine Spirit within the created order.[3]

Yet another face of "Spirit theology" comes from the seemingly opposite end of the spectrum. In the charismatic renewal movements that have swept across the denominations over the past thirty years, a traditional, more evangelical language sought also to express a radical new experience of "the gifts of the Spirit." The renewal of the Spirit moves in an immense feedback loop between the Pentecostal and the progressive poles of Christianity. This renewal is not just a minor shift of emphasis. It raises theological questions that reach deep into the heart of traditional Protestant and Roman Catholic accounts of God that have forgotten to attend to the divine face of God as Spirit. Jürgen Moltmann, a theologian whose work on pneumatology (the doctrine of the Spirit) is widely read, argues that the Pentecostal complaint about "forgetfulness of the Spirit" was a reaction against a kind of Neoorthodoxy in the Protestant churches and a response to the christocentrism in Karl Barth's theology. In other words, the resurgence of pneumatology pushes against any reduction of Christian revelation to Christ, against the temptation to focus singularly on Jesus Christ—characteristic especially of the Reformation traditions—even as it pushes toward a more radically trinitarian, and therefore ecumenical, sensibility.

Moltmann also identifies the third place that the Spirit has emerged in recent theology in ecumenical conversations moving toward a reconciliation of Western Christianity with Eastern Orthodoxy. He reminds us that it was pneumatology that split the church into East and West over a millennium ago. The split occurred in 381, when the Roman church insisted upon adding the controversial "filioque" clause to the Nicene Creed, making the Spirit proceed "from the Father *and the Son.*" From the Eastern perspective this meant an unacceptable subordination of the Spirit to the Son. Moltmann agrees with this view and explains that such a subordination eliminates the two-way motion between the second and third persons: "the way always leads from the Son to the Spirit, no longer from the Spirit to the Son. But this hard and fast conclusion is mistaken, for the Spirit accompanies the begetting of the Son, and the Son accompanies the procession of the Spirit."[4] Furthering ecumenical dialogue with the Orthodox church, for whom the Spirit is central, Moltmann argues that the Spirit of God cannot be separated from the Spirit of Christ, once Jesus has lived and died. But it precedes and exceeds the incarnation. With this argument we see there are not just feminist and Pentecostal/evangelical grounds but also altogether "orthodox" arguments for a more radical affirmation of the Spirit as not only the rather abstract third person of the Trinity but the very "Spirit of Life," the "Divine Energy of Life" itself, the immanence of God in all things, to use Moltmann's own language.

As you will see in our short history of Spirit-talk, the Christian tradition is filled with a variety of new imaginings, some of them celebrated, others repressed. As you will also see in the four constructive proposals on Spirit, the authors see the Spirit moving in radically different directions. The Spirit not only haunts ancient boundaries within and among orthodoxies in the tradition but also daunts every certainty about "right teaching" and "correct language," even in our most progressive attempts at change and hope.

Discerning the Spirit: Six Marks

The theological enterprise of mapping the doctrine of the Spirit is a complex project, one as interested in the ambiguities and poetic indeterminacy of our claims as it is in their seeming givens. As we have worked through scripture, tradition, and our own contemporary views on the matter, we have found ourselves speaking about at least six shared avenues for discerning the Spirit—six marks of Spirit's movement.

1. The Spirit is *prophetic*. The Spirit-possessed person is inspired not only to vision like other ancient seers but also to transformation: "the spirit of the Lord will possess you, and you will be in a prophetic frenzy along with them [the band of prophets] and be turned into a different person" (1 Sam. 10:6). Always in Israel the Spirit inspired the messianic hope for the resurrection of the people and the renewal of all flesh. And today it inspires the movements of liberation, of emancipation, of justice and sustainability, whereby all flesh manly and womanly, old and young, dark and light, human and animal can live in God's *shalom* (peace).
2. The Spirit is *performative*. It acts. It enacts. Or is it rather that it activates the creature to actualize itself, to realize the gift, the charisma of the Spirit—the peculiar gifts we each have received, that we each have to offer, however scorned and disdained they may be? Spirit-performance—as in the polylingual outpouring of Pentecost—provokes dramas, happenings, transformations. And it provokes them *publicly*: indeed, it produces its own new public, its *ecclesia*, its community of actors, of interpreters. And our interpretations of each other in our strangeness, our otherness, our foreign tongues and fiery spirits performs, indeed preforms, the world we hope for, the "beloved community," as Martin Luther King, Jr., called it. But in our embrace of the messianic ethics of the Spirit, we should not neglect the artistic

character of this performativity. Spirit has neither rhyme nor reason without its fleshly, soulful reverberation, without its music, its jazz.

3. The Spirit is *particular*. Always it pours or lights upon a particular situation, in a particular time and a particular place. The Spirit is not an abstraction but a particularization, a realization of particular possibilities to which you and I are particularly called. The call meets us in our particularity. Does the particularity of the Christian path sometimes embarrass us? Yet the Spirit discerned as incarnate in Jesus seeks its flesh and shape in each one of us. Unlike the abstract spirit of modernity, it does not transcend but transforms the world. It does not seek to make all people the same, but it inspires them in their specific potentials and traditions. A Christian spirituality will be neither diluted nor threatened in the encounter with the multiple particularities of a pluralistic world. The church does not possess the Spirit. But we may pray to be possessed by it, liberated not from the particularity but from the rigidity of our boundaries.
4. The Spirit is *processual*. The Spirit of scripture is said to flow, to pour, to burn, to breathe, to beat its wings, and to blow wherever it desires. It is the very movement and shift of life, a shapeshifter, not a metaphysical substance. Even as throughout the witness of scripture its own manifestations shift and evolve taking shamanic, political, messianic, christological, and apocalyptic shapes so our own flux, if we do not block it, may be the flow of the Spirit. It does not transform us once. It calls us into a process of endless transformation, of "entire sanctification," the ultimate sign of which we call the resurrection of all from death: "behold I will cause breath (*rûach*) to enter you, and you will live again" (Ezekiel 37).
5. The Spirit is *paradoxical*. Caught in the jaws of life and death, Spirit theology makes a type of contrapuntal music. Like jazz, its energy emerges in the tension that brings contradictions together. The Spirit of God and the spirit of each of us—one Spirit and many spirits; the Spirit as woman, man, bird; as elemental and personal; those who mourn and those who celebrate; those who struggle for justice and those who make peace; the mystical darkness and the daylight of activism; the human community and the elemental ecology. These contradictions ease into contrasts, forming a unity that is not a closed totality but an infinite process.
6. The Spirit is *primordial*. The Spirit is green—the Spirit is God's power of health and renewal within the primitive elements that make up physical life on our common planet home. While Christians sometimes mistake the Spirit as immaterial and invisible (so the erroneous translation of the phrase "Holy Spirit" as "Holy Ghost" in the King James Bible), the biblical texts consistently figure the Spirit as a corporeal life-form who animates and sustains the natural world. The Spirit makes alive the natural systems on which all life depends. Indeed, images of the Spirit drawn directly from nature are the

defining motif in biblical pneumatology. Consider the following metaphors and descriptions of the Spirit within the Bible: the *animating breath* that brings life and vigor to all things (Gen. 1:2; Ps. 104:29–30); the *healing wind* that conveys power and a new sense of community to those it indwells (Judges 6:34; John 3:6; Acts 2:1–4); the *living water* that vivifies and refreshes all who drink from its eternal springs (John 4:14; 7:37–38); the *cleansing fire* that alternately judges wrongdoers and ignites the prophetic mission of the early church (Acts 2:1–4; Matt. 3:11–12); and the *divine dove*, a fully embodied earth creature, a mother bird, who births creation into existence and, with an olive branch in her mouth, brings peace and renewal to a broken and divided world. This same bird (God) hovers over Jesus at his baptism to inaugurate his public ministry (Gen. 1:1–3; 8:11; Matt. 3:16; John 1:32). The Spirit is a primordial, earthen reality who is biblically figured according to the four primitive, cardinal elements—earth, wind, fire, water—that are the key components of embodied life as we know it.

A Subaltern History of God the Spirit

In much of historical Christian thought, the Spirit is the hidden and forgotten member of the Trinity, without face, appearing in animals or bushes, as unknown as galactic wind or as quiet and intimate as our breath itself. The Spirit is the Cinderella of theology—retiring, unassuming, a shadow presence in the background of the other two members of the Godhead, Father and Son. By definition, theology cannot manage the lisp and stutter of the Spirit; theology, rather, seeks constantly to speak "God" rather than blow like the wind or hover like a bird. But should the page under the reading eye burst into flame then we would have writing of Spirit. The Spirit burns but is not burned up; the Spirit is aflame but is not consumed (Exod. 3:1–7). The ancient unspoken voice says, "be not terrorized; this is just your ancestor moving." After 2,000 years of theology, of histories of Father and Son, Jewish, Byzantine and Catholic, Celtic, Germanic, Spanish Inquisitorial and Swedish liturgical, Calvinist or Kantian, what can we say about the Spirit? How can we speak about the one who seems to refuse to speak clearly for herself? Merely to mutter mundane memories, to say one more time what the mainstream tradition bent on bureaucracy has sermonized, will not do. The Spirit breaking out of Godhead from the beginning like a great mother eagle hovering, beating nestlings airwards out of the nest, beating word-thoughts out of the divine mind, launching creation like a wayward wind, provoking the chant of the Creator God in Genesis, "It is good!"—the Spirit is what in Christian faith groans in sounds too deep for words, as Paul says in Romans 8. The Spirit speaks, but in a subterranean language few of us can hear. The Spirit, then, is the irrepressible primordial groan of all beginnings, all labors, all pains auguring novelty or recreation or hope shattering the moribund surface again. There is no word, no theology adequate to this depth language. So our collective offering in this chapter is by necessity ephemeral and erratic, unplottable, not willing to submit to design or control, neither a moment within history nor an exercise in dogma.

The history of Spirit that follows is episodic and eruptive—an appearance of wind over water (Exod. 12:21); an eagle on the hunt for prey (Ps. 139:7–12; Isa. 40:31); bare fire (1 Kgs. 18:38; Acts 2:2–3); the shiver that shakes kings like Saul into quaking, raving glossolalics, or those who speak in tongues (1 Sam.10:5–13); a power that is stronger than a hurricane even in its vaguest murmur. The Spirit is active, transgressive, hyperbolic. The Spirit is Elijah on the run (1 Kgs. 19:11–13); the later, prophetic shower of Joel (Joel 2:23; Acts 2:16–21); the shout of the rout of rule-makers and wealth-hoarding reigners in palaces (Josh. 5:13 6:20); the revolutionary melody of Mary (Luke 1:46–55); the dove-diving Driver-into-the-Wilderness of Jesus (Mark 1:9–13); the Deep Cry that Paul saw undergirding all life in cosmic suffering (Rom. 8:18–27). The Spirit is the inspiration of insurgent Perpetua, adolescent mother refusing to confess empire even in the face of lion's teeth; the unscratchable Itch under Anthony's skin like a dream of desert as a scheme of Paradise; the later-comer to trinitarian confession in Constantinople; the haunt of saints and haints anonymous and innumerable throughout the West and East; as calm as clairvoyance in the *hesychasm* charism, that mystical Byzantine prayer; and the rouser of medieval rabbles riding peasant rancor into Protestant Reform and finally into French Revolution. The Spirit is the inspirer of "Enlightenment" thinkers and their "benighted" slave resisters, the black church bellowers of civil rights and interminable fights against racism, the fomenter of fierce feminist philosophy, provoker of purple-bold womanist wiles and all the styles of singing Pentecostal tongues, and the leverage of liberation proclaiming every form of domination an abomination.

As Adolf Holl's *The Left Hand of God* enumerates, the task of discerning the movement of the Spirit in history and contemporary culture is difficult indeed: it is not easy to stay simple and sanguine before a Hound of Heaven that howls and brays or only breathes mutely outside the bounds of the written text. Christianity can claim no monopoly here. The tradition itself, of slaves in exit from Egypt or of Palestinian peasants proclaiming an executed criminal as the germinal seed of God in time, resists routinization. Creeds and confessions only mark a monument against which this Wind as often as not cavorts. The Spirit hallows and haunts, moans and mobilizes, in peoples and cultures baptized and not. A Hindu Gandhi as well as an Egyptian Anthony, an apparition of Kali as well as a vision of Guadalupe, an event like breaking bread as well as breaking tyranny, *haiku* as much as Romantic poesy all these persons and events may become the "place" of being inspired, being inspirited, a holy inhabitation.

In scholarly disciplines of late, a question has emerged with great urgency, namely, how can one give an account of the consciousness or effort of history's (seeming) losers? What is the meaning of, say, a farmers' rebellion, a workers' stoppage, a wife's flight from the recurrent abuses of her husband, the infanticide of a desperate escaped slave mother such as the character in Toni Morrison's *Beloved*? Or closer to home in this chapter, how can one write theologies of the spirits of struggle from the underside? Given the above-noted insurgence of a *rûach* resisting formalization in writing, we have not appealed in what follows to the regnant sources and privileged appearances of Spirit. In fact, we have not even insisted that the name *Spirit* remain linguistically formulated and capitalized as only one and singular (there are many "spirits" with or without the capital "S"). The Bible gives hints: there may be seven or more S/spirits under the throne (Isa. 11:1–3; Rev. 4:5). Underneath the gaze of dominating literacy, the privileged rule of the eye, the code that matters is *rhythm* polymorphous, multivalent, syncopated soundings of energy that defy death before its time. Here, Spirit is life—it is intensity denying rigidity, the fecund many inside the eloquent one. To identify Spirit we must search for that elusive Something that augurs the other world inside this one like the first bursting of a snowdrop flower in the late winter snow. We have somewhat arbitrarily selected cultures and figures, movements and events that hint at the possibility from intriguing and controversial angles.

Tracking Spirit is attending to the surreptitious: after the 586 B.C.E. exile, Israel waited more than a half-millennium for the underground stream to break surface again in the bellicosity of John the Baptist's tongue. Or at least so the official version goes. But how would we know if inspired, inspirited up-wellings did not occur in multiple places, known only to unsung strugglers and a few followers or family? Undoubtedly they did. And just as undoubtedly they still do. In particular, in our own time and space of globalizing capital and imperializing America, there is a burden on a Christianity that has colluded with colonialism and its aftermath to listen and learn from beyond its borders. The year 1492 in the common era marks the full arrival of the Constantinian take-over of Christianity for purposes of conquest and control. Spirit will as often as not appear as connivance or conspiracy "against" the faith on the part of little peoples offering "errant" witness in unbiblical language to the work of a love or a labor that refuses its own suppression or stigma. Black spirituals here posit the paradigm. But so do blues and Appalachian banjos, east Indian *bhagans* and Brazilian *bossa novas*, Native American ghost dancing of the last century and rap ribaldry today. Discernment of Spirit and spirits can no longer claim to adhere to canonical views; immersion in context and collaboration in risk and concern are the only sure guides.

Our subaltern history of the Spirit has looked to contemporary vignettes and biblical sources to ground its portrayal from the underside of human experience. We now turn to the sweep of church history to track the Spirit's movements, beginning with the immediate postbiblical period. During the early patristic era—the opening of the second century C.E.—the fluidity of biblical pneumatology still characterized Christian thought. Indeed, one cannot speak of a systematic doctrine of the Holy Spirit. Spirit oscillates between three major meanings: (1) spirit as divine (as when Tertullian says that "the Word is made of Spirit" [*Against Praxeas* 7–8]); (2) spirit as human (following the Pauline trichotomy of "spirit and soul and body" [1 Thess. 5:23] and Philo's tradition of identifying the human intellect or rational soul with the spirit); (3) and spirit as the Holy Spirit, that is, as the third person of the Trinity (thus Origen observed, "Saving baptism is not complete except when performed with the authority of the whole most excellent Trinity. . . ; and . . . the name of the Holy Spirit must be joined to that of the unbegotten God the Father and his only begotten Son" [*First Principles* 1.3.2]).

During this pre-Nicene period the prophetic energy of the Spirit is still abundant, performing the infusion of the Spirit of God in the human spirit. Ignatius of Antioch, a Spirit-filled prophet and martyr, "cried aloud" in "a great voice," claiming, "What I knew was not from human flesh, but it was the Spirit who preached by my lips." But, intriguingly, the Spirit happened to be preaching church hierarchy: "Do nothing apart from the Bishop" was the prophecy. This is a hybrid transition-moment portent with significance for the future of the church: Ignatius believed both that the Holy Spirit still spoke through prophets and that the threefold ministry of bishops, presbyters, and deacons had been established by the same Spirit.

The Shepherd of Hermas manifests the survival of prophecy in the Roman church into the middle of the second century. The Shepherd's apocalyptic account of "rapture" as seizure and transportation by the Spirit into the heavens attests to an ecstatic practice, including strong distinctions between true and false prophets. Anyone who claims to be "Spirit-bearing" (*pneumatophoros*) is to be tested "by his life and his works" (*Mandate* 11). The false prophet is the one who seeks a *profit*: "who surrounds himself with luxuries . . . and takes money for prophesying." Similarly, Theophilus, sixth bishop of Antioch, sometimes identifies the "Spirit of prophecy" with the "the Word, being Spirit of God, the principality and wisdom and power of the Most High." But he goes on to distinguish the Wisdom/Sophia of God as the Holy Spirit from the Word; thus the Word and Wisdom of God form a triad with "God." Here it is that the word *trinity* (*trias*) first occurs, though not yet in the sense that would become orthodox. Theophilus adds a fourth, the human being, so we get the series: "God, the Word, Wisdom, Man."

Slightly later, Irenaeus, in his battle with "heretical" notions of multiple divine emanations, would similarly affirm the prophetic spirit as one with the spirit of creation and with Sophia. "The Word, namely the Son, was always with the Father; and that Wisdom also, which is the Spirit, was present with Him, anterior to all creation, [as] He declares by Solomon: 'God by Wisdom founded the earth'" (*Against Heresies* 4.20. 3). Thus, in his pre-Trinitarian triad, the work of creation is accomplished by God's "hands, that is, by the Son and Holy Spirit, to whom also He said, 'let us make man'."

Montanism

In the mid-second century epoch the last powerful outbreak of Spirit-prophecy occurred with the Montanist movement. Montanism was a Spirit-saturated apocalyptic movement that caught fire in the area of Phrygia, in what is today Turkey. Montanus, an early ecstatic prophet in the tradition of the biblical prophets, preached that the Spirit told him that the heavenly Jerusalem was coming soon to Phrygia. Oracle of the Spirit, Montanus proclaimed that the full outpouring of the Spirit would come to Phrygia in the second century in fulfillment of the charismatic arrival of the Spirit at Pentecost in the first century. The "New Prophecy" of Montanus, Priscilla, and Maximilla, while positioning itself in continuity with the Hebrew prophets, the church of Paul, and the Revelation of John, nonetheless released the sort of ecstatic enthusiasm that the church found dangerous. "Christ came to me in the likeness of a woman, clad in a bright robe," announced Priscilla. "And He planted wisdom in me and revealed that this place (Pepuza) is holy, and that here Jerusalem comes down from heaven." The Montanists' pneumatological apocalypticism, with its high expectation of imminent and radical world transformation, initially exercised great influence. But the emerging institutional church nonetheless found the Montanists, and indeed the very Spirit of ongoing prophecy, guilty of originality. The prophetic spirit would now rather expeditiously settle into the Holy Spirit, who inspires orthodox adherence to the beliefs and practices of the church. Though largely defended by

Tertullian as an expression of the Spirit's continuing work in the world, Montanism was later condemned by other orthodox theologians and church councils.[5]

Montanism was put on the list of heresies and thereby pushed aside, out of the way of a church that was looking for broad-based support. In principle, after the Montanist prophecy, virtually every instance whatsoever of possession by the Spirit was stigmatized and rejected for the next 1,000 years of the Sacrum Imperium that Constantine had molded. The couriers and messengers of God, both men and women, disappeared into the underground; the Holy Spirit became a theological abstraction; and the liturgy in the basilicas proceeded without further interruption.[6]

In the struggle over the proper formulation of orthodox Christianity, the church's gaze remained fixed on the second, not the third, person. But once Nicaea established that the Christ was consubstantial with the divine and not a creature—"begotten not made"—parallel questions began to arise as to the metaphysical status of the (Holy) Spirit. The architect of orthodoxy, Athanasius, argued that all of God's activity is "originated and actuated through the Word in the Spirit." But Eusebius of Caesarea maintained that the Spirit is a creature of the Son. Basil of Caesarea protested on behalf of the unity of the saving work of the Spirit with that of Father and Son and thus of the unity of their being. Now the debate about the "coessentiality" of the Spirit with the Father and Son entered into full swing. How can the Son be a "coequal person" with the Spirit, if the latter is not addressed in prayer in scripture? Because, argued Basil, we pray "in the Spirit" to God and not directly to the Spirit. Gregory of Nyssa sought to clarify that the Spirit is "neither Unbegotten nor Only-begotten, but simply is what he is."

In *The Confessions* Augustine was fascinated not with trinitarian metaphysics but with the "Spirit who dwells in us," who, in the iconography of Gen. 1:2, which can be paraphrased as, "was borne above our dark and fluid inner being." But it is his *On the Trinity*, a work written over decades, that would establish the full logic of Western pneumatology. If the Father and the Son commune eternally in a state of mutual love, the Spirit *is* their "mutual love" (*amor mutuus*): "Their common life (*communio*) must itself be consubstantial and coeternal with Them." This is a powerful assertion of the irreducibility of love to anything else. Augustine's model for understanding the Spirit as the bond of love within the inner life of Godself—what he also calls the *vinculum caritatis*—construes the Spirit as the love who unites the Father and the Son in mutual fellowship in the inner circle of the Trinity. The Spirit is the power of the eternal relationship among Creator, Redeemer, and

Sustainer within the Godhead. In a word, the Spirit is *love*—the love that is common to the three members of God's intertrinitarian family, and the love that is God's gift to all members of the human family as well. Augustine wrote,

> It follows that the Spirit himself is the God who is love. If among God's gifts there is none greater than love, and there is no greater gift of God than the Holy Spirit, we naturally conclude that he who is said to be both God and of God is himself love. And if the love whereby the Father loves the Son and the Son loves the Father displays, beyond the power of words, the communion of both, it is most fitting that the Spirit who is common to both should have the special name of love.
>
> (*The Trinity* 15.37.xix)

In the bosom of the Trinity, the Spirit is the power of communion, the bond of love, who insures the fellowship and reciprocity of the divine persons with each other. The technical term for this trinitarian commonality is *perichoresis*, which literally means "dancing around," and is used to describe the Spirit's eternal enactment of the deep love and mutuality shared by all members of the Godhead. Perichoretically, the Trinity is the Dance of Life in which the Spirit performs the role of empowering the never-ending communion and relational vitality that is God in Godself.

To stabilize his intuition of radical relationality within the terms of Greek metaphysics, Augustine established the love-spirit as its own (changeless, supernatural, platonic) "substance." Indeed, a strong sense of the work of the Holy Spirit in the soul strengthened Augustine's hand against the Donatists and the Pelagians, with their insistence upon a certain free will in our response to divine teaching and Christ's example. "This is the hidden, dreadful, poison that your heresy [Pelagianism] infuses; you would make the grace of Christ consist in His example and not in His life, saying that men are made righteous by imitating Him, not by the Holy Spirit which leads them to imitate Him, the Spirit which He poured abundantly upon His own" (*Against Julian: Opus Imperfectum* i.86.337). Elsewhere he offered a succinct analogy: "what the soul is to the human body such is the Holy Spirit to the Body of Christ" (*Sermones* 267). Thus, the substantiality of the Spirit vitalizes the true church and "makes us to abide in God, and God in us, for this is the effect of love." This love-effect paradoxically at once strengthens and disciplines the Spirit: it now becomes firmly entrenched in third place. It proceeds out of the Father-Son fellowship; thus the Spirit proceeds "from the Father and the Son" (*ex Patre Filioque*). This is the formula that would distinguish Western from Eastern orthodoxy. Its incorporation in the Latin version of the Niceno-Constantinopolitan Creed would open an unending rupture and stimulate centuries of controversy between the Greek and Latin churches.

On the northern, island edge of the emerging European society advanced by Augustine was the nature-loving, illuminated book culture of the Irish Celts. Celtic Christianity is one of the more suggestive places we can look for a trace of an "other" history of the Spirit inside the Christian tradition itself. Anonymously evangelized sometime in the third century C.E. (though more famously converted by the spiritual "combat" of St. Patrick against his Druid forebears in the fifth century), Celtic versions of the gospel life offered creative expression of the tradition in terms familiar to a nature-loving, shamanic-savvy culture of island life. Irish embodiment of Christian discipleship became the repository and saving mediation of Western Christianity during the "somber centuries" (600–1000 C.E.) on the continent, when Asian and Scandinavian invasion all but obliterated the remaining vestiges of city life and Roman aristocratic versions of the faith. Never faced with violent imposition of the gospel by an imperial army, and never reacting with the kind of savage repudiation that created Christian martyrs, Ireland gave birth to a Celtic spirituality of high literacy, deep empathy, and elaborate artistry. Tribally based, monastically organized, and entrepreneurially vitalized, early Irish Christianity invested the faith with many of the traditional practices and predilections that had already shaped the Celtic spirit in its long pilgrimage across the European landscape from Turkey to Spain, Black Sea shore to plain of Brittany, before settling on the emerald isles of Britain.

Perhaps nowhere is this ingenious Irish amalgamation of new messianism and ecological conviction more evident than in the illuminated manuscripts brought forth from monastic enclaves from the seventh to the ninth centuries. Here, even in barest glimpse, we find a mesmerizing conflation of classical Christian subject matter and Celtic mystical sensibility: Christ or the apostles stare out from the vellum page in trance-like probe of the reader, enmeshed in writhing contortions of lion mouths grasping peacock legs wrapped around angel wings sprouting from the ox or eagle representation of the Gospel writers. The designs are intricate and not sheer ornament. The newly elevated cultural artifact of this emergent religion—the written text of the New Testament—is made the vehicle for the subjugated knowledge of what is being succeeded. Gospel book is embroidered as liturgical talisman for the illiterate believer. Arguably, in this stunning decoration, older shamanistic intuition engulfs Christian tradition in a creative efflorescence, rooting gospel politics in a Spirit-animism that is characteristic of tribal cultures around the globe. The world of Spirit is not located elsewhere in such a cosmology but found "inside" of wild nature, offering plants and animals as teacher-guides for the human community. The flowing sinuosity of the bestial bodies, the Uroborous-effect of a snake eating itself apocalyptically or, read inversely, disgorging its being from within itself in the primal moment of creation, subsume linear theology in cyclical spirituality.

The eighth-century Book of Kells—which integrates classical Greco-Roman artistry into the color-thickets of Hiberno-Saxon prodigality—is associated with Ireland's premier saint, Columba, the bard-monk founder of the Iona community, whose Latin name, "dove," links the labyrinthine nature-vision of the book with the Spirit-bird of the scriptures. Columba, according to his followers, was often found in prayer with a column of light shooting up over his head, a living Pentecost of passionate invocation and an example of the ancient view of the skull as seat of spiritual power. For Columba and others, there was no need to choose between "pagan" origins and Christian belief system: in early medieval Ireland, indigenous mysticism was grafted heart and soul onto Christian charism.

Roman versus Celtic Christianity

The Synod of Whitby was hosted in 664 by the Celtic abbey of that name, a somewhat unique community of both monks and nuns, headed up by a woman, which provided the forum for debate between divergent Roman and Celtic Christian observances. Beginning in 634, Irish monks had been invited by Northumbrian royalty to evangelize Anglo-Saxon areas of eastern Britain from the island-center of Lindisfarne, just off the east coast. Only a few years earlier, a Roman monastic representative of Gregory the Great, St. Augustine of Canterbury, had arrived on the south coast and similarly begun evangelizing northwards. The ensuing clash between "Christianities" came to a head in the public dispute between Wilfred of the Anglos and Colman of the Celts. When Colman acknowledged his "theological" defeat, the Irish willingly gave up Lindisfarne and retreated to the western island monastic enclave of Iona, founded in 565 by Columba. But the defeat in doctrine (about the dating of Easter celebrations and the tonsure of monks) did not signal a defeat in influence. Lines of influence could be drawn from Lindisfarne to Iona, Kells on the Emerald Isle itself to Rome, the Holy Land in the far east to Frisia in the north. The routes of reciprocal transformations are as convoluted as the illuminated letters themselves in the Lindisfarne Gospels (700) and the Book of Kells (760), giving rise to an Anglo-Hiberno style of island sensibility that eventually fertilizes Charlemagne's cultural policy on the continent. Spirit winds its way geographically much like its shapeshifting morphology in the margins of the great illuminated manuscripts of the Irish church.

Joachim of Fiore and Hildegard of Bingen, two twelfth-century Christian mystics, give further expression to the immediate, enlivening experience of the Spirit in the life of the believer. Born in southern Italy c. 1135, Joachim of Fiore was a biblical exegete and visionary theologian who taught that world history follows a trinitarian pattern and that we are now awaiting the arrival of the Third Age, the Age of the Spirit. As a young man he received a series of revelations, one at Easter and the other at Pentecost, in which he largely divined the meaning of the Book of Revelation. He joined the Cistercian order as a monk and later left the community in order to establish a series of monastic congregations in the Sila mountains. Initially supported by a series of Popes during his lifetime, Joachim's views later influenced certain radical Franciscans, and his subsequent interpreters were condemned by papal authorities in the thirteenth century. But his apocalyptic musings about the Age of the Spirit continued to inspire his admirers, including Dante, who in his *Paradiso* locates Joachim, "endowed with prophetic spirit," in the center of a pantheon of other spiritual luminaries.

As a seer inspired by the Spirit, Joachim thought and wrote in pictures and symbols. He drew highly imaginative, triadic images of intertwining animals, vines, trees, and geometric forms to depict the threefold rhythm of world history.[7] One of his central images is of three interlocking circles to depict the alternately cyclical and progressive movement of time under the direction of God's trinitarian activity. In explaining his aesthetic vision, Joachim writes, "The first period, therefore, ought to be assigned to the Father, the second to the Son . . . [and] the third period, to the Holy Spirit. For this reason the Holy Spirit will reveal his glory in the third period, as the Son revealed his in the second, the Father his in the first."[8] The first superimposed circle in Joachim's artwork represents, therefore, the Age of the Father, the Old Testament period, in which humankind in family units lived under the Law until the coming of Christ. The second circle stands for the Age of the Son, the New Testament period, in which humankind now enjoys the offer of grace through the leadership of the clergy. The third circle is the Age of the Spirit, the new and arriving egalitarian world order, in which all persons will enjoy the immediate presence of God as Spirit as modeled by the simple and committed lives of the spiritual monastics Joachim helped to organize. Using John's Apocalypse as his key to comprehending the sweep of human history, it is Joachim's focus on this third circle that is the continuing source of his opposition and support. While still kindling much opprobrium theologian George Tavard dismisses Joachim's "picture theology" as a "posthumous failure" in which his "pictures, like his visions of history, are matters for the head, not the heart"[9]—other supporters and followers, from the Spiritual Franciscans in the medieval period to such disparate contemporary thinkers as Friedrich Schelling, Ernst Bloch, and Mircea Eliade find in the Italian abbot a voice for revolutionary Christian utopianism that is much needed in our own time.

Hildegard of Bingen is the spiritual sister of Joachim of Fiore. While there is no direct connection between these two visionaries, there are many deep affinities that underlie their respective theologies. Both thinkers were twelfth-century monastics and mystical prophets who wrote trinitarian theologies with special attention to the role of the Spirit in the world. Like Joachim, Hildegard joined a religious order. But Hildegard did so at the behest of her parents at age nine. At this early age Hildegard became an anchoress, a religious woman who lived as a recluse, walled into a monastic cell by the local bishop for the rest of her life. But Hildegard emerged from her childhood cell to become a prolific writer, musician, artist, herbalist, abbess of her growing religious community, and even statesperson as she maintained influential relationships with bishops, kings, and emperors during the high Middle Ages. She was called the "Sybil of the Rhine" for her wide-ranging impact on medieval culture through the power of her visionary writings.

In her major work entitled *Scivias* (that is, *Sci vias lucis*, "Know the Ways of Light"), Hildegard says she heard a voice from a living fire say to her, "O you who are wretched earth and, as a woman, untaught in all learning . . . cry out and relate and write these my mysteries that you see and hear in mystical visions. So do not be timid, but say those things you understand in the Spirit as I speak them through you."[10] Hildegard, being commanded by God to "cry out and write," became an oracle of the Holy Spirit. Though women were forbidden to exercise public leadership roles in the teaching ministry of the medieval church, the Spirit cut loose Hildegard's hesitant tongue and enjoined her to preach. Many of Hildegard's contemporaries, including several male clerics, saw her as filled with the Spirit and able to exercise the biblical role of prophet in a culture that needed her special message. Hildegard is a Spirit-inspired trailblazer for women today who look for God's call in their lives as a subversion of a male-dominated ecclesial and social order.

Resonant with the nature mysticism of earlier Celtic Christianity, the content of Hildegard's special message was essentially ecological, as we understand that term today. Hearkening back to the earth-centered language of the Spirit in the biblical texts—the Spirit is breath, water, fire, and earthen life-form such as a dove—Hildegard offers a nature-based model of the Spirit in relation to the other two members of the Godhead: "He who begets is the Father; he who is born is the Son; and he who in eager freshness proceeds from the Father and the Son, and sanctified the waters by moving over their face in the likeness of an innocent bird, and streamed with ardent heat over the apostles, is the Holy Spirit."[11] Hildegard's earthen spirituality was the source of her practice as a naturalist and plant-based healer. Keeper of the soil, she published extensive catalogues of the medicinal properties of the flora she cultivated and used for ailing visitors at the monastery in Bingen. She wrote and sang hymns of thanksgiving praising God for the bounty of nature and the fertility of the earth. Spiritually and physically, the earth's rich vegetation has healing properties that can refresh and renew all of God's creatures. As Elizabeth Dryer puts it,

> In addition to the Spirit's role as prophetic inspiration, Hildegard links the Holy Spirit with the term *viriditas* or "greening." She imagined the outpouring of the Spirit in natural rather than cultural metaphors. She combined images of planting, watering, and greening to speak of the presence of the Holy Spirit. Hildegard linked the flow of water on the crops with the love of God that renews the face of the earth, and by extension the souls of believers.[12]

For Hildegard, horticulture is religion because the Spirit lives in and through the natural world, bringing all things into health and fruition. Hildegard's valorization of her own female voice and her explicit correlations between God as Spirit and the fecundity of creation are significant sources for both the "gendering" and "greening" of theology in contemporary Christian feminist and environmental thought.

Thomas Müntzer, priest, preacher, and prophet, was the sixteenth-century theological heir of the medieval Spirit tradition articulated by Joachim and Hildegard. Müntzer studied theology at Leipzig and Frankfurt and served as father confessor to a group of Cistercian nuns in Thuringia. Around 1520 Müntzer became a convert to the Protestant Reformation cause in Germany and was an early supporter of Martin Luther. But he soon parted company with Luther, calling him "Brother Soft Life" because of Luther's halfway measures toward reform that did not make a full turn to a complete social revolution against the hierarchical church and feudal society. Müntzer opposed Luther's theology and its emphasis on "scripture alone" as the key to Christian identity. For Müntzer and other so-called Radical Reformers, Christianity is not a book-bound religion but consists rather of the individual believer's mystical oneness with Christ through the direct agency of the Holy Spirit. Moreover, the kingdom of God is coming to everyone who is filled with the Spirit, cried Müntzer, and it will crush all earthly rulers. Müntzer's Spirit-preaching galvanized the poor and disenfranchised peasants who regarded him as an apocalyptic prophet hell-bent on overthrowing an unjust social order. Müntzer's anti-clerical and populist emphasis on the power of the Spirit to destroy evil aimed to flatten the structures of religious and political authority in his time and made him a false prophet in the eyes of his erstwhile Protestant comrades.[13]

Müntzer taught that the church of his time was filled with false teachers who "hurl themselves against the Holy Spirit"[14] by denying the possibility that the Spirit remains alive and active in the world beyond the age of the biblical apostles. Anyone can be like the apostles because every person is a candidate for the unmediated experience of the Spirit in their heart and lives. Quoting the Books of Joel and Acts, Müntzer says that God will again "pour out his Holy Spirit over all flesh and our sons and daughters shall prophesy and shall have dreams and visions, etc. For if Christendom is not to become apostolic (Acts 2:16ff.) in the way anticipated in Joel, why should one preach at all? To what purpose then [is] the Bible with [its] visions?"[15] Müntzer's vision of a new Spirit-filled apostolic church that denies the authority of priests and bishops roused the ire of everyone around him except the common people. Direct communion with the Spirit ensures the ongoing power of divine revelation apart from clerical intervention and outside the channels of approved church teachings. The Holy Spirit is not the possession of the established church; rather, the Spirit is the inner testimony to the truth available to all persons. In Müntzer the Spirit was a wild, uncontrollable, and insurgent force for revolutionary reform. In the tradition of the medieval mystics, Müntzer identified the Spirit as the "inner light" and the "inner teacher" who can lead all persons, educated and unlearned alike, into direct communion with God. Other, later left-wing Protestant Reformers followed Müntzer in this thinking, including Menno Simons, founder of the Mennonites, and George Fox, founder of Quakerism (the Society of Friends).

But Müntzer's call for a return to primitive Christianity took an ugly turn toward armed revolt that his latter-day Mennonite and Quaker fellow travelers did not subsequently embrace. Like Simons and Fox, Müntzer called for the direct indwelling of the Spirit, but unlike Simons and Fox he linked this call to the charge to take up arms and root out the infidels who had corrupted the church and wider society. "Do not let your sword rust in its scabbard!" cried Müntzer in 1524 to a group of Protestant rulers and churchmen in an effort to stir up his audience to fight a holy war against his emerging Lutheran opposition.[16] Müntzer's call to war inspired the notorious Peasants' Revolt of

1525, in which masses of disgruntled commoners went on rampages throughout the German countryside, sacking castles and monasteries. Müntzer himself was later captured and executed for his role in the insurrection. Apocalyptic revolutionary and Spirit visionary, Müntzer's life and thought are a cautionary tale to contemporary Christians to be aware of the opportunities and the dangers inherent in seeking to lead an insurgent, Spirit-filled life.

From the early modern to the late modern period, we shift gears in our tracing of the Spirit's tracks in history. In our own time, three important examples of the Spirit working "outside" and "underneath" the mainstream Christian tradition are to be found in Afro-diaspora spiritualities, American Indian religion, and ecstatic Pentecostalism. In our first case, Afro-Caribbean and African American traditions of "working the Spirit"—in creative amalgamations of West and Central African rhythmic sensibilities with European and Amerindian cultural forms—constitute perhaps the most sustained subterranean innovations of the Holy *rûach* yet witnessed in history. (The term *African American* in this context includes Central and South American as well as North American populations of African heritage.) Here the Ghost of Groan, whom Paul perceived percolating toward freedom inside everything (Romans 8), was forced to labor pain into power in a manner that might make even Moses envious. The tradition that began its confession as a cry of the enslaved for liberation in Exodus, by the time of Columbus found itself perversely positioned as a new Pharaoh, thinking Jesus had been converted to a love of conquest in his twelve-century-long tryst with Caesar. But the tradition got it patently wrong. Indeed, contemporary Western Christianity at large cannot be comprehended apart from a thoroughgoing grasp of the way white supremacy has emerged as the bastard offspring of a confused sense of Christian superiority over other religions in the course of European colonization of the rest of the planet after 1492.

The entire modern project of subordination of peoples of color for the sake of concentrating resources and power in Western hands and lands was nowhere as ruthlessly pursued or vigorously "rationalized" as in the African slave trade. The ideology of supremacy that licensed the larceny of dark bodies from the mother continent of us all was *theologically* valorized: white skin was presumed to have a monopoly on spiritual truth and rights of reproof on all other expressions of insight. In consequence, Spirit has been driven deep into the bone of black memory of a different kind of vitality. Though differing in theological doctrine—in the Protestant black church, appearing as the One God; in older conjure traditions less colonized by white evangelicalism, appearing as multiple ancestral *personas* (*orishas* or *loas*)—Afro-diaspora celebrations of spiritual liberation everywhere move the body in recognizably African patterns.

The Faces of the Spirit

The idea that the Holy Spirit could be entertained to have more than one face or facet, more than one identity of expression, in the economy of the Trinity, is not so far removed from the Christian tradition as might be thought. In addition to biblical references that do not shy from working in the plural sense of "spirits," there is also the Pauline enumeration of the charisms of the *Hagia Pneuma*, the gifts of working that show up in the gathered community, whether in the form of tongues-speaking or healing, administrations of mercy or bellowings of prophecy, travels of apostles or trials of pastors (1 Corinthians 12–14; Eph. 4:1–16; Rom. 12:1–8). While trinitarian debate (in the Councils of Nicaea in 325 and Constantinople in 381) and christological controversy (in Ephesus in 431 and Chalcedon in 451) resulted in attempts at precise delineation of the substance and borders of shared Godhead, the Spirit's incorporation in the circulation of divine identity in 381 could only offer its operation as a primary mobility. In a word, the Spirit *moves*. Arguably, even in orthodox trinitarianism, the primary vocabulary of the Spirit's proclivity is that of dance, as we saw with Augustine in the fifth century: the *perichoresis* that circumambulates each of the three in and through the others. Here, obviously, is a site of much needed theological exploration.

Even when mainstream emphasis, West and East, tries to close the dogmatic door on allowing a radical plurality of divine moves vis-à-vis humanity, the thirst for multiple expression merely relocates its affections toward the communion of saints. If the Spirit is to be theologically straight-jacketed in the denomination of One, the living incarnation of that Spirit's work in history shows up as an ever-proliferating Many. It is at this exact point that African spiritualities—especially in the creolized modalities of the Diaspora like Voudou and Santeria, "Hoodoo" and Obeah, Jamaican Pocomania and Brazilian Cadomble—offer provocative witness. In surviving enslavement, African memory of its traditional Spirit-personas took umbrage in Roman Catholic camouflage: St. Patrick became the image of Damballah when mounting his human "horse," Mary housed Ezulie, St. George exhibited Ogu, St. Barbara showed Shango "in drag," and St. Peter embodied Eshu. That each of these manifestations of divinity in human form, for the space of a communal ritual, should rely on drum-driven dance moves as the primary idiom for identification of the arrival of spirit-in-the-flesh, should give pause. The exact parameters of inspiration may need to be re-inscribed under tutelage to this African invocation arising from the bowels of "Christian" slavery.

Arguably, rhythm is the primary vocabulary of Spirit forced underground, where it shows up in Saturday night squawk of horn as well as Sunday morning gospel song, in blues holler as well as hymn liner, in Voudou shoulder-roll as much as Baptist clap, Santeria shuffle and Candomble prance not less than AME shout—indeed, in the whole history of black laboring of impossible circumstance into antiphonal triumph of soul even inside a chain. And the public politics of such a possession-worship has again and again erupted in social movements for a better world. Drum-animated Haitian revolution (1791–1804) achieved the only successful national slave revolt in history; maroonage across the Caribbean resulted in estimable communal experiments in Amerindian-African cooperation; abolition agitation in the United States altered the Civil War focus from accommodation to elimination of slavery; Marcus Garvey's Back to Africa movement provided inspiration for initiatives of black economic and cultural independence; the North American civil rights movement dismantled Jim Crow segregation; and Black Power reversed the categories of social stigma into a public profile of pride. In the mix, Spirit took recurrent political shape as irrepressible "spiritedness." Post-slavery lynch mobs and terroristic oppression (in the southern United States), post-World War II ghettoization and discrimination (in the northern United States), post-revolutionary isolation and depravation (in Haiti), post-colonial exploitation (all around the Atlantic world) have not enervated the insurgent ribaldry of Spirit-driven creativity on the part of Afro-creolized populations, whose reggae, rap, funk, and samba improvisations of hardship-into-worship now rock church and society all around the globe. The modern mode of Spirit is *incendiary percussion*: the epiphany of God inside the infinite polyphony of sound made melodic and harmonic, rhythmically syncopated and bass-beat-weighted in a revelation that says that no space, no time, is too locked down to be cracked open by Spirit breaking in like a thief in the night.

Our second case of Spirit inside and outside the dominant religious paradigm is Native American theology and ritual. In the beginning, before Western secular and theological discourses became the dominant and revisionist languages of the global community, indigenous people conceived of a life space where the Spirit was radically incarnated into the very essence of creation. Beyond metaphor and symbol, Spirit offered multidimensional and multilingual expressions of what it means to be a life vessel. In American Indian contexts, this spiritual dynamism erupted from daily life and from the specificity of ritual and communal intention. Although individuals were invested with the authority to mediate and guide spiritual encounters, an egalitarian understanding of Spirit emanations prevailed. Spirit activity was acknowledged in all aspects of the life spectrum including the plant, animal, and human realms. Because of this common spiritual denominator, the interconnectivity of life-forces was assumed.

A Warning about Labels

American Indian or Native American cultures are unique and specific to a particular geography and tribal ancestry. Just as the term *African* locates a person or community on a particular continent but gives little or no information about the specific culture referenced, generic labels for American Indians lack reference to a more detailed understanding of particular communities along with their social and spiritual history.

In recent years indigenous people, American Indians, Asians, Africans, and others have contributed their Spirit-talk to theological discourse. American Indian cultures (like many indigenous communities) make the point that their lives are journeys through a spiritual multiverse. As Kenneth Morrison has written, "human and other-than-human mutuality . . . [are] both the social and cosmic ideal, and the goal of ritual action."[17] This way of thinking evokes varying responses from the bastions of "mainline theology" that range from curiosity and sincere acceptance to befuddlement and open resistance. Historically, Christian theological encounters with ethnic faith perspectives run the gamut from aggression and insidious cultural destruction to the more benign contestations that remind me of the children's game "Rock/Paper/Scissors." In this game, enthusiastic youngsters duel with their fingers to determine a winner—rock breaks scissors, or paper covers rock. In the terms of this children's game, then, does the book supersede the power of oral history, or do rationalism and critical thinking trump mystical experience?

These questions are powerful and instructive even without answers. But the entire question/answer game is not of paramount importance to Native people. What is important to Native communities is that they have survived. The fact that American Indian culture has continued despite the withering interpretive blasts of Western enlightenment mentality can be attributed at least in part to the trickster resiliency and creativity of the people, their spiritual and cosmological "connectedness" while under siege, and the tenacious elusiveness of their oral culture. Only in the last few decades have Western scholars conceded that direct religious and cultural connections to the unseen world are not proof of social immaturity. Rather, such embodied practices of faith and ritual create and sustain the well-being of communities and individuals.

Powwows

In recent years powwows have become increasingly popular even in non-Native communities. These events serve many purposes, including intentional reclamations of historical memory and commemorations of ancestral heritage. Typically, several tribes come together for the event, and activities include songs, dances, and prayers that evoke commonly held spiritual and cultural beliefs. However, these often open and public pan-Indian events are only the tip of the cultural iceberg. Cultural cannibals who think otherwise and expect to gain total knowledge of Native cultures through attendance at one event will feast but never obtain satisfaction.

In 1977, a position paper of the Six Nations was presented at Geneva to the Non-Governmental Organizations of the United Nations, which included this poignant quote:

> The traditional Native peoples hold the key to the reversal of the process of western civilization, which holds the promise of unimaginable suffering and destruction. Spirituality is the highest form of political consciousness. And we, the Native Peoples of the Western Hemisphere, are among the world's surviving proprietors of that kind of consciousness. We are here to impart that message.

The message has been heard loud and clear. The movement from a univocal theology to a constructive theology of word, dance, and spirit song is a gift to all. In American Indian contexts, Holy Scripture breathes revelations through syncretism, plains grasses, American Indian scholars and activists, and sweat lodges and powwows. This is sufficient proof that the Christian tradition is anchored not in the bedrock of familiarity and comfort but in the leading of a provocative and playful Spirit, who tends to lead humankind into the most unlikely and prickly places.

Womanism and Native American Religion

M. A. Jaimes Guerrero connects American Indian spirituality with African American womanism. She suggests that Alice Walker's definition of womanism is congruent with "Earth Mother," also known as the cocreator, and "Changing Woman," familiar to Southwestern American Indian communities as the "creatrix" who restores the "rightful authority" of American Indian women.[18]

A living and constructive theology embraces, enfolds, and nurtures the complexity and diversity of the human family. Each of us approaches the journey and the encounter with the Creator in ways that are particular to our cultural locations and creative innovations. When Christianity is defined and articulated in rigid and culturally biased ways, it loses the very essence of its being. Those who grasp Christian theology with tightly held epistemological fists inevitably find nothing in their sweaty palms. The story of Christian theology is a book-oriented, particular, performative, and personal saga, but one that is amenable to creative inculturation and improvisation. American Indian cultures contribute a spirituality that is deeply connected to the multiple realities of a universe not limited by our natural sight. For this gift and many others we are grateful.

A Story about Spirit

The spirit follows the parents for two years before it is born. It follows, watching. It knows everything. Even when it is born it knows everything. Until it starts walking, talking. Maybe one year old. Then it forgets, falls apart what it knows. Then, you know, it starts learning again. If the person gets old, REAL old, it will be all together again. In between is what you call living.[19]

The phenomenon of baptism in the Spirit is another case study that considers the resurgence of Spirit in our time. If the turn-of-the-twentieth-century Azusa Street Revival in Los Angeles marks the modern inception of Pentecostal experience of the Holy Spirit, it is arguable that it also marks the irruption of *Afro-spiritism* inside Christian conviction. The Spirit-baptizing and tongues-speaking fiery-ness of the resulting Assemblies of God and

Church of God in Christ (COGIC) denominations pose an incipient challenge to Christian theology: How to theorize an understanding of the Spirit that so palpably demonstrates its potency in extra-theoretical manifestations? This Spirit seizes and shouts, dances and pouts, wags tongues and shuffles feet, weeps and wails, and otherwise exceeds the bounds of middle-class propriety. And yet it remains packaged in categorical constraint. The theological content of the Pentecostal experience reinforces mainstream Christian conviction of a monopoly on truth; the form, however, augurs African possession.

The Pentecostal ecstatic experience involves a grammar of gesture that "speaks" over, under, around, and through the doctrine of the tongue in a manner of mixing Christian Spirit and African spirits. The jerk, the moan, the eye-roll, and the shoulder-shake enhance the message. Far from mere uncontrollable frenzy or ineluctable energy, the language of movement is quite pronouncedly intelligible for those in the cultural know. The recognizable appearance of spirit-personas like Shango or Yemaya, Ogu or Oshun inside the preaching of the gospel of Jesus or the glossolalia of his Spirit begs sustained theological attention. Given the history of demonization of dark things and peoples that is the modern legacy of Christian encounter with its "others," quick dismissal of such possession tropes as the "work of the devil" must be itself dismissed as more of the same racist bigotry. Christianity has yet to learn from its Azusa Street baptism. Under whose hands did it get wet with the waters of Spirit on that back avenue in the far western edge of the newly arising empire of the twentieth century?

Constructive Proposals

In this section we seek to bring together our earlier biblical and historical reflections on Spirit with constructive suggestions for a Spirit theology that is right for our time. Four different authors write micro-theologies here that lift up four aspects of Spirit—interrelational, cosmic, performative, and ecological—that we consider crucial to a full development of contemporary pneumatology.

Discerning Spirit: An Interrelational Communal Perspective

Sharon Welch

Contemplating the interrelational dimensions of the Spirit's activities has prompted me to ask, given the beauty and transforming power of Spirit, why in the history of the church has it so often been repressed? Why do many associate the Spirit with movements that skirt the dangers of heresy and chaos? Is it simply that people and communities are fearful and seek to control that which disrupts comfortable patterns of knowing and acting? While it would be reassuring to dismiss these fears as the rigid rejection of transformation, the history of the church and of the actions of people who claim the mandate of the Spirit leads us to a more complex and nuanced understanding of the dangerous paradoxes of the gifts of the Spirit.

Often the Spirit is rejected, its presence shunned, when communities of faith have not learned how to acknowledge and respond to the very real dangers of people claiming that they are being led by the Spirit and, out of that mandate, justifying the condemnation of other people, self-righteous denunciations and exclusions, and even at times violence. We cannot ignore the horror of Jonestown. A community that began as one fueled by the Spirit and committed to racial justice and social justice devolved into an isolated and fearful community in which paranoia led to mass suicide.[20] The example of Jonestown is fortunately extreme, but we commonly find people claiming to be led by the Spirit in the denunciation of others and in the confirmation of completely oppositional political views. Some believe that they are led by the Spirit in their denial of civil liberties in the name of national security; some feel led by the Spirit in their resistance to equal rights for gay, lesbian, bisexual, and transgender people; others feel led and empowered by the Spirit to protect civil liberties, led and empowered by the Spirit to extend equal rights to gay, lesbian, bisexual, and transgender people. As communities of faith, how do we assess these disparate uses of Spirit and disparate claims for the mandate of the Spirit? The dual challenge for communities of faith is not only to welcome the Spirit but to discern the Spirits.

How can we learn to discern the Spirits? How do we as individuals and as communities learn to be as critical as we are appreciative of the gifts and impulses that transform our lives? The answers are not easy, but we can learn from those communities of faith who have acknowledged the ambiguity of the Spirit's gift, who have faced the ways in which people claim the mandate of the Spirit as much to control, denounce, and exclude as to heal, embrace, and transform.[21] The story that I share is not definitive, but the insights are suggestive as we critically live out the mandate of the Spirit for us and for our time. I tell this story not as an answer but as a question, a way of posing responses to the gift and peril of the presence of the Spirit, a way of sorting through the contradictory uses that people make of the transformative powers of connection and ecstasy that are the Spirit's gift.

I was raised in a tradition in which we were taught to welcome the gifts of the Spirit. The Spirit's presence was as varied as the pulse of life itself—sometimes wild, fierce, and tumultuous, but just as often, just as important, quietly gentle, reassuring, and sustaining. The gale that transformed individuals and communities was valued, but no more so than the gentle touch that acknowledged wonder, beauty, and belonging. In this community a Spirit-filled life was one of mystery, and a Spirit-filled life was thoroughly pragmatic mystery and pragmatism, seemingly at odds, but fruitfully held in creative tension.

As much as we were taught to welcome the gifts of the Spirit, we were also taught to discern the Spirits. My uncle taught me that one can recognize that a Spirit is to be welcomed if it leads us to feel more love for other people. The first marker of the Spirit's presence, whether fierce and wild or quiet and gentle, was a profound sense of the inestimable worth, beauty, and wonder of other people. Filled with the Spirit, we saw other people as luminous gifts to life, infinitely precious and unique. We learned to question people who claimed to be led by the Spirit but used that power to denounce others or to distance themselves from others self-righteously. We questioned the Spirits who brought fear and established fear-based hierarchies.

"By their fruits you shall know them"—this community found it possible that the Spirit could lead one to stand against injustice but in so doing to stand *with* love and *in* love, not in judgment or hate. To stand for justice was to offer a gift of hope to oppressed and oppressor. Testimonies were frequent in which people described ways in which the Spirit led them to see the prior limits of their love and the need to expand it, learning to open their hearts to people they had formerly feared and condemned. I saw people raised in homophobic communities compelled by the Spirit to relinquish those prejudices and embrace, with love and gratitude, lesbian, gay, and bisexual people and to work for justice with them within the church and within society.

Discerning the Spirits in many ways simple, in many ways not. We were taught to welcome the gifts of the Spirit and to act on them. If one refused the promptings of the Spirit, they would slowly and surely stop appearing. If one responded, more would emerge. But how to respond to these gifts of insight and connection? While the criteria were clear, the implementation was not always easy.

We needed a community to help in discerning if we were following the promptings of the Spirit or were merely following our own vivid desires, hopes, and longings that were destructive of ourselves and of community. There is a heady power in self-righteous judgment, an intoxication in transgression and disruption. Many people did and do find these to be compelling and overwhelming. It was tempting to use the Spirit to control others, to mold them into a community that felt superior because of its gifts and disdainful of the rest of the world.

To discern the Spirit is to live with pragmatism and mystery, wonder and hope, chaos and order. When I was eighteen, I was fascinated by stories of angels. While at college I heard the account of someone who said that their friend had picked up a hitchhiker who told them that Jesus would soon return to earth. Immediately after this welcomed announcement, the hitchhiker disappeared. I told this story to my father, certain that he would be thrilled by an angelic report of the imminent return of the Messiah. His response was certain, measured, calm, and clear. "Well, Sharon, I don't know if he really saw an angel or not. What I would like to know is, did this encounter change his life?"

And the fruits of the Spirit are these—love, wonder, joy, courage, peace, and resilience—the ability to see our complicity with injustice and, equally important, the ability to change, to move into new horizons of love, of service, and of understanding.

The Cosmic Spirit: A Scientific Perspective

Barbara A. Holmes

The question of the cosmic aspects of the Spirit's presence in the world brings to my mind the emerging discipline of religion and science. Religion and science, I believe, remind us that the stage was set for the human drama long before we began our individual life journeys. How quickly we lose sight of the vastness and mystery of our geospiritual life space. Although it may seem that we enact our daily lives within the limited settings of home, work, school, and other familiar venues, in actuality we are moving about within the fabric of space-time. Within this matrix, our origins and endings are ensconced in the mysteries, contradictions, and anomalies that continue to ignite human curiosity. The universe is not as we supposed. It is primarily dark energy and matter; only a small percentage is visible to the human eye.

It is permeated with sound, movement, and energy that vibrates and pulsates. Within our own life space there may be eleven dimensions described by string theory. We are only equipped to perceive four—height, depth, width, and time. And so the mysteries abound!

The world of quantum physics offers a fascinating theory using language that, strangely enough, mirrors theological discourse. According to physicists, we are interconnected, not just spiritually and wishfully, but perhaps actually. David Bohm describes the entire life space as an indivisible whole that only appears to fracture into our individual life scripts. If scientists are correct, then dominance is a fallen house of cards. The assumption that the universe is a cause-and-effect clockwork space has been refuted by both science and religion.

Quantum physics tells us that the universe does not operate mechanistically. Particles burst into existence in unpredictable ways, observations of scientific experiments affect the observed, and order and rationality are not the building blocks of the life space. How can we be liberated if we are unaware of realities that have been hidden from our view by the culture, gender, sexuality, and race wars? To be truly liberated, we must realize that the physical world is different from what we imagined. Furthermore, we must enfold these differences into our theological and cultural discourses. Only then can we begin to reshape and reconstruct our ideas about identity, language, and liberation.

In this postmodern age identity and choice are shaped in the global marketplace through constant advertising and media bombardment. Awareness is the first step toward recovery. We are not consumers. We are the progeny of spirit and dust, embedded in a creative and intelligent universe. We are challenged to claim a cosmological identity that transforms the essentialisms of race, gender, class, and sexuality into jazz riffs and improvisations that diverge creatively from the main tune. The implications of these appropriations for all people—and for ethnic people in particular—are astounding.

As for language, inevitably an awakening leads to changes in the ways we talk about our lives and the world in which we live. Conflicts based on race, ethnicity, gender, class, or sexuality are power struggles that attempt through force or appropriation of the public narrative to define social acceptability. The addition of religious and scientific concepts and discourses offers a rhetorical corrective to social and legal theories about life in diverse and multicultural spaces. For example, what does race mean when darkness becomes a metaphor of power and cosmic predominance? Or similarly, who's in and who's out when connections can override distance calculated in millions of miles? What does individual and communal responsibility mean when potential and limitations are described not as social constructions but as quantum and cosmic legacies?

Primal connections to cosmological language offer a new perspective on freedom, its meaning and moral fulfillment. What does it means to be free as individuals and as members of a planetary community that includes animals, plant life, air, and water as well as human beings? The universe is a community, diverse and complex, musical, vibrant, and interdependent. It is this relational, holistic, and communal aspect of both science and religion that has been neglected to the detriment of the wider human community. The questions change when science informs discussions of theology and race. What does race mean in a scientific context, when darkness is no longer an indicator of inferiority but instead a cosmological metaphor for the power and predominance attributed to dark matter?

Biology teaches that our social separations based on difference are false. We are connected through a common human ancestry and genome. Cosmology teaches that separation is not the way of the universe. Instead, connections that defy our rational processes abound. Through the uncertainty and complementarity principles, physics teaches that our observations and attempts to know one another connect us at the most fundamental levels.

I am concerned that the discourses of science have been excluded from our imaginings about the world, our common human destiny, and all of the discussions by liberation theologians about justice and freedom. Without scientific perspectives on the life space, we create mirage-like goals that evaporate when we reach them. It was assumed that liberation was a progressive movement toward a tangible goal. The sciences teach us that the world is neither progressive nor hierarchical. Moreover, indigenous wisdom hints that our Western presumptions that the world is graspable, tangible, and concrete may be nothing more than a delightful and useful delusion.

Some of these connections are not new at all but are reclamations of indigenous ways of knowing. The world that physics and cosmology unveil is often congruent with indigenous perspectives of permeable reality structures. Rigidly ordered movements toward human flourishing have not succeeded because life itself has never unfolded in this way. The connections are broader than ethnicity or tribe; the connections are cosmological. The cure for our afflictions of the spirit lies in the knowledge that in the history of the universe, temporary oppressors are insignificant. Moreover, the universe is a mother to the motherless—an idea that flies in the face of the patriarchal assumptions of church and society.

We are beckoned toward the ancestors, toward the mysteries of faith and science that may not conform to the epistemological constraints of Western modalities. If we are to resolve our social problems we must gain a better understanding of who we are in the broader context of the universe. The discourses of difference have focused on the struggle for acceptance, equal social options, and established rights. It has been a fight for inclusion. But the study of cosmology teaches us that the fight for inclusion may be the ultimate quixotic battle. The center that lures those on the margins to seek its embrace does not exist as a stable or tangible target. Rather, issues of equality and acceptance are also matters of the Spirit that cannot be mandated or imposed. Struggles for liberation are attempts to shift realities, to invite the community to see the world differently.

The Jazz of the Spirit: A Poetic Perspective

Jim Perkinson

Serious theology remains to be done on the incarnation of God—not as flesh-of-human, but as animal and plant, dove-on-the-dunked-shoulder of Jesus, and invisible-mouth-of-mobilization addressing Moses through the bush. The two primal moments of revelation of the Christian tradition took place through desert flora and river fauna and not through the skin of our own kind. The body of the other is the haunt of the Hound of Heaven at least when on mission *for us*. This should give us pause when we raise the pen or open the eye of theology.

The Bible puts the Spirit into play as all-pervasive primordial Breath wafting over and through and as all-pervasive primordial rhythm of the cry of pain—whether in labor in the womb of a woman or in agony under the breath of a slave. The Good News places the escaping sigh on the livid lip of lacerated messiah as the ultimate question, flung skyward: Why?! Biblically, there is license to locate and liberate Spirit in all kinds of comportments in every out-of-the-way place of decay or ecstasy. Spirit is what the tradition lisps and groans, chortles and quacks after, pretends to domesticate in doctrine and lassos in catechetical lesson only to have the Flighty-Feral-Fecundity slip the noose again and again.

Of course, Spirit is either closeted as a spook or "karaoked" into mere inspiration. Spirit is the great nerve of the tongue that refuses grammar, that bunches into a hunch about unsayable orgasm and unspeakable devastation. It is not that the tradition has ignored or abstracted Spirit and now should (finally) get down to work after 2,000 years. Rather, Spirit is that which will forever tease and tantalize, trick and "telepathize," the mind moldering in an exegesis or a paraphrase. By definition Spirit cannot be put in doctrine. It is the anti-name that enamors every tongue tripped by love, seeking not a word but a kiss.

Here Christianity finds its necessary Diva of deconstruction. The Big Text does talk in tentative tremors—a galactic wind ripping large across a billion unmade worlds in Genesis (Gen. 1:2), the great mother eagle hovering over the nest of creation, flapping reluctant stars into orbit (Gen. 1:2); the rush of *rûach* beating back Red Sea waters for a hounded, harried people struggling from slavery to bravery in the wild school of Sinai (Exod. 14:21); the slight sonic touch on the cheek of an enervated Elijah, sunk in self-pity-swoon in flight from King Ahab (1 Kgs 19:12); the quake in the bone of Jeremiah (Jer. 20:9); the shake in the hip of a dancing David (2 Sam. 6:16); the slake of thirst for the woman of the well (John 4:7–15); and the groan in the ground of all for Paul (Rom. 8:18–26).

The Spirit cannot be chained in a word; its historical manner is ever the moan, the first blush of bloom in the desert when rain comes, the shiver in newborn flesh of shark, the jolt of joy when a jazz note finally leaps off the map of meaning into the improvisational nowhere of "insanity." It is before language and after time. That is its subtext in the Bible—blowing inchoate in the beginning (Gen. 1:2) or bellowing unrequited at the end (Rev. 22:17). Its mode is ever mourning or mesmerization, trauma or trance-of-titillation. Of course it is shy of theology! It is the Great Question, the Matrix of Meaning before the pen flits or the pixel pimps. Its voice will always be that of the Ghost.

But it is here in history as The Ever-Present Is animating the not-yet-answered, echoing eloquent in the undertone, the blue note, the bent sound, like a haint of midnight at every crossroads. The Spirit is the breath of black that halos every coming of light with its birth and destiny in darkness. At best, theology can attend to its erupting gestures as Question demanding not answers but quests of a lifetime. To be baptized with Spirit is to be overtaken in one's tongue, loosing a holy Babel, a tower of torrential praise and reproof, querying quiescence in God and human alike. Discernment of Spirits is thus a probe aimed at us from all the untamed spaces of our history of failures, in the unheard voices of the raped, the ravaged, the plundered, the lost. And it does not come only in coherence but rocks and jives, syncopates and celebrates, slides and "polymorphizes" around, under, and over the beat. The Spirit is laughing as the Many, showing up as Seven in Isaiah 11, as uncountable in Revelation, refusing incarceration in a numeral as much as it refuses dismissal as ephemeral. The Spirit lives underneath the book, between the lines, outside the margins in bellies and berries and bullfrogs and blizzards. The great jagged question marks of the time are its Sign, like shards of steel spiking inconsolable into a sky of silence after a tower falls, or the stare of a fly-crawling eye when hunger boils fat down to the bone. These are the zones where we might catch a glimmer or offer a slight punctuation mark that hints at the Work that Spirit is forever laboring into existence. Thematic smoke signals of the presence of the Spirit(s) include but are not limited to:

1. *Prophetic Purpose*: Jesus was driven into the wilderness by the Dove's digging dictatorial talon of summons into his shoulder (Mark 1:12–13). By all the lights of indigenous culture worldwide, this was Jesus' vision quest, the necessity to strip naked before sun and sea and sand and sink into one's own sweat and desperation. To be clear on calling, one must be clear on belonging. The vocation crystallizes only through testing up against the wildness of all else and in the trances of memory. The gift emerges from the wound of one's people discovered inside one's self, in wrestling their demon into a determination to live and die for a different possibility. Of particular import for a Christianity heretofore wedded to human domination over other life-forms on the planet is the arena of clarification: wild beasts, spirits, whispers, and wind are now allowed to speak. No other human puts in an appearance.
2. *Percussive Performance*: Here again, recognition of the appearance of the boundary-breaking Spirit in one area opens to consideration of others. If the Spirit did not ask permission of theology in order to flame the breast and frenzy the tongues of new day sons and daughters of a new latter rain on the day of Pentecost (Acts 2:17–21; Joel 2:23–29), it is likely that it will not ask Christian permission at large for work in secular folds. Black theologian James Cone has insisted on embracing the blues alongside the spirituals as a trace of the divine intention-to-save among the beaten and the broken.[22] African Americans' struggles to survive their own ongoing historical holocaust have produced a steady stream of creative upbeats of Spirited eloquence. But the question here cuts beyond the flesh of spiritual content to the bone of form. Perhaps Spirit pirouettes in history with a peculiarly sonic signature, mandating rhythmic massage as its riotous Message.

   Using a blues or jazz paradigm for theological reflection on the posture of Spirit would enjoin the primacy of a communal form of creation and a call-and-response-trained body as the necessary condition for reception. To take jazz as the clue: the whole body is enlisted as an ear sensing, anticipating, listening, hovering at the edge of the living rhythm mediated by an ensemble of others. The text is a jagged harmony: bass beats hosting the calligraphies of melody; percussive grooves suddenly reining themselves in to open the space of the "break," inviting individual virtuosity; all the blue notes and bops, the bent sounds and sliding soliloquies of filigreed improvisation; the riffs of tortured genius, tattooing the sonic membrane with entire populations of unimagined aural creatures, before being gathered back again into the polymorphic body of a complex god called "jam."

This is the human community become collective shaman, learning flight from the wedge of geese caterwauling through the sky with only the ever-shifting hologram of their own leaderless purpose for a guide. The necessity here is possession: a simultaneity of leading/following that envelops all the participatory bodies in that svelte whole that is the Spirit's gift from the winged to the gravity-struck. The drum throb encodes bone; the bass syncopates the blood; the keyboard run or sax trill cuts the interval with the possibility of infinity: transcendence even in the tiniest prison of regularity. Can theology be written in the modality of such a texture?

Even jazz's contemporary offspring—funk dance tunes, techno trances, and rap rhyme—work the interstitial infinities of the beat. Hip hop is today an entire universe launched in a flow, thickened in the synchronicity of sampled layers, quickened by the sudden syncopation of rupture. Across the entire space of postindustrial delirium and disease, a place is suddenly excised and ordered to an alternative economy of the ear in incubation, the muscle in motion, the eye of lost youth looking straight back from the door of death to defy the imperial pretense. Can God-talk allow itself to learn to walk in, taught by the very grimace it calls the devil incarnate? The question here is not orthodoxy but its polyphonic vitality in the school of percussive plurality. Can the page host the Spirit named "holy squeal?"

3. *Paradoxical Passion*: And finally, that which hip hop roars rhythmically against, underneath its often puerile cant and misogynist slant, is the violent structure of a world going global in economic exploitation and ecological annihilation. Obviously the fall of the World Trade Center towers in our time augurs ominously over the millennial moment. Here Spirit ghosts a postmodern paradox. The Manhattan site now hosts indistinct whispers in the wind where the powers of corporate divination previously focused on stocks and markets. The terror visited cannot be dismissed as only evil; it begs complex reading alongside other stories of other towers, other travails of the fallen mighty. Here is a facet of the Spirit that remains unfaced in the American epic of self-understanding: that God unansweringly watches the horrors of our violence; that no redress has yet come forth for fifty million of Africa's enslaved, untold millions of erased Amerindians, all the Salem women "be-witched" into early graves, all the *mestizo*-bloods south of the border swallowed in that border's bloody 1848 redrawing, the half-million Filipinos "liberated" into the freedom of

the corpse in our nation's first imperial venture at the dawn of industrialization, the Chinese coolies, the Arab "infidels" daring to believe Lady Liberty's summons and settle in "our" land, the "low-down" Irish, Polish, Italian, and Greek "freaks and geeks" of hard factory time, hired for a dime, forced to labor overtime, thought synonymous with crime all for the sake of bumping up the prime rate at which money is magically made into more money in the financial shrines of the land. Here are all of the heaving silences of stopped throats and broken hopes that yet await answer to their cry of "Why?" Spirit is not just cozy; it is a wind of cold, a tooth that cracks bone, a silence that does not weep in the public squares of our self-congratulation. The American story has never been "epic" (the wholly good versus the wholly evil), despite the claims otherwise of popular culture and politicians alike; from the beginning it has been more accurately a tragic tale, but told in truth only in the holds of our victims. If we would know Spirit in this land, we must learn how to listen to the blood of all our Abels yet anguishing in the soils of our cities and our souls.

The Green Spirit: An Ecological Perspective

Mark I. Wallace

In 1961 Bernard Buffet, a French artist, painted *The Baptism of Christ.* It is part of a series of large paintings depicting the life of Christ that Buffet completed in the early 1960s and that were intended to decorate the Chapelle de Château l'Arc in southern France. *The Baptism of Christ* portrays the baptism of Jesus by John the Baptist surrounded by robed supplicant women, a ministering angel, and the Holy Spirit in flight just over the head of Jesus.

What arrests my attention in this painting is Buffet's depiction of the Spirit as a wounded dove hovering over the newly baptized Savior. Buffet imagines the Spirit as thoroughly Christlike. The Spirit's wings are in full extension, stretched out to their limits, looking almost as if they have been pinned (or nailed) to their gold background. Intersecting the horizontal line of the Spirit's elongated wing pattern is an equally strong vertical line. Along this vertical line the Spirit, with bowed head and beak pointing down, is shown with its legs, like its wings, again fully extended and seemingly pinned (or nailed) to its lower abdomen and undertails, and pointing straight down like its beak. This crosswise depiction of the Spirit is repeated in the manner in which Buffet paints the Spirit's name in Latin, *Spiritus Sanctus,* by using sharp, angular, crisscrossing lines that look like a series of crosses perched high over the outstretched wings of the sacred bird.

But what I find most astonishing about Buffet's Spirit art is the depiction of the dark red wound in the Spirit's breast. Running with blood, the Spirit is pierced in its right side. I have never seen a similar crucifixion styled, or "cruciform," figuration of the Spirit in Western art. Whatever Buffet's intent in imagining the Spirit in this fashion, to me the message in this work is strikingly clear: the Spirit, like Jesus, is a victim who experiences the same suffering as does Jesus on the cross. This connection between the Spirit and Jesus is made clearer in the companion painting to the Spirit painting, in which Buffet shows John the Baptist bearing a cross as he comes to baptize Jesus. This scene falls directly underneath Buffet's image of the bleeding aviary Spirit. With the wounded Spirit above his head and the cross-bearing John the Baptist at his side, Jesus inaugurates his ministry in baptism and at the same time is preparing himself for his death on the cross. Jesus' baptism is a baptism unto his death.

Buffet's unusual painting of the Spirit cut and bleeding raises an interesting theological problem. If it is Jesus on the cross who is traditionally portrayed as pierced and crucified, then how can the Spirit be pictured by Buffet in this Christlike fashion? One source for explaining Buffet's original illustration of the cruciform Spirit is the doctrine of the Trinity. In the Trinity the three members of the Godhead are neither divided from one another nor confused with one another. Coeternal and coequal, Father, Son, and Spirit share mutual joys and common sorrows in an intimate society of love and affection. From a trinitarian perspective, the depiction of the cruciform Spirit makes sense, as one member of the Godhead, namely the Spirit, expresses in her wounded body solidarity and shared feelings with another member of the Godhead, namely the suffering Christ.

But there is another sense—a green theology sense, as it were—in which the Spirit can be understood as suffering in Christ-like fashion that I think is pointed to by Buffet's paintings (even if Buffet himself did not paint the images with this interpretation in mind). From the vantage point of green theology, the Spirit, like Jesus, also suffers loss and deprivation because the Spirit, as God's abiding and sustaining presence within nature, experiences in the depths of her person the corrosive impact of environmental depredation in our time. *Jesus suffers on the cross the sins of the world; the Spirit in the earth suffers the despoilment of the world.* Jesus suffers because he bears the sins of the world in his human flesh. The Spirit, as coeternal and coparticipatory with Jesus in the eternal Godhead, also experiences this suffering (even as does God the Father for that matter). But the Spirit also suffers in a way distinctive of her role in creation because she feels the pain of a degraded earth in her more-than-human body. The Spirit is the bird God.

The Spirit is the earthen God who indwells all things. The Spirit is the God enfleshed within all the life-forms that swim and fly and crawl and run upon the earth. Whenever, then, these life-forms suffer loss and pain, the Spirit suffers loss and pain. Whenever these life-forms are threatened and destroyed, the Spirit feels threatened and experiences death and trauma in herself. Whenever earth community is laid waste, the Spirit deeply mourns this loss and fragmentation.

To say that the Spirit is the bird God, in the manner of the scriptures, is not an empty metaphor. Christians do not think identifying Christ with the man Jesus is simply a figure of speech but rather a vital description of God actually becoming human in the person of one solitary individual 2,000 years ago. Likewise, the biblical descriptions of the Spirit as earthen being (bird) or natural element (wind or fire) is not an ornamental trope but rather a living description of the manner in which God becomes real and enfleshed in our time and place today. In Jesus, according to the Gospels, God became flesh and dwelled among us; in the Spirit, we can now say, God continually becomes flesh and dwells among us again.

John Muir's View of the Spirit

Now we observe that, in cold mountain altitudes, Spirit is but thinly and plainly clothed. . . . When a portion of Spirit clothes itself with a sheet of lichen tissue, colored simply red or yellow, or gray or black, we say that is a low form of life. Yet is it more or less radically Divine than another portion of Spirit that has gathered garments of leaf and fairy flower and adorned them with all the colors of Light, although we say that the latter creature is of a higher form of life? All of these varied forms, high and low, are simply portions of God, radiated from Him as a sun, and made terrestrial by the clothes they wear, and by the modifications of a corresponding kind in the God essence itself.[23]

The reason, then, that the Spirit suffers like Jesus on the cross—the reason Buffet's painting sets forth a profound theological truth—is not simply that the Spirit and Jesus are one in the life of God, as crucially important as that fact is. Building on Buffet's painting, we can also say that the origin of the Spirit's suffering also stems from the fact that the Spirit and the earth are one, in a certain manner of speaking. Whether manifesting herself as a living, breathing organism like a dove, or an inanimate life-force, such as wind or fire, the Spirit indwells nature as its interanimating power in order to bring all of nature into a harmonious relationship with itself. The Spirit is the vital *rûach*—God's breath that gives life to all beings. All things—rocks, trees, rivers, animals, and humans—are made of Spirit and are part of the continuous biological flow patterns that constitute life on our planet. The Spirit *ensouls* the earth as its life-giving breath, and the earth *embodies* the Spirit's mysterious interanimation of the whole creation.

The idea that Spirit and earth, interactively conceived, are one opposes the metaphysical idea of God as unchangeable and apathetic in the face of the suffering and turmoil within the creation that God spun into existence. God is not a distant abstraction but a living being who subsists in and through the natural world. Because God as Earth Spirit lives in the ground and circulates in water and wind, God suffers deeply the loss and abuse of our biological heritage through our continued assaults on our planet home. God as Spirit is pained by ongoing eco-squalor; God as Spirit undergoes deprivation and trauma through the stripping away of earth's bounty. As the earth heats up and melting polar ice fields flood shore communities and indigenous habitats, God suffers; as global economic imbalance imperils family stability and intensifies the quest for arable land in native forests, God suffers; as coral reefs bleach into decay and whole ecosystems of fish and marine life die off, God suffers; and as our planet endures what appears to be the era of the Sixth Great Extinction, like the Great Extinctions of the ice age and other mass death events, God suffers. When we plunder and lay waste to the earth, God suffers.

Today God as Spirit lives among us in great sorrow and deep anguish. From the viewpoint of green theology, just as the God who knows death through the cross of Jesus is the crucified God, so also the Spirit who enfleshes divine presence in nature is the wounded Spirit. In antiquity God's human body endured the cut marks of whips and nails; today and every day the Spirit's earth body is injured by the deep trauma we ceaselessly inflict on the planet. In Jesus, God at one time suffered the wounds of human sin and error; in the earth body of the Spirit, God is continually lacerated by chronic and thoughtless assaults upon our planet home. Herein lie the sad parallels between the crucified Jesus and the cruciform Spirit: the lash marks of human sin cut into the body of the crucified God are now even more graphically displayed across the expanse of the whole planet as the earth body of the wounded Spirit bears the incisions of further abuse. Because God as Spirit is enfleshed within creation, God experiences within the core of her deepest self the agony and suffering of an earth under siege. *The Spirit, then, as the green body of God in the world, has also become in our time the wounded God.* Earth Spirit is the wounded God who daily suffers the environmental violence wrought by humankind's unremitting ecocidal attitudes and habits. The Spirit is the wounded God even as Christ is the crucified God. As God once suffered on a tree by taking into Godself humankind's sin, so God now continually suffers another sort of agony and loss by daily bringing into Godself the environmental squalor that humankind has wrought.

But as Christ's wounds become the eucharistic blood that nourishes and inspires hope in the life of the believer, so the Spirit's agony over damage to the earth becomes a source of promise and new beginnings for persons and communities facing seemingly hopeless environmental destitution. The message of the cross is that senseless death is not foreign to God because it is through the cross that God lives in solidarity with all who suffer. The promise of new life that flows from the suffering God hanging from a tree is recapitulated in the ministry of the wounded Spirit, whose solidarity with a broken world is a token of divine forbearance and love. Hope, then, for a restored earth in our time is theologically rooted in the belief in the Spirit's benevolent cohabitation with all of the damaged and forgotten members of the biosphere human and nonhuman alike. The Spirit's abiding presence in a world wracked by human greed is a constant reminder that God desires the welfare of all members of the life web indeed, that no population of life-forms is beyond the ken of divine love, no matter how serious, even permanent, the ecological damage might be to these living communities.

Notes

Chapter 1

1. Hebrew Bible scholars have long debated the origins of monotheism. Most scholars now agree that monotheism did not fully develop in Israelite religion until the Babylonian Exile in the sixth century B.C.E. For a helpful discussion of the range of biblical scholarship on this issue, see, Robert Karl Gnuse, *No Other Gods: Emergent Monotheism in Israel*, 62–128 (Journal for the Study of the Old Testament Supplement Series 241; Sheffield, UK: Sheffield Academic Press, 1997).
2. Mary Daly, *Beyond God the Father: Toward a Philosophy of Women's Liberation* (Boston: Beacon, 1973), 19.
3. See Françoise Meltzer, *For Fear of the Fire: Joan of Arc and the Limits of Subjectivity* (Chicago: University of Chicago Press, 2001), and Amy Hollywood, *Sensible Ecstasy: Mysticism, Sexual Difference, and the Demands of History* (Chicago: University of Chicago Press, 2002).
4. See Don Compier, *What Is Rhetorical Theology? Textual Practice and Public Discourse* (Harrisburg, PA: Trinity Press International, 1999).
5. We already have examples of such crossing of methodological boundaries. I would point to the work of Douglas John Hall, for instance. See the three volumes of his *Christian Theology in a North American Context*: *Thinking the Faith*, *Professing the Faith*, and *Confessing the Faith* (Minneapolis: Fortress Press, 1989, 1993, and 1996).
6. Rebecca S. Chopp, *The Praxis of Suffering: An Interpretation of Liberation and Political Theologies* (Maryknoll, NY: Orbis, 1986).
7. See especially his *On Religion: Speeches to Its Cultured Despisers* (New York: Harper & Row, 1958).
8. Marcus J. Borg, *Jesus: A New Vision* (San Francisco: HarperSanFrancisco, 1987).
9. "When theology is divorced from spirituality it is likely to begin talking about a different god, a deity who depends on theological performance for vitality and verisimilitude." Mark A. McIntosh, *Mystical Theology: The Integrity of Spirituality and Theology* (Oxford: Blackwell, 1998). This book makes a strong case for dialogue between theology and the spiritual life.
10. A fine set of recent, very readable reflections on these themes is offered by Barbara Brown Taylor in *When God Is Silent: The 1997 Lyman Beecher Lectures on Preaching* (Cambridge, MA: Cowley, 1998). Perhaps St. John of the Cross is the most articulate "classical" explorer of this theme.
11. See *Julian of Norwich: Showings* (New York: Paulist, 1978).
12. David Hume, *Dialogues concerning Natural Religion* (London: Routledge, 1991).
13. McIntosh, *Mystical Theology*, 182.
14. The various views are nicely presented in Stephen T. Davis, ed., *Encountering Evil: Live Options in Theodicy* (Atlanta: John Knox, 1981).
15. See Jürgen Moltmann, *The Crucified God: The Cross of Christ as the Foundation and Criticism of Christian Theology*, trans. Margaret Kohl (Minneapolis: Fortress Press, 1993[1974]).

16. Gustavo Gutiérrez, *The Power of the Poor in History* (Maryknoll, NY: Orbis, 1983); and Jacquelyn Grant, "Subjectification as a Requirement of Christological Construction," in *Lift Every Voice*, ed. Susan Brooks Thistlethwaite and Mary Potter Engel, 207–20 (Maryknoll, NY: Orbis, 1998).

17. James H. Cone, "God is Black," in *Lift Every Voice*, ed. Susan Brooks Thistlethwaite and Mary Potter Engel, 101–14 (Maryknoll, NY: Orbis, 1998).

18. See James H. Cone, *God of the Oppressed* (New York: Seabury, 1975), 163–94.

19. The phrase "faith seeking understanding" (Latin: *fides quaerens intellectum*) gives expression to the most influential view of theology in the Western tradition stemming from Augustine. This view grew out of an exegesis of Isa. 7:9, which, according to the Old Latin version, read: "Unless you believe, you will not understand." Anselm of Canterbury made this idea of the theological task famous with his statement: "I do not seek to understand in order to believe, but I believe in order to understand" (*credo ut intelligam*). "An Address (*Proslogion*)," in *A Scholastic Miscellany: Anselm to Ockham*, ed. Eugene R. Fairweather (Library of Christian Classics; Philadelphia: Westminster, 1956), 74.

20. The idea, though not the exact wording, is expressed in two documents of Reformed faith. From "The Scots Confession" (1560) we find this statement: "We do not receive uncritically whatever has been declared to men under the name of general councils, for it is plain that, being human, some of them have manifestly erred, and that in matters of great weight and importance." And in "The Westminster Confession" (1647) we read: "All synods and councils since the apostles' times, whether general or particular, may err, and many have erred; therefore they are not to be made the rule of faith or practice, but to be used as a help in both." *Book of Confessions* (Louisville: Presbyterian Church, USA, 1992), 3.20 and 6.175.

21. The types are those of Alan Race, *Christians and Religious Pluralism: Patterns in the Christian Theology of Religions* (Maryknoll, NY: Orbis, 1983).

22. Cyprian of Carthage (c. 200–258), *Epistles* 72.21, in *Ante-Nicene Fathers*, ed. Alexander Roberts and James Donaldson (1886; reprint, Peabody, MA Hendrickson, 1994), 5:384.

23. On this score, see the argument of Mark Heim, *Salvations: Truth and Difference in Religion* (Maryknoll, NY: Orbis, 1995); he criticizes the "pluralist" view of Paul F. Knitter, *No Other Name: A Christian Survey of Christian Attitudes toward the World Religions* (Maryknoll, NY: Orbis, 1985).

24. Laurel C. Schneider, *Re-Imagining the Divine: Confronting the Backlash against Feminist Theology* (Cleveland: Pilgrim, 1998), 176.

Chapter 2

1. There are a number of different accounts of this incident. In his speech, "Our God Is Marching On!," given in Montgomery on March 25, 1965, Martin Luther King, Jr., described the incident as related here. In his own personal recollections of the boycott, however, Yancey Martin recalls that it was Dr. King himself who encouraged Sister Pollard to give up walking because of her age, thus eliciting her famous reply. See *A Call to Conscience: The Landmark Speeches of Martin Luther King, Jr.*, ed. Clayborne Carson and Kris Shepard (New York: Warner, 2001), 111; and Howell Raines, *My Soul Is Rested: The Story of the Civil Rights Movement in the Deep South* (New York: Penguin, 1977), 61.

2. Serene Jones, *Feminist Theory and Christian Theology: Cartographies of Grace* (Guides to Theological Inquiry; Minneapolis: Fortress Press, 2000), 22–23.

3. For English translations of works by Irenaeus, Gregory, and other early church fathers, see the website www.ccel.org/fathers2.

4. David F. Ford, *Self and Salvation: Being Transformed* (Cambridge: Cambridge University Press, 1999), 197.
5. Jörg Splett, "Body," in *Encyclopedia of Theology: The Concise Sacramentum Mundi*, ed. Karl Rahner, 157 (New York: Crossroad, 1984).
6. Ibid.
7. James R. McGovern, *Anatomy of a Lynching: The Killing of Claude Neale* (Baton Rouge: Louisiana State University Press, 1982), 2.
8. James E. Cutler, *Lynch Law: An Investigation into the History of Lynching in the United States* (New York: Longmans, Green, 1905), 175–76.
9. Trudier Harris, "Introduction," in *Selected Works of Ida B. Wells-Barnett*, compl. Trudier Harris, The Schomburg Library of Nineteenth Century Black Women Writers, 7 (1895; reprint, New York: Oxford University Press, 1991). That same year, black Catholics assembling for the third time took note of the national atmosphere and called for a formal investigation of anti-black discrimination in the church.
10. Louis-Marie Chauvet, *Symbol and Sacrament: A Sacramental Reinterpretation of Christian Existence*, trans. Patrick Madigan and Madeleine Beaumont (Collegeville, MN: Liturgical, 1995), 82.
11. Riggins R. Earl, Jr., *Dark Symbols, Obscure Signs: God, Self, and Community in the Slave Mind* (Maryknoll, NY: Orbis, 1993), 13.
12. Albert J. Raboteau, *Slave Religion: The "Invisible Institution" in the Antebellum South* (NY: Oxford, 1978), 100, 112, 113.
13. Ibid., 103.
14. Hortense J. Spillers, "Mama's Baby, Papa's Maybe: An American Grammar Book," in *The Black Feminist Reader*, ed. Joy James and T. Denean Sharpley-Whiting, 60 (Oxford: Blackwell, 2000).
15. William Goodell, *The American Slave Code in Theory and Practice: Its Distinctive Features Shown by Its Statutes, Judicial Decisions, and Illustrative Facts* (1853; reprint, New York: Negro Universities Press, 1968), 23.
16. Ibid.
17. Spillers, "Mama's Baby," 82.
18. Goodell, *The American Slave Code*, 24.
19. James Mellon, ed., *Bullwhip Days: The Slaves Remember, An Oral History* (New York: Avon, 1988), 28.
20. Solomon Northup, *Twelve Years a Slave*, ed. Sue Eakin and Joseph Logsdon (1853; reprint, Baton Rouge: Louisiana State University Press, 1968), 52.
21. Moses Grandy, *Narrative of the Life of Moses Grandy, Late a Slave in the United States of America* (Boston: O. Johnson, 1844), 11, cited in Gerda Lerner, ed., *Black Women in White America: A Documentary History* (1972; reprint, New York: Vintage, 1992), 8–9.
22. Norman R. Yetman, ed., *Voices from Slavery* (New York: Holt, Rinehart and Winston, 1970), 133.
23. Ibid., 252.
24. Ibid., 227.
25. Ibid., 151.
26. Ibid., 37.
27. Ibid., 53.

28. George M. Frederickson, *The Black Image in the White Mind: The Debate on Afro-American Character and Destiny, 1817–1914* (1971; reprint, Middletown, CT: Wesleyan University Press, 1987), 272. For some recent treatments of lynching see Orlando Patterson, *Rituals of Blood: Consequences of Slavery in Two American Centuries* (New York: Basic Civitas, 1998), and James Allen et al., *Without Sanctuary: Lynching Photography in America* (Santa Fe: Twin Palms, 2000).

29. McGovern, *Anatomy of a Lynching*, 5.

30. Frederickson, *The Black Image*, 272.

31. *Springfield (Massachusetts) Weekly Republican*, April 28, 1899, quoted in Ralph Ginzburg, ed., *One Hundred Years of Lynchings* (1962; reprint, Baltimore: Black Classic, 1988), 12.

32. *St. Louis Argus*, November 25, 1921, quoted in Ginzburg, ed., *One Hundred Years of Lynchings*, 156.

33. *Birmingham Voice of the People*, April 1, 1916, quoted in Ginzburg, ed., *One Hundred Years of Lynchings*, 102.

34. Allen et al., *Without Sanctuary*, contains essays by James Allen, Hilton Als, Congressman John Lewis, and Leon Litwack. Many churches were silent about these murders. One unnamed white Mississippian asserted that "the only way to keep the pro-lynching element in church is to say nothing which would tend to make them uncomfortable as church members" (Allen et al., *Without Sanctuary*, 21).

35. Patterson, *Rituals of Blood*, 169.

36. Johannes Betz, "Eucharist," in *Encyclopedia of Theology: The Concise Sacramentum Mundi*, ed. Karl Rahner, 157 (New York: Crossroad, 1984).

37. Miroslav Volf, *Exclusion and Embrace: A Theological Exploration of Identity, Otherness, and Reconciliation* (Nashville: Abingdon, 1996), 74.

38. Ford, *Self and Salvation*, 137, 143.

39. Marianne Sawicki, *Seeing the Lord: Resurrection and Early Christian Practices* (Minneapolis: Fortress Press, 1994), 90.

40. Ibid, 90–91.

41. Augustine, Sermon 272, Sermon 227.

42. Sawicki, *Seeing the Lord*, 264.

43. Augustine, Sermon 272.

Chapter 3

1. Christopher R. Browning, *Ordinary Men: Reserve Police Battalion 101 and the Final Solution in Poland* (New York: HarperCollins, 1992), 56–57, 61.

2. Elie Wiesel, *Night* (New York: Avon, 1960), 42, 44.

3. *Kirkliches Jahrbuch für die Evangelische Kirke in Deutschland, 1933–1944* (Gütersloh: Bertelsmann, 1948), 481.

4. Here the term *extrapersonal*, instead of *corporate*, is used to signify agents and forces larger than the individual, so that the value of the theological language of sin and evil is not lost. The terms *corporate sin* and *social evil* operate with the assumption that human persons are the only agents of sin and evil. While this is clearly a modern understanding, it cannot be applied to many in the tradition (such as Paul and Augustine), and it is questionable as to how exhaustive it is of the contemporary situation (for example, Pentecostalism).

5. Elaine Scarry, *The Body in Pain: The Making and Unmaking of the World* (New York: Oxford University Press, 1985), 3–19.
6. Paul Ricoeur, "Evil, A Challenge to Philosophy and Theology," in *Figuring the Sacred: Religion, Narrative, and Imagination*, trans. David Pellauer, ed. Mark I. Wallace (Minneapolis: Fortress Press, 1995), 251–52.
7. Paul Ricoeur, *The Symbolism of Evil*, trans. Emerson Buchanan (Boston: Beacon, 1967), 233.
8. Ibid., 255.
9. Ibid., 214.
10. Ibid.
11. See Ricoeur, "Evil," 250–51.
12. For an overview of Augustine's thought on evil, see G. R. Evans, *Augustine on Evil* (Cambridge: Cambridge University Press, 1982).
13. Augustine, *On Free Choice of the Will*, trans. A. S. Benjamin and L. H. Hackstaff (Indianapolis: Bobbs-Merill, 1964), 82–83.
14. Ibid., 6–10.
15. Ibid., 3.
16. The earliest anti-Pelagian treatise is *On the Spirit and the Letter* (written in 412), and the last is Augustine's incomplete book against Julian of Eclanum that he was writing at the time of his death in 430.
17. See Peter Brown, *The Body and Society: Men, Women, and Sexual Renunciation in Early Christianity* (New York: Columbia University Press, 1988), 387–427.
18. Augustine, *On Grace and Free Will*, in *Saint Augustine: Anti-Pelagian Writings*, ed. P. Schaff, 456 (Nicene and Post-Nicene Fathers of the Christian Church, vol. 5; 1886; reprinted Grand Rapids: Eerdmans, 1978), 456.
19. Augustine, *Confessions*, trans. By F. J. Sheed (Indianapolis: Hackett, 1942), 121.
20. Ibid.
21. Ibid., 135.
22. For a comprehensive exploration into this possibility, see Darby Ray, *Deceiving the Devil: Atonement, Abuse, and Ransom* (Cleveland: Pilgrim, 1998).
23. See Linda Mercadante, *Victims and Sinners: The Spiritual Roots of Addiction and Recovery* (Louisville: Westminster John Knox, 1996), and "Anguish: Unraveling Sin and Victimization," in *Anglican Theological Review* 82/2 (Spring 2000), 283–302.
24. The focus on relationality as a locus of sin or damage is a positive contribution of many feminist writers. See, for example, Marjorie Hewitt Suchocki, *The Fall to Violence: Original Sin in Relational Theology* (New York: Continuum, 1994); Rita Nakashima Brock, *Journeys by Heart: A Christology of Erotic Power* (New York: Crossroad, 1988); and Catherine Keller, *From a Broken Web: Sexism, Separation, and Self* (Boston: Beacon, 1986).
25. Some important works include Valerie Saiving, "The Human Situation: A Feminine View," in *Womanspirit Rising: A Feminist Reader in Religion*, ed. Carol P. Christ and Judith Plaskow, 25–42 (San Francisco: Harper & Row, 1979); and Judith Plaskow, *Sex, Sin, and Grace: Women's Experience and the Theologies of Reinhold Niebuhr and Paul Tillich* (New York: University Press of America, 1980).
26. Michel Foucault, *Power/Knowledge: Selected Interviews and Other Writings, 1972–1977*, ed. and trans. Colin Gordon et al. (New York: Pantheon, 1972), 93.

27. Ibid., 74.

28. Michel Foucault, "Nietzsche, Genealogy, History" in *Language, Counter-Memory, Practice: Selected Essays and Interviews*, trans. Donald Bouchard and Sherry Simon (Ithaca, NY: Cornell University Press, 1977), 146.

29. Ibid., 148.

30. Foucault, *Power/Knowledge*, 81. See Sharon D. Welch, *Communities of Resistance and Solidarity: A Feminist Theology of Liberation* (Maryknoll, NY: Orbis, 1985), 35ff.

31. Foucault, *Power/Knowledge*, 98.

32. Ibid., 119.

33. The allusion is to Audre Lorde's influential essay "The Master's Tools Will Never Dismantle the Master's House," in *Sister Outsider: Essays and Speeches* (Crossing Press Feminist Series; Trumansburg, NY: Crossing, 1984).

34. Musa Dube, "Postcoloniality, Feminist Spaces, and Religion," in *Postcolonialism, Feminism, and Religious Discourse*, ed. Laura E. Donaldson and Kwok Pui-lan, 117 (New York: Routledge, 2002).

35. Andrea Smith, "Walking in Balance: The Spirituality-Liberation Praxis of Native Women" in *Native American Religious Identity: Unforgotten Gods*, ed. Jace Weaver (Maryknoll, N.Y.: Orbis, 1998).

36. Gayatri Chakravorty Spivak, "Subaltern Studies: Deconstructing Historiography," in *The Spivak Reader*, ed. Donna Landry and Gerald MacLean, 213–14 (New York: Routledge, 1996).

37. Catherine Keller, "Seeking and Sucking: On Relation and Essence in Feminist Theology," in *Horizons in Feminist Theology: Identity, Tradition, and Norms*, ed. Rebecca S. Chopp and Sheila Greeve Davaney, 60 (Minneapolis: Fortress, 1997).

38. bell hooks, *Yearning: Race, Gender, and Cultural Politics* (Boston: South End, 1990), 24.

39. Paula M. L. Moya, "Postmodernism, 'Realism', and the Politics of Identity: Cherríe Moraga and Chicana Feminism," in *Feminist Genealogies, Colonial Legacies, Democratic Futures*, ed. M. Jacqui Alexander and Chandra Talpade Mohanty, 126 (New York: Routledge, 1997).

40. Jace Weaver, "From I-Hermeneutics to We-Hermeneutics: Native Americans and the Post-Colonial," in *Native American Religious Identity*, ed. Jace Weaver, 14–15 (Maryknoll, NY: Orbis, 1998).

Chapter 4

1. Brock, Rita Nakashima, and Rebecca Parker, *Proverbs of Ashes: Violence, Redemptive Suffering, and the Search for What Saves Us* (Boston: Beacon, 2001), 20–21.

2. Cuban oral tradition.

3. From the Nicene Creed, in *The Book of Confessions* (Louisville: Presbyterian Church, USA, 1992), 3.

4. As cited in J. N. D. Kelly, *Early Christian Doctrines* (New York: Harper & Row, 1978), 339–40.

5. Peter Abelard, "Exposition of the Epistle to the Romans" (An Excerpt from the Second Book), in *A Scholastic Miscellany: Anselm to Ockham*, ed. Eugene R. Fairweather, 276–87, 282–83 (Library of Christian Classics; Philadelphia: Westminster, 1981).

6. Brock and Parker, *Proverbs of Ashes*, 30.

7. *Compendium Theologiae,* chap. 239, cited in Brian Davies, *The Thought of Thomas Aquinas* (Oxford: Clarendon, 1992), 341.
8. Julian of Norwich, *Revelations of Divine Love,* trans. Clifton Wolters (New York: Penguin, 1966), 169.
9. Martin Luther, *Lectures on Galatians,* vol. 26 of *Luther's Works,* ed. Jaroslav Pelikan (Saint Louis: Concordia, and Philadelphia: Fortress Press, 1963), 166.
10. John Calvin, *Institutes of the Christian Religion,* ed. John T. McNeill, trans. Ford Lewis Battles (Library of Christian Classics; Philadelphia: Westminster, 1960), II.12.1, II.12.4.
11. Cited in *Readings in Christian Thought,* Hugh Kerr, ed. (Nashville: Abingdon, 1966), 250.
12. Jacquelyn Grant, *White Women's Christ and Black Women's Jesus: Feminist Christology and Womanist Response* (Atlanta: Scholars, 1989), 213.
13. From John Wesley's "The Lord Our Righteousness," in *The Sermons of John Wesley,* eds. Albert C. Outler and Richard P. Heitzenrater (Nashville: Abingdon, 1987), 390.
14. Friedrich Schleiermacher, "Christmas Eve Dialog on the Incarnation," in *Friedrich Schleiermacher: Pioneer of Modern Theology,* ed. Keith W. Clements (Minneapolis: Fortress Press), 200.
15. Friedrich Schleiermacher, *The Christian Faith,* ed. H. R. Mackintosh and J. S. Stewart (Philadelphia: Fortress Press, 1976), 450.
16. Cited in Trevor Hart, "The Capacity for Ambiguity," *Regarding Karl Barth: Essays toward a Reading of His Theology* (Carlisle, Cumbria, U.K.: Paternoster, 1999), 139–72, 147–48.
17. *The Barmen Declaration* (1934), 8.12, in *The Book of Confessions.*
18. Walter Rauschenbusch, *Christianity and the Social Crisis* (New York: Macmillan, 1908), 230–86.
19. Ibid.
20. Langdon Gilkey, "Neoorthodoxy," in *A New Handbook of Christian Theology,* ed. Donald W. Musser and Joseph L. Price, 334–37 (Nashville: Abingdon, 1992).
21. Gustavo Gutiérrez, *A Theology of Liberation: History, Politics and Salvation,* trans. and eds. Sister Caridad Inda and John Eagleson (Maryknoll, NY: Orbis, 1985), 176.
22. Leonardo Boff, *Jesus Christ Liberator: A Critical Christology for Our Time* (Maryknoll, NY: Orbis, 1991), 295.
23. James H. Cone, *God of the Oppressed* (San Francisco: HarperSanFrancisco, 1974), 133–34.
24. Rosemary Radford Ruether, *Sexism and God-Talk: Toward a Feminist Theology* (Boston: Beacon, 1993), 1–11.
25. Elizabeth A. Johnson, *She Who Is: The Mystery of God in Feminist Theological Discourse* (New York: Crossroad, 1993), chap. 12.
26. "One of Us," by Eric Bazilian, sung by Joan Osborne.
27. For more on Kierkegaard's understanding of "offense," see his *The Sickness unto Death,* eds. Howard Hong and Edna Hong (Princeton: Princeton University Press, 1980).
28. John the Baptist's incredulity at the prospect of contributing to the ministry of Christ, rather than simply preparing for it, is reminiscent of Mary's exclamation, "How can this be, since I am a virgin?" (Luke 1:34). Both John and Mary believed themselves incapable of bearing Christ.

29. Karen Baker-Fletcher, *Sisters of Dust, Sisters of Spirit: Womanist Wordings on God and Creation* (Minneapolis: Fortress Press, 1998).

30. Delores S. Williams, *Sisters in the Wilderness: The Challenge of Womanist God-Talk* (Maryknoll, NY: Orbis, 1993), 161–67.

31. Sharon Welch, *A Feminist Ethic of Risk* (rev. ed.; Minneapolis: Fortress Press, 2000), and Karen Baker-Fletcher, *My Sister, My Brother: Womanist and Xodus God-Talk* (Maryknoll, NY: Orbis, 1997).

32. Calvin, *Institutes of the Christian Religion*, 499.

33. Schleiermacher, *Christian Faith*, 467.

34. Ibid., 469. For an interpretation of Schleiermacher as a theologian of the middle class, see Joerg Rieger, *God and the Excluded: Visions and Blindspots in Contemporary Theology* (Minneapolis: Fortress Press, 2001), chap. 1.

35. Calvin, *Institutes of the Christian Religion*, 501, 502.

36. Schleiermacher, *Christian Faith*, 462.

37. Calvin, *Institutes*, 496.

38. Schleiermacher, *Christian Faith*, 450.

Chapter 5

1. Religion News Service, "Church Expelled for Welcoming Gays," *Washington Post*, May 3, 2003.

2. Leonard M. Hummel, *Clothed in Nothingness: Consolation for Suffering* (Minneapolis, Fortress Press, 2003), 1–2.

3. They do not represent it adequately for, by definition, a free-church tradition will take many different forms and did. These two examples combine one strain of the Anabaptist movement on the continent and an English separatist church that adopted the practice of baptism of believers. Combining these two authors as sources for these general statements creates an interpreted "type." For example, these churches did not refer to themselves as "free churches."

4. The Council of Trent dealt with many issues of ecclesial reform on a disciplinary level; it also treated the sacraments extensively, including the Eucharist, which has a bearing on the office of priestly ministry. But it did not address ecclesiology as a general topic.

5. One should note, however, that a certain number of progressive, ecumenical-minded ecclesiologists, such as Yves Congar, prepared the way for Vatican II.

6. *The Nature and Purpose of the Church: A Stage on the Way to a Common Statement*, Faith and Order Paper No. 181 (Geneva: WCC, 1998), 18–19.

7. John Macquarrie, *Principles of Christian Theology*, 2nd ed. (New York: Scribner's, 1977), 402.

8. *The Nature and Purpose of the Church*, 20–21.

9. Walter Rauschenbusch, *A Theology for the Social Gospel* (New York: Macmillan, 1917), 134.

10. MacQuarrie, *Principles*, 409.

Chapter 6

1. Adapted from Jim Perkinson, "Ogu's Iron or Jesus' Irony: Who's Zooming Who in Diasporic Possession Cult Activity?" *Journal of Religion* 81/4 (October 2001): 566–94.
2. Adapted from Dwight N. Hopkins, *Shoes That Fit Our Feet: Sources for a Constructive Black Theology* (Maryknoll, NY: Orbis, 1993), 106.
3. On the history of Syriac feminine language and imagery for the Spirit, see Susan Ashbrook Harvey, "Feminine Imagery for the Divine: The Holy Spirit, the Odes of Solomon, and Early Syriac Tradition," *Saint Vladimir's Theological Quarterly* 37 (1993): 111–40; also see regarding feminine language for the Spirit, Gary Steven Kinkel, *Our Dear Mother the Spirit: An Investigation of Count Zinzendorf's Theology and Praxis* (Lanham, MD: University Press of America, 1990), and Elizabeth A. Johnson, *She Who Is: The Mystery of God in Feminist Theological Discourse* (NY: Crossroad, 1992), 128–31.
4. Jürgen Moltmann, *The Spirit of Life: A Universal Affirmation* (Minneapolis: Fortress Press, 1992), 307.
5. See William Tabbernee, "'Will the Real Paraclete Please Speak Forth?': The Catholic-Montanist Conflict Over Pneumatology," in *Advents of the Spirit: An Introduction to the Current Study of Pneumatology*, ed. Bradford E. Hinze and D. Lyle Dabney, eds., 97–116 (Milwaukee: Marquette University Press, 2001).
6. Adolf Hull, *The Left Hand of God: A Biography of the Holy Spirit*, trans. John Cullen (New York: Doubleday, 1998), 128.
7. For reproductions and commentary, see Bernard McGinn, *The Calabrian Abbot: Joachim of Fiore in the History of Western Thought* (New York: Macmillan, 1985).
8. Joachim of Fiore, "The Book of Concordance, Book 2, Part 1, Chapters 2–12," in *Apocalyptic Spirituality*, trans. and intro. Bernard McGinn (New York: Paulist, 1979), 131.
9. George Tavard, "Apostolic Life and Church Reform," in *Christian Spirituality: High Middle Ages and Reformation*, ed. Jill Raitt, 6 (New York: Crossroad, 1988).
10. Hildegard of Bingen, *Scivias*, trans. Mother Columba Hart and Jane Bishop (New York: Paulist, 1979), 2.1, 150.
11. Hildegard of Bingen, *Scivias*, 3.7.9, 418.
12. Elizabeth Dryer, "An Advent of the Spirit: Medieval Mystics and Saints," in *Advents of the Spirit: An Introduction to the Current Study of Pneumatology*, ed. Bradford E. Hinze and D. Lyle Dabney, eds., 134 (Milwaukee: Marquette University Press, 2001).
13. See Harold J. Grimm, *The Reformation Era: 1500–1650* (2nd ed.; New York: Macmillan, 1973), 135–71.
14. Quoted in Abraham Friesen, *Thomas Müntzer, A Destroyer of the Godless: The Making of a Sixteenth-Century Religious Revolutionary* (Berkeley: University of California Press, 1990), 205.
15. Quoted in Friesen, *Thomas Müntzer*, 205–6.
16. An excerpt from Müntzer's speech can be found in William C. Placher, *Readings in the History of Christian Theology, Volume 2: From the Reformation to the Present* (Philadelphia: Westminster, 1988), 28–30.
17. Kenneth M. Morrison, "The Cosmos as Intersubjective: Native American Other-Than-Human Persons," in *Indigenous Religions: A Companion*, ed. Graham Harvey, 36 (London: Cassell, 2000).

18. M. A. Jaimes Guerrero, "Native Womanism: Exemplars of Indigenism in Sacred Traditions of Kinship" in *Indigenous Religions: A Companion,* ed. Graham Harvey, , 38, 39 (London: Cassell, 2000).

19. Mabel Mckay, Cache Creek Pomo Indian, quoted in Greg Sarris, *Keeping Slug Woman Alive: A Holistic Approach to American Indian Texts* (Berkeley: University of California Press, 1993), 34.

20. Rebecca Moore, Anthony B. Pinn, and Mary R. Sawyer, eds., *People's Temple and Black Religion in America* (Bloomington: Indiana University Press, 2003).

21. Elaine J. Lawless describes the complex uses of the Spirit within Pentecostal communities in the United States. While many women find freedom through the gifts of the Spirit, they also claim that their subordinate role to husbands and to male leaders is equally mandated by the Spirit of God. See Lawless, "Your Hair Is Your Glory." *New York Folklore* 12/3–4 (1986): 33–49, and Lawless, "Shouting for the Lord: The Power of Women's Speech in the Pentecostal Church," *Journal of American Folklore* 96/383 (1983): 434–59.

22. James H. Cone, *The Spirituals and the Blues: An Interpretation* (1972; reprint, Maryknoll, NY: Orbis, 1991), 97–127.

23. John Muir, "Yosemite Journals, March 15, 1873," *John of the Mountains: The Unpublished Journals of John Muir,* ed. Linnie Marsh Wolfe (Madison: University of Wisconsin Press, 1979), 138.

Glossary

abbess
: the female head of a monastery

abbot
: the male head of a monastery

absolve (absolution)
: the announcement by a priest of forgiveness of sins, usually as part of a penitential rite

accidents
: in Greek and medieval metaphysics, the nonessential, changeable parts of a thing

Adamic myth
: locating the origin of human sin in a primordial first couple and a paradisiacal state

adoptionism
: the notion that Jesus was merely adopted as God's son

alterity
: otherness

Anabaptist
: diverse Reformation traditions that refused infant baptism and stressed the need for adult conversion and baptism

analogy
: understanding one thing or relationship by reference to partial likenesses to another

anathema
: a ban or denunciation formally pronounced by a church body

androcentrism
: cultural centering around males

Anselm of Canterbury (1033–1109)
: medieval theologian who pioneered systematic theological reflection, especially on soteriology and the ontological argument for God's existence

Antichrist
: in Christian apocalyptic literature, a figure opposed to Christ, who is to rule the world but ultimately be vanquished by Christ

apocalypticism
: the religious notion that God will set things right through a violent cataclysm, perhaps ending the world; writings that reflect that belief

apologetics
: arguments defending Christian faith to nonbelievers

apophatic

religious experience that does not employ experiential images or categories; theology that stresses the inadequacy of our knowledge of God

apostate

a former believer who formally abandons Christian faith

apostolic (apostle)

going back to the time of the earliest followers chosen by Jesus to preach the gospel

apostolic see

a bishop's jurisdiction in a church that traces itself to New Testament times

apostolicity

the quality of sharing in apostolic ministry or the apostolic tradition

articulo mortis

Latin: at the moment of death

ascetic(ism)

disciplining the body for religious purposes, usually penitential

aseity

"itselfness," the absoute self-sufficiency and autonomy of God

Athanasius (296–373)

bishop of Alexandria who defended the consubstantiality of the son with the father

atonement

the reconciliation of God with humans through the person or work of Jesus Christ

Augustine of Hippo (354–430)

most influential of the church fathers, especially in his theologies of grace and free will, original sin, and the Trinity

auricular confession

the private telling of one's sins to a priest

ban

a formal condemnation of a person by a church authority

baptism

the Christian sacramental rite of initiation

Baptists

one of the largest Christian communions; the Reformation tradition that stressed the need for adult conversion and baptism as a basis for Christian fellowship

beatified (beatification)

being pronounced "blessed," a step toward being declared a saint by the Roman Catholic Church

benefice
a church office that includes an endowment or income

blasphemy
insult or irreverence toward God

bull (papal)
a decree or pronouncement from the pope

canonical
part of the canon, the official roster of authoritative texts

canons (canonical)
regulations or decrees from church councils

Cappadocian
relating to the three most influential fourth-century Eastern "fathers of the church"—Gregory of Nyssa, Gregory Nazianzus, and Basil of Caesarea

catechism
a course of basic religious instruction, often in question-and-answer form

catholic
universal

Chalcedon, Council of (451)
the ecumenical gathering of bishops that defined Jesus Christ as having two unconfused natures, divine and human

chastity
sexual purity or abstinence

Christendom
the realm in which Christianity was religiously and politically dominant

Christocentrism
theology that takes Christ as its starting point and norm, vs. androcentric or theocentric theologies

Christology
disciplined religious reflection on the person and work of Jesus Christ

commodification
the process by which areas of life become understood primarily through their commercial aspects or potential

communicatio idiomatum
Latin: the way in which attributes of Christ's divine and human natures are predicated of each other

conciliarism
medieval movement that claimed the authority of ecumenical councils over that of the pope

concupiscence
sinful desire, sometimes sexual

condign merit
worthy in the full sense

condignity
deemed fully worthy

Confessing church
the movement in the German church of the 1930s and 1940s that resisted the Nazi program and its takeover of the Christian church

congruity of merit
being only relatively worthy

consecrates (consecration)
ritually making holy a person or thing (e.g., a bishop, a church, eucharistic bread)

consubstantiality
the idea that the son of God is of one substance with the father

contingency
being unnecessary, the dependence of acts and creatures on God

contrition
remorse, regret, or sorrow for one's sins

correlation, method of
theological method pioneered by Paul Tillich that works by relating deep cultural questions to religious or theological answers

covenant
a pact or agreement, as between persons or between God and humans

creed
a formal statement of belief

damnation
punishment in hell for one's sins

Death of God theology
a popular theological movement in 1960s that began with the observation of the disappearance of God from contemporary culture

Deism
mechanistic and naturalistic Enlightenment notion of God, who functioned merely to create the universe and its laws and of whom there is no supernatural revelation

denomination
any of the hundreds of different official Christian bodies within American Protestant Christianity

diakonia
service; the principal function of deacons in early Christianity

Didache
early second-century document that sheds light on early liturgical and prayer practice

discipleship

following Jesus; the practical implications of Christian commitment

docetism

notion that Christ merely "seemed" (Greek = *dokein*) to be human

dogma

officially defined teaching of the Christian church

Donatism

fourth-century North African renewal movement that mandated a rigorously sinless life; opposed by Augustine

dualism

stark cosmic contrasts between good/evil, dark/light, male/female, reason/revelation, and so forth

ecclesiastic(al)

having to do with the church

ecclesiology

theological understanding of the church

embodiment

physicality, or attention to the importance of bodiliness

Enlightenment

broad cultural movement of the seventeenth and eighteenth centuries emphasizing the sufficiency of reason, the nobility and autonomy of human being, and questioning of received authorities

epiclesis

the words of consecretion of the bread and wine in the Eucharist

eschatology

Christian understanding of the "last things," traditionally death, judgment, heaven, and hell

eschaton

the final consummation of creation; traditionally, the end of the world

etymology

the roots of words

Eucharist

Christian celebration of thanksgiving, also known as Lord's Supper, the Divine Liturgy, and the mass; in Roman Catholicism, the sacrament of Christ's presence in the consecrated bread and wine

ex opere operato

Latin: "by the work worked," made effective apart from the worthiness of the agent

exclusivity, christological

the notion that Christ alone is the means of salvation for all

excommunication

formal exclusion from the church body

exegesis

interpretation, esp. of biblical texts

expiated (expiation)

making satisfaction for wrongs

extreme unction

anointing of the sick, esp. in danger of death; in Roman Catholicism a sacrament

fideism

position that reason is powerless to understand the divine, so faith and revelation are the sole means of knowledge of God

foreknowledge

God's knowledge of events before they happen

gender

the social construction of roles and meanings related to sexual difference

globalization

the economic and cultural homogenization of the planet through the spread of capitalism and mass culture

Gnosticism

movement in the first centuries of the common era, competitive with Christianity, that stressed the necessity of an esoteric saving knowledge (Greek = *gnosis*)

gospel

the Christian message or "good news"; an early account of the life of Jesus

grace

the life of God in humans; divine favor or help; unmerited help of God to humans

Gregorian Reform

widespread reform of the church, monastic orders, liturgy under Pope Gregory the Great (540–604)

hegemony

dominance or dominating influence

Hellenism

classical Greek culture, especially as influential on later centuries

Hellenistic

Greek culture of the post-classical period, after the rise of Alexander the Great

heresy

teaching judged not to be orthodox

heretic

one professing beliefs contradictory to accepted church doctrines

heteronomy
a set of alien laws and languages that violate the structures proper to human life

Hippolytus
second-century Christian writer

holistic
from the perspective of the whole

Holocaust
the destruction of European Jewry under the Nazi genocide of 1938–1945

Holy Spirit
the third person of the trinity; God

homily
a sermon preached on a biblical text

***homoiousios*–Greek**
"of like substance" with the father

***homoousios*–Greek**
"of the same substance" as the father

humanist (humanism)
the tradition of centering value on the human being, reviving classical values, sometimes rejecting theism

hybridity
based on a genetic analogy, in post-colonial studies, "the creation of new transcultural forms within the contact zone produced by colonization" (Ashcroft, Bill, et al., *Key Concepts in Post-Colonial Studies* [New York: Routledge, 1998])

hypostasis
Greek: substance or reality; used of God and of Christ

idealism
philosophical position that ideas constitute reality

idolatry
worshipping false gods

imago Dei
Latin: the image of God

impassibility
unchangeableness

impute (imputation)
to attribute or assign credit to someone

incarnate
enfleshed, made human; the doctrine that God became human in Jesus Christ

incarnation
becoming flesh; Christ is God incarnate

inclusivism

opposite of exclusivism; salvation is said to include others who do not know of Christ

inculturation

the idea that Christian teaching should be adapted to local cultures

indigenization

inculturation; the adaptation of Christian teaching to the cultures of local peoples

indulgences

church pronouncements that take away punishments due to sins

infallibility

the teaching that a pope, speaking formally as head of the Catholic church on a matter of faith or morals to be held by the whole church, cannnot err

infusion

direct gift of grace or favor from God

iniquity

sin

intercession

prayer or request to God on someone else's behalf

invocation

calling on God or a saint; a petition

justified (justification)

being deemed righteous or whole by God; being put in right relationship with God

kataphatic

religious experience that employs experiential images or categories; opposite of apophatic

kerygma

essentials of earliest Christian proclamation or preaching

keys (power of)

the apostles' power to forgive sins

Kierkegaard, Søren (1813–1855)

Danish philosopher and Protestant theologian

kingdom of God

the New Testament notion of God's reign or power; where God's reign is effective

koinonia

Greek: sharing or fellowship; early Christian community

lectio divina

Latin: divine reading; the prayerful reading of religious texts, especially scripture

Logos
Greek: Word or speech; Greek philosophical category for the eternal cosmological principle of meaning; Christian theological term for Christ as Word of God

Luther, Martin (1483–1546)
Reformer and theologian, father of the Reformation

Manichean
dualistic religious movement of late antiquity which stressed cosmic battle between forces of good and evil, light and darkness

Marcionism
named for Marcion (died c. 160), a Gnostic form of Christianity that rejected the Old Testament and its God

marginality
being outside the center of attention or power

marginalization
social process of denigration that excludes groups or traits from the center of attention or power

mass
ritual reenactment of the Last Supper of Jesus; eucharist or Lord's Supper

mediator
one who goes between, as a reconciler or redeemer or savior figure

mendicant
a religious order (e.g., Franciscan, Dominican) in which persons originally had no property or fixed residence

Mennonite
follower of Menno Simons (1496–1561), a Christian reformer who rejected infant baptism, eucharistic presence, and church organization, emphasized pacifism and nonresistance

merit
worthy of divine favor, reward or retribution

messiah
Hebrew: "annointed one"; expected one, chosen to lead or deliver the people Israel

metaphysics
the science or study of and general principles of being or reality in its most general terms

minjung
indigenous religious reflection of South Korean Christians

modernity
the post-Renaissance, post-Reformation period, through the Enlightenment, characterized by rational, empirical, objective thought

monotheism

belief in a single God

Montanism

second-century apocalyptic movement emphasizing the outpouring of the spirit in prophecy, the role of female prophets, and rigorous asceticism

mortal sin

a serious offense against God, meriting eternal punishment, in which one's relation to God is considered severed

***mujerista* theology**

liberating reflection of Hispanic women, a branch of Latina feminist theology

mysticism

intense religious experience, sometimes manifest in visions

neoorthodoxy

twentieth-century movement, associated with Karl Barth, that reasserted the role of revelation and proclamation over against the roles of reason or emotion in religion and theology

Nicaea, Council of

ecumenical council of 325 in which Arianism was rejected, the Nicene Creed was formulated, and Jesus was pronounced as "one in being with the Father"

nominalism

medieval philosophical position that human concepts are mere names with no correspondence to reality itself

normativity

having an indispensable, authoritative, or necessary role—as in scripture or tradition

omnipotent

all-powerful

ontological argument

associated with Anselm of Canterbury and René Descartes, the argument that the idea of God itself necessitates the existence of God

opere operati, non opere operantis

Latin: religious acts (e.g., forgiveness of sins) accomplished (or not) through the ritual act itself, without regard to the intent or worthiness of the agent

original righteousness

the state of intact human nature before the fall

original sin

the doctrine that a single sin by the first humans and its effects are inherited by each subsequent human

orthodox

from Greek, "right teaching"; religious teaching authoritatively judged authentic and true

ousia

Greek: being or reality or substance

papist

relating to or loyal to the pope

Paraclete

from Greek meaning "advocate"; a name for the Holy Spirit

Parousia

from Greek, the return of Christ

passion (of Christ)

the suffering and death of Jesus

patriarchalism

a system of social organization built around the power and authority of fathers

Patristic

pertaining to theologians from the second century to the seventh century C.E.

***Pax Romana*—"Roman Peace"**

the relatively stable and homogeneous economic and military situation in the first centuries of the Roman empire

Pelagianism

from Pelagius a late-fourth-century British monk and opponent of Augustine of Hippo who defended human capability to do good, avoid sin, and merit salvation without grace

penance

(a) Roman Catholic sacrament of confessing one's sins; (b) making restitution for one's sins

Pentecostal

a strain of Protestant Christianity, stemming from the American Holiness tradition, that emphasizes the gifts of the Holy Spirit, including speaking in tongues or *glossalalia*

perichoresis

from Greek, the interpenetration of the functions or roles of the three persons of the Trinity

Pharisee

a reforming movement at the time of Jesus, later influential in the beginnings of Rabbinic Judaism, often demonized by the Gospel writers

phenomenology

twentieth-century philosophical movement that attempted to isolate the phenomenon as experienced from its "objective" conceptuality

pilgrimage

religious journey to a holy site

plenary

lit. "full"; a plenary indulgence fully releases a penitent from punishment due to sins

pleroma

from Greek, "full"; the fullness of divine excellence and powers

pluralism

the idea that truth has more than one valid expression

pneumatology

theological reflection on the person and work of the Holy Spirit

polytheism

belief in many gods

pontiff

a bishop, usu. the pope

post-colonialism

critical reflection in light of the colonial legacy of Western powers

postdenominationalism

the waning of influence of official Christian bodies on the lives of believers and in North American society at large

postmodernism

critique of the assumptions of modernity and the Enlightenment

post-structuralism

associated with Jacques Derrida and Michel Foucault, a late-twentieth-century French philosophical movement that served as the theoretical and critical underpinning of postmodern thought

praxis

an understanding of the priority of practice in relation to theoretical thought

predestination

the teaching that God knows and wills the eternal destiny of each person

preferential option for the poor

notion from liberation theology that Christian teaching and theology must begin in engagement with the situation and context of the poor and excluded

Presbyterian

British and American denomination that traces its polity and confessional identity to the work of Reformers John Knox and John Calvin

prevenient

anticipatory; prevenient grace is antecedent to any human action

priesthood of all believers

conviction, enunciated by Martin Luther, that all Christians have unmediated access to the saving grace of God in Jesus Christ

process thought
pioneered by Alfred North Whitehead, the critique and reconceptualization of static, classic Western metaphysical assumptions about substance, being, causality, etc., and their replacement with more dynamic emphasis on reality as process

prophecy
a declaration by a prophet of a word from God, based on a vision, audition, or dream

prosopon
lit. Greek "mask"; person

providence
divine guidance or care; God's provision for humans

purgatory
a state after death before entering heaven in which humans' sufferings purge their souls of the punishments merited by their sins

Quaker
English and American Christian reform movement that stresses the inner light of faith and Christian pacifism

queer theory
understanding of persons and culture specifically in light of the experience of gay, lesbian, bisexual, and transgendered persons

Qumran
site of 1947 discovery of cache of manuscripts thought to be from a first-century B.C.E. and C.E. Judean sect known as the Essenes

redemption
being saved; salvation

reification
objectification, making something into a thing

relativism
the notion that things or concepts have reality or value only in relation to other things or concepts, not by themselves

remission
taking away the blame for one's sins; forgiveness

reprobation
being foreordained to damnation

Resurrection
Jesus' rising from the dead

revelation
knowing that comes from God; the process of same

rhetoric

the art of persuasion; ancient philosophical discipline; analysis of speech in terms of its purpose, intent, and audience

righteousness

being deemed worthy by or in right relation to God

Roman Curia

Catholic bureaucracy in Rome

Rule of Faith

in Latin, *regula fidei*, the essentials of Christian belief

sacrament

definitive Christian rituals, instituted by Christ, that are means of grace in Christian life; in Roman Catholicism, seven are recognized, in Lutheran Christianity two: baptism and eucharist

sacrilege

violation of or irreverence toward a sacred object or rite

sanctity (sanctification)

holiness or becoming holy

Satan

personification of evil; derived from Persian religion, developed further in Jewish and Christian thought and legend

satisfaction

reparation or payment due to God for sin

scandal of particularity

the paradox and improbability that the omnipotent God would become incarnate in a particular person, place, and set of circumstances to effect salvation of humankind

schism

a formal break in relations of disputing religious parties

scholastic theology

medieval religious thought, characterized by the use of logic and metaphysics in theology

shaman

a religious figure of power, usually associated with healing and rites of passage and reconciliation

simony

buying or selling church offices

simul iustus et peccator

lit. from Latin: at once justified and sinner; Martin Luther's idea that justification does not alter a human's status as sinner

sin

offense against God

sola scriptura
lit. from Latin: scripture alone; Martin Luther's principle that authoritative Christian teaching must be grounded in the Old and New Testaments

Sophia
the figure of Wisdom in Hebrew and Christian thought

soteriology
Christian reflection on salvation

spirituality
personal religious practice and affections

structural or social sin
systemic evils that occur through human institutions or collective mores

subaltern
derivative sciences that take their principles from higher sciences; in medieval thought, theology is thought be subaltern to God's own knowledge imparted in revelation; in contemporary thought, derived from subjugated persons or perspectives

subsidiarity, principle of
in Catholic social ethics, the conviction that social goods should not be sought at higher societal levels if they can be equally or more easily achieved at a lower level

substance
the essence or form of a thing

supernaturalism
in medieval theology, the idea that nature is overlaid by a separate level that completes and transcends nature

supersessionism
the centuries-long conviction that the Christian covenant replaces or supersedes God's covenenant with the Jewish people

sweat lodge
Native American ritual space

syncretism
the phenomenon of mutual and multiple influences of religious and philosophical strands on each other

teleology
from Greek *telos* or end; analysis through the end purpose of a thing

theism
belief in a personal God who created the universe

theocentrism
religious analysis that is centered on the action or being of God; contrast with androcentrism or Christocentrism

theodicy

a justification or defense of God's goodness in face of the fact of evil

theology of liberation

religious thought and ecclesial reform that arise from concrete religious reflection by the poor or other marginalized groups

theology

disciplined religious reflection; lit. speech about God

theotokos

Greek: "God-bearer"; affirmation of Mary as the Mother of God

Torah

the way of living for Jews, contained in written form in the first five books of the Bible

transgression

violation or sin

transubstantiation

the notion that in the Eucharist the outer characteristics of bread and wine remain while their meaning or substance changes into the body and blood of Jesus Christ

Trent, Council of

Roman Catholic council, 1545–1563, called to respond to the Reformation and to renew the life of the church

Tridentine

derived from or pertaining to the Council of Trent (1545–1563)

trinity, economic

God's being and activity considered in relation to us

trinity, immanent

God's being considered in itelf

trinity

one God as three persons

trope

use of a word as a figure of speech

universalism

the theological position that all people are saved by God

usury

lending money for interest

Vatican Council, Second

Roman Catholic council, 1962–1965, called by Pope John XXIII that led to extensive renewal and reform

venial sins

less serious offenses against God

via affirmativa

Latin: attribution of characteristics to God based on similarities to human traits

via negativa

Latin: attribution of characteristics to God based on dissimilarities to human traits

vicar

representative

voluntarism

theological account that stresses the efficacy of free will

Whitby, Synod of

English synod of 664 that settled the dating of Easter

womanist theology

distinctive theology of black women

World Council of Churches

international cooperative body of Protestant churches

Index

Electronic Resources from Fortress Pres

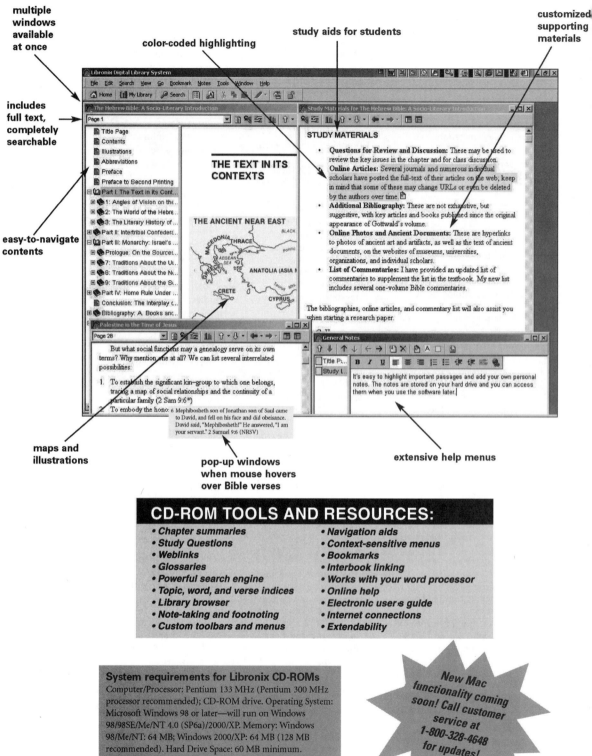

multiple windows available at once

includes full text, completely searchable

easy-to-navigate contents

maps and illustrations

color-coded highlighting

study aids for students

customized supporting materials

pop-up windows when mouse hovers over Bible verses

extensive help menus

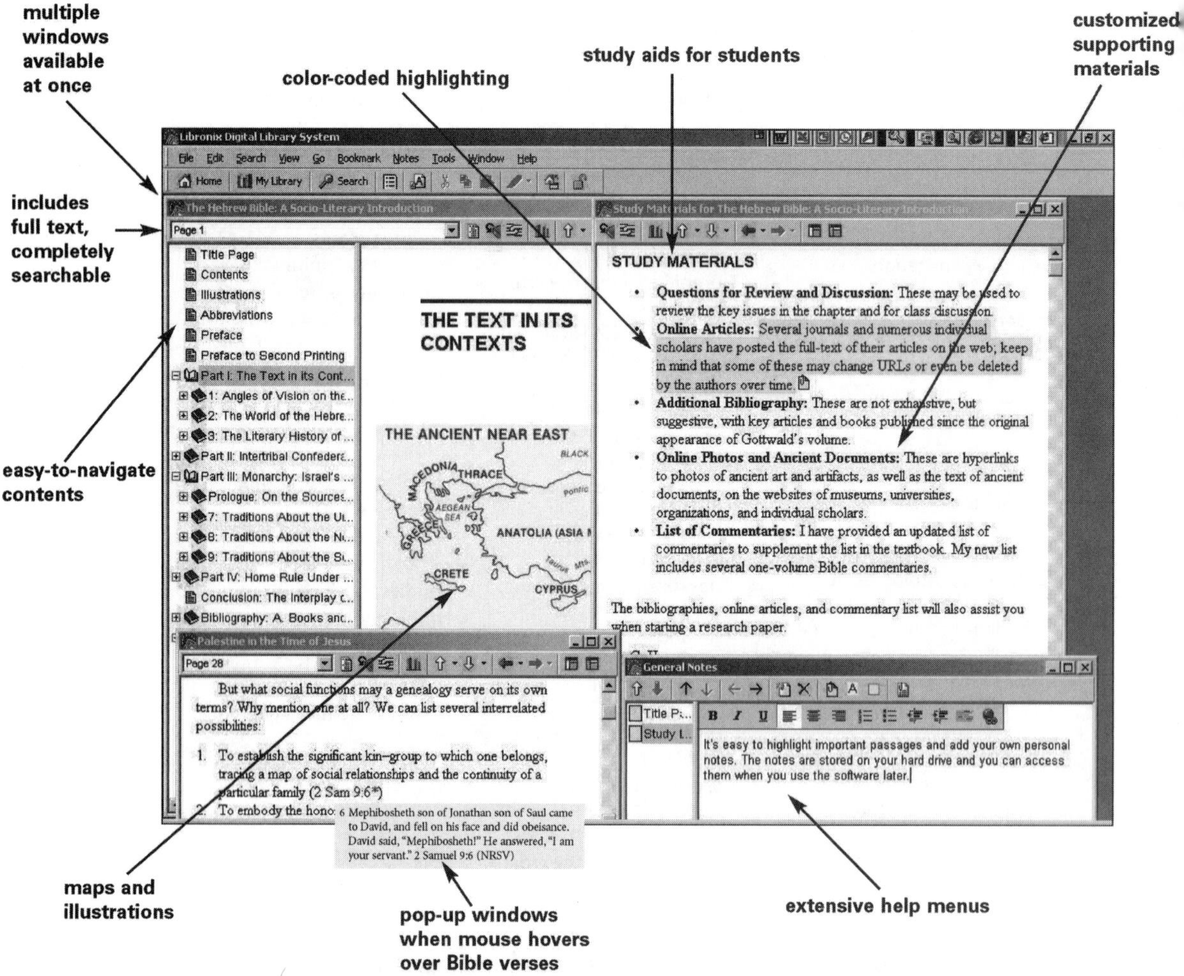

CD-ROM TOOLS AND RESOURCES:

- *Chapter summaries*
- *Study Questions*
- *Weblinks*
- *Glossaries*
- *Powerful search engine*
- *Topic, word, and verse indices*
- *Library browser*
- *Note-taking and footnoting*
- *Custom toolbars and menus*
- *Navigation aids*
- *Context-sensitive menus*
- *Bookmarks*
- *Interbook linking*
- *Works with your word processor*
- *Online help*
- *Electronic user s guide*
- *Internet connections*
- *Extendability*

System requirements for Libronix CD-ROMs

Computer/Processor: Pentium 133 MHz (Pentium 300 MHz processor recommended); CD-ROM drive. Operating System: Microsoft Windows 98 or later—will run on Windows 98/98SE/Me/NT 4.0 (SP6a)/2000/XP. Memory: Windows 98/Me/NT: 64 MB; Windows 2000/XP: 64 MB (128 MB recommended). Hard Drive Space: 60 MB minimum. Monitor Resolution: 800 x 600 or larger. Note to Macintosh users: May run on newer Macintosh computers running Windows emulation software. Performance will vary.

New Mac functionality coming soon! Call customer service at 1-800-328-4648 for updates!